LITIGATION AND ADMINISTRATIVE PRACTICE
Criminal Law and Urban Problems
Course Handbook Series
Number C-181

NEW YORK PRACTICE SKILLS
Course Handbook Series
Number F-45

Social Security and SSI Disability

Co-Chairs

Carolyn A. Kubitschek
Barbara Samuels

To order this book, call (800) 260-4PLI or fax us at (800) 321-0093.
Ask our Customer Service Department Dept. BAV5.

Practising Law Institute
810 Seventh Avenue
New York, New York 10019

"This publication is designed to provide information in regard to the subject matter covered. It is sold with the understanding that the publisher is not engaged in rendering legal, accounting or other professional service. If legal advice or other expert assistance is required, the services of a competent professional person should be sought."

—from Declaration of Principles jointly adopted by Committee of American Bar Association and Committee of Publishers and Associations

 ISBN 0-87224-585-3

Foreword

This course handbook is one of about 150 published each year by the Practising Law Institute.

Its primary function is to serve as an educational supplement to each program. It may also be used as a reference manual by attorneys and related professionals unable to attend the sessions.

The method of reproduction utilized has been chosen to insure that registrants receive these materials as quickly as possible and in the most usable form practical.

The Practising Law Institute wishes to acknowledge its debt and extend its sincere appreciation to the authors who have rendered this valuable service. They exemplify the finest tradition of our profession by sharing their expertise with their colleagues.

Prepared for distribution at the
SOCIAL SECURITY AND SSI DISABILITY
Program
March 1999

CONTENTS:

1

INTRODUCTION TO SOCIAL SECURITY AND SSI

Barbara Samuels

Part 1: INTRODUCTION TO SOCIAL SECURITY AND SSI

I. DISTINGUISHING SOCIAL SECURITY and SSI

Non-Disability Criteria Relevant to Establishing Eligibility for SSI (Supplemental Security Income) and/or SSD (Social Security Disability or Title II) Benefits

A. **SSI** is available for individuals under age 65 who are blind or disabled and poor.

1. Poor, for SSI purposes, means for an individual limited income (less than about $500 per month [1999]) and resources (less than $2,000); for a couple less than $751 per month [1999] and resources (less than $3000).

   -- Income is any money claimant receives (earned, unearned, gifts, lottery winnings, welfare, etc.) and free or below-cost food, clothing, or shelter

   -- Resources are things claimant owns that could be converted to cash or used to buy food, clothing, or shelter (e.g., bank accounts, life insurance, real property, stocks, bonds, etc.)

2. SSI eligibility entitles the claimant to Medicaid as of the date of SSI eligibility.

3. SSI benefits can be paid only from the date of filing (or, pursuant to Welfare Reform, the first month following the month of filing) of the SSI application (assuming the person is found disabled that far back).

4. The amount of SSI a person receives depends on several factors:
   -- Any non-SSI income
   -- Deeming of a income of a living-with-spouse or living-with-parent (of a child)
   -- Living arrangement (living alone or with others and meeting or not meeting fair share of costs)

5. The SSI recipient will be "suspended" (and, after a year of suspension, terminated) from benefits if he or she becomes financially or otherwise ineligible or leaves the United States for 30 days or more.

6. Under Welfare Reform, non-citizens who were lawfully residing in the United States on August 22, 1996 and who are blind or disabled may receive SSI. This includes PRUCOLS ['persons residing under color of law"]. Unless an individual was already receiving SSI on August 22, 1996, a non-citizen who was lawfully residing in the United States on that date is <u>not</u> eligible for SSI based on age, unless s/he meets one of the exceptions below, but must prove disability or blindness. Any non-citizen who entered the United States after August 22, 1996, must also meet one of the exceptions if he or she wishes to receive SSI. Briefly, the exceptions permit a non-citizen to receive SSI if he or she:

-- is a refugee or asylee, for seven years from the date he or she obtained that status;

-- has had deportation or removal withheld, for seven years from the date of obtaining that status;

-- is a Cuban/Haitian entrant, for seven years from the date entrant status is granted;

-- is an Amerasian immigrant, for seven years from the date that status is granted;

-- is a member of a limited number of Native American tribes whose jurisdiction crosses U.S. borders;

-- is an active-duty member of the United States Armed Forces or an honorably discharged veteran, or an immediate relative of such a person;

-- is a legal permanent resident who can be credited with 40 <u>qualifying quarters</u> ("QQ"s) (QQs include not only the individual's own quarters but also quarters earned by his or her spouse during the marriage and by his or her parents before he or she turned 18 years of age, but do not include any quarter after December 31, 1996 in which the non-citizen or the worker received certain federal benefits); or

-- is a battered spouse or child (or the custodial parent of a battered child), who needs SSI because of the battery, and meets certain other standards.

B. **SSD** is available for individuals under age 65 who worked under the Social Security system for ten years, or one quarter of work for each year from age 21 to the year of disability, with a minimum of at least 6 years; and who can prove that they became disabled within five years of the the last time they worked if they worked a solid five years prior to becoming disabled. If work prior to disability was sporadic, the period after alleged onset within which they can establish disability will be shorter.

1. The **date last insured** is critical: The claimant must prove that his or her disability began before the date last insured (i.e., that he or she had 20 of the last 40 quarters covered)(see Part II below).

2. SSD eligibility entitles the claimant to Medicare as of the 25th month of SSD eligibility; if income is low enough, claimant may also qualify for Medicaid, but Medicaid is only automatic if an individual also receives an SSI benefit.

3. SSD benefits can be paid for as much as 12 months prior to the date of application, but will never be paid for the first five full months of established disability.

   EXAMPLES: 1) Oscar applied for SSD benefits on January 5, 1995, claiming he had been disabled since March 1993. Assuming he proves disability as of the earlier date, he can be paid from January 1994, one year prior to his application date. 2) Felix also applied for SSD on January 5, 1995, but he has only claimed disability since January 4, 1995. Assuming he wins, he can only be paid from July 1995, the first month following five full months of disability.

4. The amount of SSD a person receives depends on his or her earnings as reflected in an "earnings record" kept by Social Security (see Part II below).

5. Dependents of a wage-earner entitled to SSD may also be able to get benefits based on the disability person's earnings (see below). Survivors of a deceased insured worker, may also collect benefits(see Part III below).

6. Non-citizens who are lawfully residing in the United States can receive SSD benefits if they are insured.

II. DISABILITY INSURANCE COVERAGE[1]

Social Security Disability is an insurance program. Like any other insurance program to be entitled to a benefit an individual must be "covered". One becomes "covered" by paying taxes [FICA, for employees; self-employment tax for persons who are self-employed] into the system for a certain number of quarters. How many quarters are required depends on an individual's age when an application is filed and the type of benefits sought. For disability purposes, "coverage" [insured status] lasts for only a limited period of time. To be eligible to receive a benefit payment, one must be covered and one must establish disability before the expiration of one's covered period, e.g. before the **"date last insured"** [**DLI**].

In order to comprehend how this system works, and what an earnings record can tell you about an individual client, it is important to understand a number of basic concepts which are discussed below:

A. **Quarters of Coverage**, In general:

Each calendar year contains four quarters: the first quarter is January thru March; the second quarter is April through June; the third quarter is July through September, and the fourth quarter is October through December. When Social security began in 1936, it cost $50. of earnings in any quarter to purchase one quarter of credited coverage. With the passage of time, the cost has risen, so that in 1999, one quarter of coverage requires earnings of $720. Up to 1977, coverage was purchased on a quarterly basis; hence, work had to be done during a quarter for coverage to be earned. Since 1978, coverage has been annualized, so that currently earnings of $2,880.00 at any time during a calendar year will purchase coverage for the whole year, e.g. 4 quarters. [20 CFR 404.140 et. seq.]

B. **FULLY**, **CURRENTLY** and **DISABILITY** Insured:

To be eligible for disability insurance an individual must be "**fully**" or "**currently**" and "**disability**" insured.

1. Generally, to be "**fully**" insured an individual must have 40 quarters [or, 10 years] of credited earnings. In the alternative, depending on one's age when applying for benefits, it may be enough to have one quarter of coverage for every year from 1950, or age 21, to the year application is made for disability, with at least

---

[1] Other rules apply to insured status for old age purposes. See POMS RS 00301.00 et. seq. Also, see below, §III.C.

4

a minimum of 6 quarters for very young persons.[20 CFR 404.110][2]

2. To be "**currently**" insured an individual must have 6 quarters of coverage out of the 13 quarter period ending in the quarter in which disability occurred. This concept applies to individuals who become disabled before age 31. [The "current" insurance concept also applies as an alternative to protect survivors [e.g. mother with young children, dependent children, etc.] of young wage-earners who die without being "fully" insured.[20 CFR 404.120]

3. "**Disability**" insured status generally requires that an individual must have worked at least 20 quarters [e.g. 5 years] during the 40 quarters [e.g. 10 years] immediately before becoming disabled. However, if the disabled claimant is less than 31 years old, s/he needs coverage for one-half the quarters starting with the quarter after his/her 21st birthday up through the onset of disability, but never less than 6 quarters. [Example: To calculate the coverage needed by a 30 year old claimant: There are 9 years (or 36 quarters) between age 21 and 30, one-half of which would be 18 quarters.] [20 CFR 404.130]

C. **Determining "date last insured", in general**

An earnings record should be included in every Title II disability file. If it is not in the file ask SSA produce it. If the earnings record has been properly completed the "date last insured" will be indicated. If the earnings record is not fully developed it is not usually hard to figure out the "DLI".

Each year in the earning record is followed by four letters or symbols. Each letter or symbol represents one quarter of that year. The most common letters are "C" which stands for "covered", and "N" which stands for "not covered". The most common symbols are an asterisk [*] or a number sign [#], each of which means that that quarter "might be covered".[3]

---

[2] The rules governing these concepts are complicated. Any attempt to summarize them is fraught with the danger of misconstruction. Reference should, therefore, be made to the statute [42 USC §414, 423(c)] and regulations [20 CFR 404.110 - 133] when questions arise in individual cases. See also POMS RS 00301 et. seq.

[3] If any quarters indicated by these symbols are essential to the question of whether the individual is insured, the earnings record will be manually reviewed for those quarters. Since 1978, earnings have been credited on an annualized, not quarterly, basis. From that year on there should not be any further use of symbols because coverage is given on the basis of the amount of earnings in a calendar year not on the basis of which quarter it was earned in.

An individual is insured for disability purposes for a maximum period of five years following the quarter in which s/he last worked. This period is shortened by every non-credited quarter during the last five years preceding the onset of disability. To determine the last date of insured status simply count the "C" quarters starting with the most recent and counting backwards until you have counted 20 "C" quarters. The DLI will be 10 years from the earliest (e.g. 20th) "C" quarter.

For example, below are the credited quarters in the earnings record of George Jones:

1985	CC*C
1986	CCCN
1987	CCCC
1988	CCCC
1989	CNCC
1990	CCCC
1991	CCNC
1992	NNCC
1993	CCNN
1994	CCCC
1995	CCN

According to his earnings record, George last worked in the 2nd quarter of 1995. During the last 5 years he worked he missed a number of quarters [due to illnee or layoffs]. In order to find George's DLI, count back 20 quarters starting with the 2nd quarter of 1995. The 20th quarter is the 1st quarter of 1989. Ten years (e.g. 40 quarters) from the 1st quarter of 1989 is the 4th quarter of 1999. Since a "DLI" always ends on the last day of a quarter, George is covered for disability purposes through December 31, 1999.[4]

Thus, George must establish that his disability (as defined by SSA) began <u>on or before December 31, 1994</u>. If he succeeds, his Social Security benefits could, theoretically, continue for the rest of his life or until he reaches age 65 and is automatically converted to retirement benefits. If, however, he does not establish the onset of disability by or before his "DLI" [for, example, if he suffers a massive heart attack on January 1, 1995,

---

[4] Coverage during any quarter always extends to the last day of the quarter. Therefore, for "DLI" purposes it is not necessary to know the month or day a claimant ceased to work. If one is covered for the 1st quarter of a year, one is covered through March 31st of that year; if one is covered through the 2nd quarter of the year, one is covered through June 30th of that year; if covered for the 3rd quarter, coverage extends through September 30th; and for the 4th quarter through December 31st.

and cannot show evidence of the existence of a heart condition before that date], then he will not get any Social Security disability benefit because he was no longer insured on the date the disabling impairment began.

D. **Determining DLI for younger workers**

When a younger worker, e.g. below age 31, files for disability s/he may either prove "fully insured" status or "currently" insured status. How is DLI determined for persons who need less than 20 out of 40 quarters of coverage?

If a 24 year old individual becomes disabled s/he must have 6 quarters of coverage prior to onset of disability to be covered. Go back to the earliest quarter necessary to establish 6 out of 13 quarters and from that earliest quarter count 13 quarters into the future to find the DLI. For example:

1991 NNNN
1992 CNNC
1993 NNNN
1994 CCCC
1995 CCNN
1996 NNNN
1997 NNNN
1998 NNNN

The earliest quarter of coverage needed to establish 6 out of the last 13 quarters for this individual is the 1st quarter of 1994. Counting 13 quarters forward from the first quarter of 1994, the DLI of this individual would be March 31, 1997 (the end of the 13th quarter).

E. **Calculating Benefit Amounts**: Essential Concepts

1. **Period of Disability**: is a period of time during which the worker meets the definition of disability if s/he is or was insured for disability purposes when the disabling impairment began [e.g. if the disability began prior to the expiration of the "date last insured"].

A **Period of Disability begins** on the date the disability began if the worker has disability insured status as of that date; or, it can begin on the first day of the first calendar quarter after the disability began in which the worker acquires disability insured status.

A **Period of Disability ends** with the last day of whichever of the following months happens earliest: the second month after the month in which the disability ceases; the month before the month in which the worker reaches age 65; or the month in which the worker dies. [20 CFR 404.320 et. seq.]

2. **Disability Freeze**: If a period of disability is established, the worker's earnings record is "frozen" and the period of disability may be excluded in determining whether the person is fully or currently insured, and in figuring the amount of benefit entitlement. This means that any months of work within the period of disability will not be counted in figuring the claimant's **"average earnings"**. [20 CFR 404.320]

But note the period of disability is **not excluded** in figuring the disabled person's (or the survivor's) right to receive Social Security benefits or the amount of such benefits, if excluding it would be to the claimant's disadvantage. For example, the period of disability would not be excluded when the disabled person has potential quarters of coverage in the disability period (that is, calendar quarters which could be quarters of coverage except for the fact that they are within a period of disability. This could include work activity during a trial work period, an unsuccessful work attempt, vocational rehabilitation, or some special situations[5]).

3. **Primary Insurance Amount [PIA]**: This is the highest amount of benefits which can be paid on an individual's Social Security account, and is available on retirement at or after age 65 or on establishing a period of disability. [20 CFR 404.201 et. seq.; 20 CFR 404.317]. **PIA** is generally calculated on the basis of **Average Indexed Monthly Earning** [**AIME**] [20 CFR 404.210]; but for

---

[5] Jernigan v. Chater, 973 F Supp 534 (D Md 1997)(Claimant could invoke less stringent definition of disability to utilize inclusive average-monthly-wage methods of calculating benefits so that his earnings during "period of disability" could be considered in determining his PIA amount, which then would result in greater DIB. Claimant, who was born in 1926 and was statutorily blind since birth, was awarded a period of disability in 1952 on the basis of blindness, but performed SGA from 1958 to 1989, so did not become eligible for a benefit until the end of 1989. There are two methods for calculating PIA. If, prior to 1979, the worker reached age 62, became disabled or died, then his PIA is computed under the average-monthly-wage method. If none of these events occurred before 1979, then the AIME is used to determine the PIA. The Commissioner must determine plaintiff's benefit amount to be "the highest of all those computed under the methods of which he is eligible." [Under the AIME his PIA is $951.40; under the AMW method [excluding period of disability work) his PIA is $231.90; under the AMW (inclusion of earnings during period of disability) his PIA is $1300. In this case, the claimant was allowed to include his earnings during his period of disability in calculating his PIA under the old method, AMW).

older workers other formulas may be available.[6]

4. **<u>Average Indexed Monthly Earnings [AIME]</u>**: is based on a combination of the number of years of credited work and the amount of earnings credited in each year. Not all credited years are counted in calculating **AIME**. How many years are counted depend on the claimant's date of birth. [20 CFR 404.211] Generally, the concept of "indexing" earnings, means that earnings from earlier years can be equalized in value with inflated earnings from more recent years. Indexing values change each year based on the average wage nationwide in that year.[7]

First annual indexed earnings are calculated; then monthly indexed earnings have to be figured. Once that is done, bend points are applied to determine the actual PIA. Bend points change each year: In 1999, the following bend points apply:

1) Bend points for computing PIA for initial entitlement in 1998:[8]

90% of AIME for 1st $505, plus
32% of AIME over $505 and through $3,043, plus
15% of AIME over $3,043.

2) Bend points for computing family maximum for retirement and survivor programs[9] in 1998:

150% of 1st $645 of worker's PIA, plus
272% of worker's PIA over $645 through $931, plus
134% of worker's PIA over $931 through $1,214, plus
175% of worker's PIA over $1,214.

F. **Correcting An Earnings Record**

Up through 1989 incorrectly posted earnings could only be corrected if correction was initiated within 3 years, 3 months and 15 days of

---

[6] See above n. 5.

[7] This calculation is not an easy one because the numbers used change each year. To obtain the appropriate indexing numbers for a given year consult SSA or the POMS. Additonally, an inexpensive and very useful volume, <u>The Guide to Social Security and Medicare</u>, is published annually by William M. Mercer, Inc. 1500 Meidinger Tower, Louisville, Kentucky 40202-3415, [502] 561-4541; and contains worksheets with indexing numbers and other helpful tools for figuring out disability, retirement and survivor benefits.

[8] 63 Fed Reg 58450 (October 30, 1998).

[9] 63 Fed Reg 58450 (October 30, 1998).

the year of earnings, with one exception. If no earnings at all were posted in a given year, correction could be made any time. However, if even a few dollars were posted [incorrectly] any change would have to be requested within the time limit noted above.

Pursuant to P.L. 101-239 (Omnibus Budget Reconcialition Act of 1989), the time limit for correction of earnings records was lifted so that erroneously posted earnings can be corrected any time. However, the burden of proof is on the individual seeking correction to show the correct amount "by evidence satisfactory to the Secretary". To date SSA has not issued regulations defining what evidence will be found "satisfactory to the Secretary". However, in the past, evidence satisfactory to the Secretary has been limited to tax returns of wages or of self-employment earnings(if timely filed with the IRS), or a wage report of a state. [20 CFR 404.822]. Pay stubs might also be acceptable.

G. **Checking An Earnings Record**

Pursuant to Pub. L. 101-239 (OBRA, 1989), SSA was required, not later than October 1, 1990, to provide all persons age 25 and over with a Social Security account statement, including a statement of earnings, an estimate of the person's contribution to the program, and an estimate of future retirement benefits. Beginning 1995, all persons age 60 and over will automatically receive a statement with a notice that earnings are updated annually and can be requested. And by 1999, earnings statements will automatically be sent biannually to people under age 60.

Any person who has a Social Security number is entitled to know what earnings have been posted to his/her account for each year and can request such information in writing. [20 CFR 404.810]
SSA has developed a simple form for obtaining earnings record and estimated benefit information [SSA-7004-PC-OP1].

Because both employers and SSA can err, and because the longer one waits to find out whether an error has occurred the harder it will be to produce proof to correct it, everyone should check their Social Security records at least once every three years.

III. SOCIAL SECURITY DEPENDENCY AND SURVIVOR INSURANCE

A. In general: Social Security pays monthly benefits to covered individuals who are elderly, disabled or blind and to their dependents and survivors under certain circumstances. The Social Security Act is codified at 42 USC §401 et. seq. Social Security regulations are found at 20 CFR part 404.

B. Insured Status of the Wage-earner is a Prerequisite to Coverage of Dependents and Survivors

Listed below are the types of insurance coverage needed for a wage-earner to have "insured" status for her/himself and, therefore, protection for his/her dependents and survivors.

<u>Monthly benefits can be paid to</u>:	<u>If the wage-earner is</u>:
1. Retired worker age 62 and over	Fully insured
2. Disabled worker under age 65	Fully & disability
3. Disabled worker under age 31	Currently, disability
4. Spouse of Disabled or retired worker	fully, currently; and disability depending on age
5. Dependent child	same as #4
6. Widow(er)[including divorced spouse]	fully insured
7. widow(er) with dependent child	fully or currently
8. Disabled widow(er) [including disabled divorced spouse]	fully insured
9. Mother's/father's	fully or currently
10. Dependent parent	fully insured

C. Potential Auxiliary Beneficiaries

1. Wage-earner[10]: An insured worker is entitled to full coverage when s/he reaches age 65. "Full coverage" means the maximum amount to which the worker is entitled based on what s/he has paid into the Social Security system. Social Security's term for the maximum amount payable on a worker's account is the "Primary Insurance Amount" or PIA. A worker can take early retirement as early as age 62 but they will receive only a percentage of the PIA they would get if they waited until age 65 to collect a benefit. Once a worker takes early retirement his/her benefit will always be a reduced amount. If a worker chooses to wait until after his/her 65th birthday to claim a benefit an increment is added to the PIA for each month from age 65 to age 70 during which the individual was eligible to receive a benefit.

2. Spouse: The spouse of a covered worker can receive a reduced old age benefit at age 62, but receives a full one-half of the worker's PIA if s/he waits until reaching age 65. A widow/er receives the full amount to which the worker was entitled before his/her death depending on the age at which the worker chose to start receiving his/her benefit. An eligible divorced spouse can receive a benefit on the worker's account even though the worker

[10] Throughout this paper the term "wage-earner" is used to denote the worker on whose Social Security account or number benefits are sought and through whom dependents and survivors claim entitlement to Social Security payments. Nothing in this section relates to the SSI program which <u>does not</u> provide for benefits to family members.

delays receiving a benefit. [Spousal benefits as well as other dependency and survivor benefits are discussed at greater length below].

3. Dependency and Survivors: Benefits are available under certain circumstances for the the following categories of dependents and survivors: wife/husband, mother/father (of the wage-earner's eligible children), widow/er, parents (of the wage-earner), children (minor and/or disabled), stepchildren, or grandchildren. In order for a survivor to receive a benefit the wage-earner on whose account the benefit is sought must be fully insured.

D. Retirement and Insured status:

1. "Fully insured": To qualify for old age insurance the wage-earner must be "fully insured". To be fully insured a wage-earner must have the requisite number of quarters of coverage. Quarters of coverage are earned through payroll taxes. The cost of a quarter of coverage has risen over the years. Up to 1977 a quarter of coverage cost $50.00. In 1978, the cost went up to $250 per quarter. In 1999 the cost will be $740 per quarter.

In general an individual who has 40 quarters (or 10 years) of coverage is fully insured. Alternatively, a person is fully insured if s/he has at least one quareter of coverage for each calendar year after 1950, or, if later, after the year in which s/he attained age 21, and prior to the year in which s/he attains age 62 or dies (or becomes disabled) whichever occurs earlier.

2. Earnings After Retirement: An individual can receive Social Security old age benefits and still work as long as his/her income does not exceed the maximum allowable amount. What the maximum allowable earnings are depends on one's age. In 1999, for individuals who are age 65 through 69, the maximum allowable earnings will be $15,500 per year. For individuals age 62 through 64 the maximum allowable earnings will be $9,600 per year. For those age 70 and over, there is no limit on earnings.

If earnings exceed the allowable amount, Social Security benefits will be reduced. For those age 65 through 69, $1.00 of Social Security benefits will be lost for each $3.00 of earnings above the allowable limit; for individuals age 62 through 64, $1.00 of Social Security will be lost for each $2.00 of earnings above the limit. [These earnings limits apply only to old age benefits; other standards apply to the earnings of disabled or blind beneficiaries.]

3. Non-wage Income: Since Social Security is not a needs-based (welfare) program there is no resource test or non-wage income limit. Thus income from stocks, bonds, or any sources other than wages from a job do not count against a Social Security recipient's

benefits.

4. Benefit Payment Levels: The amount of a monthly Social Security payment depends both on the number of years the individual paid into the system and the level at which s/he paid in each year. Monthly benefits can range from less than $200 to more than $1300 for an individual wage-earner. A husband/wife at age 65 receives one-half of whatever his/her spouse is entitled to; while a widow/er at age 65 or above gets the full amount to which his/her spouse was entitled. Benefits received prior to age 65 are a percentage of the PIA. Generally, the formula applied to determine a reduced amount is: 19/40th of 1% for each month below age 65.

Cost of living increases, which generally occur annually based on increases in the consumer price index, apply to the basic PIA benefit payment plus any prior cost of living increases. Cost of living increases occur the first month of each calendar year.

5. Taxing Social Security Benefits: Some portion of Social Security benefits may be subject to federal income tax. The portion may vary from 50 to 85% of the annual benefit amount, depending on an individual's total taxable income.

6. Other Old Age Benefits: Individuals eligible for Social Security directly or through a wage-earner are also eligible for Medicare when they reach age 65. Others who reach age 65 may, under certain circumstances, buy into the Medicare program.

7. Aliens and Payment of Social Security Benefits: Special rules apply to aliens who work under our Social Security system for a period of time and return to their own country. Whether or not they can receive a Social Security benefit in their home country may depend on how long they lived in the United States and which country they return to. In general, if their homeland has a social insurance program which pays benefits to a qualified U.S. citizen who worked in that country, then our system will pay the qualified alien. There are many nations with which the U.S. now has treaties or "Totalization Agreements" covering these issues. See 20 CFR 404.463 for list of countries with which such agreements exist [as of 1997] and for a list of countries to which we do not send Social Security benefits. For the most recent list contact Social Security Administration Office of International Policy, Baltimore, MD.

E. Specific Criteria for Entitlement to Dependent and Survivor Benefit Eligibility[11]

---

[11] This paper is an overview, intended to make survivor and dependency benefits more accessible to the advocate. DO NOT RELY on it as the ultimate statement of authority on auxiliary benefits in any particular fact situation. Make sure to refer to the Code of Federal Regulations [20 CFR 404.301 et. seq.] when assessing a

A monthly Social Security benefit can be paid to the following non-wage-earner dependents and survivors if the wage-earner is/was insured at the time of the event which forms the basis of the claim, e.g. retirement, disability or death.[12]

1. SPOUSES:

A) Spouse of Living Wage-earner: Husband's or Wife's Benefit [20 CFR 404.330;.333;.344 et. seq.]

The husband or wife of an insured, living wage-earner is covered on the wage-earner's account if the following criteria are met:

i. The wage-earner is covered and entitled to retirement or disability benefits;

ii. the wage-earner and the claimant spouse are validly married[13] or, if not, may be "deemed" validly married[14]

---

client's entitlement to benefits.

[12] While not repeated in these materials, a written application is a pre-condition to entitlement for any benefit. Unless and until a written application is filed no benefit is payable. Also, if the wage-earner is alive s/he is usually (but not always) required to apply for benefits before a dependent will be eligible for payment. Finally, an individual may be eligible for more than one benefit or on more than one account [e.g. disabled adult child on insured parent's Social Security account and on his/her own Social Security account]. In such a case, the individual will receive whichever benefit is highest.

[13] See 20 CFR 404.344 -.346. The validity of a marriage is determined by the law of the state in which the marriage took place. This includes "common law" marriages if such a marriage is recognized in the state in which it is alleged to have occurred. See also note 6.

[14] A claimant may be a "deemed" spouse if s/he, in good faith, went through a marriage ceremony which would have been valid but for a legal impediment [i.e. unbeknownst to the claimant, the wage-earner had not divorced his/her previous spouse] not known to the claimant at the time of the marriage, and the claimant continued to live with the wage-earner in the same household when s/he applied for benefits. [20 CFR 404.346].

See Burton v. Chater, Unemp Ins Rep (CCH) ¶15,168B (ED Ark 1996)(ALJ properly determined that a claimant was not entitled to widow's insurance benefits where the decedent married his first

and are living in the same household at the time the application for benefits is filed, and one of the following criteria is met:

a. the marital relationship has lasted at least one year;
b. claimant and the insured are the natural parents of a child; or
c. In the month before the claimant married the insured s/he was entitled, or potentially entitled[15], to any of the following benefits: wife's, husband's, widow's, widower's, parent's, disabled child; or annuity payments under the railroad retirement act.

iii. the claimant is 62 years old or older and meets all other conditions of entitlement; or, the claimant is the insured's husband or wife and has in his/her care a child who is entitled on the wage-earner's account who is either under age 16 or disabled;

iv. the claimant is not entitled to an old age or disability benefit based on a PIA that is equal to or greater than the full wife's or husband's benefit, e.g. one-half the wage-earner's PIA.

B) Spouse of Deceased Wage-earner: Widow and Widower Benefits [20 CFR 404.335-.338]

The widow or widower of a deceased wage-earner is entitled to a benefit on the deceased wage-earner's account if the following criteria are met:

i. The claimant and the insured wage-earner were validly married or "deemed" validly married[16], and one of the

---

wife in 1938, and that marriage never ended in divorce; the claimant and the decedent were allegedly married in Chicago in 1950 or 1952; at the time of the marriage, the claimant knew that the decedent was not divorced from his first wife; the claimant's alleged marriage was not valid under Illinois law, nor was the claimant a putative spouse under such law; and Arkansas, the state where the decedent was domiciled and died, would not deem the alleged marriage valid since it was not valid under Illinois law).

[15] "Potentially" entitled means if the claimant had applied and had been old enough s/he could have been entitled in one of the categories. [20 CFR 404.335].

[16] Effective January 1, 1991, a deemed spouse and a legal spouse may simultaneously collect a benefit on the account of the same wage-earner under some circumstances. [Pub. L. 101-508, §5119,

15

following applies:

a. Claimant and the insured were married for at least 9 months immediately before the insured wage-earner died; or
b. the relationship did not last nine months before the insured died but it was reasonably expected that the insured would live for 9 months, and
c. the death of the insured was accidental (this includes death of a service person in the line of duty); or
d. the claimant had been previously married to the insured for at least 9 months; or

ii. Claimant and insured wage-earner were the natural parents of a child; or one of the marital partners adopted the other's child during the course of the marriage; or both partners adopted a child who was under age 18, or

iii. In the month before claimant married the insured, the claimant was entitled to or potentially entitled to any of the following benefits: widow's or widower's; father's or mother's; wife's or husband's; parent's or disabled child; or to an annuity under the Railroad Retirement Act, and

iv. Claimant is not entitled to an old-age benefit that is equal to or greater than the insured wage-earner's PIA; and

v. The claimant

a. is age 60 or above; or
b. is between age 50 - 59 and disabled and the disabling impairment began within 7 years of the wage-earner's death or within 7 years of the termination of mother's or father's benefits received on account of the wage-earner's child(ren); or
c. has in his/her care a child under the age of 16, or disabled, who is entitled to benefits on the wage-earner's account. [See Mother's/father's benefits, at §III A.4.].

C) Divorced Spouses' Benefits: [20 CFR 404.335;.336;.340]

i. Divorced Spouse of Living Wage-earner [20 CFR 404.331]

The divorced spouse [husband or wife] of an insured wage-

---

amending 42 USC §416(h)].

16

earner is covered on the wage-earner's account if the following criteria are met:

a. The wage-earner is insured and is disabled or at least age 62;
b. Claimant and the insured were validly married under state law for at least 10 years immediately before the divorce became final;
c. Claimant is not married;
d. Claimant is age 62 or older;
e. The claimant is not entitled to a retirement or disability insurance benefit based on a primary insurance amount which equals or exceeds one-half of the wage-earner's PIA; and
f. Claimant has been divorced from the insured wage-earner for at least two years. [Exception: Effective January 1, 1991, if spouse's retirement benefits were received prior to the divorce, the claimant can continue to receive benefits without a waiting period. Pub.L. 101-508, §5127, amending 42 UCS §402(b),(c)].

ii. Surviving Divorced Spouse [20 CFR 404.336]

The surviving divorced wife or husband of an insured wage-earner may be entitled to a widow or widower's benefit if:

a. The claimant is the insured's surviving divorced husband or wife, e.g. was validly married to the insured and the marriage lasted at least 10 years before the divorce became final;
b. Claimant is at least 60 years old; or at least 50 and is disabled and the disability began not later than 7 years after the insured died or within 7 years of the last entitlement to mother's or father's benefits or to widow's or widower's benefits based on disability;
c. Claimant is not entitled to an old-age benefit that is equal to or greater than the insured's PIA; and
d. Claimant is unmarried, <u>or after 1983</u>:
   - claimant remarried after age 60; or
   - claimant remarried after age 50 but before reaching age 60 and was entitled to disabled widow(er)'s benefits or met the disability requirements at the time of the remarriage.

D) <u>Mother's and Father's</u>: [20 CFR 404.339-.341;.347-349]

i. Mother's and father's benefits are an alternate form of widow(er)[including divorced widow(er)] benefits for spouses who are not old enough to receive retirement widow(er) benefits and where[17]:

a. the mother or father has the wage-earner's child in his/her care; and
b. Such child is under the age of 16, or if older than 16, is disabled and is receiving a benefit on the wage-earner's account; and
c. The mother's or father's earnings do not exceed the allowable maximum[18].

Having a child "in care" means either "exercising control and responsibility" for the welfare and care of a child under age 16 or a mentally incompetent child age 16 or over; or performing personal services for a disabled mentally competent child age 16 or over.

ii. Parental "control and responsibility" means:
a. displaying a strong interest in the proper rearing of the child;
b. supervising the child's activities;
c. participating in the important decisions about the child's physical needs and mental development; and
d. Measurably controlling the child's upbringing and development. [20 CFR 404.348]

Parental responsibility can be exercised directly, as when the parent and child live together, or indirectly by instructing the child's custodian (whether individual or institution) and making sure the instructions are carried out.

iii. A parent cannot meet the "in care" requirements if:
a. The child is in the armed forces;
b. the child is 16 or over (unless the child is disabled); or
c. the parent and child are not living together and
   1. The child is living with the other parent; or
   2. The parent is mentally incompetent; or
   3. The child was removed from the parent's custody by court order; or
   4. The parent has given up the right to custody to some other person or agency; or
   5. The separation is for a period of more than 6 months and the child is age 16 or over and disabled but is mentally competent. Attendance at school, however, will not preclude a parent from having the child in

---

[17] Mother's and father's benefits depend on the entitlement of a child or children under age 16 or disabled before age 22.

[18] The allowable maximum is the amount an individual can earn who is less than 65 years old [20 CFR 404.415].

his/her care as long as the school does not have exclusive control and jurisdiction of the child; and the child spends an annual vacation of at least 30 days with the parent (unless it is not feasible for the child to return home during vacation). [20 CFR 404.347;.349]

2. CHILDREN: [20 CFR 404.350 et. seq.]

A) The category of "children" potentially includes not only legitimate children but illegitimate children, stepchildren, adopted children, grandchildren and stepgrandchildren. [20 CFR 404.354] A presumption of dependency, however, generally applies only to natural, legitimate and some adopted children. In other situations dependency requirements are indicated below.

B) In general: Children are eligible to receive benefits on the account of a insured disabled, retired or deceased wage-earner up to the age of 18 (or up to age 19 if the child is still a full-time student), or age 18 or over if the child is under a disability which began before age 22. Additionally, the child must be dependent on the wage-earner, and must be unmarried. However, if a disabled child marries an individual receiving disability benefits the marriage does not terminate the disabled child's benefit entitlement. [20 CFR 404.350-352;.367]

i. Legitimate children: are the natural (biological) children of a wage-earner born during a valid marriage, or where the wage-earner and mother of the child intermarried at a later date. Legitimate children are presumed dependent. [20 CFR.404.355]

ii. Illegitimate children: are children born out of wedlock [20 CFR 404.355]. To be eligible for a benefit on the account of the wage-earner father an illegitimate child must establish:[19]

a. written acknowledgement; or

b. a judicial decree of paternity; or

c. a court order for support based on a finding that the child is the son or daughter of the wage-earner; or

---

[19] Where the putative father is deceased, proof is a major problem in cases of illegitimacy absent a written acknowledgement or court order of paternity. Questions of proof exceed the intended parameters of this paper. In general, however, the intestacy laws of the State of New York require that, absent a finding of paternity, a marriage between the parents, or a signed acknowledgement, paternity may be established by clear and convincing evidence and by the father's open and notorious acknowledgment of the child as his own, (Estates, Powers and Trusts [EPT], §4-1.2.). Generally, to be clear and convincing, such evidence must come from the father's side of the family.

d. if the wage-earner is deceased, if the child can show by satisfactory evidence that s/he would be entitled to inherit under the intestacy laws of the state in which the wage-earner was domiciled; or

e. if other satisfactory evidence shows that the wage-earner was the father of the child <u>and</u> the child was either living with the wage-earner or the wage-earner was contributing to the support of the child at the time of the wage-earner's death. [20 CFR 404.355; .360-.361;.366]

iii. Adopted Children:[20] Children adopted <u>before</u> the wage-earner becomes eligible for benefits [e.g. before onset of disability, retirement or death] are presumed dependent. [20 CFR 404.356;.359; .362;.365] Additionally, pursuant to legislation enacted in 1988, a child adopted <u>after</u> a wage-earner becomes eligible for Social Security benefits will be eligible for child's insurance benefits on the same basis as a child born to an eligible wage-earner. Adoption can be either actual or equitable. [P.L. 101-239, amending §202 of the Social Security Act, 42 U.S.C. §402, 1988]. However, adoption by a surviving spouse must be initiated prior to the wage-earner's death or completed within two years of the wage-earner's death, and the child must either live with the wage-earner or must have received one-half support from the wage-earner in the year prior to his death. [P.L. 101-508, §5104, 1990]

iv. Disabled Adult Children: must be age 18 or older with a disability which began before age 22. The parent on whose account the disabled adult child seeks benefits must be covered and receiving disability or retirement benefits or must be deceased. Disability for the child is determined under the same standards and by the same process as for a disabled adult. [See generally 20 CFR 404.1501 et. seq.]. Disabled adult benefits will continue as long as the child continues to meet the disability standard, and remains unmarried unless the disabled adult child marries an individual who is also receiving disability benefits. [20 CFR 404.352;.368]

v. Grandchildren[21]: are entitled to benefits on the account of a covered, recipient grandparent [e.g. the wage-earner] if the

---

[20] The right of an adopted child to inherit from, or to seek benefits on the account of, a natural parent may be dependent on whether the child was adopted before or after the natural parent's death and on the law of the state of the natural parent's domicile.

[21] There are a number of possible permutations for grandchildren which include step-grandchildren and adopted grandchildren. For the former consider both criteria in this section and the criteria set forth in the section on stepchildren; and for the latter, look to the section on adopted children.

grandchild's natural or adoptive parents are disabled or deceased <u>and</u> the grandchild is dependent on the grandparent for support. "Dependency" means that the child began living with the grandparent before age 18; and that s/he lived with the grandparent in the U.S. and <u>received</u> at least one-half support from the grandparent during the year before the grandparent became entitled to retirement or disability insurance benefits or died; or, if the grandparent had a period of disability that lasted until s/he became entitled to benefits or died, for the year immediately before the month in which the period of disability began. [20 CFR 404.358;.364]

vi. Stepchildren: an individual becomes a stepchild when a wage-earner marries the child's natural parent or marries the child's adopting parent after the adoption[22]. Death of the stepparent does not end the relationship, although divorce will.[23] Either way, however, there is no termination of a stepchild's existing established entitlement to a child's benefit as the child of the stepparent.

In order to become a stepchild of a living stepparent the child must have lived with the stepparent for at least one year before the application is filed. If the stepparent is deceased, to qualify for survivor's benefits, the child must have been the wage-earner's stepchild for at least 9 months immediately preceding the day on which the wage-earner died, unless the wage-earner's death was accidental.

Additionally, the child must establish dependency on the stepparent. Prior to July, 1996, dependency could be demonstrated either by the child have been living with the stepparent <u>or</u> by the stepparent contributing at least one-half the child's support. Effective with initial monthly benefit payments for July 1996 or later, the only way for a step-child to show dependency, and therefore entitlement to benefits on the step-parent's record, is to show that the step-parent was contributing one half support at whichever of the following times applies: at the beginning of the step-parent's period of disability, at the time the step-parent becomes eligible for retirement benefits, at the time the child's application was filed, or at the time of the step-parent's death.[24]

---

[22] A stepchild can become an adopted child if the wage-earner actually adopts the child(ren) of his/her spouse.

[23] But see Taylor v. Chater, 907 F Supp 306 (ND Ind 1995). DIB benficiaries' stepchildren were entitled to child's insurance benefits where they had been his stepchildren and they lived with him for a full year; subsequent divorce of stepchildren's mother from recipient did not affect their continued entitlement to benefits.

[24] Pub L 104-121, §104 (enacted March 29, 1996).

[20 CFR 404.357;.358;.363-.364]

3. PARENTS:[25] [20 CFR 404.370 et. seq.]

The parent(s) [including natural, adoptive or stepparent(s)] of a deceased wage-earner is entitled to an insurance benefit if the wage-earner was fully insured at the time of death, the parent has reached age 62, and the parent is not entitled to any retirement benefit [a minimum benefit or a benefit on another account] which is equal to, or larger than, the parent's benefit available on the wage-earner's account, and the parent was receiving at least one-half support from the wage-earner at the time the wage-earner died, or at the beginning of a period of disability if that period continued up to the month of the wage-earner's death.[26] Parents benefits may end with the parent's remarriage. [20 CFR 404.370-.374]

F. Benefit Limitations: Family maximum

1. Family Maximum: The Social Security Act limits the amount of monthly benefits that can be paid for any month on the earnings of an insured individual. If the total benefits to which all persons are entitled on one earnings record exceed the maximum amount available on that account then those benefits will be reduced to a level consistent with the available family maximum for that account. [20 CFR 404.304;.403-407]. In general, the lower the Primary Insurance Amount (PIA)[27], the smaller the family maximum[28].

2. Applicable Family Maximum formula: The family maximum is determined by the type of benefit to which the wage-earner is entitled, e.g. disability or retirement. Where the wage-earner is disabled the family maximum is limited to the lesser of (a) 85% of the AIME or 100% of the PIA, if larger, or (b) 150% of the PIA.

---

[25] Parents benefits can apply to natural, adoptive or stepparents with somewhat differing criteria applicable to each category. [See 20 CFR 404.374].

[26] Time Limit for Filing Proof of Support: Proof of support must be filed within 2 years of the wage-earner's death or within 2 years of the establishment of the wage-earner's period of disability, whichever point is being used. The latter may be many years prior to the year in which a parent can actually qualify for a benefit.

[27] See generally, Appendix I.

[28] If the PIA is low enough (e.g. around $200), there will be nothing left over for auxiliary benefits.

Where the wage-earner receives a retirement benefit (or is deceased), the family maximum would be based on the wage-earner's PIA in the year of original eligibility enhanced by a percentage factor as the PIA rises[29].

The formulas for calculating family maximums are complex and tend to change annually.[30] [See generally, 20 CFR 404.403]. However, a family maximum never results in the reduction of the benefits payable to the wage-earner; if reduction is necessary because of imposition of a family maximum it is the auxiliary beneficiaries (spouse, children, parents, etc.) whose benefits are reduced. [20 CFR 404.404]. Additionally, if benefits are payable to both a legal spouse and a divorced spouse, the payment to the divorced spouse does not fall within the parameters of the family maximum; however, all benefits due a wage-earner's children, whether legitimate or not, come out of and must fit within, the family maximum.

3. Percentage of PIA available for Particular Auxiliary Beneficiaries.

    a. Husband/wife: one-half of the wage-earner's PIA. [20 CFR 404.333]

    b. Widow(er): an amount equal to the wage-earner's PIA, unless the wage-earner began to receive benefits before he reached age 65 or died before reaching age 62, but not less than 82 1/2% of the wage-earner's PIA. [20 CFR 404.338]

    c. Mother's or father's: 75% of the wage-earner's PIA, with potential reductions for "excess" earnings. [20 CFR 404.342; 404.304;.410-413]

    d. Child's: one-half of the wage-earner's PIA if the insured is alive; 3/4 of the wage-earner's PIA if the insured is deceased.[20 CFR 404.353]

    e. Parent(s): 82 1/2% of the wage-earner's PIA if only one parent is eligible; 75% of the wage-earner's PIA if both parents are eligible. [20 CFR 404.373].

---

[29] For example, if a retired wage-earner, whose eligibility year is 1993, has a PIA up to $513 the family maximum is 150% of the PIA; if the wage-earner's PIA is between $513.01 and $740, the family max will be $769.50 plus 272% of the excess PIA over $513. A PIA above $740.01 would be enhanced by a different percentage factor.

[30] Family maximum, along with PIA, are usually found already calculated in the wage-earner's earnings record.

However, even though a statutorily specified percentage of benefits is generally payable to a particular auxiliary beneficiary [e.g. widow, child, parent, etc.], the stated percentage may not actually be available in a given case because of the constraints imposed by application of the family maximum.

Part 2: INTRODUCTION TO WORK INCENTIVES UNDER SOCIAL SECURITY and SSI FOR DISABLED INDIVIDUALS

I. SSI Income and Resource Rules

1. Types of income

   A. Earned
   B. Unearned
   C. Deemed

2. Earned Income

   A. Gross wages or net self employment income
   B. Includes income from sheltered workshop, royalties from publication of individual's work or honoria for services rendered; bonuses, commissions and severance pay.
   C. Calculating effect of income on SSI
      a. deduct first $65 (or $85, if no unearned income)
      b. deduct 1/2 the rest
      c. remainder is countable earned income
      d. deduct countable earned income from SSI benefit which would otherwise be available (considering living arrangement).
      e. SSI benefit remains.

   D. EXAMPLE: George lives alone. His only income is $885 from his job. To calculate SSI:

      Step 1: Calculating countable income

	$885	
-	85	
=	$800	÷ 2 = $400
-	400	
=	$400	countable income

      Step 2: Calculating SSI benefit

	$580	(SSI: living alone rate)
-	400	
	$180	(SSI benefit)

      Step 3: John's actual monthly income

	$885	(gross earnings)
+	180	(SSI benefit)
	$1065	(total monthly income)

3. Unearned income:

   A. anything that is not wages or self-employment income,

including any benefit.

B. Countable benefits: SSA, VA, workers' comp. Unemployment, private pension, annuity, interest or dividend income, gifts, etc.

C. Other forms of unearned income: alimony, child support, rental income (unless renting is business), prizes and awards.

D. Non-countable unearned income: first $20, only.

E. EXAMPLE: George receives a birthday gift of $300. SSI will deduct $280 from his benefit for that month, since the only part that will not be counted is the first $20.

F. In-kind income:

i. Is a form of unearned income;
ii. It is food, clothing or shelter provided by someone (inside or outside the claimant's household) inkind, not in cash.
ii. Is counted in ne of two ways depending on the individual's living arrangement:

a. If an individual "lives in the household of another", inkind support is counted as a flat, irrebutable 1/3 reduction of the federal benefit rate (FBR). This reduction is called a VTR, "value of the one-third reduction";

- living in the household of another means receiving a subsidy for <u>both</u> food and shelter.

- In 1999 the FBR = $500. 1/3 the FBR = $166.66 1/3 reduction leaves an SSI benefit of: $331.34

b. for any other living arrangement, inkind support is counted as a rebuttable deduction of 1/3 the FBR + $20.00. This calculation is called a PMV, "presumed maximum value".

- The PMV in 1999 is $186.66;

- The maximum reduction for inkind support, no matter how valuable the support may be, is $186.66, leaving an SSI benefit of $311.34.

- If the actual amount of inkind support is less than the PMV, and the claimant has the evidence to prove it, only the actual value will be charged against the claimant's SSI.

iii. EXAMPLE: George receives a free bag of groceries from his supermarket for being the one millionth customer to check out in the store's first year. The value of the groceries in the bag is $70. George's SSI in the month in which he receives the groceries will be reduced by $70 [i.e. the fair market value of the groceries, rather than by the PMV). If SSI learns about the groceries later, the $70 will be charged as an overpayment.

4. Deemed income: income presumed to be available whether it is or not. Applies in three situations:

A. Spousal: between couples who are living together and are:
i. legally married; or
ii. common law (in states which recognize common law); or
iii. holding themselves out as married

Deeming ceases when the couple ceases to live together.

B. Parent to child: until the child reaches age 18.

C. Sponsor to alien:

i. for individuals who entered the country before 8/22/96, for the first 3 years;

ii. for individuals who entered after 8/22/96, generally, until the alien is naturalized or earns 40 quarters (10 years of work credits).

iv. pursuant to the Personal Responsibility and Work Opportunity Act of 1996, a sponsorship agreement is a legally enforcible document, and a sponsor of an alien can be held financially liable for any public benefits received by a sponsored alien until the alien is naturalized or has earned 40 quarters of work credit.

D. Deemed income may totally wipe out SSI eligibility or result in reduced amount of benefit.

5. Income exclusions

A. Earned income tax credit

B. $10 of infrequent or irregular income;

C. Student earnings (for students under age 22) up to $400/month but not more than $1,620 per calendar year;

D. Impairment-related work expenses (applies to both initial and continuing eligibility);

E. Blind work expenses (for blind SSI recipients only);

F. amounts set aside in a PASS plan;

G. Needs-based assistance funded by state or city;

H. home produce;

I. disaster relief;

J. Foster care assistance for ineligible child;

K. Interest on burial fund;

L. home energy assistance;

M. Any support assistance provided by a non-profit organization for food, clothing or shelter, including a rental subsidy paid directly to the landlord.

N. Federal relocation assistance;

O. For a child SSI recipient, 1/3 of the support paid by an absent parent;

P. Transportation tickets for domestic travel received as a gift (if paid for directly to the vendor and the ticket is nonrefundable to the recipient);

Q. Money borrowed or money received as repayment of a loan;

R. Medical care and services (not paid for by Medicaid); or social services;

S. Bills paid or gifts of any non-food, clothing or shelter items, if paid directly to the vendor;

T. See generally 416.1100 et. seq.

II. Title II work incentives

1. Avoiding consequences of the SGA $500 rule (applies only to SSD recipients)

A. Rebutting the presumption of SGA

1. Unsuccessful Work Attempt (UWA)
   a. less than 6 month of work, ceased because
   b. of disabling impairment or
   c. removal or loss of special work conditions

2. Subsidized or make work: SSA counts only that portion of an individual's wages which is <u>not</u> subsidized (i.e. which constitutes competitive work activity)

   a. Nature of work or special conditions must show person not fully earning his pay

      - if person needs special supervision, or extra help to do simple tasks, or a job coach
      - on the job training supported by state VR, usually involves a subsidy

   b. Sheltered work may or may not be SGA

3. Reduce wages by offset

   a. impairment related work expenses, or

      - reasonable cost of items and services needed to perform work
      - only deductible if paid for by worker, not third party

   b. business-related work expenses (self-employment)

      - reasonable cost of expenses
      - vehicle, supplies, telephone

   c. NO blind work expenses for SSD

4. Calculating SGA

   a. figure out value of subsidy (document from employer, sheltered work shop, co-workers) whether in cash or in-kind;

   b. deduct subsidy from gross income

   c. if this leaves less than $500/mon, SGA is generally rebutted

5. Income averaging

   a. start with gross wages, after any allowable deductions

   b. If work is steady and continuous, divide total

wages by number of months worked;

c. If work is seasonal, wages averaged over the actual period of time worked

d. during TWP, income averaging does not apply.

e. if work is sporadic because of impairment, then individual should go back on benefits when wages fall below $500/mon during EPE

f. In 2nd Circuit states, income averaging applies after the EPE ends (Conley, p. 36);

g. In the rest of the country, SSA policy: SSA limits income averaging to applicants; if person earns $500/mon in any month following TWP and EPE, benefits can be terminated.

2. Trial work period

   1. Not applicable if Medical improvement occurs

   2. includes any 9 months with earnings at or above $200/mon

   3. claimant retains all earnings and benefits during first 9 months + 3 transitional months, then benefits end if earnings continue at or above $500/mon

3. EPE

   1. 36 months following end of TWP
   2. benefits will not be paid for any month of SGA
   3. benefits will be paid for any month below SGA
   4. if work ceases, claimant will be reinstated
   5. benefits cease if medical improvement occurs

4. Extended medicare

   1. continuation of Medicare for 39 months after end of TWP
   2. in some cases person can continue Medicare by "buy=in" after extended Medicare ends (called Health Insurance for Working Disabled) (p 38 -39)

II. SSI work incentives

A. SGA $500 rules only applies to applicants

- can be rebutted using:
  - impairment-related work expenses,
  - blind work expenses
  - business expenses

30

- subsidized work, make work, etc.

B. TWP period does not apply; EPE does not apply

C. work incentives inapplicable if medical improvement occurs

D. In determining countable income, certain exclusions apply:

- calculate earned, unearned and deemed income (as above)
- deduct value of subsidized work
- exclusion for student's earned income ($400/mon up to $1,620/yr.

E. Break-even points (<u>based on benefits claimant would receive if no countable income</u>).

- if there is no income other than earned income, for an individual living alone with no other deductions (e.g. deeming, ISM, etc.), break-even point is reached using the following formula: 2 x (FBR + SSP) + $85

- In 1999 (in NYS): 2 x $586 = $1166 + $85 = $1,251/mon

- an SSI recipient in NYS who earns $1,251 or more per month is no longer eligible for even $1.00 of SSI; and, therefore, is not automatically eligible for Medicaid.

- an SSI recipient in NYS who earns $1,250 or less per month is eligible for at least $1.00 of SSI and is, therefore, automatically entitled to Medicaid as well.

F. Blind work expenses (applies only to blind SSI recipients)

G. IRWE

H. Extended Medicaid: §1619-b allows former SSI recipients to continue eligibility for Medicaid when SSI benefits cease because wages are too high. The annual income limits governing §1619-b eligibility for New Yorkers during 1998 is $28,736/year. So long as annual income is below this figure and other eligibility criteria are met, the individual will remain automatically eligible for Medicaid. Additionally, persons who have extremely high Medicaid-reimbursable health care costs, including cost for home health care, may have a much higher allowable annual income.

Prepared by Barbara Samuels, Legal Services for New York City, 350 Broadway, New York, New York 10009. [212]431-7200. January, 1999.

NOTES

2

DISABILITY STANDARDS AND CONCEPTS

Carolyn A. Kubitschek

1

DISABILITY STANDARDS AND CONCEPTS

Carolyn A. Kubitschek

Social Security Disability Insurance Benefits and Supplemental Security Income were created by Congress. In creating the programs, Congress originated the definitions.

Statutory Definition of Disability.

The United States Supreme Court has ruled that the Social Security Act is a piece of remedial legislation.[1] It was designed to be "unusually protective" of claimants.[2] Because of its remedial character, the courts have repeatedly held the statute is to be construed liberally, and not in a "constricted and crabbed" manner.[3] Specifically, the determination should be whether the claimant is able to "perform the requisite physical acts day in and day out, in the sometimes competitive and stressful conditions in which real people work in the real world."[4]

The statute defines disability as "inability to engage in any substantial gainful activity by reason of any medically determinable physical or mental impairment which can be expected to result in death or which has lasted or can be expected to last for a continuous period of not less than 12 months. . . ."[5]

The statute sets up several obvious criteria. First, the person must have a medical problem. "[A] 'physical or mental impairment' is an impairment that results from anatomical, physiological, or psychological abnormalities which are demonstrable by medically acceptable clinical and laboratory diagnostic techniques."[6] If neither a physician nor a psychologist can verify the patient's health problem, then the individual is not disabled, regardless of how incapacitated he or she feels.

Second, the individual must be unable to do "any substantial gainful activity," i.e., work. However, there are some exceptions to that blanket rule: people who are unable to do their former jobs but capable of doing some work will nonetheless be found disabled for Social Security purposes, if their advanced age, poor education, and limited work experience make them so unattractive to prospective employers that they are, as a practical matter, unemployable. (See discussion, infra.) In accordance with that exception, the Social Security Act provides that:

An individual shall be

> determined to be under a disability only if his physical or mental impairment or impairments are of such severity that he is not only unable to do his previous work but cannot, considering his age, education, and work experience, engage in any other kind of substantial gainful work which exists in the national economy.[7]

Durational Requirement

In order to be disabling, an impairment must last for at least twelve months or cause death.[8] An impairment which improves to the point that the claimant is capable of returning to work in less than twelve months is not a disabling impairment, not matter how much it incapacitates the individual.

The Supplemental Security Income program contains the same twelve-month requirement.[9]

Note: the law refers to an impairment which "has lasted or can be expected to last for a continuous period of not less than twelve months."[10] The individual does not have to wait to apply for benefits until he or she has been disabled for twelve consecutive months. S/he may apply for benefits at any time, and will qualify for benefits at the inception of the disabling impairment as long as the impairment is terminal or will last for twelve months.

The Sequential Evaluation.

The statute provides that an individual:

shall be determined to be under

> a disability only if his physical or mental impairment or impairments are of such severity that he is not only unable to do his previous work but cannot, considering his age, education, and work experience, engage in any other kind of substantial gainful work which exists in the national economy, regardless of whether such work exists in the immediate area in which he lives, or whether a specific job vacancy exists, for him, or whether he would be hired if he applied for work.[11]

The statute is designed with two steps in mind. The first step is to determine whether the claimant can do his or her previous work. If not, the second step is to determine whether the claimant can do any other work in the national economy.[12] Both determinations require an individualized assessment of the claimant's impairments,[13] the ability of the claimant to function in the workplace given those impairments, and her capacity to reenter the labor force after retraining.[14]

The two-step process of the above statute has, in turn, been expanded by the Social Security Administration into a five-step method called the "sequential evaluation process." The sequential evaluation process replaces the individual assessment of each claimant with a categorized approach -- the process creates categories and then establishes standards for each category. In order to allay misunderstanding and to encourage a more uniform application of

Social Security Administration (SSA) policy, every step of the sequential evaluation process is governed by detailed regulations.

Step One --Substantial Gainful Activity

First, SSA determines whether or not the claimant is currently engaged in "substantial gainful activity," i.e., whether the claimant is working.[15] People who work will not be found disabled if they are gainfully employed, not matter how sick or injured they are.

"Gainful activity" is defined as "work activity that you do for pay or profit."[16] It does not encompass any activity that does not provide for monetary compensation: social activities, hobbies, taking care of oneself, performing household tasks, etc.[17]

"Substantial gainful activity" is defined as "work activity that is both substantial and gainful."[18] The work performed must involve mental or physical activities that are significant, productive and that result in (or are intended for) pay or profit.[19] The bottom line for the Social Security practitioner is that not all work qualifies as substantial gainful activity.

How does the Social Security Administration determine whether a claimant's work activity is substantial and gainful? As can be expected, the amount of earnings is an important factor. Low earnings are considered proof that the claimant has not been engaging in substantial gainful activity.[20] A minimum amount has been established by the agency, at which point SSA "generally" concludes that the claimant has not engaged in substantial gainful activity.[21] That amount changes with the fluctuations of the economy, and has ranged from $130.00 per month in years prior to 1976,[22] to $300.00 per month since 1990.[23]

There is also an income ceiling, and earnings above that level are "considered" substantial gainful activity.[24] The ceiling has ranged from $200.00 per month in years prior to 1976,[25] up to $500.00 per month from 1990 to the present.[26] Claimants who have earned between $300.00 and $500.00 per month do not receive either the presumption that they are working or the presumption that they are not working.

Even if the claimant has earned less than the maximum amount established, the agency will also examine the actual value of the work performed in making its determination. For example, if a carpenter spends several hundred hours repairing a house, and charges only $499.00 for his labors, the Social Security Administration will use the market value of the work as the claimant's actual earnings. Thus, if the value of the work performed exceeds the maximum dollar amount established, then the work is substantial gainful activity, despite the fact that the claimant has earned less than the maximum.[27]

Part-time work may qualify as substantial gainful activity.[28] In fact, a claimant's ability to work part-time may indicate an ability to perform full-time work.[29]

The SSA averages the monthly earnings of a claimant measured over the course of a year -- if the claimant's average monthly income is below the $300.00 minimum, then the work performed during the year is not considered substantial. Thus, even if the claimant's income was above the maximum for one or more months, the claimant will not be considered to have engaged in substantially gainful activity as long as the annual earnings are less than $3600.00.[30]

A history of "transitory" or "sporadic" employment is deemed not to be substantial gainful activity.[31] Unsuccessful attempts at securing employment fall into this category: "Work that you are forced to stop after a short time because of your impairment," does not constitute substantial gainful activity.[32] A work attempt is unsuccessful if it lasts less than three months,[33] while work which exceeds six months is considered a successful attempt.[34] Work attempts between three and six months are subject to further evaluation -- what is at issue here is the reason why the job ended. If the job ended because the claimant's impairments led to frequent absences, unsatisfactory performance, or if the claimant worked during a period of temporary remission or under special conditions, then that work is also considered an unsuccessful attempt at substantial gainful activity.[35]

Special rules are in effect for determining whether self-employed claimants have participated in substantial gainful activity. The agency does not make its determination based exclusively on income but instead quantifies the value of the claimant's activities to the business.[36] Therefore, a self-employed claimant earning less than the specified minimum dollar amounts may still be considered to be taking part in substantial gainful activity.

Claimants whose impairments necessitate a higher degree of supervision, emotional support, and tolerance or who require concessions such as a slower pace of work than would normally be expected in a competitive workplace, and, consequentially, a significantly lower level of productivity, are not taking part in what constitutes substantial gainful activity.[37] The nature as well as level of supervision and productivity of the claimant's work are the determining factors in establishing whether or not substantial gainful activity was performed.

The sheltered workshop is a prime example of a workplace in which claimants, particularly those suffering from mental impairments, receive special treatment.[38] Part-time work in a sheltered workshop is not considered evidence of the claimant's ability to work full-time, and if the claimant's earnings in a sheltered workshop were less than $500.00 per month, the agency will presume that the work does not qualify as substantial gainful activity.[39]

Step Two -- Severity

The second step in the sequential evaluation is the determination of whether the impairment is "severe." An impairment or combination of impairments "is not severe if it does not significantly limit your physical or mental abilities to do basic work activities." Basic work activities are "the abilities and aptitudes necessary to do most jobs." Examples of these include--

(1) Physical functions such as walking, standing, sitting,

> lifting, pushing, pulling, reaching, carrying, or handling;
>
> (2) Capacities for seeing, hearing, and speaking;
>
> (3) Understanding, carrying out, and remembering simple instructions;
>
> (4) Use of judgment;
>
> (5) Responding appropriately to supervision, co-workers and usual work situations; and
>
> (6) Dealing with changes in a routine work setting.[40]

The severity regulations were found to be consistent with the statute by the United States Supreme Court, in Bowen v. Yuckert[41]:

> [The Social Security Act] restricts eligibility for disability benefits to

> claimants whose medically severe impairments prevent them from doing their previous work <u>and</u> also prevent them from doing any other substantial gainful work in the national economy. If a claimant is unable to show that he has a medically severe impairment, he is not eligible for disability benefits. In such a case, there is no reason for the Secretary to consider the claimant's age, education, and work experience.[42]

Therefore, since 1984, the Social Security Administration has considered the combined effect of all of a claimant's impairments in determining severity:

> [W]e will consider the combined

> effect of all of your impairments without regard to whether any such impairment, if considered separately, would be of sufficient severity. If we do find a medically severe combination of impairments, the combined impact of the impairments will be considered throughout the disability determination process.[43]

If the claimant does suffer from a severe impairment, SSA will then proceed to the third step in the sequential evaluation process.

Step Three -- Listings of Impairments

Step 3 is a determination of whether or not the claimant's illness or injury is identical to, or medically equivalent to, one of several hundred illnesses "considered severe enough to prevent a person from doing any gainful activity."[44] This list is called the Listing of Impairments.[45] The claimant is automatically found disabled when he or she has an impairment that matches or is equivalent to one (or more) of the impairments on the Listing.[46] It does not matter if the claimant would actually be able to work; meeting a Listing means an automatic finding of disability.

Since the list contains impairments which would preclude the performance of any gainful activity, not merely substantial gainful activity,[47] a claimant who meets a Listing will be more severely impaired than is necessary to qualify for benefits under the statute's functional test.

The list of automatically disabling impairments has been divided by the SSA into fourteen categories for adults, representing different body systems, and fourteen additional categories for children, although children may also be evaluated under the adult Listings. The 14 adult categories are:

1.00 Musculoskeletal System.

2.00 Special Senses (vision and hearing) and Speech.

3.00 Respiratory System.

4.00 Cardiovascular System.

5.00 Digestive System.

6.00 Genito-Urinary System.

7.00 Hemic and Lymphatic System.

8.00 Skin.

9.00 Endocrine System.

10.00 Multiple Body Systems.

11.00 Neurological Disorders.

12.00 Mental Disorders.

13.00 Neoplastic Diseases, Malignant.

14.00 Immune System.[48]

Each of the 14 categories contains numerous impairments, and measures the degree of each impairment necessary to be disabling under the law.

The actual ability to work is irrelevant when the claimant meets a Listing.[49] For example: numerous paraplegics work. One, Franklin Roosevelt, became President. The List of Impairments, on the other hand, provides that the loss of major function of both legs[50] is a disabling impairment. Therefore, all paraplegics are automatically disabled, as long as they are not actually gainfully employed.

Only medical criteria are contained in the Listings.[51] Neither functional ability nor vocational factors are relevant. Thus, when a claimant meets the Listings, the fact that s/he has worked in the past (while meeting the listings) is irrelevant.

A claimant whose impairment or impairments do not meet the Listings may still be found disabled if the impairment is medically equivalent to one or more impairments on the list, or if the combined effect of all of the claimant's impairments is medically equivalent to a listed impairment.[52] Medical equivalence means equivalence in both severity and duration to a listed impairment.[53] Medical equivalence, however, may include only medical factors, not vocational factors, such as claimant's age, education, or past work experience.[54]

Because the Listings can make or break a determination of disability, the possibility that a claimant might meet or equal a Listing should encourage counsel to produce evidence on that issue.

Moreover, the Administrative Law Judge must develop the record with all component parts of that listing in mind.[55] The ALJ should make sure that the Listings (much like the Social Security Act itself) are construed broadly, and not interpreted in a "constricted and crabbed manner."[56]

Claimants who suffer from impairments for which a Listing exists, but whose impairments do not satisfy every criterion of the Listing, may be found automatically disabled if their impairments are medically equivalent to an appropriate listing. Medical equivalence occurs in this situation when "one or more of the specified medical findings is missing from the evidence ... [but] other findings of equal or greater clinical significance and relating to the same impairment are present in the medical evidence."[57]

Furthermore, residual functional capacity must also be considered by the SSA in determining medical equivalence.[58] The practitioner should keep in mind that the Listings encompass those impairments whose severity prevent a claimant from engaging in any gainful activity. Therefore, if the claimant's residual functional capacity is so restricted that she cannot take part in any gainful activity, the claimant must, by definition, have an impairment that is medically equivalent to a Listed impairment. In the words of the Second Circuit:

> If a claimant's residual functional capacity leaves her unable to perform any gainful activity, her impairment, even if unlisted, must be at the

level of severity of an impairment included in the Secretary's Listings.[59]

If a claimant has an impairment which does not meet any Listing, that impairment must be compared to a listed impairment which is most similar to that of the claimant.[60]

If a claimant's impairments do not meet or equal any on the list, s/he must proceed to Step Four of the sequential evaluation process.

Step Four -- Ability to do Past Relevant Work

The fourth step undertaken by the Social Security Administration is a determination of the claimant's "residual functional capacity"[61] and whether that capacity enables the claimant to perform past relevant work. That evaluation entails the claimant's actual ability to function and perform daily tasks. The evaluation would include the degree to which the claimant can sit, stand, walk, lift, carry, push, pull, climb, bend, tolerate various temperatures, concentrate, obey orders, and understand instructions.

The Social Security Administration also takes into consideration the functional demands of the claimant's former employment. The claimant's residual functional capacity is measured against the demands of the claimant's previous jobs. If his or her residual functional capacity is equivalent to or greater than the demands of past work performed, then the claimant is capable of returning to a former job, and is, hence, not disabled.[62]

Step Five -- Ability to do Other Work

If the claimant's residual

functional capacity is insufficient to meet the physical and/or mental demands of former employment, the Social Security Administration will proceed to the fifth and last step. The agency will ascertain whether or not other jobs exist in the national economy which the claimant can perform, considering the fact that s/he lacks the capacity to return to a former job, and given his or her particular functional limitations.[63]

Some people who are actually able to work -- though not capable of performing their past jobs -- will still be found disabled because, by reason of vocational factors, they are unemployable. The agency has developed a set of tables known as the "Grids," because they are, in fact, printed on a series of grids. Their purpose is to distinguish between claimants who either are disabled or are not disabled based upon vocational factors.[64]

The Grids, which can be found in an appendix to the Social Security Regulations,[65] deem the following categories of claimants to be disabled:

1. Claimants who are capable of performing only sedentary work, are 50 years of age or older, have a limited -- i.e., seventh through eleventh grade[66] -- education, and previously did unskilled work or no work at all;[67]

2. Claimants who are capable of performing only sedentary work, are 50 years of age or older, have a limited education, and previously did skilled or semi-skilled work but lack transferable skills;[68]

3. Claimants who are capable of performing only sedentary work, are 50 years of age or older, have graduated

from high school but not recently, and previously did unskilled work or no work at all;[69]

4. Claimants who are capable of performing only sedentary work, are 50 years of age or older, have graduated from high school but not recently, and previously did skilled or semi-skilled work but lack transferable skills;[70]

5. Claimants who are capable of performing only sedentary work, are between 45 and 49 years of age, are illiterate or unable to communicate in English, and previously did unskilled work or no work at all;[71]

6. Claimants who are capable of performing light work, are 55 years of age or older, have a limited education, and previously did unskilled work or no work at all;[72]

7. Claimants who are capable of

performing light work, are 55 years of age or older, have a limited education, and previously did skilled or semi-skilled work but lack transferable skills;[73]

8. Claimants who are capable of performing light work, are 55 years of age or older, graduated from high school, but not recently, and previously did unskilled work or no work at all;[74]

9. Claimants who are capable of performing light work, are 55 years of age or older, graduated from high school, but not recently, and previously did skilled or semi-skilled work but lack transferable skills;[75]

10. Claimants who are capable of performing light work, are between 50 and 54 years of age, are illiterate or unable to communicate in English, and previously did unskilled work or no work at all;[76]

11. Claimants who are capable of performing medium work, are 60 years of age or older, have at most a marginal education (sixth grade or less),[77] and previously did unskilled work or no work at all;[78] and

12. Claimants who are capable of performing medium work, are 55 years of age or older, have a limited education, and never worked.[79]

All other claimants who are capable of doing a full range of work at a certain exertional level, and whose vocational profile matches a Grid category, are deemed not to be disabled.

However, many individuals have vocational profiles which do not fit neatly into one or another grid category. Many individuals have impairments which limit their capabilities to less than the full range of work at any exertional level. And many individuals have non-exertional impairments, which limit the range of job that they can perform at any given exertional level. For all of those individuals, the Grids do not apply. Instead, the Social Security Administration must make individualized determinations as to their ability to work.

The agency's five-step process has come under criticism for creating "pigeonholes,"[80] based upon such empirical criteria as the Listings and the Grids, while at the same time dispensing with the individualized evaluation envisioned by the statute. The United States Supreme Court, however, has found that the use of pigeonholes in the sequential evaluation process "contribute[s] to the uniformity and efficiency of disability determinations."[81]

Weighing Medical Opinions

The medical information in a claimant's file may include reports and records from three different types of physicians: treating physicians, examining physicians, and non-examining physicians. Those reports are given different amounts of weight.

Treating Physicians

One of the most important sources of evidence regarding a claimant's condition is the medical treating source. The law gives "special evidentiary weight to the opinion of the treating physician."[82] The regulations promulgated by the Commissioner explicitly agree. "Generally, we give more weight to opinions from [the claimant's] treating sources. . . ."[83]

An ALJ has the obligation to "make

every reasonable effort to obtain from the individual's treating physician . . . all medical evidence, including diagnostic tests, necessary in order to properly make [a disability] determination. . . ."[84] To fulfill that obligation, the ALJ must obtain reports from the treating physicians,[85] and copies of the claimant's treatment records.[86] Specifically, the ALJ must "request a medical source statement describing the types of work that the applicant is still capable of performing."[87] The ALJ's duty to develop the record exists whether or not the claimant is represented by counsel.[88] Moreover, if the treating physician provides medical evidence to the ALJ, but the evidence is "inadequate, it [is] the ALJ's duty to seek additional information."[89]

Reports of the treating physician

are the most important type of medical reports. If those reports are supported by objective medical evidence, they are binding on the Social Security Administration.

Examining Physicians

Examining physicians are those who do not actually provide treatment to the claimant over a period of time. Instead, they examine the claimant once, sometimes at the request of the Social Security Administration.[90]

A consultative physician who sees an individual on one occasion for an examination cannot obtain the necessary long term medical history and can therefore provide limited information.[91] Accordingly, in the Second Circuit, opinions of consulting physicians are entitled to less weight than those of treating physicians.

Non-examining Physicians

Non-examining physicians generally fall into one of two categories. They may be what SSA calls "review physicians," physicians hired by the agency to review the claimant's medical records and determine whether the claimant is disabled under Social Security rules. Or they may be physicians called to testify as advisors at hearings.

Opinions of non-examining physicians are entitled to very little weight in the Second Circuit.[92] Opinions of medical advisors are likewise entitled to little weight. The function of medical advisors is to "explain complex medical problems in terms understandable to lay examiners."[93]

Other courts are similarly unimpressed by non-examining physicians. The Eighth Circuit refers to the conclusions of a doctor who has never seen the patient as "medical sophistry."[94]

ENDNOTES

1. Bowen v. City of New York, 476 U.S. 467, 486 n. 14, 106 S.Ct. 2022, 2033 n. 14, 90 L.Ed.2d 462, 479 n. 14 (1986).

2. Bowen v. City of New York, 476 U.S. 467, 480, 106 S.Ct. 2022, 2030, 90 L.Ed.2d 462, 475 (1986), quoting from Heckler v. Day, 467 U.S. 104, 106, 104 S.Ct. 2249, 2251, 81 L.Ed.2d 88 (1984).

3. Williams on behalf of Williams v. Bowen, 858 F.2d 255, 260 (2d Cir. 1988).

4. Kouril v. Bowen, 912 F.2d 971 (8th Cir. 1990).

5. 42 U.S.C. §423(d)(1)(A), Social Security Disability Income Benefits; 42 U.S.C. §1382c(a)(3)(A), Supplemental Security Income benefits.

6. 42 U.S.C. §423(d)(3).

7. 42 U.S.C. §§423(d)(2); 1382c(3)(B).

8. 42 U.S.C. §§416(i)(1)(A), 423(d)(1)(A); 20 C.F.R. §§404.1505(a), 416.905(a).

9. 42 U.S.C §1382c(a)(3)(A).

10. 20 C.F.R. §§404.1505(s); 416.905(a).

11. 42 U.S.C. §423(d)(2)(A).

12. 42 U.S.C. §423(d)(2)(A).

13. Heckler v. Campbell, 461 U.S. 458, 103 S.Ct. 1952, 76 L.Ed.2d 66 (1983).

14. Id.

15. 20 C.F.R. §§404.1520(b), 416.920(b).

16. 20 C.F.R. §§404.1572(b); 416.972(b). The regulation clarifies that a person need not actually realize a profit to be engaging in substantial gainful activity.

17. 20 C.F.R. §§404.1572(c), 416.972(c); attending law school; Neumerski v. Califano, 513 F.Supp. 1011 (E.D. Pa. 1981).

18. 20 C.F.R. §§404.1572, 416.972.

19. 20 C.F.R. §§404.1510; 416.910.

20. Fogarty v. Secretary of Health and Human Services, 690 F.Supp. 166 (W.D.N.Y. 1988).

21. 20 C.F.R. §§404.1574(b)(3); 416.974(b)(3).

22. 20 C.F.R. §§404.1574(b)(3)(i); 416.974(b)(3)(i).

23. 20 C.F.R. §§404.1574(b)(3)(vii); 416.974(b)(3)(vii).

24. 20 C.F.R. §§404.1574(b)(2); 416.974(b)(2).

25. 20 C.F.R. §§404.1574(b)(2)(i); 416.974(b)(2)(i).

26. 20 C.F.R. §§404.1574(b)(2)(vii); 416.974(b)(2)(vii).

27. 20 C.F.R. §§404.1574(b)(6); 416.974(b)(6).

28. 20 C.F.R. §§404.1572(a); 416.972(a).

29. 20 C.F.R. §§404.1571, 416.971.

30. Conley v. Bowen, 859 F.2d 261, 265 (2d Cir. 1988).

31. Storyk v. Secretary of Health, Education and Welfare, 462 F.Supp. 152, 158 (S.D.N.Y. 1978)

32. 20 C.F.R. §§404.1574(a)(1); 416.974(a)(1).

33. SSR 84-25. See also, Preston v. Secretary of Health and Human Services, 854 F.2d 815, 817 (6th Cir. 1988), where the claimant's work lasted for 10 days.

34. SSR 84-25.

35. SSR 84-25 (1984).

36. 20 C.F.R. §§404.1575(a); 416.975(a).

37. Fogarty v. Secretary of Health and Human Services, 690 F.Supp. 166 (W.D.N.Y. 1988).

38. 20 C.F.R. §§404.1574(a)(3); 416.974(a)(3).

39. 20 C.F.R. §§404.1574(b)(4)(vii); 416.974(b)(4)(vii).

40. 20 C.F.R. §§404.1521; 416.921 (1985).

41. 482 U.S. 137, 107 S.Ct. 2287, 96 L.Ed.2d 119 (1987).

42. Bowen v. Yuckert, 482 U.S. 137, 148, 107 S.Ct. 2287, 2294-95, 96 L.Ed.2d 119, 131 (1987).

43. 20 C.F.R. §§404.1523, 416.923.

44. 20 C.F.R. §§404.1525(a); 416.925(a); Sullivan v. Zebley, 493 U.S. 521, 110 S.Ct. 885, 892, 107 L.Ed.2d 967 (1990).

45. The list is found at 20 C.F.R. Part 404, Subpart P, Appendix 1.

46. 20 C.F.R. §§404.1520(d), 416.920(d).

47. Sullivan v. Zebley, 493 U.S. 521, 110 S.Ct. 885, 892, 107 L.Ed.2d 967 (1990).

48. 20 C.F.R. Part 404, Subpart P, Appendix 1.

49. Gambill v. Bowen, 823 F.2d 1998 (6th Cir. 1987).

50. 20 C.F.R. Part 404, Subpart P, §1.09B.

51. 20 C.F.R. §§404.1525(b)(1); 416.925(b)(1).

52. 20 C.F.R. §§404.1526(a); 416.926(a).

53. 20 C.F.R. §§404.1526(a); 416.926(a).

54. 20 C.F.R. §§404.1526(b); 416.926(b).

55. Johnson v. Secretary of Health and Human Services, 794 F.2d 1106 (6th Cir. 1986); Tingling v. Secretary of Health and Human Services, 575 F.Supp. 905 (S.D.N.Y. 1983).

56. Williams on behalf of Williams v. Bowen, 859 F.2d 255, 260 (2d Cir. 1988).

57. SSR 83-19.

58. Kier v. Sullivan, 888 F.2d 244, 247 (2d Cir. 1989).

59. Kier v. Sullivan, 888 F.2d 244, 247 (2d Cir. 1989).

60. 20 C.F.R. §§404.1526(a); 416.926(a).

61. 20 C.F.R. §§404.1545, 416.945.

62. 20 C.F.R. §§404.1520(e); 416.920(e).

63. 20 C.F.R. §§404.1520(f)(1); 416.920(f)(1).

64. 20 C.F.R. §§404.1569, 416.969.

65. 20 C.F.R. Part 404, Subpart P, Appendix 2.

66. 20 C.F.R. §§404.1564(b)(3); 416.964(b)(3).

67. 20 C.F.R. Part 404, Subpart P, Appendix 2, §§201.01, 201.09.

68. 20 C.F.R. Part 404, Subpart P, Appendix 2, §§201.02, 201.10.

69. 20 C.F.R. Part 404, Subpart P, Appendix 2, §§201.04, 201.12.

70. 20 C.F.R. Part 404, Subpart P, Appendix 2, §§201.06, 201.14.

71. 20 C.F.R. Part 404, Subpart P, Appendix 2, §201.17.

72. 20 C.F.R. Part 404, Subpart P, Appendix 2, §202.01.

73. 20 C.F.R. Part 404, Subpart P, Appendix 2, §202.02.

74. 20 C.F.R. Part 404, Subpart P, Appendix 2, §202.04.

75. 20 C.F.R. Part 404, Subpart P, Appendix 2, §202.06.

76. 20 C.F.R. Part 404, Subpart P, Appendix 2, §202.09.

77. 20 C.F.R. §§404.1564(b)(2); 416.964(b)(2).

78. 20 C.F.R. Part 404, Subpart P, Appendix 2, §203.01.

79. 20 C.F.R. Part 404, Subpart P, Appendix 2, §§203.02, 203.10.

80. Marcus v. Bowen, 696 F. Supp. 364 (N.D. Ill. 1988); subsequent decision Marcus v. Sullivan, 926 F.2d 604 (7th Cir. 1991).

81. Bowen v. Yuckert, 482 U.S. 137, 153, 107 S.Ct. 2287, 2297, 96 L.Ed.2d 119, 134 (1987), citing Heckler v. Campbell, 461 U.S. 458, 461, 103 S.Ct. 1952, 1954, 76 L.Ed.2d 66, 71 (1983).

82. Clark v. Commissioner of Social Security, 143 F.3d 115, 118 (2d Cir. 1998).

83. 20 C.F.R. §§404.1527(d)(2); 416.927(d)(2).

84. 42 U.S.C. § 423(d)(2)(B).

85. 20 C.F.R. §§404.1512(d)(1); 416.912(d)(1).

86. 20 C.F.R. §§404.1512(e)(1); 416.912(e)(1).

87. Ripley v. Chater, 67 F.3d 552, 557 (5th Cir. 1995); 20 C.F.R. §§404.1513(b)(6); 416.913(b)(6).

88. Pratts v. Chater, 94 F.3d 34, 37 (2d Cir. 1996).

89. Schaal v. Apfel, 134 F.3d 496, 505 (2d Cir. 1998); 20 C.F.R. §§404.1513(e)(1); 416.913(e)(1).

90. 20 C.F.R. §§404.1517, 416.917.

91. <u>Cruz v. Sullivan</u>, 912 F.2d 8, 13 (2d Cir. 1990); Fernandez-Sosa v. Bowen, 701 F.Supp. 74 (S.D.N.Y. 1988); Torres v. Bowen, 700 F. Supp. 1306 (S.D.N.Y. 1988).

92. Hidalgo v. Bowen, 822 F.2d 294 (2d Cir. 1987).

93. Vargas v. Sullivan, 898 F.2d 293 (2d Cir. 1990).

94. Nelson v. Heckler, 712 F.2d 346 (8th Cir. 1983).

NOTES

3

PREPARING A DISABILITY CLAIM

Pamela Levine

PREPARING A DISABILITY CLAIM

Pamela Levine

I. INITIAL CLIENT INTERVIEW

Getting Information

A. Biographical and personal information
   1. address
   2. telephone for client and/or another contact
   3. date of birth
   4. education level
   5. family information
      a. auxiliary benefits
   6. another type of Social Security claim - eg SSI, ADC, etc
   7. current sources of income and insurance
      a. medical insurance
         i. private medical insurance
         ii. medicare or medicaid
         iii. workers' compensation
      b. receipt of other benefits
         i. workers' compensation
         ii. short or long term disability
         iii. veterans benefits
         iv. public assistance

B. Work history
   1. seasonal work or "off the books" work activity
   2. job duties: physical and mental
   3. 15 years (See 20 C.F.R. §404.1565)
   4. work attempts
   5. insured status

C. Treatment information
   1. Treating sources
      a. length and frequency of treatment
      b. type of treatment
      c. doctor's specialty, if any
      d. 20 C.F.R §§404.1527(d), 416.927(d); SSR 96-2p
   2. Consultative Examinations
      a. Independent Medical Examinations
      b. Consultative Examiners
         i. Social Security

ii. Workers' Compensation
iii. Long-Term Disability Insurance carrier

D. Assessing whether there is a meritorious claim
   1. is durational requirement met or expected to be met?
      a. Title II: 20 C.F.R §404.1509
      b. SSI: 20 C.F.R. §416.905
   2. does client understand the Social Security standard for disability?
   3. is there medical support for proof disability?

E. Application for disability benefits:
   1. Title II only, SSI only, or concurrent claim
   2. Any other type of SS claims pending or appropriate
   3. Prior application information
   4. Filing of application or determining stage pending

II. AUTHORIZATIONS

A. Appointment of Representative Forms: SSA 1696

B. Medical Authorization Forms

C. Authorization to Release Information to Social Security: SSA 827

D. Specialized Authorizations
   1. Hospital specific
   2. Sensitive information - e.g. HIV, psychiatric

E. Retainer Agreement

III. GETTING EVIDENCE TO PROVE YOUR CLAIM

A. Medical
   1. Physical
      a. Narratives
      b. Treatment records
      c. RFCs
   2. Psychiatric
      a. Narratives
      b. Treatment records
      c. RFCs

   3. Independent Medical Examinations
   4. Contacting other attorneys for additional information

B. Vocational
   1. work attempt information
   2. "light duty"
   3. VESID

C. Copying the OHA file
   1. Reviewing work background and education level
   2. Reviewing dates
      a. application filing date
      b. previous denials
      c. onset
   3. Reviewing medical information
      a. reports from treating sources
      b. consultative examination reports
      c. non-examining review physicians
   4. Reviewing earnings records for Title II claims
      a. verifying insured status
      b. post-onset earnings

D. Requesting Subpoenas

IV. PREPARING FOR TESTIMONY OF CLIENTS & WITNESSES

A. Nuts and Bolts of Hearing Procedure
   1. Audiotape recording
   2. Oath/affirmation

B. Who is your audience
   1. Your client
   2. The ALJ
   3. Appeals Council
   4. Federal Court

C. Focusing on the issues for this claim

D. Developing Testimony
   1. see attached: Hearing Questionnaire/Checklist
   2. see SSR 96-7p

E. Evaluating the OHA file
   1. See above section III(C).
   2. Checking for Additional Information
      1. earnings
      2. consultative examination reports
      3. non-examining review physician reports
      4. reports of contact

V. PREPARING FOR EXPERT TESTIMONY

A. MEDICAL ADVISORS (MA)
   1. Evaluating the Medical Advisor's Qualifications
   2. Why was the MA called?
   3. MA's testimony
      a. Meets a Listing
      b. Equals a Listing
      c. No past relevant work
      d. Grids
      e. Less than sedentary
   4. Cross-examination of the MA
      a. the record
      b. medical resources
      c. client's testimony
   5. Obtaining additional medical evidence

B. VOCATIONAL EXPERT (VE)
   1. Evaluating the Vocational Expert's Qualifications
   2. Why was the VE called?
   3. Developing your client's testimony
      a. past relevant work activity
      b. RFC
      c. limitations
   4. Check the GRIDs
   5. Hypotheticals
      a. reflective of the record
      b. objecting to exhibits in the record
      c. clarity of record
   6. VE's response
      a. sampling or exhaustive list of jobs
      b. a significant numbers of jobs
   7. Definition of terms used
   8. Eliminating the jobs cited by the VE
      a. cross-examination by medical evidence

b. cross-examination by contradictory vocational evidence
c. client's testimony
d. referring to the Dictionary of Occupational Titles
e. Social Security Ruling 96-9p

CLIENT INTERVIEW INFORMATION

Claim Information:
Case Type: ______________________
Prior applications: ______________________
Referral Source: ______________________
Other pending legal matters: ______________________
Name/Address of other representing attorneys: ____________
____

Personal History:
Name: ______________________
Aliases: ______________________
Social Security Number: ______________________
Date of Birth/Age: ______________________
Address: ______________________
____
Telephone Number: ______________________
Other contact number: ______________________
Education Level: ______________________
Past Work History: ______________________
____
____
____
Work Attempts: ______________________
Disability Description: ______________________
____
Onset of Disability: ______________________
Date Last Worked: ______________________

Medical Information:

Name of Doctor: ______________________________
Address: ______________________________
____
Telephone and Fax Numbers: ______________________________
____
Doctor's Specialty: ______________________________
First date of treatment: ______________________________
Last date of treatment: ______________________________
Frequency of treatment: ______________________________
Type of treatment: ______________________________

Name of Doctor: ______________________________
Address: ______________________________
____
Telephone and Fax Numbers: ______________________________
____
Doctor's Specialty: ______________________________
First date of treatment: ______________________________
Last date of treatment: ______________________________
Frequency of treatment: ______________________________
Type of treatment: ______________________________

Name of Doctor: ______________________________
Address: ______________________________
____
Telephone and Fax Numbers: ______________________________
____
Doctor's Specialty: ______________________________
First date of treatment: ______________________________
Last date of treatment: ______________________________
Frequency of treatment: ______________________________
Type of treatment: ______________________________

Name of Doctor: ______________________________
Address: ______________________________
____
Telephone and Fax Numbers: ______________________________
____
Doctor's Specialty: ______________________________
First date of treatment: ______________________________
Last date of treatment: ______________________________
Frequency of treatment: ______________________________
Type of treatment: ______________________________

Hospital: ______________________________
Patient Identification Number: ______________________________
Inpatient:
Dates of admission and discharge: ______________________________
Reason for admission: ______________________________
Outpatient:
First date of treatment: ______________________________
Last date of treatment: ______________________________
Frequency of treatment: ______________________________
Clinics attended: ______________________________
Type of treatment: ______________________________

Hospital: ______________________________
Patient Identification Number: ______________________________
Inpatient:
Dates of admission and discharge: ______________________________
Reason for admission: ______________________________
Outpatient:
First date of treatment: ______________________________
Last date of treatment: ______________________________
Frequency of treatment: ______________________________
Clinics attended: ______________________________
Type of treatment: ______________________________

Hospital: ______________________________
Patient Identification Number: ______________________________
Inpatient:
Dates of admission and discharge: ______________________________
Reason for admission: ______________________________
Outpatient:
First date of treatment: ______________________________
Last date of treatment: ______________________________
Frequency of treatment: ______________________________
Clinics attended: ______________________________
Type of treatment: ______________________________

Hospital: ______________________________
Patient Identification Number: ______________________________
Inpatient:
Dates of admission and discharge: ______________________________
Reason for admission: ______________________________
Outpatient:
First date of treatment: ______________________________
Last date of treatment: ______________________________

HEARING QUESTIONNAIRE/CHECKLIST

I. BIOGRAPHICAL INFORMATION

Name:
Social Security Number:
Hearing Date:
Name of ALJ:
Location of Hearing Office:

Application Date:
Date of denials:
Prior application information:

Date Last Worked:
Date of Onset:
Post-onset work attempt(s):
- Dates of attempt(s):
- Job duties:
- Reason ended:
- Gross earnings:

Past relevant work information:
- Job:
- Length of time on job:
- Job duties:
- Why ended:

Education:
- Ability to read/write/speak English:

Vocational Training:

II. DISABILITY INFORMATION

Description of Disability:
- (List Impairments)

Name of Treating Source (for each impairment)
Specialty of Doctor (if any):
Date Treatment Began:
Still Treating?:
Frequency of Treatment:
Type of treatment:
Prognosis:

Hospital Admission(s)
Dates:
Reason:

Medication(s) Prescribed:
Dosage:
Reason for Medication(s):
Side effects(s):

Use of any assistive device of aids:
    Prescribed by medical source?:

RFC:

Pain:
    Location:
    Description:
    Frequency:
    Duration:
    Aggravating Factors:
    Mitigating Factors:
    Intensity:

III. ACTIVITIES OF DAILY LIVING

Who do you live with?
    if children, obtain ages

Type of housing:
    Private house or apartment:
    Stairs or elevator?

Household chores: Who performs?
    Cooking
    Cleaning: dust, mop, sweep, vacuum
    Grocery shopping
    Laundry

Ability to Use Public Transportation:
    Any difficulty?:
Drive a car?
    Frequency:
    Distance driven:
    Any difficulty?:

Description of Typical Day:

Attendance at groups, organizations, religious services:
    Distance from home:
    Mode of travel used:
    Frequency of attendance:

Hobbies:

Changes since disability onset?
    family life:
    social life:
    returned to work:

Social Security Ruling SSR 96–9p., Titles II and XVI: Determining Capability To Do Other Work—Implications of a Residual Functional Capacity for Less Than a Full Range of Sedentary Work

AGENCY: Social Security Administration.

ACTION: Notice of Social Security Ruling.

SUMMARY: In accordance with 20 CFR 422.406(b)(1), the Commissioner of Social Security gives notice of Social Security Ruling SSR 96–9p. This Ruling explains the Social Security Administration's policies regarding the impact of a residual functional capacity assessment for less than a full range of sedentary work on an individual's ability to do other work.

EFFECTIVE DATE: July 2, 1996.

FOR FURTHER INFORMATION CONTACT: Joanne K. Castello, Division of Regulations and Rulings, Social Security Administration, 6401 Security Boulevard, Baltimore, MD 21235, (410) 965–1711.

SUPPLEMENTARY INFORMATION: Although we are not required to do so pursuant to 5 U.S.C. 552(a)(1) and (a)(2), we are publishing this Social Security Ruling in accordance with 20 CFR 422.406(b)(1).

Social Security Rulings make available to the public precedential decisions relating to the Federal old-age, survivors, disability, supplemental security income, and black lung benefits programs. Social Security Rulings may be based on case decisions made at all administrative levels of adjudication, Federal court decisions, Commissioner's decisions, opinions of the Office of the General Counsel, and other policy interpretations of the law and regulations.

Although Social Security Rulings do not have the force and effect of the law or regulations, they are binding on all components of the Social Security Administration, in accordance with 20 CFR 422.406(b)(1), and are to be relied upon as precedents in adjudicating cases.

If this Social Security Ruling is later superseded, modified, or rescinded, we will publish a notice in the Federal Register to that effect.

(Catalog of Federal Domestic Assistance, Programs 96.001 Social Security—Disability Insurance; 96.002 Social Security—Retirement Insurance; 96.004 Social Security—Survivors Insurance; 96.005 Special Benefits for Disabled Coal Miners; 96.006 Supplemental Security Income)

Dated: June 7, 1996.

Shirley S. Chater,

Commissioner of Social Security.

Policy Interpretation Ruling—Titles II and XVI: Determining Capability To Do Other Work—Implications of a Residual Functional Capacity for Less Than a Full Range of Sedentary Work

Purpose: To explain the Social Security Administration's policies regarding the impact of a residual functional capacity (RFC) assessment for less than a full range of sedentary work on an individual's ability to do other work. In particular, to emphasize that:

1. An RFC for less than a full range of sedentary work reflects very serious limitations resulting from an individual's medical impairment(s) and is expected to be relatively rare.

2. However, a finding that an individual has the ability to do less than a full range of sedentary work does not necessarily equate with a decision of "disabled." If the performance of past relevant work is precluded by an RFC for less than the full range of sedentary work, consideration must still be given to whether there is other work in the national economy that the individual is able to do, considering age, education, and work experience.

Citations (Authority): Sections 223(d) and 1614(a) of the Social Security Act (the Act), as amended; Regulations No. 4, sections 404.1513(c), 404.1520, 404.1520a, 404.1545, 404.1546, 404.1560, 404.1561, 404.1562, 404.1563 through 404.1567, 404.1569, 404.1569a; appendix 1 of subpart P, section 12.00; appendix 2 of subpart P, sections 200.00 and 201.00; Regulations No. 16, sections 416.913(c), 416.920, 416.920a, 416.945, 416.946, 416.960, 416.961, 416.962, 416.963 through 416.967, 416.969 and 416.969a.

Introduction: Under the sequential evaluation process, once it has been determined that an individual is not engaging in substantial gainful activity and has a "severe" medically determinable impairment(s) which, though not meeting or equaling the criteria of any listing, prevents the individual from performing past relevant work (PRW), it must be determined whether the individual can do any other work, considering the individual's RFC, age, education, and work experience.

RFC is what an individual can still do despite his or her functional limitations and restrictions caused by his or her medically determinable physical or mental impairments. It is an administrative assessment of the extent to which an individual's medically determinable impairment(s), including any related symptoms, such as pain, may cause physical or mental limitations or restrictions that may affect his or her capacity to perform work-related physical and mental activities. RFC is assessed by adjudicators at each level of the administrative review process based on all of the relevant evidence in the case record, including information about the individual's symptoms and any "medical source statements"—i.e., opinions about what the individual can still do despite a severe impairment(s)—submitted by an individual's treating source(s) or other acceptable medical source.[1]

[1] For a detailed discussion of the difference between the RFC assessment, which is an administrative finding of fact, and the opinion evidence called the "medical source statement" or "MSS," see SSR 96–5p, "Titles II and XVI: Medical Source Opinions on Issues Reserved to the Commissioner."

RFC is the individual's maximum remaining ability to perform sustained work on a regular and continuing basis; i.e., 8 hours a day, for 5 days a week, or an equivalent work schedule. It is not the least an individual can do, but the most, based on all of the information in the case record. The RFC assessment considers only those limitations and restrictions that are caused by an individual's physical or mental impairments. It does not consider limitations or restrictions due to age or body habitus, since the Act requires that an individual's inability to work must result from the individual's physical or mental impairment(s). (See SSR 96–8p, "Titles II and XVI: Assessing Residual Functional Capacity in Initial Claims.")

Initially, the RFC assessment is a function-by-function assessment based upon all of the relevant evidence of an individual's ability to perform work-related activities. This RFC assessment is first used for a function-by-function comparison with the functional demands of an individual's PRW as he or she actually performed it and then, if necessary, as the work is generally performed in the national economy.[2]

However, at the last step of the sequential evaluation process, the RFC assessment is used to determine an individual's "maximum sustained work capability" and, where solely non-exertional impairments are not involved, must be expressed in terms of the exertional classifications of work: sedentary, light, medium, heavy, and very heavy work. The rules of appendix 2 of subpart P of Regulations No. 4 take administrative notice of the existence of numerous unskilled occupations within each of these exertional levels. The rules are then used to direct decisions about whether an individual is disabled or, when the individual is unable to perform the full range of work contemplated by an exertional level(s), as a framework for decisionmaking considering the individual's RFC, age, education, and work experience.

The impact of an RFC for less than a full range of sedentary work is especially critical for individuals who have not yet attained age 50. Since age,

[2] RFC may be expressed in terms of an exertional category, such as "light," if it becomes necessary to assess whether an individual is able to perform past relevant work as it is generally performed in the national economy. However, without the initial function-by-function accounting of the individual's capacities, it may not be possible to determine whether the individual is able to perform past relevant work as it is generally performed in the national economy because particular occupations may not require all of the exertional and nonexertional demands necessary to perform the full range of work at a given exertional level. See SSR 96–8p, "Titles II and XVI: Assessing Residual Functional Capacity in Initial Claims."

education, and work experience are not usually significant factors in limiting the ability of individuals under age 50 to make an adjustment to other work,[3] the conclusion whether such individuals who are limited to less than the full range of sedentary work are disabled will depend primarily on the nature and extent of their functional limitations or restrictions. On the other hand, since the rules in Table No. 1 of appendix 2, "Residual Functional Capacity: Maximum Sustained Work Capability Limited to Sedentary Work as a Result of Severe Medically Determinable Impairment(s)," direct a decision of "disabled" for individuals age 50 and over who are limited to a full range of sedentary work, unless the individual has transferable skills or education that provides for direct entry into skilled sedentary work, the impact of an RFC for less than the full range of sedentary work in such individuals is less critical.

Policy Interpretation: Under the regulations, "sedentary work" represents a significantly restricted range of work. Individuals who are limited to no more than sedentary work by their medical impairments have very serious functional limitations. For the majority of individuals who are age 50 or older and who are limited to the full range of sedentary work by their medical impairments, the rules and guidelines in appendix 2 require a conclusion of "disabled."

Nevertheless, the rules in Table No. 1 in appendix 2 take administrative notice that there are approximately 200 separate unskilled sedentary occupations, each representing numerous jobs, in the national economy.[4] Therefore, even though "sedentary work" represents a significantly restricted range of work, this range in itself is not so prohibitively restricted as to negate work capability for substantial gainful activity in all individuals.

Moreover, since each occupation administratively noticed by Table No. 1 represents numerous jobs, the ability to do even a *limited* range of sedentary work does not in itself establish disability in all individuals, although a finding of "disabled" usually applies when the full range of sedentary work is significantly eroded (see *Using the Rules in Table No. 1 as a Framework: "Erosion" of the Occupational Base* below). In deciding whether an individual who is limited to a partial range of sedentary work is able to make an adjustment to work other than any PRW, the adjudicator is required to make an individualized determination, considering age, education, and work experience, including any skills the individual may have that are transferable to other work, or education that provides for direct entry into skilled work, under the rules and guidelines in the regulations.

Sedentary Work

The ability to perform the full range of sedentary work requires the ability to lift no more than 10 pounds at a time and occasionally to lift or carry articles like docket files, ledgers, and small tools. Although a sedentary job is defined as one that involves sitting, a certain amount of walking and standing is often necessary in carrying out job duties. Jobs are sedentary if walking and standing are required occasionally and other sedentary criteria are met. "Occasionally" means occurring from very little up to one-third of the time, and would generally total no more than about 2 hours of an 8-hour workday. Sitting would generally total about 6 hours of an 8-hour workday. Unskilled sedentary work also involves other activities, classified as "nonexertional," such as capacities for seeing, manipulation, and understanding, remembering, and carrying out simple instructions.

The Occupational Base for Sedentary Work

The term "occupational base" means the approximate number of occupations that an individual has the RFC to perform considering all exertional and nonexertional limitations and restrictions. (See SSR 83–10, "Titles II and XVI: Determining Capability to Do Other Work—The Medical-Vocational Rules of Appendix 2" (C.E. 1981–1985, p. 516).) A full range of sedentary work includes all or substantially all of the approximately 200[5] unskilled sedentary occupations administratively noticed in Table No. 1.

Thus, the RFC addressed by a particular rule in Table No. 1 establishes an occupational base that at a minimum includes the full range of unskilled sedentary occupations administratively noticed. The base may be broadened by the addition of specific skilled or semiskilled occupations that an individual with an RFC limited to sedentary work can perform by reason of his or her education or work experience. However, if the individual has no transferable skills or no education or training that provides for direct entry into skilled work, the occupational base represented by the rules in Table No. 1 comprises only the sedentary unskilled occupations in the national economy that such an individual can perform.

The rules in Table No. 1 direct conclusions as to disability where the findings of fact coincide with all of the criteria of a particular rule; i.e., RFC (a maximum sustained work capability for sedentary work) and the vocational factors of age, education, and work experience. In order for a rule in Table No. 1 to direct a conclusion of "not disabled," the individual must be able to perform the full range of work administratively noticed by a rule. This means that the individual must be able to perform substantially all of the strength demands defining the sedentary level of exertion, as well as the physical and mental nonexertional demands that are also required for the performance of substantially all of the unskilled work considered at the sedentary level. Therefore, in order for a rule to direct a conclusion of "not disabled," an individual must also have no impairment that restricts the nonexertional capabilities to a level below those needed to perform unskilled work, in this case, at the sedentary level.

---

[3] However, "younger individuals" age 45–49 who are unable to communicate in English or who are illiterate in English and who are limited to even a *full* range of sedentary work must be found disabled under rule 201.17 in Table No. 1.

[4] An "occupation" refers to a grouping of numerous individual "jobs" with similar duties. Within occupations (e.g., "carpenter") there may be variations among jobs performed for different employers (e.g., "rough carpenter").

[5] The regulations specify that this is an approximation. The revised fourth edition of the Dictionary of Occupational Titles and its companion volumes (the DOT, 1991) lists 137 separate occupations. However, the introduction to Volume I explains that the fourth edition of the DOT (1977) "substantially modified or combined with related definitions" several thousand definitions from the third edition. In 1992, we published a notice in the Federal Register explaining that an analysis of the revised fourth edition of the DOT and available data for the then upcoming volume of the Selected Characteristics of Occupations Defined in the Revised Dictionary of Occupational Titles (SCO) showed "that the range of work of which the medical-vocational rules take administrative notice continues to represent more occupations than would be required to represent significant numbers," and that "we have received no significant data or other evidence to indicate that * * * the unskilled occupational base * * * has changed substantially." (See 57 FR 43005, September 17, 1992.) In February 1996, contact with the North Carolina Occupational Analysis Field Center, the organization that compiles the data the Department of Labor uses in the SCO, confirmed that there are no precise updated data but that the regulatory estimate of approximately 200 sedentary unskilled occupations is still valid, because some of the 137 occupations in the current edition of the DOT comprise more than one of the separate occupations of which we take administrative notice.

Using the Rules in Table No. 1 as a Framework: "Erosion" of the Occupational Base

Where any one of the findings of fact does not coincide with the corresponding criterion of a rule in Table No. 1 (except in those cases where the concept of borderline age applies[6]), the rule does not direct a decision. In cases such as the following, the medical-vocational rules must be used as a framework for considering the extent of any erosion of the sedentary occupational base:

- Any one of an individual's exertional capacities is determined to be less than that required to perform a full range of sedentary work; or
- Based on an individual's exertional capacities, a rule in Table No. 1 would direct a decision of "not disabled," but the individual also has a nonexertional limitation(s) that narrows the potential range of sedentary work to which he or she might be able to adjust (i.e., the individual has the exertional capacity to do the full range of sedentary work, but the sedentary occupational base is reduced because of at least one nonexertional limitation).

When there is a reduction in an individual's exertional or nonexertional capacity so that he or she is unable to perform substantially all of the occupations administratively noticed in Table No. 1, the individual will be unable to perform the full range of sedentary work: the occupational base will be "eroded" by the additional limitations or restrictions. However, the mere inability to perform substantially all sedentary unskilled occupations does not equate with a finding of disability. There may be a number of occupations from the approximately 200 occupations administratively noticed, and jobs that exist in significant numbers, that an individual may still be able to perform even with a sedentary occupational base that has been eroded.

Whether the individual will be able to make an adjustment to other work requires adjudicative judgment regarding factors such as the type and extent of the individual's limitations or restrictions and the extent of the erosion of the occupational base; i.e., the impact of the limitations or restrictions on the number of sedentary unskilled occupations or the total number of jobs to which the individual may be able to adjust, considering his or her age, education, and work experience, including any transferable skills or education providing for direct entry into skilled work. Where there is more than a slight impact on the individual's ability to perform the full range of sedentary work, if the adjudicator finds that the individual is able to do other work, the adjudicator must cite examples of occupations or jobs the individual can do and provide a statement of the incidence of such work in the region where the individual resides or in several regions of the country.

Exertional and Nonexertional Limitations and Restrictions

Exertional capacity addresses an individual's limitations and restrictions of physical strength and defines the individual's remaining ability to perform each of seven strength demands: Sitting, standing, walking, lifting, carrying, pushing, and pulling. An exertional limitation is an *impairment-caused* limitation of any one of these activities.

Nonexertional capacity considers any work-related limitations and restrictions that are not exertional. Therefore, a nonexertional limitation is an *impairment-caused* limitation affecting such capacities as mental abilities, vision, hearing, speech, climbing, balancing, stooping, kneeling, crouching, crawling, reaching, handling, fingering, and feeling. Environmental restrictions are also considered to be nonexertional.

Thus, it is the *nature of an individual's limitations and restrictions*, not certain impairments or symptoms, that determines whether the individual will be found to have only exertional limitations or restrictions, only nonexertional limitations or restrictions, or a combination of exertional and nonexertional limitations or restrictions. For example, even though mental impairments often affect nonexertional functions, they may also limit exertional capacity affecting one of the seven strength demands; e.g., from fatigue or hysterical paralysis. Likewise, symptoms, including pain, are not intrinsically exertional or nonexertional; when a symptom causes a limitation in one of the seven strength demands, the limitation must be considered exertional. (See SSR 96–8p, "Titles II and XVI: Assessing Residual Functional Capacity in Initial Claims.")

Guidelines for Evaluating the Ability To Do Less Than a Full Range of Sedentary Work

The following sections provide adjudicative guidance as to the impact of various RFC limitations and restrictions on the unskilled sedentary occupational base. The RFC assessment must include a narrative that shows the presence and degree of any specific limitations and restrictions, as well as an explanation of how the evidence in file was considered in the assessment. The individual's maximum remaining capacities to perform sustained work on a regular and continuing basis (what he or she can still do 8 hours a day, for 5 days a week, or an equivalent work schedule) must be stated.

An accurate accounting of an individual's abilities, limitations, and restrictions is necessary to determine the extent of erosion of the occupational base, the types of sedentary occupations an individual might still be able to do, and whether it will be necessary to make use of a vocational resource. The RFC assessment must be sufficiently complete to allow an adjudicator to make an informed judgment regarding these issues.

Exertional Limitations and Restrictions

Lifting/carrying and pushing/pulling: If an individual is unable to lift 10 pounds or occasionally lift and carry items like docket files, ledgers, and small tools throughout the workday, the unskilled sedentary occupational base will be eroded. The extent of erosion will depend on the extent of the limitations. For example, if it can be determined that the individual has an ability to lift or carry slightly less than 10 pounds, with no other limitations or restrictions in the ability to perform the requirements of sedentary work, the unskilled sedentary occupational base would not be significantly eroded; however, an inability to lift or carry more than 1 or 2 pounds would erode the unskilled sedentary occupational base significantly. For individuals with limitations in lifting or carrying weights between these amounts, consultation with a vocational resource may be appropriate.

Limitations or restrictions on the ability to push or pull will generally have little effect on the unskilled sedentary occupational base.

Standing and walking: The full range of sedentary work requires that an individual be able to stand and walk for a total of approximately 2 hours during an 8-hour workday. If an individual can stand and walk for a total of slightly less than 2 hours per 8-hour workday, this, by itself, would not cause the occupational base to be significantly eroded. Conversely, a limitation to standing and walking for a total of only a few minutes during the workday would erode the unskilled sedentary occupational base significantly. For individuals able to stand and walk in between the slightly less than 2 hours and only a few minutes, it may be

[6] See 20 CFR 404.1563(a) and 416.963(a) and SSR 83–10.

appropriate to consult a vocational resource.

Sitting: In order to perform a full range of sedentary work, an individual must be able to remain in a seated position for approximately 6 hours of an 8-hour workday, with a morning break, a lunch period, and an afternoon break at approximately 2-hour intervals. If an individual is unable to sit for a total of 6 hours in an 8-hour work day, the unskilled sedentary occupational base will be eroded. The extent of the limitation should be considered in determining whether the individual has the ability to make an adjustment to other work. *See Alternate sitting and standing* below.

The fact that an individual cannot do the sitting required to perform the full range of sedentary work does not necessarily mean that he or she cannot perform other work at a higher exertional level. In unusual cases, some individuals will be able to stand and walk longer than they are able to sit. If an individual is able to stand and walk for approximately 6 hours in an 8-hour workday (and meets the other requirements for light work), there may be a significant number of light jobs in the national economy that he or she can do even if there are not a significant number of sedentary jobs.

Alternate sitting and standing: An individual may need to alternate the required sitting of sedentary work by standing (and, possibly, walking) periodically. Where this need cannot be accommodated by scheduled breaks and a lunch period, the occupational base for a full range of unskilled sedentary work will be eroded. The extent of the erosion will depend on the facts in the case record, such as the frequency of the need to alternate sitting and standing and the length of time needed to stand. The RFC assessment *must* be specific as to the frequency of the individual's need to alternate sitting and standing. It may be especially useful in these situations to consult a vocational resource in order to determine whether the individual is able to make an adjustment to other work.

Medically required hand-held assistive device: To find that a hand-held assistive device is medically required, there must be medical documentation establishing the need for a hand-held assistive device to aid in walking or standing, and describing the circumstances for which it is needed (i.e., whether all the time, periodically, or only in certain situations; distance and terrain; and any other relevant information). The adjudicator must always consider the particular facts of a case. For example, if a medically required hand-held assistive device is needed only for prolonged ambulation, walking on uneven terrain, or ascending or descending slopes, the unskilled sedentary occupational base will not ordinarily be significantly eroded.

Since most unskilled sedentary work requires only occasional lifting and carrying of light objects such as ledgers and files and a maximum lifting capacity for only 10 pounds, an individual who uses a medically required hand-held assistive device in one hand may still have the ability to perform the minimal lifting and carrying requirements of many sedentary unskilled occupations with the other hand.[7] For example, an individual who must use a hand-held assistive device to aid in walking or standing because of an impairment that affects one lower extremity (e.g., an unstable knee), or to reduce pain when walking, who is limited to sedentary work because of the impairment affecting the lower extremity, and who has no other functional limitations or restrictions may still have the ability to make an adjustment to sedentary work that exists in significant numbers. On the other hand, the occupational base for an individual who must use such a device for balance because of significant involvement of both lower extremities (e.g., because of a neurological impairment) may be significantly eroded.

In these situations, too, it may be especially useful to consult a vocational resource in order to make a judgment regarding the individual's ability to make an adjustment to other work.

Nonexertional Limitations and Restrictions

Postural limitations: Postural limitations or restrictions related to such activities as climbing ladders, ropes, or scaffolds, balancing, kneeling, crouching, or crawling would not usually erode the occupational base for a full range of unskilled sedentary work significantly because those activities are not usually required in sedentary work. In the SCO, "balancing" means maintaining body equilibrium to prevent falling when walking, standing, crouching, or running on narrow, slippery, or erratically moving surfaces. If an individual is limited in balancing only on narrow, slippery, or erratically moving surfaces, this would not, by itself, result in a significant erosion of the unskilled sedentary occupational base. However, if an individual is limited in balancing even when standing or walking on level terrain, there may be a significant erosion of the unskilled sedentary occupational base. It is important to state in the RFC assessment what is meant by limited balancing in order to determine the remaining occupational base. Consultation with a vocational resource may be appropriate in some cases.

An ability to stoop occasionally; i.e., from very little up to one-third of the time, is required in most unskilled sedentary occupations. A *complete* inability to stoop would significantly erode the unskilled sedentary occupational base and a finding that the individual is disabled would usually apply, but restriction to occasional stooping should, by itself, only minimally erode the unskilled occupational base of sedentary work. Consultation with a vocational resource may be particularly useful for cases where the individual is limited to less than occasional stooping.

Manipulative limitations: Most unskilled sedentary jobs require good use of both hands and the fingers; i.e., bilateral manual dexterity. Fine movements of small objects require use of the fingers; e.g., to pick or pinch. Most unskilled sedentary jobs require good use of the hands and fingers for repetitive hand-finger actions.

Any *significant* manipulative limitation of an individual's ability to handle and work with small objects with both hands will result in a significant erosion of the unskilled sedentary occupational base. For example, example 1 in section 201.00(h) of appendix 2, describes an individual who has an impairment that prevents the performance of *any* sedentary occupations that require bilateral manual dexterity (i.e., "limits the individual to sedentary jobs which do not require bilateral manual dexterity"). When the limitation is less significant, especially if the limitation is in the non-dominant hand, it may be useful to consult a vocational resource.

The ability to feel the size, shape, temperature, or texture of an object by the fingertips is a function required in very few jobs and impairment of this ability would not, by itself, significantly erode the unskilled sedentary occupational base.

Visual limitations or restrictions: Most sedentary unskilled occupations require working with small objects. If a visual limitation prevents an individual from seeing the small objects involved in most sedentary unskilled work, or if an individual is not able to avoid ordinary hazards in the workplace, such as boxes

[7] Bilateral manual dexterity is needed when sitting but is not generally necessary when performing the standing and walking requirements of sedentary work.

on the floor, doors ajar, or approaching people or vehicles, there will be a significant erosion of the sedentary occupational base. These cases may require the use of vocational resources.

Communicative limitations: Basic communication is all that is needed to do unskilled work. The ability to hear and understand simple oral instructions or to communicate simple information is sufficient. If the individual retains these basic communication abilities, the unskilled sedentary occupational base would not be significantly eroded in these areas.

Environmental restrictions: An "environmental restriction" is an impairment-caused need to avoid an environmental condition in a workplace. Definitions for various workplace environmental conditions are found in the SCO; e.g., "extreme cold" is exposure to nonweather-related cold temperatures.

In general, few occupations in the unskilled sedentary occupational base require work in environments with extreme cold, extreme heat, wetness, humidity, vibration, or unusual hazards. The "hazards" defined in the SCO are considered unusual in unskilled sedentary work. They include: moving mechanical parts of equipment, tools, or machinery; electrical shock; working in high, exposed places; exposure to radiation; working with explosives; and exposure to toxic, caustic chemicals. Even a need to avoid all exposure to these conditions would not, by itself, result in a significant erosion of the occupational base.

Since all work environments entail some level of noise, restrictions on the ability to work in a noisy workplace must be evaluated on an individual basis. The unskilled sedentary occupational base may or may not be significantly eroded depending on the facts in the case record. In such cases, it may be especially useful to consult a vocational resource.

Restrictions to avoid exposure to odors or dust must also be evaluated on an individual basis. The RFC assessment must specify which environments are restricted and state the extent of the restriction; e.g., whether only excessive or even small amounts of dust must be avoided.

Mental limitations or restrictions: A substantial loss of ability to meet any one of several basic work-related activities on a sustained basis (i.e., 8 hours a day, 5 days a week, or an equivalent work schedule), will substantially erode the unskilled sedentary occupational base and would justify a finding of disability. These mental activities are generally required by competitive, remunerative, unskilled work:

- Understanding, remembering, and carrying out simple instructions.
- Making judgments that are commensurate with the functions of unskilled work—i.e., simple work-related decisions.
- Responding appropriately to supervision, co-workers and usual work situations.
- Dealing with changes in a routine work setting.

A less than substantial loss of ability to perform any of the above basic work activities may or may not significantly erode the unskilled sedentary occupational base. The individual's remaining capacities must be assessed and a judgment made as to their effects on the unskilled occupational base considering the other vocational factors of age, education, and work experience. When an individual has been found to have a limited ability in one or more of these basic work activities, it may be useful to consult a vocational resource.

Use of Vocational Resources

When the extent of erosion of the unskilled sedentary occupational base is not clear, the adjudicator may consult various authoritative written resources, such as the DOT, the SCO, the Occupational Outlook Handbook, or County Business Patterns.

In more complex cases, the adjudicator may use the resources of a vocational specialist or vocational expert.[8] The vocational resource may be asked to provide any or all of the following: An analysis of the impact of the RFC upon the full range of sedentary work, which the adjudicator may consider in determining the extent of the erosion of the occupational base, examples of occupations the individual may be able to perform, and citations of the existence and number of jobs in such occupations in the national economy.

Effective Date: This Ruling is effective on the date of its publication in the Federal Register.

Cross-References: SSR 86-8, "Titles II and XVI: The Sequential Evaluation Process" (C.E. 1986, p. 78), SSR 83-10, "Titles II and XVI: Determining Capability to Do Other Work—The Medical-Vocational Rules of Appendix 2" (C.E. 1981-1985, p. 516), SSR 83-12, "Titles II and XVI: Capability to Do Other Work—The Medical-Vocational Rules as a Framework for Evaluating Exertional Limitations Within a Range of Work or Between Ranges of Work" (C.E. 1981-1985, p. 529), SSR 83-14, "Titles II and XVI: Capability to Do Other Work—The Medical-Vocational Rules as a Framework for Evaluating a Combination of Exertional and Nonexertional Impairments" (C.E. 1981-1985, p. 535), SSR 85-15, "Titles II and XVI: Capability to Do Other Work—The Medical-Vocational Rules as a Framework for Evaluating Solely Nonexertional Impairments" (C.E. 1981-1985, p. 543), SSR-96 8p, "Titles II and XVI: Assessing Residual Functional Capacity in Initial Claims;" Program Operations Manual System, sections DI 24510.001, DI 24510.005, DI 24510.010, DI 24510.050, DI 24515.061, DI 25001.001, DI 25010.001, DI 25020.005, DI 25020.010, DI 25020.015, DI 25025.001 and DI 28005.015; and Hearings, Appeals, and Litigation Law Manual, sections I-2-548 and I-2-550.

[8] At the hearings and appeals levels, vocational experts (VEs) are vocational professionals who provide impartial expert opinion during the hearings and appeals process either by testifying or by providing written responses to interrogatories. A VE may be used before, during, or after a hearing. Whenever a VE is used, the individual has the right to review and respond to the VE evidence prior to the issuance of a decision. The VE's opinion is not binding on an adjudicator, but must be weighed along with all other evidence.

[FR Doc. 96-16692 Filed 7-01-96; 8:45 am]
BILLING CODE 4190-29-P

[Social Security Ruling (SSR) 96-7p]

Titles II and XVI: Evaluation of Symptoms in Disability Claims: Assessing the Credibility of an Individual's Statements

AGENCY: Social Security Administration.

ACTION: Notice of Social Security ruling.

SUMMARY: In accordance with 20 CFR 422.406(b)(1), the Commissioner of Social Security gives notice of Social Security Ruling 96-7p. This Ruling clarifies when the evaluation of symptoms, including pain, under 20 CFR 404.1529 and 416.929 requires a finding about the credibility of an individual's statements about pain or other symptom(s) and its functional effects; explains the factors to be considered in assessing the credibility of the individual's statements about symptoms; and states the importance of explaining the reasons for the finding about the credibility of the individual's statements in the disability determination or decision. This Ruling also incorporates and elaborates upon the policy interpretation and procedures in SSR 95-5p, "Titles II and XVI: Considering Allegations of Pain and Other Symptoms in Residual Functional Capacity and Individualized Functional Assessments and Explaining Conclusions Reached" (published in the

Federal Register on October 31, 1995, at 60 FR 55406). Consequently, this Ruling supersedes SSR 95-5p.

EFFECTIVE DATE: July 2, 1996.

FOR FURTHER INFORMATION CONTACT: Joanne K. Castello, Division of Regulations and Rulings, Social Security Administration, 6401 Security Boulevard, Baltimore, MD 21235, (410) 965-1711.

SUPPLEMENTARY INFORMATION: Although we are not required to do so pursuant to 5 U.S.C. 552 (a)(1) and (a)(2), we are publishing this Social Security Ruling in accordance with 20 CFR 422.406(b)(1).

Social Security Rulings make available to the public precedential decisions relating to the Federal old-age, survivors, disability, supplemental security income, and black lung benefits programs. Social Security Rulings may be based on case decisions made at all administrative levels of adjudication, Federal court decisions, Commissioner's decisions, opinions of the Office of the General Counsel, and other policy interpretations of the law and regulations.

Although Social Security Rulings do not have the force and effect of the law or regulations, they are binding on all components of the Social Security Administration, in accordance with 20 CFR 422.406(b)(1), and are to be relied upon as precedents in adjudicating cases.

If this Social Security Ruling is later superseded, modified, or rescinded, we will publish a notice in the Federal Register to that effect.

(Catalog of Federal Domestic Assistance, Programs 96.001 Social Security—Disability Insurance; 96.002 Social Security—Retirement Insurance; 96.004 Social Security—Survivors Insurance; 96.005 Special Benefits for Disabled Coal Miners; 96.006 Supplemental Security Income.)

Dated: June 7, 1996.

Shirley S. Chater,

Commissioner of Social Security.

Policy Interpretation Ruling—Titles II and XVI: Evaluation of Symptoms in Disability Claims: Assessing the Credibility of an Individual's Statements

This Ruling supersedes Social Security Ruling (SSR) 95-5p, "Titles II and XVI: Considering Allegations of Pain and Other Symptoms in Residual Functional Capacity and Individualized Functional Assessments and Explaining Conclusions Reached."

Purpose: The purpose of this Ruling is to clarify when the evaluation of symptoms, including pain, under 20 CFR 404.1529 and 416.929 requires a finding about the credibility of an individual's statements about pain or other symptom(s) and its functional effects; to explain the factors to be considered in assessing the credibility of the individual's statements about symptoms; and to state the importance of explaining the reasons for the finding about the credibility of the individual's statements in the disability determination or decision.[1] In particular, this Ruling emphasizes that:

1. No symptom or combination of symptoms can be the basis for a finding of disability, no matter how genuine the individual's complaints may appear to be, unless there are medical signs and laboratory findings demonstrating the existence of a medically determinable physical or mental impairment(s) that could reasonably be expected to produce the symptoms.

2. When the existence of a medically determinable physical or mental impairment(s) that could reasonably be expected to produce the symptoms has been established, the intensity, persistence, and functionally limiting effects of the symptoms must be evaluated to determine the extent to which the symptoms affect the individual's ability to do basic work activities. This requires the adjudicator to make a finding about the credibility of the individual's statements about the symptom(s) and its functional effects.

3. Because symptoms, such as pain, sometimes suggest a greater severity of impairment than can be shown by objective medical evidence alone, the adjudicator must carefully consider the individual's statements about symptoms with the rest of the relevant evidence in the case record in reaching a conclusion about the credibility of the individual's statements if a disability determination or decision that is fully favorable to the individual cannot be made solely on the basis of objective medical evidence.

4. In determining the credibility of the individual's statements, the adjudicator must consider the entire case record, including the objective medical evidence, the individual's own statements about symptoms, statements and other information provided by treating or examining physicians or psychologists and other persons about the symptoms and how they affect the individual, and any other relevant evidence in the case record. An individual's statements about the intensity and persistence of pain or other symptoms or about the effect the symptoms have on his or her ability to work may not be disregarded solely because they are not substantiated by objective medical evidence.

5. It is not sufficient for the adjudicator to make a single, conclusory statement that "the individual's allegations have been considered" or that "the allegations are (or are not) credible." It is also not enough for the adjudicator simply to recite the factors that are described in the regulations for evaluating symptoms. The determination or decision must contain specific reasons for the finding on credibility, supported by the evidence in the case record, and must be sufficiently specific to make clear to the individual and to any subsequent reviewers the weight the adjudicator gave to the individual's statements and the reasons for that weight.

Citations (Authority): Sections 216(i), 223(d), and 1614(a)(3) of the Social Security Act, as amended; Regulations No. 4, sections 404.1528(a), 404.1529, and 404.1569a; and Regulations No. 16, sections 416.928(a), 416.929, and 416.969a.

Introduction: A symptom is an individual's own description of his or her physical or mental impairment(s).[2] Under the regulations, an individual's statement(s) about his or her symptoms is not enough in itself to establish the existence of a physical or mental impairment or that the individual is disabled.

The regulations describe a two-step process for evaluating symptoms, such as pain, fatigue, shortness of breath, weakness, or nervousness:

- First, the adjudicator must consider whether there is an underlying medically determinable physical or mental impairment(s)—i.e., an impairment(s) that can be shown by medically acceptable clinical and laboratory diagnostic techniques—that could reasonably be expected to produce the individual's pain or other symptoms.[3] The finding that an

[1] For clarity, the discussions in this Ruling refer only to claims of individuals claiming disability benefits under title II and individuals age 18 or older claiming disability benefits under title XVI. However, the same basic principles with regard to determining whether statements about symptoms are credible also apply to claims of individuals under age 18 claiming disability benefits under title XVI.

[2] For an individual under age 18 claiming disability benefits under title XVI who is unable to adequately describe his or her symptom(s), the adjudicator will accept as a statement of this symptom(s) the description given by the person most familiar with the individual, such as a parent, other relative, or guardian. 20 CFR 416.928(a).

[3] The adjudicator must develop evidence regarding the possibility of a medically determinable mental impairment when the record contains information to suggest that such an impairment exists, and the individual alleges pain or other symptoms, but the medical signs and laboratory findings do not substantiate any physical impairment(s) capable of producing the pain or other symptoms.

individual's impairment(s) could reasonably be expected to produce the individual's pain or other symptoms does not involve a determination as to the intensity, persistence, or functionally limiting effects of the individual's symptoms. If there is no medically determinable physical or mental impairment(s), or if there is a medically determinable physical or mental impairment(s) but the impairment(s) could not reasonably be expected to produce the individual's pain or other symptoms, the symptoms cannot be found to affect the individual's ability to do basic work activities.

• Second, once an underlying physical or mental impairment(s) that could reasonably be expected to produce the individual's pain or other symptoms has been shown, the adjudicator must evaluate the intensity, persistence, and limiting effects of the individual's symptoms to determine the extent to which the symptoms limit the individual's ability to do basic work activities. For this purpose, whenever the individual's statements about the intensity, persistence, or functionally limiting effects of pain or other symptoms are not substantiated by objective medical evidence, the adjudicator must make a finding on the credibility of the individual's statements based on a consideration of the entire case record. This includes the medical signs and laboratory findings, the individual's own statements about the symptoms, any statements and other information provided by treating or examining physicians or psychologists and other persons about the symptoms and how they affect the individual, and any other relevant evidence in the case record. This requirement for a finding on the credibility of the individual's statements about symptoms and their effects is reflected in 20 CFR 404.1529(c)(4) and 416.929(c)(4). These provisions of the regulations provide that an individual's symptoms, including pain, will be determined to diminish the individual's capacity for basic work activities to the extent that the individual's alleged functional limitations and restrictions due to symptoms can reasonably be accepted as consistent with the objective medical evidence and other evidence in the case record.

When additional information is needed to assess the credibility of the individual's statements about symptoms and their effects, the adjudicator must make every reasonable effort to obtain available information that could shed light on the credibility of the individual's statements. In recognition of the fact that an individual's symptoms can sometimes suggest a greater level of severity of impairment than can be shown by the objective medical evidence alone, 20 CFR 404.1529(c) and 416.929(c) describe the kinds of evidence, including the factors below, that the adjudicator must consider in addition to the objective medical evidence when assessing the credibility of an individual's statements:

1. The individual's daily activities;
2. The location, duration, frequency, and intensity of the individual's pain or other symptoms;
3. Factors that precipitate and aggravate the symptoms;
4. The type, dosage, effectiveness, and side effects of any medication the individual takes or has taken to alleviate pain or other symptoms;
5. Treatment, other than medication, the individual receives or has received for relief of pain or other symptoms;
6. Any measures other than treatment the individual uses or has used to relieve pain or other symptoms (e.g., lying flat on his or her back, standing for 15 to 20 minutes every hour, or sleeping on a board); and
7. Any other factors concerning the individual's functional limitations and restrictions due to pain or other symptoms.

Once the adjudicator has determined the extent to which the individual's symptoms limit the individual's ability to do basic work activities by making a finding on the credibility of the individual's statements, the impact of the symptoms on the individual's ability to function must be considered along with the objective medical and other evidence, first in determining whether the individual's impairment or combination of impairments is "severe" at step 2 of the sequential evaluation process for determining disability and, as necessary, at each subsequent step of the process.[4] (See SSR 96–3p, "Titles II and XVI: Considering Allegations of Pain and Other Symptoms in Determining Whether a Medically Determinable Impairment is Severe," and SSR 96–8p, "Titles II and XVI: Assessing Residual Functional Capacity in Initial Claims.")

Policy Interpretation: A symptom is an individual's own description of his or her physical or mental impairment(s). Once the existence of a medically determinable physical or mental impairment(s) that could reasonably be expected to produce pain or other symptoms has been established, adjudicators must recognize that individuals may experience their symptoms differently and may be limited by their symptoms to a greater or lesser extent than other individuals with the same medical impairments and the same medical signs and laboratory findings. Because symptoms, such as pain, sometimes suggest a greater severity of impairment than can be shown by objective medical evidence alone, any statements of the individual concerning his or her symptoms must be carefully considered if a fully favorable determination or decision cannot be made solely on the basis of objective medical evidence.

If an individual's statements about pain or other symptoms are not substantiated by the objective medical evidence, the adjudicator must consider all of the evidence in the case record, including any statements by the individual and other persons concerning the individual's symptoms. The adjudicator must then make a finding on the credibility of the individual's statements about symptoms and their functional effects.

Credibility

In general, the extent to which an individual's statements about symptoms can be relied upon as probative evidence in determining whether the individual is disabled depends on the credibility of the statements. In basic terms, the credibility of an individual's statements about pain or other symptoms and their functional effects is the degree to which the statements can be believed and accepted as true. When evaluating the credibility of an individual's statements, the adjudicator must consider the entire case record and give specific reasons for the weight given to the individual's statements.

The finding on the credibility of the individual's statements cannot be based on an intangible or intuitive notion about an individual's credibility. The reasons for the credibility finding must be grounded in the evidence and articulated in the determination or

[4] In determining whether the impairment(s) of an individual claiming disability benefits under title II or an individual age 18 or older claiming disability benefits under title XVI is medically equivalent to a listed impairment in appendix 1 of subpart P of 20 CFR Part 404, the adjudicator will not substitute allegations of pain or other symptoms for a missing or deficient sign or laboratory finding to raise the severity of the individual's impairment(s) to that of a listed impairment. 20 CFR 404.1529(d)(3) and 416.929(d)(3). In determining whether the impairment(s) of an individual under age 18 claiming disability benefits under title XVI is equivalent to a listed impairment, if the adjudicator cannot find equivalence based on medical evidence only, the adjudicator will consider pain or another symptom(s) under 20 CFR 416.926a(b)(3) in determining whether the individual has an impairment(s) that results in overall functional limitations that are the same as the disabling functional consequences of a listed impairment. 20 CFR 416.929(d)(3).

decision. It is not sufficient to make a conclusory statement that "the individual's allegations have been considered" or that "the allegations are (or are not) credible." It is also not enough for the adjudicator simply to recite the factors that are described in the regulations for evaluating symptoms. The determination or decision must contain specific reasons for the finding on credibility, supported by the evidence in the case record, and must be sufficiently specific to make clear to the individual and to any subsequent reviewers the weight the adjudicator gave to the individual's statements and the reasons for that weight. This documentation is necessary in order to give the individual a full and fair review of his or her claim, and in order to ensure a well-reasoned determination or decision.

In making a finding about the credibility of an individual's statements, the adjudicator need not totally accept or totally reject the individual's statements. Based on a consideration of all of the evidence in the case record, the adjudicator may find all, only some, or none of an individual's allegations to be credible. The adjudicator may also find an individual's statements, such as statements about the extent of functional limitations or restrictions due to pain or other symptoms, to be credible to a certain degree. For example, an adjudicator may find credible an individual's statement that the abilities to lift and carry are affected by symptoms, but find only partially credible the individual's statements as to the extent of the functional limitations or restrictions due to symptoms; i.e., that the individual's abilities to lift and carry are compromised, but not to the degree alleged. Conversely, an adjudicator may find credible an individual's statement that symptoms limit his or her ability to concentrate, but find that the limitation is greater than that stated by the individual.

Moreover, a finding that an individual's statements are not credible, or not wholly credible, is not in itself sufficient to establish that the individual is not disabled. All of the evidence in the case record, including the individual's statements, must be considered before a conclusion can be made about disability.

Factors in Evaluating Credibility

Assessment of the credibility of an individual's statements about pain or other symptoms and about the effect the symptoms have on his or her ability to function must be based on a consideration of all of the evidence in the case record. This includes, but is not limited to:

- The medical signs and laboratory findings;
- Diagnosis, prognosis, and other medical opinions provided by treating or examining physicians or psychologists and other medical sources; and
- Statements and reports from the individual and from treating or examining physicians or psychologists and other persons about the individual's medical history, treatment and response, prior work record and efforts to work, daily activities, and other information concerning the individual's symptoms and how the symptoms affect the individual's ability to work.

The adjudicator must also consider any observations about the individual recorded by Social Security Administration (SSA) employees during interviews, whether in person or by telephone. In instances where the individual attends an administrative proceeding conducted by the adjudicator, the adjudicator may also consider his or her own recorded observations of the individual as part of the overall evaluation of the credibility of the individual's statements.

Consideration of the individual's statements and the statements and reports of medical sources and other persons with regard to the seven factors listed in the regulations,[5] along with any other relevant information in the case record, including the information described above, will provide the adjudicator with an overview of the individual's subjective complaints. The adjudicator must then evaluate all of this information and draw appropriate inferences and conclusions about the credibility of the individual's statements.

The following sections provide additional guidelines for the adjudicator to consider when evaluating the credibility of an individual's statements.

Consistency

One strong indication of the credibility of an individual's statements is their consistency, both internally and with other information in the case record. The adjudicator must consider such factors as:

- The degree to which the individual's statements are consistent with the medical signs and laboratory findings and other information provided by medical sources, including information about medical history and treatment.
- The consistency of the individual's own statements. The adjudicator must compare statements made by the individual in connection with his or her claim for disability benefits with statements he or she made under other circumstances, when such information is in the case record. Especially important are statements made to treating or examining medical sources and to the "other sources" defined in 20 CFR 404.1513(e) and 416.913(e). The adjudicator must also look at statements the individual made to SSA at each prior step of the administrative review process and in connection with any concurrent claim or, when available, prior claims for disability benefits under titles II and XVI. Likewise, the case record may contain statements the individual made in connection with claims for other types of disability benefits, such as workers' compensation, benefits under programs of the Department of Veterans Affairs, or private insurance benefits. However, the lack of consistency between an individual's statements and other statements that he or she has made at other times does not necessarily mean that the individual's statements are not credible. Symptoms may vary in their intensity, persistence, and functional effects, or may worsen or improve with time, and this may explain why the individual does not always allege the same intensity, persistence, or functional effects of his or her symptoms. Therefore, the adjudicator will need to review the case record to determine whether there are any explanations for any variations in the individual's statements about symptoms and their effects.
- The consistency of the individual's statements with other information in the case record, including reports and observations by other persons concerning the individual's daily activities, behavior, and efforts to work. This includes any observations recorded by SSA employees in interviews and observations recorded by the adjudicator in administrative proceedings.

Medical Evidence

Symptoms cannot be measured objectively through clinical or laboratory diagnostic techniques; however, their effects can often be clinically observed. The regulations at 20 CFR 404.1529(c)(2) and 416.929(c)(2) provide that objective medical evidence "is a useful indicator to assist us in making reasonable conclusions about the intensity and persistence of" an individual's symptoms and the effects those symptoms may have on the

[5] The seven factors are also set out in the "Introduction," above.

individual's ability to function. The examples in the regulations (reduced joint motion, muscle spasm, sensory deficit, and motor disruption) illustrate findings that may result from, or be associated with, the symptom of pain. When present, these findings tend to lend credibility to an individual's allegations about pain or other symptoms and their functional effects.

When there are medical signs and laboratory findings demonstrating the existence of a medically determinable physical or mental impairment(s) that could reasonably be expected to produce the pain or other symptoms, the adjudicator must always attempt to obtain any available objective medical evidence concerning the intensity and persistence of the pain or other symptoms, and, when such evidence is obtained, must consider it in evaluating the individual's statements. However, allegations concerning the intensity and persistence of pain or other symptoms may not be disregarded *solely* because they are not substantiated by objective medical evidence. A report of negative findings from the application of medically acceptable clinical and laboratory diagnostic techniques is one of the many factors that appropriately are to be considered in the overall assessment of credibility. However, the absence of objective medical evidence supporting an individual's statements about the intensity and persistence of pain or other symptoms is only one factor that the adjudicator must consider in assessing an individual's credibility and must be considered in the context of all the evidence.

Over time, there may also be medical signs and laboratory findings that, though not directly supporting or refuting statements about the intensity or persistence of pain or other symptoms, demonstrate worsening or improvement of the underlying medical condition. Such signs and findings may also help an adjudicator to draw appropriate inferences about the credibility of an individual's statements.

Apart from the medical signs and laboratory findings, the medical evidence, especially a longitudinal medical record, can be extremely valuable in the adjudicator's evaluation of an individual's statements about pain or other symptoms.

Important information about symptoms recorded by medical sources and reported in the medical evidence may include:

- Onset, description of the character and location of the symptoms, precipitating and aggravating factors, frequency and duration, course over time (e.g., whether worsening, improving, or static), and daily activities. Very often, this information will have been obtained by the medical source from the individual and may be compared with the individual's other statements in the case record. However, the evidence provided by a medical source may also contain medical opinions of the source about the individual's symptoms and their effects, and such opinions must be weighed applying the factors in 20 CFR 404.1527 and 416.927.
- A longitudinal record of any treatment and its success or failure, including any side effects of medication.
- Indications of other impairments, such as potential mental impairments, that could account for the allegations.

Although longitudinal records showing regular contact with a treating source are the most desirable, longitudinal medical records can be valuable even when they are not treating source records. For example, an individual may receive treatment at a clinic and see different physicians, but the clinic records may still show a longitudinal history of complaints and attempts at relief.

Medical Treatment History

In general, a longitudinal medical record demonstrating an individual's attempts to seek medical treatment for pain or other symptoms and to follow that treatment once it is prescribed lends support to an individual's allegations of intense and persistent pain or other symptoms for the purposes of judging the credibility of the individual's statements. Persistent attempts by the individual to obtain relief of pain or other symptoms, such as by increasing medications, trials of a variety of treatment modalities in an attempt to find one that works or that does not have side effects, referrals to specialists, or changing treatment sources may be a strong indication that the symptoms are a source of distress to the individual and generally lend support to an individual's allegations of intense and persistent symptoms.[6]

On the other hand, the individual's statements may be less credible if the level or frequency of treatment is inconsistent with the level of complaints, or if the medical reports or records show that the individual is not following the treatment as prescribed and there are no good reasons for this failure. However, the adjudicator must not draw any inferences about an individual's symptoms and their functional effects from a failure to seek or pursue regular medical treatment without first considering any explanations that the individual may provide, or other information in the case record, that may explain infrequent or irregular medical visits or failure to seek medical treatment. The adjudicator may need to recontact the individual or question the individual at the administrative proceeding in order to determine whether there are good reasons the individual does not seek medical treatment or does not pursue treatment in a consistent manner. The explanations provided by the individual may provide insight into the individual's credibility. For example:

- The individual's daily activities may be structured so as to minimize symptoms to a tolerable level or eliminate them entirely, avoiding physical or mental stressors that would exacerbate the symptoms. The individual may be living with the symptoms, seeing a medical source only as needed for periodic evaluation and renewal of medications.
- The individual's symptoms may not be severe enough to prompt the individual to seek ongoing medical attention or may be relieved with over-the-counter medications.
- The individual may not take prescription medication because the side effects are less tolerable than the symptoms.
- The individual may be unable to afford treatment and may not have access to free or low-cost medical services.
- The individual may have been advised by a medical source that there is no further, effective treatment that can be prescribed and undertaken that would benefit the individual.
- Medical treatment may be contrary to the teaching and tenets of the individual's religion.

Other Sources of Information

Other sources may provide information from which inferences and conclusions may be drawn about the credibility of the individual's statements. Such sources may provide information about the seven factors listed in the regulations and may be especially helpful in establishing a longitudinal record. Examples of such sources include public and private agencies, other practitioners, and nonmedical sources such as family and friends.

[6] The adjudicator must also remember that medical treatment need not always be specifically for the relief of a symptom. Often, treatment will be aimed at ameliorating the underlying medical condition which, in turn, may result in improvement in symptoms. The treatment may also cause symptoms as a side effect.

Observations of the Individual

In instances in which the adjudicator has observed the individual, the adjudicator is not free to accept or reject the individual's complaints solely on the basis of such personal observations, but should consider any personal observations in the overall evaluation of the credibility of the individual's statements.

In evaluating the credibility of the individual's statements, the adjudicator must also consider any observations recorded by SSA personnel who previously interviewed the individual, whether in person or by telephone.

Consideration of Findings by State Agency and Other Program Physicians and Psychologists at the Administrative Law Judge and Appeals Council Levels of Administrative Review

Under 20 CFR 404.1527(f) and 416.927(f), administrative law judges and the Appeals Council are required to consider findings of fact by State agency medical and psychological consultants and other program physicians and psychologists about the existence and severity of an individual's impairment(s), including the existence and severity of any symptoms, as opinions of nonexamining physicians and psychologists. Administrative law judges and the Appeals Council are not bound by any State agency findings, but they may not ignore these opinions and must explain the weight given to the opinions in their decisions. Therefore, if the case record includes a finding by a State agency medical or psychological consultant or other program physician or psychologist on the credibility of the individual's statements about limitations or restrictions due to symptoms, the adjudicator at the administrative law judge or Appeals Council level of administrative review must consider and weigh this opinion of a nonexamining source under the applicable rules in 20 CFR 404.1527 and 416.927 and must explain the weight given to the opinion in the decision. (See SSR 96-6p, "Titles II and XVI: Consideration of Administrative Findings of Fact by State Agency Medical and Psychological Consultants and Other Program Physicians and Psychologists at the Administrative Law Judge and Appeals Council Levels of Administrative Review; Medical Equivalence.")

Effective Date: This Ruling is effective on July 2, 1996.

Cross-References: SSR 96-3p, "Titles II and XVI: Considering Allegations of Pain and Other Symptoms in Determining Whether a Medically Determinable Impairment is Severe," SSR 96-8p, "Titles II and XVI: Assessing Residual Functional Capacity in Initial Claims," SSR 96-6p, "Titles II and XVI: Consideration of Administrative Findings of Fact by State Agency Medical and Psychological Consultants and Other Program Physicians and Psychologists at the Administrative Law Judge and Appeals Council Levels of Administrative Review; Medical Equivalence;" and Program Operations Manual System, sections DI 24515.061 and DI 24515.064.B.3.

[FR Doc. 96-16690 Filed 7-1-96; 8:45 am]

BILLING CODE 4190-29-P

Social Security Ruling (SSR) 96-4p. Titles II and XVI: Symptoms, Medically Determinable Physical and Mental Impairments, and Exertional and Nonexertional Limitations

AGENCY: Social Security Administration.

ACTION: Notice of Social Security Ruling.

SUMMARY: In accordance with 20 CFR 422.406(b)(1), the Commissioner of Social Security gives notice of Social Security Ruling 96-4p. This Ruling clarifies the Social Security Administration's longstanding policy on the evaluation of symptoms in the adjudication of claims for disability benefits under Title II, Federal Old-Age, Survivors, and Disability Insurance Benefits, and Title XVI, Supplemental Security Income for the Aged, Blind, and Disabled, of the Social Security Act.

EFFECTIVE DATE: July 2, 1996.

FOR FURTHER INFORMATION CONTACT: Joanne K. Castello, Division of Regulations and Rulings, Social Security Administration, 6401 Security Boulevard, Baltimore, MD 21235, (410) 965-1711.

SUPPLEMENTARY INFORMATION: Although we are not required to do so pursuant to 5 U.S.C. 552(a)(1) and (a)(2), we are publishing this Social Security Ruling in accordance with 20 CFR 422.406(b)(1).

Social Security Rulings make available to the public precedential decisions relating to the Federal old-age, survivors, disability, supplemental security income, and black lung benefits programs. Social Security Rulings may be based on case decisions made at all administrative levels of adjudication, Federal court decisions, Commissioner's decisions, opinions of the Office of the General Counsel, and other policy interpretations of the law and regulations.

Although Social Security Rulings do not have the force and effect of the law or regulations, they are binding on all components of the Social Security Administration, in accordance with 20 CFR 422.406(b)(1), and are to be relied upon as precedents in adjudicating cases.

If this Social Security Ruling is later superseded, modified, or rescinded, we will publish a notice in the Federal Register to that effect.

(Catalog of Federal Domestic Assistance, Programs 96.001 Social Security—Disability Insurance; 96.002 Social Security—Retirement Insurance; 96.004 Social Security-Survivors Insurance; 96.005 Special Benefits for Disabled Coal Miners; 96.006 Supplemental Security Income)

Dated: June 7, 1996.

Shirley S. Chater,

Commissioner of Social Security.

Policy Interpretation Ruling—Titles II and XVI: Symptoms, Medically Determinable Physical and Mental Impairments, and Exertional and Nonexertional Limitations

Purpose: The purpose of this Ruling is to clarify longstanding policy of the Social Security Administration on the evaluation of symptoms in the adjudication of claims for disability benefits under title II and title XVI of the Social Security Act (the Act). In particular, this Ruling emphasizes that:

1. A "symptom" is not a "medically determinable physical or mental impairment" and no symptom by itself can establish the existence of such an impairment.

2. In the absence of a showing that there is a "medically determinable physical or mental impairment," an individual must be found not disabled at step 2 of the sequential evaluation process. No symptom or combination of symptoms can be the basis for a finding of disability, no matter how genuine the individual's complaints may appear to be, unless there are medical signs and laboratory findings demonstrating the existence of a medically determinable physical or mental impairment.

3. The terms "exertional" and "nonexertional" in the regulations describe types of functional limitations or restrictions resulting from a medically determinable physical or mental impairment; i.e., exertional limitations affect an individual's ability to meet the strength demands of jobs, and nonexertional limitations or restrictions affect an individual's ability to meet the nonstrength demands of jobs. Therefore, a symptom in itself is neither exertional nor nonexertional. Rather, it is the nature of the functional limitations or restrictions caused by an

impairment-related symptom that determines whether the impact of the symptom is exertional, nonexertional, or both.

4. The application of the medical-vocational rules in appendix 2 of subpart P of Regulations No. 4 depends on the nature of the limitations and restrictions imposed by an individual's medically determinable physical or mental impairment(s), and any related symptoms.

Citations (Authority): Sections 216(i), 223(d) and 1614(a)(3) of the Social Security Act, as amended; Regulations No. 4, sections 404.1505, 404.1508, 404.1520, 404.1528(a), 404.1529, 404.1569a and subpart P, appendix 2; and Regulations No. 16, sections 416.905, 416.908, 416.920, 416.924, 416.928(a), 416.929 and 416.969a.

Policy Interpretation

Need To Establish the Existence of a Medically Determinable Physical or Mental Impairment

The Act defines disability as the inability to do any substantial gainful activity by reason of any medically determinable physical or mental impairment that can be expected to result in death or which has lasted or can be expected to last for a continuous period of not less than 12 months.[1] An "impairment" must result from anatomical, physiological, or psychological abnormalities that can be shown by medically acceptable clinical and laboratory diagnostic techniques. Although the regulations provide that the existence of a medically determinable physical or mental impairment must be established by medical evidence consisting of signs, symptoms,[2] and laboratory findings, the regulations further provide that under no circumstances may the existence of an impairment be established on the basis of symptoms alone. Thus, regardless of how many symptoms an individual alleges, or how genuine the individual's complaints may appear to be, the existence of a medically determinable physical or mental impairment cannot be established in the absence of objective medical abnormalities; i.e., medical signs and laboratory findings.

No symptom or combination of symptoms by itself can constitute a medically determinable impairment. In claims in which there are no medical signs or laboratory findings to substantiate the existence of a medically determinable physical or mental impairment, the individual must be found not disabled at step 2 of the sequential evaluation process set out in 20 CFR 404.1520 and 416.920 (or, for an individual under age 18 claiming disability benefits under title XVI, 20 CFR 416.924).

In addition, 20 CFR 404.1529 and 416.929 provide that an individual's symptoms, such as pain, fatigue, shortness of breath, weakness, or nervousness, will not be found to affect the individual's ability to do basic work activities (or, for an individual under age 18 claiming disability benefits under title XVI, to function independently, appropriately, and effectively in an age-appropriate manner) unless medical signs and laboratory findings show that there is a medically determinable physical or mental impairment(s) that could reasonably be expected to produce the symptom(s) alleged.

Exertional and Nonexertional Limitations

Once the existence of a medically determinable physical or mental impairment(s) that could reasonably be expected to produce the pain or other symptoms alleged has been established on the basis of medical signs and laboratory findings, allegations about the intensity and persistence of the symptoms must be considered with the objective medical abnormalities, and all other evidence in the case record, in evaluating the functionally limiting effects of the impairment(s). In addition, for determinations or decisions at step 5 of the sequential evaluation process for individuals claiming disability benefits under title II and individuals age 18 or older claiming disability benefits under title XVI, 20 CFR 404.1569a and 416.969a explain that an individual's impairment(s) and related symptoms, such as pain, may cause limitations of function or restrictions that limit an individual's ability to meet certain demands of jobs. These sections divide limitations or restrictions into three classifications: Exertional, nonexertional, and combined exertional and nonexertional. Exertional limitations or restrictions affect an individual's ability to meet the seven strength demands of jobs (sitting, standing, walking, lifting, carrying, pushing, and pulling), while nonexertional limitations or restrictions affect an individual's ability to meet the nonstrength demands of jobs (all physical limitations and restrictions that are not reflected in the seven strength demands, and mental limitations and restrictions). The nature of the limitations or restrictions affects whether the rules in appendix 2 to subpart P of Regulations No. 4 may be used to direct a decision or must be used as a framework for decisionmaking.

Likewise, under the regulations, symptoms in themselves are neither exertional nor nonexertional. An individual's symptoms, however, can cause limitations or restrictions that are classified as exertional, nonexertional, or a combination of both. For example, pain can result in an exertional limitation if it limits the ability to perform one of the strength activities (e.g., lifting), or a nonexertional limitation if it limits the ability to perform a nonstrength activity (e.g., fingering or concentrating). It is the nature of the limitations or restrictions resulting from the symptom (i.e., exertional, nonexertional, or both) that will determine whether the medical-vocational rules in appendix 2 may be used to direct a decision or must be used as a framework for decisionmaking. For additional discussion of this longstanding policy, see SSR 96–8p, "Titles II and XVI: Assessing Residual Functional Capacity in Initial Claims."

Effective Date: This Ruling is effective on July 2, 1996.

Cross-References: SSR 96–3p, "Titles II and XVI: Considering Allegations of Pain and Other Symptoms in Determining Whether a Medically Determinable Impairment is Severe," SSR 96–7p, "Titles II and XVI: Evaluation of Symptoms in Disability Claims: Assessing the Credibility of an Individual's Statements," and SSR 96–8p, "Titles II and XVI: Assessing Residual Functional Capacity in Initial Claims;" and Program Operations Manual System, sections DI 24501.020, DI 24515.061, and DI 24515.063.

[FR Doc. 96–16687 Filed 7–1–96; 8:45 am]
BILLING CODE 4190–29–P

[1] This definition of disability applies to individuals claiming disability benefits under title II and individuals age 18 or older claiming disability benefits under title XVI. For title XVI, an individual under age 18 will be considered disabled if he or she is suffering from a medically determinable physical or mental impairment of comparable severity to an impairment that would disable an adult.

[2] 20 CFR 404.1528, 404.1529, 416.928, and 416.929 provide that symptoms, such as pain, fatigue, shortness of breath, weakness or nervousness, are an individual's own perception or description of the impact of his or her physical or mental impairment(s). (20 CFR 416.928 further provides that, for an individual under age 18 who is unable to adequately describe his or her symptom(s), the adjudicator will accept as a statement of this symptom(s) the description given by the person most familiar with the individual, such as a parent, other relative, or guardian.) However, when any of these manifestations is an anatomical, physiological, or psychological abnormality that can be shown by medically acceptable clinical diagnostic techniques, it represents a medical "sign" rather than a "symptom."

[Social Security Ruling (SSR) 96–2p.]

Titles II and XVI: Giving Controlling Weight To Treating Source Medical Opinions

AGENCY: Social Security Administration.

ACTION: Notice of Social Security Ruling.

SUMMARY: In accordance with 20 CFR 422.406(b)(1), the Commissioner of Social Security gives notice of Social Security Ruling 96–2p. This Ruling explains terms used in the Social Security Administration regulations on evaluating medical opinions concerning when treating source medical opinions are entitled to controlling weight, and clarifies how the policy is applied.

EFFECTIVE DATE: July 2, 1996.

FOR FURTHER INFORMATION CONTACT: Joanne K. Castello, Division of Regulations and Rulings, Social Security Administration, 6401 Security Boulevard, Baltimore, MD 21235, (410) 965–1711.

SUPPLEMENTARY INFORMATION: Although we are not required to do so pursuant to 5 U.S.C. 552 (a)(1) and (a)(2), we are publishing this Social Security Ruling in accordance with 20 CFR 422.406(b)(1).

Social Security Rulings make available to the public precedential decisions relating to the Federal old-age, survivors, disability, supplemental security income, and black lung benefits programs. Social Security Rulings may be based on case decisions made at all administrative levels of adjudication, Federal court decisions, Commissioner's decisions, opinions of the Office of the General Counsel, and other policy interpretations of the law and regulations.

Although Social Security Rulings do not have the force and effect of the law or regulations, they are binding on all components of the Social Security Administration, in accordance with 20 CFR 422.406(b)(1), and are to be relied upon as precedents in adjudicating cases.

If this Social Security Ruling is later superseded, modified, or rescinded, we will publish a notice in the Federal Register to that effect.

(Catalog of Federal Domestic Assistance, Programs 96.001 Social Security—Disability Insurance; 96.002 Social Security—Retirement Insurance; 96.004 Social Security—Survivors Insurance; 96.005 Special Benefits for Disabled Coal Miners; 96.006 Supplemental Security Income)

Dated: June 7, 1995.

Shirley S. Chater,

Commissioner of Social Security.

Policy Interpretation Ruling

Titles II and XVI: Giving Controlling Weight To Treating Source Medical Opinions

Purpose: To explain terms used in our regulations on evaluating medical opinions concerning when treating source medical opinions are entitled to controlling weight, and to clarify how the policy is applied. In particular, to emphasize that:

1. A case cannot be decided in reliance on a medical opinion without some reasonable support for the opinion.

2. Controlling weight may be given only in appropriate circumstances to medical opinions, i.e., opinions on the issue(s) of the nature and severity of an individual's impairment(s), from treating sources.

3. Controlling weight may not be given to a treating source's medical opinion unless the opinion is well-supported by medically acceptable clinical and laboratory diagnostic techniques.

4. Even if a treating source's medical opinion is well-supported, controlling weight may not be given to the opinion unless it also is "not inconsistent" with the other substantial evidence in the case record.

5. The judgment whether a treating source's medical opinion is well-supported and not inconsistent with the other substantial evidence in the case record requires an understanding of the clinical signs and laboratory findings and what they signify.

6. If a treating source's medical opinion is well-supported and not inconsistent with the other substantial evidence in the case record, it *must* be given controlling weight; i.e., it must be adopted.

7. A finding that a treating source's medical opinion is not entitled to controlling weight does not mean that the opinion is rejected. It may still be entitled to deference and be adopted by the adjudicator.

Citations (Authority): Sections 205(a), 216(i), 223(d), 1614(a)(3), and 1631(d) of the Social Security Act, as amended; Regulations No. 4, sections 404.1502 and 404.1527, and Regulations No. 16, sections 416.902 and 416.927.

Pertinent History: Our regulations at 20 CFR 404.1502, 404.1527, 416.902, and 416.927 were revised on August 1, 1991, to define who we consider to be a "treating source" and to set out detailed rules for evaluating treating source medical opinions and other opinions. Among the provisions of these rules is a special provision in 20 CFR 404.1527(d)(2) and 416.927(d)(2) that requires adjudicators to adopt treating source medical opinions (i.e., opinions on the issue(s) of the nature and severity of an individual's impairment(s)) in one narrowly defined circumstance. As we stated in the preamble to the publication of the final rules:

> The provision recognizes the deference to which a treating source's medical opinion should be entitled. It does not permit us to substitute our own judgment for the opinion of a treating source on the issue(s) of the nature and severity of an impairment when the treating source has offered a medical opinion that is well-supported by medically acceptable clinical and laboratory diagnostic techniques and is not inconsistent with other substantial evidence.

56 FR 36932, 36936 (1991).

Policy Interpretation: Explanation of Terms

Controlling weight. This is the term used in 20 CFR 404.1527(d)(2) and 416.927(d)(2) to describe the weight we give to a medical opinion from a treating source that must be adopted. The rule on controlling weight applies when *all* of the following are present:

1. The opinion must come from a "treating source," as defined in 20 CFR 404.1502 and 416.902. Although opinions from other acceptable medical sources may be entitled to great weight, and may even be entitled to more weight than a treating source's opinion in appropriate circumstances, opinions from sources other than treating sources can never be entitled to "controlling weight."

2. The opinion must be a "medical opinion." Under 20 CFR 404.1527(a) and 416.927(a), "medical opinions" are opinions about the nature and severity of an individual's impairment(s) and are the only opinions that may be entitled to controlling weight. (See SSR 96–5p, "Titles II and XVI: Medical Source Opinions on Issues Reserved to the Commissioner.")

3. The adjudicator must find that the treating source's medical opinion is "well-supported" by "medically acceptable" clinical and laboratory diagnostic techniques. The adjudicator cannot decide a case in reliance on a medical opinion without some reasonable support for the opinion.

4. Even if well-supported by medically acceptable clinical and laboratory diagnostic techniques, the treating source's medical opinion also must be "not inconsistent" with the other "substantial evidence" in the individual's case record.

If any of the above factors is not satisfied, a treating source's opinion cannot be entitled to controlling weight. It is an error to give an opinion controlling weight simply because it is the opinion of a treating source if it is not well-supported by medically acceptable clinical and laboratory diagnostic techniques or if it is inconsistent with the other substantial evidence in the case record. However, when all of the factors are satisfied, the adjudicator *must* adopt a treating source's medical opinion irrespective of any finding he or she would have made in the absence of the medical opinion.

For a medical opinion to be *well-supported* by medically acceptable clinical and laboratory diagnostic techniques, it is not necessary that the opinion be *fully* supported by such evidence. Whether a medical opinion is well-supported will depend on the facts of each case. It is a judgment that adjudicators must make based on the extent to which the opinion is supported by medically acceptable clinical and laboratory diagnostic techniques and requires an understanding of the clinical signs and laboratory findings in the case record and what they signify.

It is not unusual for a single treating source to provide medical opinions about several issues; for example, at least one diagnosis, a prognosis, and an opinion about what the individual can still do. Although it is not necessary in every case to evaluate each treating source medical opinion separately, adjudicators must always be aware that one or more of the opinions may be controlling while others may not. Adjudicators must use judgment based on the facts of each case in determining whether, and the extent to which, it is necessary to address separately each medical opinion from a single source.

Medically acceptable. This term means that the clinical and laboratory diagnostic techniques that the medical source uses are in accordance with the medical standards that are generally accepted within the medical community as the appropriate techniques to establish the existence and severity of an impairment. The requirement that controlling weight can be given to a treating source medical opinion only if it is well-supported by medically acceptable clinical and laboratory diagnostic techniques helps to ensure that there is a sound medical basis for the opinion.

Not inconsistent. This is a term used to indicate that a well-supported treating source medical opinion need not be supported directly by all of the other evidence (i.e., it does not have to be *consistent* with all the other evidence) as long as there is no other substantial evidence in the case record that contradicts or conflicts with the opinion.

Whether a medical opinion is "not inconsistent" with the other substantial evidence is a judgment that adjudicators must make in each case. Sometimes, there will be an obvious inconsistency between the opinion and the other substantial evidence; for example, when a treating source's report contains an opinion that the individual is significantly limited in the ability to do work-related activities, but the opinion is inconsistent with the statements of the individual's spouse about the individual's actual activities, or when two medical sources provide inconsistent medical opinions about the same issue. At other times, the inconsistency will be less obvious and require knowledge about, or insight into, what the evidence means. In this regard, it is especially important to have an understanding of the clinical signs and laboratory findings and any treatment provided to determine whether there is an inconsistency between this evidence and medical opinions about such issues as diagnosis, prognosis (for example, when deciding whether an impairment is expected to last for 12 months), or functional effects. Because the evidence is in medical, not lay, terms and information about these issues may be implied rather than stated, such an inconsistency may not be evident without an understanding of what the clinical signs and laboratory findings signify.

Substantial evidence. This term describes a quality of evidence. Substantial evidence is "* * * more than a mere scintilla. It means such relevant evidence as a reasonable mind might accept as adequate to support a conclusion." (*Richardson* v. *Perales*, 402 U.S. 389 (1971), SSR 71-53c, C.E. 1971-1975, p. 418.) The term is intended to have this same meaning in 20 CFR 404.1527(d)(2) and 416.927(d)(2). It is intended to indicate that the evidence that is inconsistent with the opinion need not prove by a preponderance that the opinion is wrong. It need only be such relevant evidence as a reasonable mind would accept as adequate to support a conclusion that is contrary to the conclusion expressed in the medical opinion.

Depending upon the facts of a given case, any kind of medical or nonmedical evidence can potentially satisfy the substantial evidence test. For example, a treating source's medical opinion on what an individual can still do despite his or her impairment(s) will not be entitled to controlling weight if substantial, nonmedical evidence shows that the individual's actual activities are greater than those provided in the treating source's opinion. The converse is also true: Substantial evidence may demonstrate that an individual's ability to function may be less than what is indicated in a treating source's opinion, in which case the opinion will also not be entitled to controlling weight.

When a Treating Source's Medical Opinion Is Not Entitled to Controlling Weight

Adjudicators must remember that a finding that a treating source medical opinion is not well-supported by medically acceptable clinical and laboratory diagnostic techniques or is inconsistent with the other substantial evidence in the case record means only that the opinion is not entitled to "controlling weight," not that the opinion should be rejected. Treating source medical opinions are still entitled to deference and must be weighed using all of the factors provided in 20 CFR 404.1527 and 416.927. In many cases, a treating source's medical opinion will be entitled to the greatest weight and should be adopted, even if it does not meet the test for controlling weight.

Also, in some instances, additional development required by a case—for example, to obtain more evidence or to clarify reported clinical signs or laboratory findings—may provide the requisite support for a treating source's medical opinion that at first appeared to be lacking or may reconcile what at first appeared to be an inconsistency between a treating source's medical opinion and the other substantial evidence in the case record. In such instances, the treating source's medical opinion will become controlling if, after such development, the opinion meets the test for controlling weight. Conversely, the additional development may show that the treating source's medical opinion is not well-supported by medically acceptable clinical and laboratory diagnostic techniques or may create an inconsistency between the medical opinion and the other substantial evidence in the case record, even though the medical opinion at first appeared to meet the test for controlling weight. Ordinarily, development should not be undertaken for the purpose of determining whether a treating source's medical opinion should receive controlling weight if the case record is otherwise adequately developed. However, in cases at the administrative law judge (ALJ) or Appeals Council (AC) level, the ALJ or the AC may need to consult a medical expert to gain more insight into what the clinical signs and laboratory findings signify in order to decide whether a medical opinion is well-supported or whether it is not inconsistent with other substantial evidence in the case record.

Explanation of the Weight Given to a Treating Source's Medical Opinion

Paragraph (d)(2) of 20 CFR 404.1527 and 416.927 requires that the adjudicator will always give good reasons in the notice of the determination or decision for the weight given to a treating source's medical opinion(s), i.e., an opinion(s) on the nature and severity of an individual's impairment(s). Therefore:

• When the determination or decision:

—Is not fully favorable, e.g., is a denial; or

—is fully favorable based in part on a treating source's medical opinion, e.g., when the adjudicator adopts a treating source's opinion about the individual's remaining ability to function;

the notice of the determination or decision must contain specific reasons for the weight given to the treating source's medical opinion, supported by the evidence in the case record, and must be sufficiently specific to make clear to any subsequent reviewers the weight the adjudicator gave to the treating source's medical opinion and the reasons for that weight.

• When the determination or decision is fully favorable and would be even without consideration of a treating source's medical opinion, the notice of the determination or decision must contain an explanation of the weight given to the treating source's medical opinion. This explanation may be brief.

Effective Date: This Ruling is effective on July 2, 1996.

Cross-References: SSR 96–5p, "Titles II and XVI: Medical Source Opinions on Issues Reserved to the Commissioner;" Program Operations Manual System, sections DI 22505.001, and DI 24515.001–24515.003; Hearings, Appeals, and Litigation Law manual, sections I–2–530, I–2–532, I–2–534, I–2–539, I–2–540, I–2–825, I–3–111, I–3–712, I–3–812, and Temporary Instruction 5–310.

[FR Doc. 96–16685 Filed 7–1–96; 8:45 am]

BILLING CODE 4190–29–P

COMMITTEE FOR THE IMPLEMENTATION OF TEXTILE AGREEMENTS

Adjustment of Import Limits for Certain Cotton, Wool and Man-Made Fiber Textile Products Produced or Manufactured in Costa Rica

June 26, 1996.

AGENCY: Committee for the Implementation of Textile Agreements (CITA).

ACTION: Issuing a directive to the Commissioner of Customs increasing limits.

EFFECTIVE DATE: June 27, 1996.

FOR FURTHER INFORMATION CONTACT: Jennifer Aldrich, International Trade Specialist, Office of Textiles and Apparel, U.S. Department of Commerce, (202) 482–4212. For information on the quota status of these limits, refer to the Quota Status Reports posted on the bulletin boards of each Customs port or call (202) 927–5850. For information on embargoes and quota re-openings, call (202) 482–3715.

SUPPLEMENTARY INFORMATION:

Authority: Executive Order 11651 of March 3, 1972, as amended; section 204 of the Agricultural Act of 1956, as amended (7 U.S.C. 1854); Uruguay Round Agreements Act.

The current limits for certain categories are being increased for carryover.

A description of the textile and apparel categories in terms of HTS numbers is available in the CORRELATION: Textile and Apparel Categories with the Harmonized Tariff Schedule of the United States (see Federal Register notice 60 FR 65299, published on December 19, 1995). Also see 61 FR 3002, published on January 30, 1996.

The letter to the Commissioner of Customs and the actions taken pursuant to it are not designed to implement all of the provisions of the Uruguay Round Agreements Act and the Uruguay Round Agreement on Textiles and Clothing, but are designed to assist only in the implementation of certain of their provisions.

D. Michael Hutchinson,

Acting Chairman, Committee for the Implementation of Textile Agreements.

Committee for the Implementation of Textile Agreements

June 26, 1996.

Commissioner of Customs,

Department of the Treasury, Washington, DC 20229.

Dear Commissioner: This directive amends, but does not cancel, the directive issued to you on January 24, 1996, by the Chairman, Committee for the Implementation of Textile Agreements. That directive concerns imports of certain cotton, wool and man-made fiber textile products, produced or manufactured in Costa Rica and exported during the twelve-month period which began on January 1, 1996 and extends through December 31, 1996.

Effective on June 27, 1996, you are directed to increase the limits for the following categories, as provided for under the Uruguay Round Agreements Act and the Uruguay Round Agreement on Textiles and Clothing:

Category	Adjusted twelve-month limit [1]
340/640	987,044 dozen.
342/642	364,373 dozen.
347/348	1,663,387 dozen.
443	216,806 numbers.
447	12,517 dozen.

[1] The limits have not been adjusted to account for any imports exported after December 31, 1995.

The guaranteed access levels for the foregoing categories remain unchanged.

The Committee for the Implementation of Textile Agreements has determined that these actions fall within the foreign affairs exception to the rulemaking provisions of 5 U.S.C. 553(a)(1).

Sincerely,

D. Michael Hutchinson,

Acting Chairman, Committee for the Implementation of Textile Agreements.

[FR Doc. 96–16820 Filed 7–1–96; 8:45 am]

BILLING CODE 3510–DR–F

Establishment of an Import Limit for Certain Cotton and Man-Made Fiber Textile Products Produced or Manufactured in El Salvador

June 26, 1996.

AGENCY: Committee for the Implementation of Textile Agreements (CITA).

ACTION: Issuing a directive to the Commissioner of Customs establishing a limit.

EFFECTIVE DATE: June 27, 1996.

FOR FURTHER INFORMATION CONTACT: Jennifer Aldrich, International Trade Specialist, Office of Textiles and Apparel, U.S. Department of Commerce, (202) 482–4212. For information on the quota status of this limit, refer to the Quota Status Reports posted on the bulletin boards of each Customs port or call (202) 927–5850. For information on embargoes and quota re-openings, call (202) 482–3715. For information on categories on which consultations have been requested, call (202) 482-3740.

SUPPLEMENTARY INFORMATION:

Authority: Executive Order 11651 of March 3, 1972, as amended; section 204 of the

[Code of Federal Regulations]
[Title 20, Volume 2, Parts 400 to 499]
[Revised as of April 1, 1998]
From the U.S. Government Printing Office via GPO Access
[**CITE: 20CFR404.1565**]

[Page 370]

TITLE 20--EMPLOYEES' BENEFITS

CHAPTER III--SOCIAL SECURITY ADMINISTRATION

PART 404--FEDERAL OLD-AGE, SURVIVORS AND DISABILITY INSURANCE (1950-)--Table of

Subpart P--Determining Disability and Blindness

Sec. 404.**1565** Your work experience as a vocational factor.

(a) General. Work experience means skills and abilities you have acquired through work you have done which show the type of work you may be expected to do. Work you have already been able to do shows the kind of work that you may be expected to do. We consider that your work experience applies when it was done within the last 15 years, lasted long enough for you to learn to do it, and was substantial gainful activity. We do not usually consider that work you did 15 years or more before the time we are deciding whether you are disabled (or when the disability insured status requirement was last met, if earlier) applies. A gradual change occurs in most jobs so that after 15 years it is no longer realistic to expect that skills and abilities acquired in a job done then continue to apply. The 15-year guide is intended to insure that remote work experience is not currently applied. If you have no work experience or worked only ''off-and-on'' or for brief periods of time during the 15-year period, we generally consider that these do not apply. If you have acquired skills through your past work, we consider you to have these work skills unless you cannot use them in other skilled or semi-skilled work that you can now do. If you cannot use your skills in other skilled or semi-skilled work, we will consider your work background the same as unskilled. However, even if you have no work experience, we may consider that you are able to do unskilled work because it requires little or no judgment and can be learned in a short period of time.

(b) Information about your work. Under certain circumstances, we will ask you about the work you have done in the past. If you cannot give us all of the information we need, we will try, with your permission, to get it from your employer or other person who knows about your work, such as a member of your family or a co-worker. When we need to consider your work experience to decide whether you are able to do work that is different from what you have done in the past, we will ask you to tell us about all of the jobs you have had in the last 15 years. You must tell us the dates you worked, all of the duties you did, and any tools, machinery, and equipment you used. We will need to know about the amount of walking, standing, sitting, lifting and carrying you did during the work day, as well as any other physical or mental duties of your job. If all of your work in the past 15 years has been arduous and unskilled, and you have very little education, we will ask you to tell us about all of your work from the time you first began working. This information could help you to get disability benefits.

[Code of Federal Regulations]
[Title 20, Volume 2, Parts 400 to 499]
[Revised as of April 1, 1998]
From the U.S. Government Printing Office via GPO Access
[**CITE: 20CFR404.1527**]

[Page 357-360]

TITLE 20--EMPLOYEES' BENEFITS

CHAPTER III--SOCIAL SECURITY ADMINISTRATION

PART 404--FEDERAL OLD-AGE, SURVIVORS AND DISABILITY INSURANCE (1950-)--Table of

Subpart P--Determining Disability and Blindness

Sec. 404.**1527** Evaluating medical opinions about your impairment(s) or disability.

(a) General. (1) You can only be found disabled if you are unable to do any substantial gainful activity by reason of any medically determinable physical or mental impairment which can be expected to result in death or which has lasted or can be expected to last for a continuous period of not less than 12 months. See Sec. 404.1505. Your impairment must result from anatomical, physiological, or psychological abnormalities which are demonstrable by medically acceptable clinical and laboratory diagnostic techniques. See Sec. 404.1508.

(2) Evidence that you submit or that we obtain may contain medical opinions. Medical opinions are statements from physicians and psychologists or other acceptable medical sources that reflect judgments about the nature and severity of your impairment(s), including your symptoms, diagnosis and prognosis, what you can still do despite impairment(s), and your physical or mental restrictions.

(b) How we consider medical opinions. In deciding whether you are disabled,

[[Page 358]]

we will always consider the medical opinions in your case record together with the rest of the relevant evidence we receive.

(c) Making disability determinations. After we review all of the evidence relevant to your claim, including medical opinions, we make findings about what the evidence shows.

(1) If all of the evidence we receive, including all medical opinion(s), is consistent, and there is sufficient evidence for us to decide whether you are disabled, we will make our determination or decision based on that evidence.

(2) If any of the evidence in your case record, including any medical opinion(s), is inconsistent with other evidence or is internally inconsistent, we will weigh all of the evidence and see whether we can decide whether you are disabled based on the evidence we have.

(3) If the evidence is consistent but we do not have sufficient evidence to decide whether you are disabled, or if after weighing the evidence we decide we cannot reach a conclusion about whether you are disabled, we will try to obtain additional evidence under the provisions of Secs. 404.1512 and 404.1519 through 404.1519h. We will request additional existing records, recontact your treating sources or any other examining sources, ask you to undergo a consultative examination at our expense, or ask you or others for more information. We will consider any additional evidence we receive together with the evidence we already have.

(4) When there are inconsistencies in the evidence that cannot be resolved, or when despite efforts to obtain additional evidence the evidence is not complete, we will make a determination or decision based

on the evidence we have.

(d) How we weigh medical opinions. Regardless of its source, we will evaluate every medical opinion we receive. Unless we give a treating source's opinion controlling weight under paragraph (d)(2) of this section, we consider all of the following factors in deciding the weight we give to any medical opinion.

(1) Examining relationship. Generally, we give more weight to the opinion of a source who has examined you than to the opinion of a source who has not examined you.

(2) Treatment relationship. Generally, we give more weight to opinions from your treating sources, since these sources are likely to be the medical professionals most able to provide a detailed, longitudinal picture of your medical impairment(s) and may bring a unique perspective to the medical evidence that cannot be obtained from the objective medical findings alone or from reports of individual examinations, such as consultative examinations or brief hospitalizations. If we find that a treating source's opinion on the issue(s) of the nature and severity of your impairment(s) is well-supported by medically acceptable clinical and laboratory diagnostic techniques and is not inconsistent with the other substantial evidence in your case record, we will give it controlling weight. When we do not give the treating source's opinion controlling weight, we apply the factors listed below, as well as the factors in paragraphs (d) (3) through (5) of this section in determining the weight to give the opinion. We will always give good reasons in our notice of determination or decision for the weight we give your treating source's opinion.

(i) Length of the treatment relationship and the frequency of examination. Generally, the longer a treating source has treated you and the more times you have been seen by a treating source, the more weight we will give to the source's medical opinion. When the treating source has seen you a number of times and long enough to have obtained a longitudinal picture of your impairment, we will give the source's opinion more weight than we would give it if it were from a nontreating source.

(ii) Nature and extent of the treatment relationship. Generally, the more knowledge a treating source has about your impairment(s) the more weight we will give to the source's medical opinion. We will look at the treatment the source has provided and at the kinds and extent of examinations and testing the source has performed or ordered from specialists and independent laboratories. For example, if your ophthalmologist notices that you have complained of neck pain during your eye examinations, we will consider his

[[Page 359]]

or her opinion with respect to your neck pain, but we will give it less weight than that of another physician who has treated you for the neck pain. When the treating source has reasonable knowledge of your impairment(s), we will give the source's opinion more weight than we would give it if it were from a nontreating source.

(3) Supportability. The more a medical source presents relevant evidence to support an opinion, particularly medical signs and laboratory findings, the more weight we will give that opinion. The better an explanation a source provides for an opinion, the more weight we will give that opinion. Furthermore, because nonexamining sources have no examining or treating relationship with you, the weight we will give their opinions will depend on the degree to which they provide supporting explanations for their opinions. We will evaluate the degree to which these opinions consider all of the pertinent evidence in your claim, including opinions of treating and other examining sources.

(4) Consistency. Generally, the more consistent an opinion is with the record as a whole, the more weight we will give to that opinion.

(5) Specialization. We generally give more weight to the opinion of a specialist about medical issues related to his or her area of

specialty than to the opinion of a source who is not a specialist.

(6) Other factors. When we consider how much weight to give to a medical opinion, we will also consider any factors you or others bring to our attention, or of which we are aware, which tend to support or contradict the opinion.

(e) Medical source opinions on issues reserved to the Commissioner--(1) Opinions that you are disabled. We are responsible for making the determination or decision about whether you meet the statutory definition of disability. In so doing, we review all of the medical findings and other evidence that support a medical source's statement that you are disabled. A statement by a medical source that you are ''disabled'' or ''unable to work'' does not mean that we will determine that you are disabled.

(2) Other opinions on issues reserved to the Commissioner. We use medical sources, including your treating source, to provide evidence, including opinions, on the nature and severity of your impairment(s). Although we consider opinions from treating and examining sources on issues such as whether your impairment(s) meets or equals the requirements of any impairment(s) in the Listing of Impairments in appendix 1 of this subpart, your residual functional capacity (see Secs. 404.1545 and 404.1546), or the application of vocational factors, the final responsibility for deciding these issues is reserved to the Commissioner. We will not give any special significance to the source of the opinion on these issues.

(f) Opinions of nonexamining medical and psychological consultants and other nonexamining physicians and psychologists. We consider all evidence from nonexamining physicians and psychologists to be opinion evidence. When we consider the opinions of nonexamining sources on the nature and severity of your impairments, we apply the rules set forth in paragraphs (a) through (e) of this section. In addition, the following rules apply to State agency medical and psychological consultants, and to medical advisors we consult in connection with administrative law judge hearings and Appeals Council review.

(1) At the initial and reconsideration steps in the administrative review process, except in disability hearings, State agency medical and psychological consultants are members of the teams that make the determinations of disability. A State agency medical or psychological consultant will consider the evidence in your case record and make findings of fact about the medical issues, including, but not limited to, the existence and severity of your impairment(s), the existence and severity of your symptoms, whether your impairment(s) meets or equals the requirements for any impairment listed in appendix 1 to this subpart, and your residual functional capacity. These administrative findings of fact are based on the evidence in your case record but are not themselves evidence at these steps.

(2) Administrative law judges are responsible for reviewing the evidence

[[Page 360]]

and making findings of fact and conclusions of law. Administrative law judges are not bound by any findings made by State agency medical or psychological consultants. However, these findings are considered at the hearing level. See Sec. 404.1512(b)(6). When administrative law judges consider these findings, they will evaluate them using the rules set forth in paragraphs (a) through (e) of this section. Also, administrative law judges may ask for and consider the opinions of medical advisors on the nature and severity of your impairment(s) and whether your impairment(s) equals the requirements of any listed impairment in appendix 1 to this subpart.

(3) When the Appeals Council makes a decision, it will follow the same rules for considering opinion evidence as administrative law judges follow.

[56 FR 36960, Aug. 1, 1991, as amended at 62 FR 38451, July 18, 1997]

[Code of Federal Regulations]
[Title 20, Volume 2, Parts 400 to 499]
[Revised as of April 1, 1998]
From the U.S. Government Printing Office via GPO Access
[**CITE: 20CFR416.927**]

[Page 734-737]

TITLE 20--EMPLOYEES' BENEFITS

CHAPTER III--SOCIAL SECURITY ADMINISTRATION

PART 416--SUPPLEMENTAL SECURITY INCOME FOR THE AGED, BLIND, AND DISABLED--Table of

Subpart I--Determining Disability and Blindness

Sec. 416.**927** Evaluating medical opinions about your impairment(s) or disability.

(a) General. (1) If you are an adult, you can only be found disabled if you are unable to do any substantial gainful activity by reason of any medically determinable physical or mental impairment which can be expected to result in death or which has lasted or can be expected to last for a continuous period of not less than 12 months. (See Sec. 416.905.) If you are a child, you can be found disabled only if you have a medically determinable physical or mental impairment(s) that causes marked and severe functional limitations and that can be expected to result in death or that has lasted or can be expected to last for a continuous period of not less than 12 months. (See Sec. 416.906.) Your impairment must result from anatomical, physiological, or psychological abnormalities which are demonstrable by medically acceptable clinical and laboratory diagnostic techniques. (See Sec. 416.908.)

(2) Evidence that you submit or that we obtain may contain medical opinions. Medical opinions are statements from physicians and psychologists or other acceptable medical sources that reflect judgments about the nature and severity of your impairment(s), including your symptoms, diagnosis and prognosis, what you can still do despite impairment(s), and your physical or mental restrictions.

(b) How we consider medical opinions. In deciding whether you are disabled, we will always consider the medical opinions in your case record together with the rest of the relevant evidence we receive.

(c) Making disability determinations. After we review all of the evidence relevant to your claim, including medical opinions, we make findings about what the evidence shows.

(1) If all of the evidence we receive, including all medical opinion(s), is consistent, and there is sufficient evidence for us to decide whether you are disabled, we will make our determination or decision based on that evidence.

(2) If any of the evidence in your case record, including any medical opinion(s), is inconsistent with other evidence or is internally inconsistent, we

[[Page 735]]

will weigh all of the evidence and see whether we can decide whether you are disabled based on the evidence we have.

(3) If the evidence is consistent but we do not have sufficient evidence to decide whether you are disabled, or, if after weighing the evidence we decide we cannot reach a conclusion about whether you are disabled, we will try to obtain additional evidence under the provisions of Secs. 416.912 and 416.919 through 416.919h. We will request additional existing records, recontact your treating sources or any other examining sources, ask you to undergo a consultative examination at our expense, or ask you or others for more information. We will

consider any additional evidence we receive together with the evidence we already have.

(4) When there are inconsistencies in the evidence that cannot be resolved, or when despite efforts to obtain additional evidence the evidence is not complete, we will make a determination or decision based on the evidence we have.

(d) How we weigh medical opinions. Regardless of its source, we will evaluate every medical opinion we receive. Unless we give a treating source's opinion controlling weight under paragraph (d)(2) of this section, we consider all of the following factors in deciding the weight we give to any medical opinion.

(1) Examining relationship. Generally, we give more weight to the opinion of a source who has examined you than to the opinion of a source who has not examined you.

(2) Treatment relationship. Generally, we give more weight to opinions from your treating sources, since these sources are likely to be the medical professionals most able to provide a detailed, longitudinal picture of your medical impairment(s) and may bring a unique perspective to the medical evidence that cannot be obtained from the objective medical findings alone or from reports of individual examinations, such as consultative examinations or brief hospitalizations. If we find that a treating source's opinion on the issue(s) of the nature and severity of your impairment(s) is well-supported by medically acceptable clinical and laboratory diagnostic techniques and is not inconsistent with the other substantial evidence in your case record, we will give it controlling weight. When we do not give the treating source's opinion controlling weight, we apply the factors listed below, as well as the factors in paragraphs (d) (3) through (5) of this section in determining the weight to give the opinion. We will always give good reasons in our notice of determination or decision for the weight we give your treating source's opinion.

(i) Length of the treatment relationship and the frequency of examination. Generally, the longer a treating source has treated you and the more times you have been seen by a treating source, the more weight we will give to the source's medical opinion. When the treating source has seen you a number of times and long enough to have obtained a longitudinal picture of your impairment, we will give the source's opinion more weight than we would give it if it were from a nontreating source.

(ii) Nature and extent of the treatment relationship. Generally, the more knowledge a treating source has about your impairment(s) the more weight we will give to the source's medical opinion. We will look at the treatment the source has provided and at the kinds and extent of examinations and testing the source has performed or ordered from specialists and independent laboratories. For example, if your ophthalmologist notices that you have complained of neck pain during your eye examinations, we will consider his or her opinion with respect to your neck pain, but we will give it less weight than that of another physician who has treated you for the neck pain. When the treating source has reasonable knowledge of your impairment(s), we will give the source's opinion more weight than we would give it if it were from a nontreating source.

(3) Supportability. The more a medical source presents relevant evidence to support an opinion, particularly medical signs and laboratory findings, the more weight we will give that opinion. The better an explanation a source provides for an opinion, the more weight we will give that opinion. Furthermore, because nonexamining sources

[[Page 736]]

have no examining or treating relationship with you, the weight we will give their opinions will depend on the degree to which they provide supporting explanations for their opinions. We will evaluate the degree to which these opinions consider all of the pertinent evidence in your claim, including opinions of treating and other examining sources.

(4) Consistency. Generally, the more consistent an opinion is with the record as a whole, the more weight we will give to that opinion.

(5) Specialization. We generally give more weight to the opinion of a specialist about medical issues related to his or her area of specialty than to the opinion of a source who is not a specialist.

(6) Other factors. When we consider how much weight to give to a medical opinion, we will also consider any factors you or others bring to our attention, or of which we are aware, which tend to support or contradict the opinion.

(e) Medical source opinions on issues reserved to the Commissioner--(1) Opinions that you are disabled. We are responsible for making the determination or decision about whether you meet the statutory definition of disability. In so doing, we review all of the medical findings and other evidence that support a medical source's statement that you are disabled. A statement by a medical source that you are ''disabled'' or ''unable to work'' does not mean that we will determine that you are disabled.

(2) Other opinions on issues reserved to the Commissioner. We use medical sources, including your treating source, to provide evidence, including opinions, on the nature and severity of your impairment(s). Although we consider opinions from treating and examining sources on issues such as whether your impairment(s) meets or equals the requirements of any impairment(s) in the Listing of Impairments in appendix 1 to subpart P of part 404 of this chapter, your residual functional capacity (see Secs. 416.945 and 416.946), or the application of vocational factors, the final responsibility for deciding these issues is reserved to the Commissioner. We will not give any special significance to the source of the opinion on these issues.

(f) Opinions of nonexamining medical and psychological consultants and other nonexamining physicians and psychologists. We consider all evidence from nonexamining physicians and psychologists to be opinion evidence. When we consider the opinions of nonexamining sources on the nature and severity of your impairments, we apply the rules set forth in paragraphs (a) through (e) of this section. In addition, the following rules apply to State agency medical and psychological consultants, and to medical advisors we consult in connection with administrative law judge hearings and Appeals Council review.

(1) At the initial and reconsideration steps in the administrative review process, except in disability hearings, State agency medical and psychological consultants are members of the teams that make the determinations of disability. A State agency medical or psychological consultant will consider the evidence in your case record and make findings of fact about the medical issues, including, but not limited to, the existence and severity of your impairment(s), the existence and severity of your symptoms, whether your impairment(s) meets or equals the requirements for any impairment listed in appendix 1 to subpart P of part 404 of this chapter, and your residual functional capacity. These administrative findings of fact are based on the evidence in your case record but are not themselves evidence at these steps.

(2) Administrative law judges are responsible for reviewing the evidence and making findings of fact and conclusions of law. Administrative law judges are not bound by any findings made by State agency medical or psychological consultants. However, these findings are considered at the hearing level. See Sec. 416.912(b)(6). When administrative law judges consider these findings, they will evaluate them using the rules set forth in paragraphs (a) through (e) of this section. Also, administrative law judges may ask for and consider the opinions of medical advisors on the nature and severity of your impairment(s) and whether your impairment(s) equals the requirements of any

[[Page 737]]

listed impairment in appendix 1 to subpart P of part 404 of this chapter.

(3) When the Appeals Council makes a decision, it will follow the same rules for considering opinion evidence as administrative law judges follow.

[56 FR 36968, Aug. 1, 1991, as amended at 62 FR 6428, Feb. 11, 1997; 62 FR 13538, Mar. 21, 1997; 62 FR 38454, July 18, 1997]

[Code of Federal Regulations]
[Title 20, Volume 2, Parts 400 to 499]
[Revised as of April 1, 1998]
From the U.S. Government Printing Office via GPO Access
[**CITE: 20CFR404.1509**]

[Page 341]

TITLE 20--EMPLOYEES' BENEFITS

CHAPTER III--SOCIAL SECURITY ADMINISTRATION

PART 404--FEDERAL OLD-AGE, SURVIVORS AND DISABILITY INSURANCE (1950-   )--Table of

Subpart P--Determining Disability and Blindness

Sec. 404.**1509** How long the impairment must last.

Unless your impairment is expected to result in death, it must have lasted or must be expected to last for a continuous period of at least 12 months. We call this the duration requirement.

[Code of Federal Regulations]
[Title 20, Volume 2, Parts 400 to 499]
[Revised as of April 1, 1998]
From the U.S. Government Printing Office via GPO Access
[**CITE**: **20CFR416.905**]

[Page 704]

TITLE 20--EMPLOYEES' BENEFITS

CHAPTER III--SOCIAL SECURITY ADMINISTRATION

PART 416--SUPPLEMENTAL SECURITY INCOME FOR THE AGED, BLIND, AND DISABLED--Table of

Subpart I--Determining Disability and Blindness

Sec. 416.**905** Basic definition of disability for adults.

(a) The law defines disability as the inability to do any substantial gainful activity by reason of any medically determinable physical or mental impairment which can be expected to result in death or which has lasted or can be expected to last for a continuous period of not less than 12 months. To meet this definition, you must have a severe impairment, which makes you unable to do your previous work or any other substantial gainful activity which exists in the national economy. To determine whether you are able to do any other work, we consider your residual functional capacity and your age, education, and work experience (see Sec. 416.920).

(b) There are different rules for determining disability for individuals who are statutorily blind. We discuss these in Secs. 416.981 through 416.985.

[45 FR 55621, Aug. 20, 1980, as amended at 56 FR 5553, Feb. 11, 1991]

HEALTH AND HUMAN SERVICES
SOCIAL SECURITY ADMINISTRATION

NAME (Claimant) (Print or Type)	SOCIAL SECURITY NUMBER

Section I **APPOINTMENT OF REPRESENTATIVE**

I appoint this individual ____
(Name and Address)

to act as my representative in connection with my claim or asserted right under:

☐ Title II (RSDI) ☐ Title XVI (SSI) ☐ Title IV FMSHA (Black Lung) ☐ Title XVIII (Medicare Coverage)

I authorize this individual to make or give any request or notice; to present or elicit evidence; to obtain information; and t receive any notice in connection with my pending claim or asserted right wholly in my stead.

SIGNATURE (Claimant)	ADDRESS
TELEPHONE NUMBER (Area Code)	DATE

Section II **ACCEPTANCE OF APPOINTMENT**

I, ______________________________, hereby accept the above appointment. I certif that I have not been suspended or prohibited from practice before the Social Security Administration; that I am not, as a currer or former officer or employee of the United States, disqualified from acting as the claimant's representative; and that I will nc charge or receive any fee for the representation unless it has been authorized in accordance with the laws and regulatior referred to on the reverse side hereof. In the event that I decide not to charge or collect a fee for the representation, I will notif the Social Security Administration (completion of Section II (optional) satisfies this requirement).

I am a / an ____
(Attorney, union representative, relative, law student, etc.)

SIGNATURE (Representative)	ADDRESS
TELEPHONE NUMBER (Area code)	DATE

Section III (Optional) **WAIVER OF FEE**

I waive my right to charge and collect a fee under Section 206 of the Social Security Act, and I release my client (the claiman from any obligations, contractual or otherwise, which may be owed to me for services I have performed in connection wit my client's claim or asserted right.

SIGNATURE (Representative)	DATE

WAIVER OF DIRECT PAYMENT

I ONLY waive my right to direct certification of a fee from the withheld past-due benefits of my client (the claimant). I NOT, however, waive my right to petition for and be authorized to charge and collect a fee directly from my client.

SIGNATURE (Representative)	DATE

TO BE COMPLETED BY SSA
NUMBER HOLDER
SOCIAL SECURITY NUMBER
EMPLOYEE/CLAIMANT/BENEFICIARY *(If other than Number Holder)*

AUTHORIZATION FOR SOURCE TO RELEASE INFORMATION TO THE SOCIAL SECURITY ADMINISTRATION (SSA)

INFORMATION ABOUT SOURCE— PLEASE PRINT, TYPE, OR WRITE CLEARLY

NAME AND ADDRESS OF SOURCE *(Include Zip Code)*	RELATIONSHIP TO CLAIMANT/BENEFICIARY

INFORMATION ABOUT CLAIMANT/BENEFICIARY – PLEASE PRINT, TYPE, OR WRITE CLEARLY

NAME AND ADDRESS *(If known)* AT TIME CLAIMANT/BENEFICIARY HAD CONTACT WITH SOURCE *(Include Zip Code)*	DATE OF BIRTH	CLAIMANT/BENEFICIARY I.D. NUMBER *(If known and different than SSN) (Clinic/Patient No.)*

APPROXIMATE DATES OF CLAIMANT/BENEFICIARY CONTACT WITH SOURCE *(e.g., dates of hospital admission, treatment, discharge, etc.)*

TO BE COMPLETED BY CLAIMANT/BENEFICIARY OR PERSON AUTHORIZED TO ACT IN HIS/HER BEHALF

GENERAL AND SPECIAL AUTHORIZATION TO RELEASE MEDICAL AND OTHER INFORMATION IN ACCORDANCE WITH THE PROVISIONS OF THE SOCIAL SECURITY ACT; THE PUBLIC HEALTH SERVICE ACT, SECTIONS 523 AND 527; AND TITLE 38 U.S.C. VETERANS BENEFITS, SECTION 4132.

I hereby authorize the above-named source to release or disclose to the Social Security Administration or State agency the following information for the period(s) identified above:

1) All medical records or other information regarding my treatment, hospitalization, and/or outpatient care for my impairment(s), including psychological or psychiatric impairment(s), drug abuse, alcoholism, sickle cell anemia, acquired immunodeficiency syndrome (AIDS), or tests for or infection with human immunodeficiency virus (HIV);
2) Information about how my impairment(s) affects my ability to complete tasks and activities of daily living;
3) Information about how my impairment(s) affected my ability to work.

I understand that this authorization, except for action already taken, may be voided by me at anytime. If I do not void this authorization, it will automatically end when a final decision is made on my claim. If I am already receiving benefits, the authorization will end when a final decision is made as to whether I can continue to receive benefits.

READ IMPORTANT INFORMATION ON REVERSE BEFORE SIGNING FORM BELOW.

SIGNATURE OF CLAIMANT/BENEFICIARY OR PERSON AUTHORIZED TO ACT IN HIS/HER BEHALF	RELATIONSHIP TO CLAIMANT/ BENEFICIARY	DATE
STREET ADDRESS		TELEPHONE NUMBER (Area Code)
CITY	STATE	ZIP CODE

The signature and address of a person who either knows the person signing this form or is satistifed as to that person's identity is requested below. This is not required by the Social Security Administration, but without it the source may not honor this authorization.

SIGNATURE OF WITNESS	STREET ADDRESS	
CITY	STATE	ZIP CODE

Form SSA-827 (1-91) Use Prior Editions

(OVER)

NOTES

4

THE ALJ HEARING

Barbara Samuels

THE ALJ HEARING

I. HEARINGS: 20 C.F.R. §§ 404.929 et seq. and 416.1429 et seq.

A. In general: claimant may submit additional evidence; claimant may request ALJ subpoena evidence; claimant (and witnesses) may testify, claimant and decision-maker meet face to face for the first, and only, time - it is a de novo review which should be independent of all previous evaluations and decisions.

B. Duration: Hearings generally last from 20 minutes to 2 hours, depending on the judge, the advocate, the issues and the claimant.

C. Procedure: The procedure is generally informal. The rules of evidence do not apply. In most cases, the judge will do direct examination of your client, only letting you come in to do cross-examination of your own client. The judge will also question any experts first, letting you cross-examine. HOWEVER, be prepared in case the judge wants the advocate to do the direct.

D. Participants: ALJ, his/her assistant (to operate tape recorder), claimant, claimant's witnesses (if any); medical expert and/or vocational expert (possible)

E. Elements of hearing:

1. ALJ introduction and opening statements (will vary from judge to judge);
2. swearing witness(es);
3. admission of evidence (objections may be offered).
4. Representative opening statement, may be optional or ALJ may request statement by rep of theory of the case.
5. Testimony: claimant generally testifies first, followed by claimant's witnesses (if any), and ALJ's witness(es) (if any). Each witness may be cross examined following his or her direct testimony. ALJ may do initial examination of claimant or ask representative to examine the claimant. Representative should be prepared to do the examination if asked.
6. Motions (or requests): to keep the record open for submission of additional evidence; for one or more post-hearing consultative examinations; for time to submit a written closing argument, etc.

7. Closing argument: Should it be done? What should it cover? Should it be presented orally or submitted in writing.

8. Hearing decision: ALJs do not generally announce their decision at the end of the hearing and it may take weeks to months to receive a written decision. If anything significant changes for the claimant after the hearing but before the decision is issued, additional evidence can be submitted to the ALJ.

F. The function of Medical Experts and vocational experts

1. Who calls them? The hearing notice should indicate that an expert will appear, but not necessarily the expert's name.

2. A copy of the expert's resume should be included in the hearing file prior to the hearing; if it is not, ask the ALJ's assistant to provide it.

3. When and why are they used?

4. Preparing for expert testimony: If an ME or VE is scheduled to testify, evaluate the record trying to anticipate issues they will be asked to consider. Prepare for their testimony. Consider the following:

   a. For a VE: evaluate the physical mental demands of each of the claimant's past relevant jobs; look up each job in the DOT; compare how your claimant described his/her work with the DOT description; consider what functions (exertional and nonexertional) were essential to each job; compare those requirements with claimant's current RFC; consider whether claimant has any skills and whether they are transferable, and, if so, whether anything would prevent the claimant from utilizing those skills currently. Does the Grid apply? If so, does it help? If not, are their non-exertional impairments which preclude use of the Grid? Consider the claimant's age and education? At what level of exertion can the claimant win? How severe is each nonexertional impairment? In what ways do they limit activity necessary to performance of any type of work which would win the claim?

   b. For an ME: evaluate the medical evidence, especially focusing on objective test results and diagnoses. Look up each diagnosed condition in an appropriate medical text. What objective findings, signs and symptoms are related to each diagnosis? Does the record support claimant contentions of pain, weakness, fatigue or any other subjective symptom? In the PDR or another relevant source, look up each medication? What is it prescribed for? Does the dosage prescribed suggest any level of severity? What RFC does the treating physician give? Is that opinion supported by relevant findings and test results? How close are CE findings to treating source findings? How close is any DDS RFC to the treating source RFC? Is the duration requirement met?

II. The impact and importance of 1996 Social Security Rulings:

A. What do they cover?

B. How are they being used?

III. Standards of Conduct for Representatives: Rights, Responsibilities and Ethical Obligations of an Authorized Representative

A. SSA Standards of Conduct [63 Fed Reg 41404 (8/4/98), amending regulations at, 20 CFR 404.1740 - .1750, .1765, .1770, .1799; 416.1540 - .1550, .1565, .1599]. [Copy of the regulations, attached].

1. Rules of conduct and standards of responsibility for representatives, 20 CFR 404.1740; 416.1540, subsection(b), Affirmative Duties, include:

a. "Act with reasonable promptness to obtain information and evidence that the claimant wants to submit in support of his or her claim, and forward same to SSA for consideration as soon as practicable..."

b. "Assist the claimant in complying, as soon as possible, with [SSA] requests for information or evidence at any stage of the administrative decisionmaking process..."

c. "Conduct his or her dealings in a manner that furthers the efficient, fair and orderly conduct of the administrative decisionmaking process, [including],

i. Provide competent representation to a claimant. Competent representation requires the knowledge, skill, thoroughness and preparation reasonably necessary for the representation, [including] knowing the significant issue(s) in a claim and having a working knowledge of the applicable provisions of the Social Security Act...the regulations and the Rulings; and

3

ii. Act with reasonable diligence and promptness in representing a claimant."

2. Other considerations

a. Disclosing the parameters of representation

i. what will you do for the claimant?
ii. how long will representation continue?
iii. will you assist after the ALJ hearing? If so, in what capacity?

b. Giving to and obtaining information from SSA: Issues of privacy and confidentiality

i. If adverse information is in an SSA file, can you inform the claimant?
ii. must all evidence be submitted to SSA?
iii. If not, how do you choose?
iv. Submitting information your client may not want considered?[1]
v. Timeliness of submitting evidence

c. Advocates role at the hearing and beyond

d. Obligations to the claimant after the ALJ decision is rendered.

---

[1] EXAMPLE: Mr. J. comes to you complaining of a variety of physical impairments. Upon review of the medical record it becomes clear that the claimant's physical impairments are under good control or insignificant. When you confront Mr. J. about the lack of helpful medical evidence, he gets very excited and tells you that you, like everyone else, is in league with the devil, that his "voices" have told him he must take care of himself and maybe he'll just have to "off" the judge. Trying to calm him, you suggest that he have a psychological evaluation, at which point, Mr. J. screams, "I'm not crazy and nobody's gonna make out I'm crazy". This conversation convinces you that Mr. J. has serious mental problems. Since the client refuses to cooperate with you, the only thing you can think to do is to contact the ALJ and request that he order a psychological evaluation. Can you do this? Given the claimant's threat, do you have any obligation to warn the ALJ that Mr. J. is potentially dangerous?

Reporting and recordkeeping requirements.

Dated: July 24, 1998.

Kenneth S. Apfel,

Commissioner of Social Security.

For the reasons set forth in the preamble, part 404, subpart R, and part 416, subpart O, chapter III of title 20 of the Code of Federal Regulations are amended as set forth below.

PART 404—FEDERAL OLD-AGE, SURVIVORS AND DISABILITY INSURANCE (1950—)

Subpart R—[Amended]

1. The authority citation for subpart R of part 404 continues to read as follows:

Authority: Secs. 205(a), 206, and 702(a)(5) of the Social Security Act (42 U.S.C. 405(a), 406, and 902(a)(5)).

2. Section 404.1740 is revised to read as follows:

§ 404.1740 Rules of conduct and standards of responsibility for representatives.

(a) *Purpose and scope.* (1) All attorneys or other persons acting on behalf of a party seeking a statutory right or benefit shall, in their dealings with us, faithfully execute their duties as agents and fiduciaries of a party. A representative shall provide competent assistance to the claimant and recognize the authority of the Agency to lawfully administer the process. The following provisions set forth certain affirmative duties and prohibited actions which shall govern the relationship between the representative and the Agency, including matters involving our administrative procedures and fee collections.

(2) All representatives shall be forthright in their dealings with us and with the claimant and shall comport themselves with due regard for the nonadversarial nature of the proceedings by complying with our rules and standards, which are intended to ensure orderly and fair presentation of evidence and argument.

(b) *Affirmative duties.* A representative shall, in conformity with the regulations setting forth our existing duties and responsibilities and those of claimants (see § 404.1512 in disability and blindness claims):

(1) Act with reasonable promptness to obtain the information and evidence that the claimant wants to submit in support of his or her claim, and forward the same to us for consideration as soon as practicable. In disability and blindness claims, this includes the obligations to assist the claimant in bringing to our attention everything that shows that the claimant is disabled or blind, and to assist the claimant in furnishing medical evidence that the claimant intends to personally provide and other evidence that we can use to reach conclusions about the claimant's medical impairment(s) and, if material to the determination of whether the claimant is blind or disabled, its effect upon the claimant's ability to work on a sustained basis, pursuant to § 404.1512(a);

(2) Assist the claimant in complying, as soon as practicable, with our requests for information or evidence at any stage of the administrative decisionmaking process in his or her claim. In disability and blindness claims, this includes the obligation pursuant to § 404.1512(c) to assist the claimant in providing, upon our request, evidence about:

(i) The claimant's age;

(ii) The claimant's education and training;

(iii) The claimant's work experience;

(iv) The claimant's daily activities both before and after the date the claimant alleges that he or she became disabled;

(v) The claimant's efforts to work; and

(vi) Any other factors showing how the claimant's impairment(s) affects his or her ability to work. In §§ 404.1560 through 404.1569, we discuss in more detail the evidence we need when we consider vocational factors; and

(3) Conduct his or her dealings in a manner that furthers the efficient, fair and orderly conduct of the administrative decisionmaking process, including duties to:

(i) Provide competent representation to a claimant. Competent representation requires the knowledge, skill, thoroughness and preparation reasonably necessary for the representation. This includes knowing the significant issue(s) in a claim and having a working knowledge of the applicable provisions of the Social Security Act, as amended, the regulations and the Rulings; and

(ii) Act with reasonable diligence and promptness in representing a claimant. This includes providing prompt and responsive answers to requests from the Agency for information pertinent to processing of the claim.

(c) *Prohibited actions.* A representative shall not:

(1) In any manner or by any means threaten, coerce, intimidate, deceive or knowingly mislead a claimant, or prospective claimant or beneficiary, regarding benefits or other rights under the Act;

(2) Knowingly charge, collect or retain, or make any arrangement to charge, collect or retain, from any source, directly or indirectly, any fee for representational services in violation of applicable law or regulation;

(3) Knowingly make or present, or participate in the making or presentation of, false or misleading oral or written statements, assertions or representations about a material fact or law concerning a matter within our jurisdiction;

(4) Through his or her own actions or omissions, unreasonably delay or cause to be delayed, without good cause (see § 404.911(b)), the processing of a claim at any stage of the administrative decisionmaking process;

(5) Divulge, without the claimant's consent, except as may be authorized by regulations prescribed by us or as otherwise provided by Federal law, any information we furnish or disclose about a claim or prospective claim;

(6) Attempt to influence, directly or indirectly, the outcome of a decision, determination or other administrative action by offering or granting a loan, gift, entertainment or anything of value to a presiding official, Agency employee or witness who is or may reasonably be expected to be involved in the administrative decisionmaking process, except as reimbursement for legitimately incurred expenses or lawful compensation for the services of an expert witness retained on a non-contingency basis to provide evidence; or

(7) Engage in actions or behavior prejudicial to the fair and orderly conduct of administrative proceedings, including but not limited to:

(i) Repeated absences from or persistent tardiness at scheduled proceedings without good cause (see § 404.911(b));

(ii) Willful behavior which has the effect of improperly disrupting proceedings or obstructing the adjudicative process; and

(iii) Threatening or intimidating language, gestures or actions directed at a presiding official, witness or Agency employee which results in a disruption of the orderly presentation and reception of evidence.

3. Section 404.1745 is revised to read as follows:

§ 404.1745 Violations of our requirements, rules, or standards.

When we have evidence that a representative fails to meet our qualification requirements or has violated the rules governing dealings with us, we may begin proceedings to suspend or disqualify that individual from acting in a representational capacity before us. We may file charges seeking such sanctions when we have evidence that a representative:

(a) Does not meet the qualifying requirements described in § 404.1705;

(b) Has violated the affirmative duties or engaged in the prohibited actions set forth in § 404.1740; or

(c) Has been convicted of a violation under section 206 of the Act.

4. Section 404.1750 is amended by revising paragraphs (a) and (d) to read as follows:

§ 404.1750 Notice of charges against a representative.

(a) The Deputy Commissioner for Disability and Income Security Programs (or other official the Commissioner may designate), or his or her designee, will prepare a notice containing a statement of charges that constitutes the basis for the proceeding against the representative.

* * * * *

(d) The Deputy Commissioner for Disability and Income Security Programs (or other official the Commissioner may designate), or his or her designee, may extend the 30-day period for good cause.

* * * * *

5. Section 404.1765 is amended by revising paragraph (a), the second sentence of paragraph (e), and paragraph (g)(3) to read as follows:

§ 404.1765 Hearing on charges.

(a) *Scheduling the hearing.* If the Deputy Commissioner for Disability and Income Security Programs (or other official the Commissioner may designate), or his or her designee, does not take action to withdraw the charges within 15 days after the date on which the representative filed an answer, we will hold a hearing and make a decision on the charges.

* * * * *

(e) *Parties.* * * * The Deputy Commissioner for Disability and Income Security Programs (or other official the Commissioner may designate), or his or her designee, shall also be a party to the hearing.

* * * * *

(g) * * *

(3) If the representative did file an answer to the charges, and if the hearing officer believes that there is material evidence available that was not presented at the hearing, the hearing officer may at any time before mailing notice of the hearing decision reopen the hearing to accept the additional evidence.

* * * * *

6. Section 404.1770 is amended by revising the first sentence of paragraph (a)(3) and paragraph (b)(3) to read as follows:

§ 404.1770 Decision by hearing officer.

(a) * * *

(3) The hearing officer shall mail a copy of the decision to the parties at their last known addresses. * * *

(b) * * *

(3) If the final decision is that a person is suspended for a specified period of time from being a representative in dealings with us, he or she will not be permitted to represent anyone in dealings with us during the period of suspension unless authorized to do so under the provisions of § 404.1799.

7. Section 404.1799 is amended by revising the first sentence of paragraph (c) and the second sentence of paragraph (e) to read as follows:

§ 404.1799 Reinstatement after suspension or disqualification—period of suspension not expired.

* * * * *

(c) The Deputy Commissioner for Disability and Income Security Programs (or other official the Commissioner may designate), or his or her designee, upon notification of receipt of the request, shall have 30 days in which to present a written report of any experiences with the suspended or disqualified person subsequent to that person's suspension or disqualification. * * *

* * * * *

(e) * * * It shall also mail a copy to the Deputy Commissioner for Disability and Income Security Programs (or other official the Commissioner may designate), or his or her designee.

* * * * *

PART 416—SUPPLEMENTAL SECURITY INCOME FOR THE AGED, BLIND, AND DISABLED

Subpart O—[Amended]

8. The authority citation for subpart O of part 416 continues to read as follows:

Authority: Secs. 702(a)(5) and 1631(d) of the Social Security Act (42 U.S.C. 902(a)(5) and 1383(d)).

9. Section 416.1540 is revised to read as follows:

§ 416.1540 Rules of conduct and standards of responsibility for representatives.

(a) *Purpose and scope.* (1) All attorneys or other persons acting on behalf of a party seeking a statutory right or benefit shall, in their dealings with us, faithfully execute their duties as agents and fiduciaries of a party. A representative shall provide competent assistance to the claimant and recognize the authority of the Agency to lawfully administer the process. The following provisions set forth certain affirmative duties and prohibited actions which shall govern the relationship between the representative and the Agency, including matters involving our administrative procedures and fee collections.

(2) All representatives shall be forthright in their dealings with us and with the claimant and shall comport themselves with due regard for the nonadversarial nature of the proceedings by complying with our rules and standards, which are intended to ensure orderly and fair presentation of evidence and argument.

(b) *Affirmative duties.* A representative shall, in conformity with the regulations setting forth our existing duties and responsibilities and those of claimants (see § 416.912 in disability and blindness claims):

(1) Act with reasonable promptness to obtain the information and evidence that the claimant wants to submit in support of his or her claim, and forward the same to us for consideration as soon as practicable. In disability and blindness claims, this includes the obligations to assist the claimant in bringing to our attention everything that shows that the claimant is disabled or blind, and to assist the claimant in furnishing medical evidence that the claimant intends to personally provide and other evidence that we can use to reach conclusions about the claimant's medical impairment(s) and, if material to the determination of whether the claimant is blind or disabled, its effect upon the claimant's ability to work on a sustained basis, pursuant to § 416.912(a);

(2) Assist the claimant in complying, as soon as practicable, with our requests for information or evidence at any stage of the administrative decisionmaking process in his or her claim. In disability and blindness claims, this includes the obligation pursuant to § 416.912(c) to assist the claimant in providing, upon our request, evidence about:

(i) The claimant's age;

(ii) The claimant's education and training;

(iii) The claimant's work experience;

(iv) The claimant's daily activities both before and after the date the claimant alleges that he or she became disabled;

(v) The claimant's efforts to work; and

(vi) Any other factors showing how the claimant's impairment(s) affects his or her ability to work, or, if the claimant is a child, his or her functioning. In

§§ 416.960 through 416.969, we discuss in more detail the evidence we need when we consider vocational factors; and

(3) Conduct his or her dealings in a manner that furthers the efficient, fair and orderly conduct of the administrative decisionmaking process, including duties to:

(i) Provide competent representation to a claimant. Competent representation requires the knowledge, skill, thoroughness and preparation reasonably necessary for the representation. This includes knowing the significant issue(s) in a claim and having a working knowledge of the applicable provisions of the Social Security Act, as amended, the regulations and the Rulings; and

(ii) Act with reasonable diligence and promptness in representing a claimant. This includes providing prompt and responsive answers to requests from the Agency for information pertinent to processing of the claim.

(c) *Prohibited actions.* A representative shall not:

(1) In any manner or by any means threaten, coerce, intimidate, deceive or knowingly mislead a claimant, or prospective claimant or beneficiary, regarding benefits or other rights under the Act;

(2) Knowingly charge, collect or retain, or make any arrangement to charge, collect or retain, from any source, directly or indirectly, any fee for representational services in violation of applicable law or regulation;

(3) Knowingly make or present, or participate in the making or presentation of, false or misleading oral or written statements, assertions or representations about a material fact or law concerning a matter within our jurisdiction;

(4) Through his or her own actions or omissions, unreasonably delay or cause to be delayed, without good cause (see § 416.1411(b)), the processing of a claim at any stage of the administrative decisionmaking process;

(5) Divulge, without the claimant's consent, except as may be authorized by regulations prescribed by us or as otherwise provided by Federal law, any information we furnish or disclose about a claim or prospective claim;

(6) Attempt to influence, directly or indirectly, the outcome of a decision, determination or other administrative action by offering or granting a loan, gift, entertainment or anything of value to a presiding official, Agency employee or witness who is or may reasonably be expected to be involved in the administrative decisionmaking process, except as reimbursement for legitimately incurred expenses or lawful compensation for the services of an expert witness retained on a non-contingency basis to provide evidence; or

(7) Engage in actions or behavior prejudicial to the fair and orderly conduct of administrative proceedings, including but not limited to:

(i) Repeated absences from or persistent tardiness at scheduled proceedings without good cause (see § 416.1411(b));

(ii) Willful behavior which has the effect of improperly disrupting proceedings or obstructing the adjudicative process; and

(iii) Threatening or intimidating language, gestures or actions directed at a presiding official, witness or Agency employee which results in a disruption of the orderly presentation and reception of evidence.

10. Section 416.1545 is revised to read as follows:

§ 416.1545 Violations of our requirements, rules, or standards.

When we have evidence that a representative fails to meet our qualification requirements or has violated the rules governing dealings with us, we may begin proceedings to suspend or disqualify that individual from acting in a representational capacity before us. We may file charges seeking such sanctions when we have evidence that a representative:

(a) Does not meet the qualifying requirements described in § 416.1505;

(b) Has violated the affirmative duties or engaged in the prohibited actions set forth in § 416.1540; or

(c) Has been convicted of a violation under section 1631(d) of the Act.

11. Section 416.1550 is amended by revising paragraphs (a) and (d) to read as follows:

§ 416.1550 Notice of charges against a representative.

(a) The Deputy Commissioner for Disability and Income Security Programs (or other official the Commissioner may designate), or his or her designee, will prepare a notice containing a statement of charges that constitutes the basis for the proceeding against the representative.

* * * * *

(d) The Deputy Commissioner for Disability and Income Security Programs (or other official the Commissioner may designate), or his or her designee, may extend the 30-day period for good cause.

* * * * *

12. Section 416.1565 is amended by revising paragraph (a), the second sentence of paragraph (e), and paragraph (g)(3) to read as follows:

§ 416.1565 Hearing on charges.

(a) *Scheduling the hearing.* If the Deputy Commissioner for Disability and Income Security Programs (or other official the Commissioner may designate), or his or her designee, does not take action to withdraw the charges within 15 days after the date on which the representative filed an answer, we will hold a hearing and make a decision on the charges.

* * * * *

(e) *Parties.* * * * The Deputy Commissioner for Disability and Income Security Programs (or other official the Commissioner may designate), or his or her designee, shall also be a party to the hearing.

* * * * *

(g) * * *

(3) If the representative did file an answer to the charges, and if the hearing officer believes that there is material evidence available that was not presented at the hearing, the hearing officer may at any time before mailing notice of the hearing decision reopen the hearing to accept the additional evidence.

* * * * *

13. Section 416.1599 is amended by revising the first sentence of paragraph (c) and the second sentence of paragraph (e) to read as follows:

§ 416.1599 Reinstatement after suspension or disqualification—period of suspension not expired.

* * * * *

(c) The Deputy Commissioner for Disability and Income Security Programs (or other official the Commissioner may designate), or his or her designee, upon notification of receipt of the request, shall have 30 days in which to present a written report of any experiences with the suspended or disqualified person subsequent to that person's suspension or disqualification. * * *

* * * * *

(e) * * * It shall also mail a copy to the Deputy Commissioner for Disability and Income Security Programs (or other official the Commissioner may designate), or his or her designee.

* * * * *

[FR Doc. 98–20760 Filed 8–3–98; 8:45 am]

BILLING CODE 4190–29–P

United States of America
DEPARTMENT OF HEALTH AND HUMAN SERVICES
SOCIAL SECURITY ADMINISTRATION
OFFICE OF HEARINGS AND APPEALS

SUBPENA

In the case of .... (Claimant)

Claim for ....

.... (Wage Earner) (Leave blank if same as above)

.... (Social Security Number)

To:

You are hereby required to SUBMIT *in the above case at a hearing to be held by* ________________, *an Administrative Law Judge of the Office of Hearings and Appeals. The hearing will be held on the* ________ *day of* ________ *at* ________ *o'clock in Room* 2938 *of the* JACOB K. JAVITS *Building, at* 26 FEDERAL PLAZA *(Number and Street)*, NEW YORK *(City)*, N.Y. *(State)*.

You are further required to bring with you and produce at said hearing the following books, correspondence, papers, records or other documents: ALL TREATMENT NOTES, X-RAYS, LAB TESTS RESULTS, OR OTHER MEDICAL DOCUMENTATION YOU HAVE FOR THIS PATIENT, FOR THE PERIOD

and any other evidence in your possession relating to the above matter.

IMPORTANT.–BRING THIS SUBPENA WITH YOU TO THE HEARING

YOUR PERSONAL APPEARANCE WILL NOT BE REQUIRED PROVIDED RECORDS ARE RECEIVED.

D.O.B:
CHART#:
PLEASE RESPOND WITHIN 10 DAYS

SECRETARY OF HEALTH AND HUMAN SERVICES

By ....

ADMINISTRATIVE LAW JUDGE
(Title)

26 FEDERAL PLAZA, RM. 2909
(Address)

NEW YORK, N.Y. 10278
(City, State, and ZIP Code)

Date ....

Form HA-511 (2-86)
Prior edition may be used until supply is exhausted

Social Security Administration

Form Approved
OMB No. 0960-0527

Please read the back of the last copy before you complete this form.

Name (Claimant) (Print or Type)	Social Security Number
Wage Earner (If Different)	Social Security Number

Part I **APPOINTMENT OF REPRESENTATIVE**

I appoint this person, ____ ,
(Name and Address)

to act as my representative in connection with my claim(s) or asserted right(s) under:

☐ Title II (RSDI) ☐ Title XVI (SSI) ☐ Title IV FMSHA (Black Lung) ☐ Title XVIII (Medicare Coverage)

This person may, entirely in my place, make any request or give any notice; give or draw out evidence or information; get information; and receive any notice in connection with my pending claim(s) or asserted right(s).

☐ I am appointing, or I now have, more than one representative. My main representative is ____ .
(Name of Principal Representative)

Signature (Claimant)	Address
Telephone Number (with Area Code) ( )	Date

Part II **ACCEPTANCE OF APPOINTMENT**

I, ______________________________ , hereby accept the above appointment. I certify that I have not been suspended or prohibited from practice before the Social Security Administration; that I am not disqualified from representing the claimant as a current or former officer or employee of the United States; and that I will not charge or collect any fee for the representation, even if a third party will pay the fee, unless it has been approved in accordance with the laws and rules referred to on the reverse side of the representative's copy of this form. If I decide not to charge or collect a fee for the representation, I will notify the Social Security Administration. (Completion of Part III satisfies this requirement.)

☐ I am an attorney. ☐ I am not an attorney. (Check one.)

Signature (Representative)	Address
Telephone Number (with Area Code) ( )	Date

Part III (Optional) **WAIVER OF FEE**

I waive my right to charge and collect a fee under sections 206 and 1631(d)(2) of the Social Security Act. I release my client (the claimant) from any obligations, contractual or otherwise, which may be owed to me for services I have provided in connection with my client's claim(s) or asserted right(s).

Signature (Representative)	Date

Part IV (Optional) **ATTORNEY'S WAIVER OF DIRECT PAYMENT**

I waive only my right to direct payment of a fee from the withheld past-due retirement, survivors, disability insurance or black lung benefits of my client (the claimant). I do not waive my right to request fee approval and to collect a fee directly from my client or a third party.

Signature (Attorney Representative)	Date

(See Important Information on Reverse) FILE COPY

SOCIAL SECURITY ADMINISTRATION

Refer to:

Office of Hearings and Appeal:
Room 2909
26 Federal Plaza
New York, NY 10278-0035
Telephone: (212)264-8819

Dear [redacted]

We have received your request for a hearing before an Administrative Law Judge (ALJ). This letter tells you about the hearing process and things you should do now to prepare for your hearing. We will mail a Notice of Hearing to you at least 20 days before the date of the hearing to tell you its time and place.

The Hearing

At the hearing, you may present your case to the ALJ who will hear and decide it. The ALJ will consider the issue(s) you have raised and the evidence now in your file and any additional evidence you provide. The ALJ may consider other issues as well and, if necessary, change parts of the previous decision that were favorable to you. The Notice of Hearing will state the issues the ALJ plans to consider at the hearing.

Because the hearing is your time to show the ALJ that the issues should be decided in your favor, we need to make sure that your file has everything you want the ALJ to consider. We can help you get needed evidence. After the ALJ reviews the evidence in your file, he or she may request more evidence to consider at your hearing.

Your Right To Representation

You may choose to be represented by a lawyer or other person. A representative can help you get evidence, prepare for the hearing, and present your case at the hearing. If you decide to have a representative, you should find one immediately so that he or she can start preparing your case.

Some private lawyers charge a fee only if you receive benefits. Some organizations may be able to represent you free of charge. Your representative may not charge or receive any fee unless we approve it.

We have enclosed the leaflet "Social Security and Your Right to Representation." We are also enclosing a list of groups that can help you find a representative.

See Next Page

If you get a representative, you or that person should call us to give us his or her name, address and telephone number. You also will need to complete our Form SSA-1696-U4 Appointment of Representative. Any local Social Security office can give you this form.

Providing Additional Evidence

If there is more evidence you want the ALJ to see, get it to us as soon as possible. If you need help, you should immediately contact our office, your local Social Security office, or your representative (if you appoint one). Evidence you cannot get to us before the hearing may be brought to the hearing. You may ask the ALJ to issue a subpoena that requires a person to submit documents or testify at your hearing.

You May See The Evidence In Your File

If you wish to see the evidence in your file, you may do so on the date of the hearing or before that date. If you wish to review your file before the date of the hearing, please call us.

If You Have Any Questions

If you have any questions, please call or write us. Our telephone number and address are shown on the first page of this letter.

Sincerely yours,

Administrative Law Judge

Enclosures

Social Security Administration
SSA Publication No. 05-10075
March 1998

Your Right To Representation

You can choose to have a representative help you when you do business with Social Security. We will work with your representative, just as we would with you.

Your representative cannot charge or collect a fee from you without first getting written approval from the Social Security Administration, even if your claim is denied. However, your representative may accept money in advance as long as he or she holds it in a trust or escrow account.

Both you and your representative are responsible for providing Social Security with accurate information. It is wrong to knowingly and willingly furnish false information. doing so may result in criminal prosecution.

What A Representative Can Do

Once appointed, your representative can act for you in most Social Security matters. For example, he or she can:

- get information from your Social Security file;
- help you get medical records or information to support your claim;
- come with you, or for you, to any interview, conference or hearing you have with us;
- request a reconsideration, hearing or Appeals Council review; and
- help you and your witnesses prepare for a hearing and question any witnesses.

Your representative also will receive a copy of the decision(s) we make on your claim(s).

Choosing A Representative

You can choose an attorney or other qualified person to represent you. You also can have more than one representative.

Some organizations can help you find an attorney or give you free legal services if you qualify. Some attorneys don't charge unless you receive benefits. Your Social Security office has a list of organizations that can help you find a representative.

You can appoint one or more **persons** in a firm, corporation or other organization as your representative(s), but you **may not** appoint the firm, corporation or organization itself. You also may not appoint a person who has been suspended or disqualified from representing others before the Social Security Administration or who may not, by law, act as a representative.

Once you choose a representative, you must tell us **in writing** as soon as possible. To do this, you can get a Form SSA-1696-U4, *Appointment of Representative*, from any Social Security office.

You must give the name of the person you are appointing and sign your name. If the person is not an attorney, he or she must, in writing, give his or her name; state that he or she accepts the appointment; and sign the form.

What Your Representative May Charge

To charge you a fee for his or her services, your representative first must file either a fee agreement or a fee petition with us. Your representative cannot charge you more than the fee amount we approved. If either you or your representative disagree with the fee we approved, you or your representative can ask us to look at it again.

A representative who charges or collects a fee without our approval, or charges or collects too much, may be suspended or disqualified from representing anyone before the Social Security Administration. He or she also may face criminal prosecution.

Filing A Fee Agreement

If you and your representative have a written fee agreement, your representative may ask us to approve it any time before we decide your claim. Usually, we'll approve the agreement and tell you in writing how much your representative may charge as long as:

- you both signed the agreement;
- the fee you agreed on is no more than 25 percent of past-due benefits, or $4,000, whichever is less; and
- your claim was approved and resulted in past-due benefits.
- If we don't approve the fee agreement, we will tell you and your representative in writing that your representative must file a fee petition.

Filing A Fee Petition

Your representative may give us a fee petition when he or she has finished working on your claim(s). This written request, accounting for the fee, describes in detail the amount of time spent on each service provided. Your representative must give you a copy of the fee petition and each attachment. If you disagree with the information shown, contact us within 20 days. We will consider the reasonable value of the services provided and tell you in writing the amount of the fee we approve.

How Much You Pay

The amount of the fee we decide your representative may charge is the most you owe him or her, except for out-of-pocket expenses. It might be different from the amount you agreed to pay.

If an attorney represents you, we usually withhold 25 percent of your past-due benefits to pay toward the fee for you. Later, we pay the attorney's fee from this money and send you any money left over.

You must pay your representative directly:

- the rest you owe
  - if the amount of the fee is more than the amount of money we withheld and paid your attorney for you;
- all of the fee you owe
  - if we did not withhold past-due benefits; for example, when your representative is not an attorney or the benefits are Supplemental Security Income (SSI) or;
  - if we withheld, but later paid you the money because your attorney did not either ask for approval until after 60 days of the date of your notice of award or tell us on time that he or she planned to ask for a fee.

Also, you must pay directly for out-of-pocket expenses your representative incurs or expects to incur, such as the cost of getting your doctor's or hospital records. Our approval is not needed for such expenses.

If Someone Else Pays Your Representative

Even when someone else will pay the fee for you (for example, an insurance company), we must approve the fee unless:

- it's a nonprofit organization or federal, state, county or city agency that will pay the fee and any expenses from government funds; or
- your representative gives us a written statement that you will not have to pay any fee or expenses.

If You Go Before A Federal Court

The court can allow a reasonable fee for your attorney. The fee usually will not exceed 25 percent of all past-due benefits which result from the court's decision. Your attorney cannot charge any additional fee for services before the court.

For More Information

If you have any questions about your right to representation, call our toll-free number, 1-800-772-1213.

The Social Security Administration treats all calls confidentially --whether they're made to our toll-free number or to one of our local offices. We also want to ensure that you receive accurate and courteous service. That is why we have a second Social Security representative listen to some incoming and outgoing telephone calls.

****

IF YOU WANT TO OBTAIN A PRIVATE ATTORNEY to represent your case, then the following organizations listed will help. You will be referred to a private practicing attorney who is familiar with representing Social Security claimants. **SOME PRIVATE ATTORNEYS MAY TAKE YOUR CASE UNDER A FEE AGREEMENT WHEREBY NO FEE WILL BE CHARGED UNLESS YOUR CLAIM IS ALLOWED.** The attorney must first obtain approval from an Administrative Law Judge for ANY fee charged.

****

New York County Lawyers Association
14 Vesey Street
New York, N.Y. 10007
(212) 267-6646

National Organization of Social Security Claimants' Representatives (NOSSCR) ****Referral Service Only****
6 Prospect Street
Midland Park, N.J. 07432
(1-800) 431-2804

****

IF YOU ARE NOT ABLE TO PAY FOR REPRESENTATION AND YOU BELIEVE THAT YOU MIGHT QUALIFY FOR FREE LEGAL REPRESENTATION, YOU SHOULD CONTACT ONE OF THE ORGANIZATIONS LISTED ON THE FOLLOWING PAGES.

****

M A N H A T T A N S E R V I C E S

MFY Legal Services
299 Broadway, 4th Floor
New York, NY 10007
(212) 417-3700

Law Center for the Disabled
217 Broadway
New York, NY 10007
(212) 732-4494

Legal Services for The Elderly
130 West 42nd Street, 17th Floor
New York, N.Y. 10036
(212) 391-0120

Legal Aid Society Volunteer Division/Community Law Offices
230 East 106th Street, 9th Floor
New York, N.Y. 10029
(212) 426-3000 (212) 722-2000

Legal Aid Society

841 Broadway, 3rd Floor
New York, N.Y. 10003
(212) 387-2220

2090 Seventh Avenue
New York, N.Y. 10027
(212) 663-3293

****

M A N H A T T A N   S E R V I C E S (CONTINUED)

****

Legal Services for New York City
Legal Support Unit
350 Broadway, 6th Floor
New York, N.Y. 10013
(212) 431-7200

BLS Legal Services
Senior Citizen Law Office
1 Boerum Plaza, 3rd Fl.
Brooklyn, NY 11201
(718) 488-7448

Center for Immigrant's Rights, Inc.
48 St. Marks Place
New York, N.Y. 10003
(212) 505-6890

Disabled American Veterans
252 Seventh Avenue
New York, N.Y. 10001
(212) 620-6644

Harlem Legal Services, Inc.

144 West 125th Street
New York, N.Y. 10027
(212) 222-7800

47-55 Sickles Street
New York, N.Y. 10040
(212) 567-8119

CeDAR - Center for Disability Advocacy Rights, Inc.
841 Broadway (between 13th & 14th Streets), Suite 605
New York, New York 10003
TEL: (212) 979-0505; FAX: (212) 979-8778; TDD: (212) 979-7880

****

B R O O K L Y N   S E R V I C E S

****

Brooklyn Office of the Aging
1685 East 15th Street
Brooklyn, N.Y. 11229
(718) 645-3111

Legal Aid Society

166 Montague Street
Brooklyn, NY 11201
(718) 722-3100

3159 Coney Island Ave
Brooklyn, NY 11235
(718) 934-2989

186 Joralemon St
Brooklyn, NY 11201
(718) 852-8888

Brooklyn Legal Services

260 Broadway
Brooklyn, N.Y. 11211
(718) 782-6195

105 Court Street
Brooklyn, N.Y. 11201
(718) 237-5500

80 Jamaica Avenue
Brooklyn, NY 11207
(718) 345-6200

Bedford Stuyvesant Community Legal Services
1368-90 Fulton Street
Brooklyn, N.Y. 11216

(718) 636-1155

STATEN ISLAND SERVICES

Richmond County Bar Association
2012 Victory Blvd.
Staten Island, N.Y. 10314
(718) 442-4500

Legal Aid Society

60 Bay Street
Staten Island, N.Y. 10301
(718) 273-6677

QUEENS SERVICES

Queens County Bar Association
90-35 148th Street
Jamaica, N.Y. 11435-4097
(718) 739-4100

Legal Aid Society
20-11 Mott Avenue
Far Rockaway, N.Y. 11691
(718) 337-4900

Queens Legal Services

89-02 Sutphin Blvd.
Jamaica, N.Y. 11435
(718) 657-8611

42-15 Cresent Street, 9th Floor
Long Island City, N.Y. 11101
(718) 392-5646

BRONX SERVICES

Bronx County Bar Association
851 Grand Concourse
Bronx, N.Y. 10451
(718) 293-5600

Legal Aid Society

953 Southern Blvd.
Bronx, N.Y. 10459
(718) 991-4600

2605 Grand Concourse
Bronx, N.Y. 10468
(718) 220-0030

579 Courtlandt Avenue
Bronx, N.Y. 10451
(718) 993-6250

SOCIAL SECURITY ADMINISTRATION

Refer to:

Office of Hearings and Appeals
26 Federal Plaza Room 2909
New York, N.Y. 10278
Telephone: 212-264-8819
Date:

NOTICE OF HEARING

I have scheduled your hearing for:

Day: **Date:** **Time:**

Room: 2938 **Address:** 26 FEDERAL PLAZA, NEW YORK, NY 10278

It is Important That You Come To Your Hearing

I have set aside this time to hear your case. If you do not appear at the hearing and I do not find that you have good cause for failing to appear, I may **dismiss** your request for hearing. I may do so without giving you further notice.

Complete The Enclosed Card

Please complete and return the enclosed card to let me know you to me within 5 days.

If You Cannot Come To Your Scheduled Hearing

To request a change, you must state why you object to the time or place set. You also must state the time and place you want the hearing held. You should do this in writing if at all possible.

If I find that you have good reason, I will reschedule the hearing for a time and place I set. I will also mail you another notice at least 20 days before the date of the hearing.

See Next Page

Travel Costs

When you, a representative, or needed witnesses will travel more than 75 miles one way to the hearing, we can pay certain travel costs. I am enclosing a sheet telling about our rules for doing that. Please call if you want more information.

You May Choose To Have A Person Represent You

If you want to have a representative, please get one right away. You should show this notice to anyone you may appoint. You or that person should also call this office to give us his or her name, address, and telephone number.

Issues I Will Consider In Your Case

The hearing concerns your application of , for a period of disability and disability insurance benefits under sections 216(i) and 223(a) of the Social Security Act (Act). The hearing also concerns your application of , for Supplemental Security Income (SSI) and whether you may be eligible for SSI as a disabled person under section 1614(a)(3) of the Act.

I will decide if you have enough earnings under Social Security to be insured for disability insurance benefits. If you do, I must decide if you became disabled while insured.

Under the Act, I may find you disabled for those benefits or SSI only if you have a physical or mental impairment that:

- has prevented you from doing any substantial gainful work; and
- has lasted 12 straight months or can be expected to last for that time or result in death.

To decide if you are disabled, I will follow a step-by-step process until I can make a decision. The issues in this process concern:

- any work you have done since you got sick:
- the severity of your impairment(s); and
- your ability to do the kind of work you did in the past and, considering your age, education and work experience, any other work that exists in the national economy.

Our regulations explain the rules for deciding if you are disabled and, if so, when you became disabled. These rules appear in the Code of Federal Regulations, Title 20, Chapter III, Part 404 (Subpart P), and Part 416 (Subpart I).

More About The Issues

If you qualify for benefits based on disability, I will also decide if your disability continues. I will consider whether there has been any medical improvement in your impairment(s) or whether one of the exceptions to medical improvement stated in the regulations applies. Unless certain exceptions apply, I will find you still disabled if you have not become able to work.

If You Object To The Issues

If you object to the issues I have stated, you must tell me in writing why you object. You must do this as soon as possible before the hearing.

You May Submit Additional Evidence And Review Your File

If there is more evidence you want to submit, get it to me right away. If you cannot get the evidence to me before the hearing, bring it to the hearing. If you want to see your file **before** the date of the hearing, call this office.

Your Right To Request A Subpoena

I may issue a subpoena that requires a person to submit documents or testify at your hearing. I will issue a subpoena if it is reasonably necessary for the full presentation of your case.

If you want me to issue a subpoena, you must submit a written request. You should submit the request as soon as possible before the hearing. The request must identify the needed documents or witnesses and their location, state the important facts the document or witness is expected to prove, and indicate why you cannot prove these facts without a subpoena.

What Happens At The Hearing

- You may review your file. If you wish to do so, please arrive 30 minutes before the time set for the hearing. Call us if you want more time.
- You will have a chance to testify and tell me about your case.
- You and, if you appoint one, your representative may submit documents, present and question witnesses, state your case, and present written statements about facts and law.
- I will question you and any other witnesses about the issues in your case. You and any other witnesses must normally testify under oath or affirmation. My staff will record the hearing.

My Decision

After the hearing, I will issue a written decision explaining my findings of fact and conclusions of law. I will base my decision on all of the evidence of record, including the testimony at the hearing. I will mail a copy of the decision to you.

If You Have Any Questions

If you have any questions, please call or write this office. Our telephone number and address are shown on the first page of this notice.

____

Administrative Law Judge

Enclosures

When we can pay travel expenses

If you must travel more than 75 miles one way from your home or office to attend the hearing, we can pay certain costs. Here are the rules that apply:

- We can pay your transportation expenses such as the cost of a bus ticket or expenses for driving your car.

- In certain circumstances, you may need meals, lodging, or taxicabs. The Administrative Law Judge (ALJ) must approve these special travel costs **before the hearing unless** the costs were unexpected and unavoidable.

- The ALJ may also approve payment of similar travel expenses for your representative and any witnesses he or she determines are needed at the hearing.

- You must submit a written request for payment of travel expenses to the ALJ at the time of the hearing or as soon as possible after the hearing. List what you spent and include supporting receipts. If you requested a change in the scheduled location of the hearing to a location farther from your residence, we cannot pay you for any **additional** travel expenses.

- If you need money for travel costs in advance, you should tell the ALJ as soon as possible **before the hearing**. We can make an advance payment only if you show that without it you would not have the funds to travel to or from the hearing.

- If you receive travel money in advance, you must give the ALJ an itemized list of your actual travel costs and receipts within 20 days after your hearing.

- If we gave you an advance payment that is more than the amount you are due for travel costs, you must pay back the difference within 20 days after we tell you how much you owe us.

ACKNOWLEDGMENT OF NOTICE OF HEARING

(Complete this card and return it **at once** in the envelope provided. No postage is necessary.)

CLAIMANT	SOCIAL SECURITY NUMBER
WAGE EARNER	HEARING OFFICE

(Check only one)

☐ **I will be present** at the time and place shown on the Notice of Hearing. If an emergency arises after I mail this form and I cannot be present, I will immediately notify you at the telephone number shown on the Notice of Hearing.

☐ **I cannot be present** at the time or place shown on the Notice of Hearing. I request that you reschedule my hearing because: ______________________________

(Use the reverse side for additional remarks.)

NOTE: YOUR REQUEST FOR HEARING MAY BE DISMISSED IF YOU DO NOT ATTEND THE HEARING AND CANNOT GIVE A GOOD REASON FOR NOT ATTENDING. THE TIME OR PLACE OF THE HEARING WILL BE CHANGED IF YOU HAVE A GOOD REASON FOR YOUR REQUEST.

SIGNATURE	DATE	AREA CODE AND TELEPHONE NO.

☐ I have recently moved. My new address is on the reverse side.

Form **HA-504** (12-87)

Form Approved
OMB No 0960-0289

CLAIMANT'S MEDICATIONS

PRIVACY STATEMENT

PRIVACY ACT/PAPERWORK ACT NOTICE: THE COLLECTION OF INFORMATION ON THIS FORM IS AUTHORIZED BY SECTIONS 205 (a), 702, 1631 (e)(1)(A) AND (B), AND 1869 (b)(1) AND (c) OF THE SOCIAL SECURITY ACT, AS APPROPRIATE. THE INFORMATION PROVIDED WILL BE USED TO FURTHER PROCESS YOUR CLAIM. INFORMATION REQUESTED ON THIS FORM IS VOLUNTARY, BUT FAILURE TO PROVIDE ALL OR ANY PART OF THE REQUESTED INFORMATION MAY AFFECT THE DECISION ON YOUR CLAIM. INFORMATION YOU FURNISH ON THIS FORM MAY BE DISCLOSED BY THE SOCIAL SECURITY ADMINISTRATION TO ANOTHER PERSON OR GOVERNMENT AGENCY ONLY WITH RESPECT TO SOCIAL SECURITY PROGRAMS AND TO COMPLY WITH FEDERAL LAWS REQUIRING THE DISCLOSURE OF INFORMATION OR THE EXCHANGE OF INFORMATION BETWEEN THE SOCIAL SECURITY ADMINISTRATION AND OTHER AGENCIES.

(Claimant and Social Security Number)	(Wage Earner and Social Security Number) (Leave blank if same as claimant)

(To be completed by hearing office before mailing to claimant)

PLEASE PRINT

PLEASE LIST BELOW THE PRESCRIPTION MEDICATIONS WHICH YOU ARE PRESENTLY TAKING. IF THE NAME OF THE MEDICATION IS NOT SHOWN ON THE PRESCRIPTION CONTAINER, YOU MAY VERIFY THE NAME WITH YOUR PHARMACIST.

NAME OF MEDICATION & DOSAGE	DATE FIRST PRESCRIBED	DAILY AMOUNT TAKEN	REASON FOR MEDICATION	NAME OF PHYSICIAN

(If additional space is needed, use back of form.)

PLEASE LIST BELOW THE NONPRESCRIPTION MEDICATIONS YOU ARE TAKING AND THE REASONS YOU TAKE THEM.

(If additional space is needed, use back of form.)

Knowing that anyone making a false statement or representation of a material fact for use in determining the right to payment under the Social Security Act commits a crime punishable under Federal law, I certify that the above statements are true.

SIGNATURE	DATE

FORM HA-4632 (3-85) Prior edition may be used until exhausted

SOCIAL SECURITY ADMINISTRATION

Form Approved.
OMB No. 0960-0052

MEDICAL REPORT
(General)

PRIVACY ACT/PAPERWORK REDUCTION ACT NOTICE: The Social Security Administration is authorized to collect the information on this form under sections 205(a), 223(d) and 1633(a) of the Social Security Act. The information on this form is needed by Social Security to complete processing of the named patient's claim. While giving us the information on this form is voluntary, failure to provide the requested information may prevent an accurate or timely decision on the named patient's claim. Although the information you furnish on this form is almost never used for any purpose other than making a determination about disability, such information may be disclosed by the Social Security Administration to another person or governmental agency only with respect to Social Security programs and to comply with federal laws requiring the exchange of information between Social Security and another agency.

TIME IT TAKES TO COMPLETE THIS FORM: We estimate that it will take you about 30 minutes to complete this form. This includes the time it will take to read the instructions, gather the necessary facts and fill out the form. If you have comments or suggestions on this estimate, write to the Social Security Administration, ATTN: Reports Clearance Officer, 1-A-21 Operations Bldg., Baltimore, MD 21235-0001. **Send only comments relating to our estimate or other aspects of this form to the office listed above. All requests for Social Security cards and other claims-related information should be sent to your local Social Security office, whose address is listed under Social Security Administration in the U.S. Government section of your telephone directory.**

Identifying Information *(To be completed by Requesting Office)*	PATIENT'S NAME	DATE OF BIRTH	SOCIAL SECURITY NO.
	WAGE EARNER'S NAME *(If different from patient)*	NAME AND ADDRESS OF REQUESTING OFFICE	
	NAME OF DOCTOR		

NOTICE TO PHYSICIAN:

PLEASE INCLUDE SUFFICIENT DETAILS OF HISTORY, PHYSICAL AND DIAGNOSTIC FINDINGS, CLINICAL COURSE, THERAPY AND RESPONSE TO ENABLE A REVIEWING PHYSICIAN TO MAKE AN INDEPENDENT DETERMINATION AS TO THE SEVERITY AND DURATION OF THE IMPAIRMENT.

I. HISTORY:

DATE YOU FIRST EXAMINED PATIENT	FREQUENCY OF VISITS	DATE OF MOST RECENT EXAMINATION

Form **SSA-3826-F4** (5-88) 1 Printed on recycled paper

II. PHYSICAL FINDINGS: Please show all pertinent findings *(with dates)*.

HEIGHT	WEIGHT

III. LABORATORY AND SPECIAL STUDIES: Give Results of all Pertinent Studies With Dates. *(In the case of ECG's please attach a copy of the tracing or a detailed description thereof.)*

IV. DIAGNOSES:

1.

2.

3.

V. TREATMENT and RESPONSE

REPORTING PHYSICIAN'S NAME AND ADDRESS *(Type or Print)*	SIGNATURE	TITLE
	TELEPHONE NUMBER *(Include area code)*	DATE

Form SSA-3826-F4 (5-88) 4 *U.S. Government Printing Office: 1995 — 387-008/20088

MEDICAL ASSESSMENT OF ABILITY TO DO WORK-RELATED ACTIVITIES (PHYSICAL)

NAME OF INDIVIDUAL SOCIAL SECURITY NUMBER

To determine this individual's ability to do work-related activities on a day-to-day basis in a regular work setting, please give us an assessment-BASED ON YOUR EXAMINATION-of how the individual's physical capabilities are affected by the impairment(s). Consider the medical history, the chronicity of findings (or lack thereof), and the expected duration of any work-related limitations, but not the individual's age, sex, or work experience.

For each activity shown below:

(1) Check the Appropriate block;

(2) Respond to the questions concerning the individual's ability to perform the activity; and

(3) Identify the particular medical findings (i.e., physical exam findings, x-ray findings, laboratory test results, history, symptoms (including pain), etc. which support your assessment of any limitations.

IT IS IMPORTANT THAT YOU RELATE PARTICULAR MEDICAL FINDINGS TO ANY ASSESSED EDUCATION IN CAPACITY. THE USEFULNESS OF YOUR ASSESSMENT DEPENDS ON THE EXTENT TO WHICH YOU DO THIS.

1. Are LIFTING/CARRYING affected by impairment? What are the medical findings that support this assessment?

( ) No
( ) Yes

If "yes", how many pounds can the individual lift and/or carry?

Maximum Occasionally (from very little up to 1/3 of an 8-hour day)________

Maximum Frequently (from 1/3 to 2/3 of an 8-hour day)________

II. Are STANDING/WALKING affected by impairment?

( ) No
( ) Yes

If "yes", how many hours in an 8-hour work day can the individual stand and/or walk? total______

without interruption?_______

What are the medical findings that support this assessment?

III. Is SITTING affected that by impairment?

( ) No
( ) Yes

If "yes", how many hours in an 8-hour work day can the individual sit? total________

without interruption?________

What are the medical findings support this assessment?

IV. How often can the individual perform following POSTURAL ACTIVITIES?

	Frequently	*Occasionally	**Never
Climb			
Balance			
Stoop			
Crouch			
Kneel			

What are the medical findings support this assessment?

*Frequently: from 1/3 to 2/3 of an 8-hour day
**Occasionally: from very little up to 1/3 of an 8-hour day.

Crawl			

V. Are the following PHYSICAL FUNCTIONS affected by the impairment?

	No	Yes
Reaching		
Handling		
Feeling		
Pushing/Pulling		
Seeing		
Hearing		
Speaking		

A. How are these physical functions affected?

B. What are the medical findings that support this assessment

VI. Are there ENVIRONMENTAL RESTRICTIONS caused by the impairment?

	No	Yes
Heights		
Moving Machinery		
Temperature Extremes		
Dust		
Noise		
Fumes		
Humidity		
Vibration		
Other		

A. How do the checked restrictions affect the individual's activities?

B. What are the medical findings that support this assessment.

VII. State any other work-related activities which are affected by the impairment, and indicate how the activities are affected. What are the medical findings that support this assessment?

VII. State any other work-related activities which are affected by the impairment, and indicate how the activities are affected. What are the medical findings that support this assessment?

PHYSICIAN'S SIGNATURE DATE

ASSESSMENT OF ABILITY TO ENGAGE IN WORK-RELATED ACTIVITIES (MENTAL)

Individual ______________________ Social Security Number ______________

To help us determine this individual's ability to do work-related activities on a day-to-day basis in a regular work setting, please give us an assessment - BASED ON YOUR EXAMINATION - of how the individual's functional capabilities are affected by the impairment(s). Consider the medical history, the chronicity of findings (or lack thereof), and the expected duration of any work-related limitations, but not the individual's age, sex, or work experience. **YOUR ASSESSMENT SHOULD BE BASED ON YOUR CLINICAL FINDINGS AND PROFESSIONAL OPINION AND NOT UPON THE SUBJECTIVE STATEMENTS OF THE INDIVIDUAL.**

1. For each activity shown below, describe the functional limitations which exist as a result of the individual's mental impairments by checking the most closely applicable term.

2. Identify the particular medical findings (i.e. mental status examination, behavior, intelligence testing, symptoms, etc.) which support your assessment of any limitations.

IT IS IMPORTANT THAT YOU RELATE PARTICULAR MEDICAL FINDINGS TO ANY ASSESSED REDUCTION IN CAPACITY. THE HELPFULNESS OF YOUR ASSESSMENT DEPENDS ON THE EXTENT TO WHICH YOU DO THIS.

DEFINITION OF RATING TERMS

None:	No impairment in this area.
Slight:	Suspected impairment of slight importance which does not affect functional ability.
Moderate:	An impairment which reduces but does not preclude ability to function.
Marked:	An impairment which seriously affects ability to function.
Extreme:	Functional ability precluded.

I. MAKING OCCUPATIONAL ADJUSTMENTS

CHECK THE TERM REPRESENTING THE INDIVIDUAL'S ABILITY TO ADJUST TO A JOB AND COMPLETE ITEM 9.

1. Follow work rules

[ ] None [ ] Slight [ ] Moderate [ ] Marked [ ] Extreme [ ] Insufficient Evidence

2. Relate to coworkers

[ ] None [ ] Slight [ ] Moderate [ ] Marked [ ] Extreme [ ] Insufficient Evidence

3. Deal with the public

[ ] None [ ] Slight [ ] Moderate [ ] Marked [ ] Extreme [ ] Insufficient Evidence

4. Use judgment

[ ] None [ ] Slight [ ] Moderate [ ] Marked [ ] Extreme [ ] Insufficient Evidence

5. Interact with supervisor(s)

[ ] None [ ] Slight [ ] Moderate [ ] Marked [ ] Extreme [ ] Insufficient Evidence

6. Deal with work stresses

[ ] None [ ] Slight [ ] Moderate [ ] Marked [ ] Extreme [ ] Insufficient Evidence

7. Function independently

[ ] None [ ] Slight [ ] Moderate [ ] Marked [ ] Extreme [ ] Insufficient Evidence

8. Maintain attention/concentration

[ ] None [ ] Slight [ ] Moderate [ ] Marked [ ] Extreme [ ] Insufficient Evidence

9. Describe any limitations and include the medical/clinical findings that support this assessment.

II. MAKING PERFORMANCE ADJUSTMENTS

CHECK THE TERM REPRESENTING THE INDIVIDUAL'S ABILITY TO ADJUST TO A JOB AND COMPLETE ITEM 4.

1. Understand, remember, and carry out complex job instructions

[ ] None [ ] Slight [ ] Moderate [ ] Marked [ ] Extreme [ ] Insufficient Evidence

2. Understand, remember and carry out detailed but not complex job instructions

[ ] None [ ] Slight [ ] Moderate [ ] Marked [ ] Extreme [ ] Insufficient Evidence

3. Understand, remember and carry out simple job instructions

[ ] None [ ] Slight [ ] Moderate [ ] Marked [ ] Extreme [ ] Insufficient Evidence

4. Describe any limitations and include the medical/clinical findings that support this assessment (e.g. intellectual ability, thought organization, memory, comprehension, etc.)

III. MAKING PERSONAL-SOCIAL ADJUSTMENTS

CHECK THE TERM REPRESENTING THE INDIVIDUAL'S LIMITATIONS TO ADJUST PERSONALLY AND SOCIALLY AND COMPLETE ITEM 5.

1. Maintain acceptable personal appearance

[ ] None [ ] Slight [ ] Moderate [ ] Marked [ ] Extreme [ ] Insufficient Evidence

2. Behave in an emotionally stable manor

[ ] None [ ] Slight [ ] Moderate [ ] Marked [ ] Extreme [ ] Insufficient Evidence

3. Behave predictably in social situations

[ ] None [ ] Slight [ ] Moderate [ ] Marked [ ] Extreme [ ] Insufficient Evidence

4. Demonstrate reliability

[ ] None [ ] Slight [ ] Moderate [ ] Marked [ ] Extreme [ ] Insufficient Evidence

5. Describe any limitations and include the medical/clinical findings that support the assessment.

IV. OTHER WORK-RELATED ACTIVITIES

State any other work-related activities which are adversely affected by the impairment(s), indicate how the activities are affected, and what medical clinical findings support this assessment.

V. CAPABILITY TO MANAGE BENEFITS

Can the individual manage monetary benefits in his/her own best interests? [ ] YES [ ] NO

VI. ADDITIONAL COMMENTS

Physician's Signature Date

Request for Review of Hearing Decision/Order

DEPARTMENT OF HEALTH AND HUMAN SERVICES
SOCIAL SECURITY ADMINISTRATION/OFFICE OF HEARINGS AND APPEALS

Form Approved
OMB No 0960-0277

REQUEST FOR REVIEW OF HEARING DECISION/ORDER

(Take or mail original and all copies to your local Social Security office)

See Privacy Act Notice on Reverse

CLAIMANT

WAGE EARNER (Leave blank if same as above)

SOCIAL SECURITY NUMBER

SPOUSE'S NAME AND SOCIAL SECURITY NUMBER
(Complete ONLY in Supplemental Security Income Case)

NAME | SSN

(Check ONE)
Initial Entitlement ☐ Termination or other Postentitlement Action ☐

Type Claim (Check ONE)

- Retirement or Survivors .... Only ☐ (RSI)
- Disability, Worker or Child .... Only ☐ (DIWC)
- Disability, Widow or Widower .... Only ☐ (DIWW)
- Health Insurance, Part A .... Only ☐ (HIA)
- SSI, Aged ...... Only ☐ (SSIA) With Title II Claim ☐ (SSAC)
- SSI, Blind ...... Only ☐ (SSIB) With Title II Claim ☐ (SSBC)
- SSI, Disability ... Only ☐ (SSID) With Title II Claim ☐ (SSDC)
- Other (Specify)

I disagree with the action taken on the above claim and request review of such action by the Appeals Council of the Office of Hearings and Appeals. My reasons for disagreement are:

____

____

ADDITIONAL EVIDENCE

Any additional evidence which you wish to submit must be either attached to this form or forwarded within 15 days to the Appeals Council at the address shown below. It is important that you write your Social Security number on any letter or material you send us. Where the evidence is not submitted within 15 days of this date, or within any extension of time granted by the Appeals Council, the Council will proceed to take its action based on the evidence of record.

Knowing that anyone making a false statement or representation of a material fact for use in determining the right to payment under the Social Security Act commits a crime punishable under Federal law, I certify that the above statements are true.

Signed by: (Either the claimant or representatives should sign—Enter addresses for both)

SIGNATURE OR NAME OF CLAIMANT'S REPRESENTATIVE ☐ ATTORNEY ☐ NON-ATTORNEY		CLAIMANT SIGNATURE
STREET ADDRESS		STREET ADDRESS
CITY, STATE, AND ZIP CODE		CITY, STATE, AND ZIP CODE
AREA CODE AND TELEPHONE NUMBER	DATE	AREA CODE AND TELEPHONE NUMBER

Claimant should not fill in below this line

TO BE COMPLETED BY SOCIAL SECURITY ADMINISTRATION

Is this request filed timely? ☐ Yes ☐ No — If "NO" is checked: (1) attach claimant's explanation for delay; (2) attach any pertinent letter, material or information in Social Security Office.

ACKNOWLEDGEMENT OF RECEIPT OF REQUEST FOR REVIEW OF HEARING DECISION/ORDER

This request for Review of Hearing Decision/Order was filed on ______________ at ______________
The APPEALS COUNCIL will notify you of its action on your request.

APPEALS COUNCIL
OFFICE OF HEARINGS AND APPEALS, SSA
P.O. BOX 3200
ARLINGTON, VA 22203

For the Social Security Administration:

SIGNATURE BY:	
TITLE	
STREET ADDRESS	
CITY	
STATE	ZIP CODE
SERVICING SOCIAL SECURITY OFFICE CODE	

Form HA-520-US (6/88)

CLAIMS FOLDER

NOTES

NOTES

5

APPEALS COUNCIL PRACTICE AND PROCEDURE

James M. Baker

APPEALS COUNCIL PRACTICE AND PROCEDURE

James M. Baker

Introduction

The Appeals Council is an entity within the Social Security Administration's Office of Hearings and Appeals. Its primary function is to conduct discretionary reviews of decisions made by administrative law judges ("ALJs") in individual claims for benefits arising under Titles II, XVI, and XVIII of the Social Security Act. In the multi-layered appeals process that governs Social Security cases, the Appeals Council comes between the ALJ hearing and the appeal to federal court. It is the last appeal within the SSA bureaucracy. You must appeal to the Appeals Council in order to appeal beyond it to federal court.

Appealing to the Appeals Council is by and large an unrewarding activity. Reversal rates are low. In 1997, for instance, the Appeals Council "affirmed" or dismissed appeals in in 79% of cases, remanded for further ALJ proceedings in 18%, and awarded benefits outright in only 3%. (The rates are for all claimants; presumably rates for represented claimants are better.) Low as they are, rates were substantially lower in the past. In the early to mid-1980s, when I began to handle disability claims, the Appeals Council regularly "affirmed" the ALJ in more than 98% of claims.

The secret to successful Appeals Council practice, in my view, is not to devote too much time to it. A basic Appeals Council letter should not exceed 2-4 pages in length and should not consume much more than half a work day of your time. If you spend a week writing a 30 page Memorandum of Law to the Appeals Council you will not, in my opinion, appreciably enhance your chances for success and you will enormously increase your level of frustration when, 12-18 months later, your receive in the mail the Appeals Council's one page, form-letter-format, denial of your "Request for Review." Save it for district court.

Sources of Law

The formal rules governing Appeals Council practice and procedure are located at 20 C.F.R. §§ 404.966-984 (Title II claims), 416.1466-1484 (Title XVI claims). The Appeals Council is a creature of regulation, not statute. That is, the Social Security Act does not require SSA to maintain an appellate body to hear appeals from adverse ALJ decisions. SSA has chosen by regulation to create such an entity and could chose to abolish it. Indeed, there are serious efforts afoot to do just that, whereof more anon.

Formal Practice Requirements

There are few formalities in Appeals Council practice. SSA has optional "Request for Review" forms but any written communication from the claimant or her representative which expresses a desire to appeal an adverse ALJ decision is sufficient. I generally write a letter containing factual and legal argument in lieu of a formal memorandum. (A sample letter follows.) If I submit additional medical evidence, I simply send it along with the letter. If I have not already appeared on the client's behalf at an earlier stage of proceedings, I will also submit one of SSA's "Appointment of Representative" forms.

Where and When to Appeal

The Request for Review can be filed at any SSA office or directly with the Appeals Council at 5107 Leesburg Pike, Falls Church, VA 22041-3255. 20 C.F.R. § 404.968(a)(2). You have 60 days to appeal after receipt of the ALJ's decision. 20 C.F.R. § 404.968(a)(1). There is a rebuttable presumption that the ALJ's decision is received five days after the date which appears on the decision which means, as a practical matter, that it is usually safe to file on the 65th day. Caution is warranted, however. If your office in fact received the ALJ decision 2 days after it was dated, you have only 62 days to file (though SSA will probably have no way of knowing you got it earlier). Conversely, if you received the decision 12 days after the date, you can technically file on the 72nd day, but you had better be prepared to prove late receipt.

When you do file, it is extremely good practice to get a receipt, if you file in person, or to use certified mail, return receipt requested, if you mail. I have had two cases in 18 years of practice where the Appeals Council adamantly insisted -- until I produced my certified mail receipt -- that no Request for Review had ever been filed.

If you miss the deadline, the Appeals Council can extend it if you show "good cause." See 20 C.F.R. §§ 404.968, 404.911. Be prepared to grovel abjectly.

Provided you have filed the Request for Review on time, you can then ask the Appeals Council to extend your time to submit legal argument and/or new evidence. The Appeals Council is usually willing to grant at least one short extension. Moreover, it will routinely grant a request for a copies of the written exhibits received by the ALJ and the hearing tape. 20 C.F.R. § 404.974. This, as a practical matter, will extend your deadline for months.

Grounds for Appeal

The Appeals Council will consider any grounds for appeal that could be urged in district court, *e.g.*, that the ALJ committed legal errors in the interpretation of the statute or regulations, or failed to conduct a fair proceeding, or that her findings of fact were not supported by substantial evidence. In addition, the claimant has an absolute right to submit new evidence at the Appeals Council level without having to excuse her failure to offer it earlier. If new evidence is submitted, the Appeals Council reviews the entire record *de novo* and reverses the ALJ if it decides that her decision was "contrary to the weight of the evidence currently of record." 20 C.F.R. § 404.970(b). This is a much better deal -- at least in theory -- than what the claimant gets if no new evidence is submitted: a review to see if the ALJ's decision was supported by "substantial evidence." 20 C.F.R. § 404.970(a)(3). In practice, I think cases submitted with new evidence do tend to get looked at more carefully and more favorably than cases without.

New evidence submitted at the Appeals Council level must "relate to the period on or before the date of the [ALJ] decision." 20 C.F.R. § 404.970(b). Given the least excuse, the Appeals Council will assume that the new evidence you submit reflects medical developments that arose only after the ALJ decision. It is usually possible to anticipate the problem and have the evidence, such as the doctor's report, explicitly recite that it describes the claimant's pre-decision condition.

The right to submit new evidence to the Appeals Council is an extremely valuable one since it allows you to fix evidentiary problems, as well as legal ones, on appeal. For this reason, SSA has been most eager to limit it. Several years ago, SSA attempted to persuade the federal courts that evidence first submitted at the Appeals Council level could not be relied upon by the claimant once the case reached the courts. The Second Circuit rejected this argument, however. Perez v. Chater, 77 F.3d 41 (2d Cir. 1995).

SSA has recently had more success with an argument that the claimant cannot raise legal arguments in district court that she failed to raise before the Appeals Council. E.g., Griffith v. Callahan, 138 F.3d 1150 (7th Cir. 1998); Brewer v. Chater, 103 F.3d 1384 (7th Cir. 1997). The Second Circuit has not yet spoken on this issue of "issue preclusion"; and it is to be hoped that the Court will ultimately not apply issue preclusion against claimants who were unrepresented at the Appeals Council level. The message for representatives who practice before the Appeals Council is clear, however: You should take care to raise before the Appeals Council any legal issue you even might want to assert in district court.

Outcomes

The Appeals Council can dispose of a Request for Review

essentially in three ways: (1) It can affirm the ALJ. (2) It can reverse the ALJ and order further proceedings at the ALJ level, usually a new hearing. (3) It can reverse and order payment of benefits. Remands can happen over and over again: It is not uncommon for a case to bounce up and down between the Appeals Council and ALJ two or three times. In one unfortunate case which took nearly six years to complete, I lost four hearings before the same ALJ, with the Appeals Council remanding on the first three appeals and finally awarding benefits on the fourth. (Nowadays, there is a policy that a case will only go back to the same ALJ once.)

For curious doctrinal reasons, the Appeals Council rarely, if ever, "affirms" an ALJ decision. If it doesn't think the appeal has merit, it will "refuse to review" it, letting the ALJ decision stand as SSA's "final" decision in the case. If it decides for the claimant, it will first "accept" the case for review and then reverse. The Appeals Council goes through these linguistic contortions for strategic purposes which are basically beyond the scope of this outline but which include allowing it to disclaim responsibility for affirming unusually egregious ALJ errors.

<u>Own Motion Review</u>

In addition to reviewing ALJ decisions at the request of dissatisfied claimants, the Appeals Council also possesses the authority to review cases on its own motion. 20 C.F.R. § 404.969. Theoretically, that is, you could obtain a favorable ALJ decision today only to be notified, six weeks from now, that the Appeals Council has decided that your client isn't disabled after all. If the Appeals Council is going to conduct an "own motion review," it must act within 60 days of the ALJ decision. Id. Historically, the Appeals Council's exercise of this authority has been extraordinarily rare. (It has happened to a client of mine just once in 18 years.) On the other hand, people much more knowledgeable than I about the inner workings of SSA have reported that SSA plans a vast expansion of own motion review at the same time that it is testing elimination of Appeals Council review initiated by the claimant. (See below.) If this occurs, the Appeals Council may be transformed from an entity which hears appeals by claimants to one which polices ALJs with excessively high reversal rates.

Elimination of Appeals Council Review

For years, there have been proposals that SSA eliminate one or more steps in its multi-level review process, the favorite targets being reconsideration and Appeals Council review. Recently, SSA has begun to test the feasibility of eliminating the latter in certain parts of the country, including New York City. The regulations governing these cases are set out at 20 C.F.R. § 404.966. Basically, what happens is that, in certain randomly-selected cases, SSA informs the claimant in the notice announcing the ALJ decision that the decision is SSA's final decision and that the claimant, if dissatisfied, must appeal directly to district court. 20 C.F.R. § 404.966(c). The Appeals Council still retains the authority to conduct an own motion review but must act before a district court complaint is filed, *i.e.*, within 60 days of the ALJ decision (or less if the claimant files sooner.) 20 C.F.R. § 404.966(b)(2).

BRONX LEGAL SERVICES
DISABILITY LAW PROJECT
579 COURTLANDT AVENUE
BRONX, NEW YORK 10451
TEL: (718) 993-6250
FAX: (718) 993-3672

DENNIS C. GARDNER
Chairperson

WALKER T. THOMPSON
Project Director

GUILENE CHERENFANT EDOUARD
Acting Director of Litigation

September 27, 1996

Appeals Council
Office of Hearings and Appeals, SSA
5107 Leesburg Pike
Falls Church, Va. 22041-3255

Re: Luisa C______
SSN: 123-45-9789

Dear Members:

I am writing to request review of the September 13, 1996 decision of ALJ Robin J. Arzt which denied Luisa C____'s claim for SSI benefits based upon disability. My Appointment of Representative form is already on file.

This is a relatively simple and straightforward case. The claimant was 49 years old on the date of the administrative hearing. She had acquired a ninth grade education in her native Puerto Rico but did not speak English. Ms. C____ had no past relevant work experience, having spent most of her adult life caring for her extremely ill mother, who died about two years prior to the hearing. At the hearing, Ms. C____ agreed that none of her physical impairments was incapacitating. She claimed, however, that she was unable to work because of the severe depression which she had experienced since her mother's death.

The entire medical record on the nature and extent of Ms. C____'s psychiatric disability consists of three documents. There is an initial "Psychiatric Consultation Report" prepared by Patricia Daniels, Ph.D., on October 11, 1994. Exh. 15, p. 1. There are also two "Psychiatric Assessment" forms completed by Dr. Daniels on April 25, 1995 (Exh. 15, pp. 2-5) and May 9, 1995. (Exh. 18, 1-4.)

The initial report diagnoses Ms. C____ as suffering from major depression with weight loss, decreased appetite, insomnia, memory loss and headaches. Mood was depressed. There was vague suicidal ideation. There was considerable social isolation. The report mentions other, unspecified "signs of depression." Exh. 15, p.1. Ms. C____'s symptoms were attributed to the death of her mother which had occurred about 18 months before. The report states:

> "The patient's mother died 18 months ago and the patient who lived with her, attributes most of her symptoms to her mother's death. The patient's mother was diabetic and had to have both legs amputated and the patient devoted all her time to caring for her mother. The mother had become blind after 6 operations of her eyes. The patient was an only child and never married. She devoted her whole life to caring for her mother, who was always sickly." Exh. 15, p. 1.

The first of the two psychiatric assessment forms, completed on April 25, 1995, indicates that there had been little improvement in Ms. C____'s condition after six months of therapy. Exh. 15, p. 3. Ms. C___ was still experiencing fatigue, lack of energy, sleep disturbance, and appetite disturbance. Id. Dr. Daniels stated that Ms. C____ was impaired to a "marked" or "severe" degree in virtually every rating category. Id. at 4-5. She also indicated that Ms. C____'s condition had lasted, or was expected to last, more than twelve months. Id. at 3.

The second form, completed a mere two weeks after the first, expresses essentially the same assessment of functional capacity. Exh. 18, pp. 3-4. Ms. C____'s symptoms included depression, fatigue, lack of energy, sleep disturbance, difficulty concentrating, and some anxiety. Id. at 1-2. She was socially isolated. Id. On mental status examination, Ms. C____ was anxious and dysthymic. There were other, unspecified signs of depression. Id. at 1. Prognosis was said to be "poor" and her depression was described as a "very chronic" condition. Id. at 2.

In her decision of September 13, 1995, ALJ Arzt acknowledged that Ms. C____'s treating psychologist believed her to be disabled but nevertheless denied benefits. This decision was in error and should be reversed.

First, under the Commissioner's version of the "treating physician rule" now codified at 20 C.F.R. § 416.927(d)(2), the opinion of a treating physician that a claimant is disabled is entitled to "controlling weight" if "well-supported by medically acceptable clinical and laboratory diagnostic techniques" and not inconsistent with other substantial evidence. Dr. Daniels' reports are entitled to controlling weight under this standard. Although ALJ Arzt states that the psychologist's assessment of the degree of functional impairment is "not supported by objective findings" (Decision, p. 4), the basis for this statement is totally unclear. Possibly ALJ Arzt believes that a person suffering from a disabling degree of depression ought to exhibit symptoms in addition to those Ms. C____ exhibits, i.e., depressed mood, appetite disturbance, sleep disturbance, fatigue and decreased energy, and difficulty concentrating. There is, however, no medical evidence to support the ALJ's lay opinion on this subject. Her opinion is also decidedly wrong, since the symptoms Ms. C____ has are exactly what one needs to satisfy the listing for depression.*

Second, even if Dr. Daniels' opinion was not "well-supported by medically acceptable clinical and laboratory diagnostic techniques," it is nevertheless entitled to be weighed against contradictory medical opinion in terms of specific factors identified in the regulations. 20 C.F.R. § 416.927(d). Those factors are: examining relationship, treating relationship, supportability, consistency, and specialization. Id. If Dr. Daniels' opinion, even though not "well-supported," is nevertheless superior to the evidence which contradicts it in terms of these five variables, it must be preferred. Id. Here, Dr. Daniels' opinion that Ms. C____ is psychiatrically disabled is totally uncontradicted in this record. Although the regulations do not specifically address this situation, the result for Ms. C____ can hardly be worse than if Dr. Daniels' opinion had been contradicted by some "inferior" report.

Third, and finally, if ALJ Arzt believed that Dr. Daniels' evidence was inadequate for any reason, she was absolutely obligated by the Social Security Act, the Commissioner's regulations, and innumerable court decisions to develop the record further. She should do this, in the first instance, by re-contacting Dr. Daniels. 20 C.F.R. § 416.912(e). ("We will seek additional evidence or clarification from your medical source when the report from your medical source contains a conflict or ambiguity that must be resolved, the report does not contain all the necessary information, or does not appear to be based on medically acceptable clinical and laboratory techniques.") If the missing information is not available from the treating source, SSA must arrange for a consultative examination. 20 C.F.R. § 416.912(f). ("If the information we need is not readily available from the records of your treatment source, ... we will ask you to attend one or more consultative examinations at our expense.") (Emphasis added.) See also 20 C.F.R. §§ 416.919, 416.919a(b)

---

* That is, Part A of Listing 12.04 is satisfied if the claimant has depressive syndrome plus at least four of the signs or symptoms enumerated in section 12.04A.1. Ms. C____ certainly exhibits (b) appetite disturbance with change in weight, (c) sleep disturbance, (e) decreased energy, and (g) difficulty concentrating or thinking. She probably also exhibits anhedonia and feelings of guilt or worthlessness, although these are not expressly mentioned by Dr. Daniels. Three out of four part B criteria are also satisfied. Exhs. 15, pp. 4-5; 18, pp. 3-4.

("Situations requiring a consultative examination.") (Emphasis added.) Nothing in the regulations permits the Commissioner to deny benefits to a claimant who might be disabled solely because needed information is not readily forthcoming from treating sources.

For the foregoing reasons, the decision of ALJ Arzt should be reversed and benefits awarded on the basis of the treating psychologist's opinion that Ms. C____ is disabled and satisfies the requirements of Listing 12.04. In the alternative, Ms. C____'s claim should be remanded for development of a complete medical record.

Very truly yours,

James M. Baker
Attorney

JMB/jb

CERTIFIED MAIL, RETURN RECEIPT REQUESTED

NOTES

NOTES

6

SOCIAL SECURITY DISABILITY AND SSI CLAIMS IN THE FEDERAL COURTS

James M. Baker

SOCIAL SECURITY DISABILITY AND SSI CLAIMS IN THE FEDERAL COURTS

James M. Baker

Introduction

Claimants dissatisfied with Social Security Administration ("SSA") determinations of their claims for disability benefits may have them reviewed by the federal courts under 42 U.S.C. § 405(g). Claims for such judicial review are initially heard in the district courts and can be appealed to the courts of appeals and to the U.S. Supreme Court. The federal courts have the power to affirm SSA's determination, reverse the determination and order further proceedings at the administrative level (which may, in turn, lead to additional court proceedings), or reverse SSA outright and award benefits to the claimant.

Although the claim for review is filed in the federal trial court, the nature of the proceeding is strictly appellate. Pleadings are unimportant; there is no discovery or trial. The government produces a transcript of the proceedings that took place before the administrative agency and the parties are basically stuck with that record. Mostly what you do in federal court, if you're a Social Security practitioner, is write briefs.

The other basic thing the beginner needs to know about the practice in federal court is that you often win -- at least if you're at all careful about picking your fights. Despite a lot of language in the court decisions about the narrow scope of review and the great deference the courts must pay to the administrative agency, reversal rates are high, especially for competently represented plaintiffs. If your client has serious health problems and a good work record, most federal district court judges can usually be persuaded to order SSA to take a second look at the case. It is considerably more difficult, however, to get an outright award of benefits.

Prerequisites to Suit

Judicial review of SSA determinations is available only under 42 U.S.C. § 405(g). There is no general federal question jurisdiction over SSA for this purpose. To invoke § 405(g), the plaintiff must have exhausted administrative remedies, which means that she must have proceeded through the entire, four-step administrative appeal process (initial determination, reconsideration, ALJ hearing, Appeals Council review). If the plaintiff skips any of these steps -- say, for instance, that she never had an ALJ hearing because the ALJ erroneously dismissed her hearing request on the grounds of untimely filing -- she may not proceed under § 405(g).[1]

Suit must be commenced within 60 days of receipt of SSA's final decision, which is normally the denial of review by the Appeals Council. The 60 day limitations period is strictly enforced. It is not, however, jurisdictional and therefore can be waived. If plaintiff misses the deadline, she may petition the Appeals Council for waiver, which will be granted if the Appeals Council finds "good cause." 20 C.F.R. §§ 404.982, 404.911. The courts also possess authority to relieve litigants from the consequences of missing the 60 day limit but exercise it sparingly, such as when mental illness prevents the claimant from filing. Cf. Canales v. Sullivan, 936 F.2d 755 (2d Cir. 1991).

The only proper venue for a claim brought under 42 U.S.C. 405(g) is the district of the plaintiff's residence at the time of commencement of suit. 42 U.S.C. § 405(g). The objection to venue is waivable, however. I have known of cases where the government agreed to venue in the district where the administrative proceedings took place after the plaintiff had moved across the country.

Procedures

Although procedures vary somewhat between districts and among individual judges, the basic pattern of Social Security disability litigation is the following: Plaintiff begins things by filing a summons and complaint within 60 days of the final administrative determination. The government has 60 days to answer but will inevitably request and receive one or more extensions because it takes a number of months for it to prepare the transcript of administrative proceedings which must be filed with the answer. After the answer and transcript are filed, both parties will normally move for judgment on the pleadings under Federal Rule 12(c). The judge will decide the motions and do one of three things: affirm SSA's decision, reverse the decision and send the case back for a new hearing before the agency, or award benefits to the claimant.

Cases do not invariably follow this pattern: Occasionally the government will move to dismiss the complaint if it feels the court should not reach the merits for some reason, such as untimely filing. Sometimes the government itself moves for a remand to the agency if it feels that the administrative decision is indefensible and wishes to head off an outright award of benefits. The vast majority of cases, however, are decided by cross-motions for judgment on the pleadings: The parties write what are essentially appellate briefs arguing that SSA's decision denying benefits was or was not correct and the court decides the issue based on the briefs and its review of the administrative record. Some judges hear oral argument; others do not.

As a practical matter, writing the brief is about 95% of the lawyer's work in one of these cases. Some attorneys devote considerable time and ingenuity to drafting the complaint, but I feel this is largely a waste of time: The complaint in an individual Social Security disability case performs the function of a notice of appeal. (A sample complaint follows.) I would be surprised to learn that many judges even look at them.

The Scope of Review

In theory, the district court approaches legal and factual issues very differently. On questions of law, the court exercises plenary powers of review and will reverse SSA's determination if it feels that the Commissioner committed any error of law that affected the outcome. On questions of fact, the court's power is much more limited. It must affirm SSA's findings of fact as long as they are supported by "substantial evidence." 42 U.S.C. § 405(g). This is a pretty low standard, "substantial evidence" being defined as "such relevant evidence as a reasonable mind might accept as adequate to support a conclusion." Richardson v. Perales, 402 U.S. 389, 401 (1971). In other words, the district court judge is not allowed to disturb SSA's determination of no disability merely because she finds the evidence of disability more persuasive. To reverse, the court must decide that <u>no reasonable person</u> could look at the evidence that was before the Commissioner and come up with the Commissioner's findings.

Human nature being what it is, the substantial evidence rule is formidable on paper but not in practice. If the district court judge can be persuaded that your client is disabled, she is going to do something helpful for your client, not reluctantly defer to the supposed greater expertise of a government bureaucrat. In fact, judicial hostility to the substantial evidence rule has been so pronounced that in the 1970s and 1980s the Second Circuit evolved something known as the "treating physician rule," which virtually stood the substantial evidence rule on its head: If the plaintiff's doctor said she was disabled, she got benefits even if all of the other doctors said she wasn't. <u>See</u>, <u>e</u>.<u>g</u>., <u>Schisler v. Bowen</u>, 851 F. 2d Cir. 1988). Although the Court has subsequently retreated from its most extreme embrace of the treating physician rule -- for reasons that are beyond the scope of this outline -- it remains the case that the substantial evidence rule is not an important obstacle for a sympathetic client.

Although the court and the parties are largely bound by the factual record amassed below, there is a limited right to submit new evidence. Under Sentence 6 of 42 U.S.C. § 405(g), the plaintiff may submit evidence of disability never considered below to the court. The court will accept the evidence only if persuaded that it is material, <u>i</u>.<u>e</u>., might have changed the result below if SSA had considered it, and if the plaintiff can produce a pretty good excuse for not having offered it earlier.

See generally Tirado v. Bowen, 842 F.2d 595 (2d Cir. 1988).[2] What the plaintiff gets in this situation is not an award of benefits but only an opportunity to present her case, with the new evidence, to the Commissioner. Id. Note that the right to offer new evidence is much more limited in district court than before the Appeals Council, where there is no requirement that the claimant excuse not having offered it earlier.

Outcomes

As noted, the district court can affirm, reverse and remand for further proceedings, or reverse outright and order benefits. The Second Circuit has not developed a coherent body of case law on the "remand vs. reversal" question. In one oft-repeated but lamentably vague formulation, the Court has stated that the district court should reverse outright "when the record provides persuasive proof of disability and a remand for further evidentiary proceedings would serve no purpose..." Parker v. Harris, 626 F. 2d 225, 235 (2d Cir. 1980). One situation where the odds of getting an outright reversal are reasonably good is where the ALJ has erroneously denied your client's claim at Step 5 of the sequential evaluation process after finding, at Step 4, that she can no longer do her past relevant work. Generally speaking, in this situation, the courts will not give SSA a second crack at Step 5 -- where it has the burden of proof -- unless it can satisfy the "good cause" test for new evidence remands. Carroll v. Secretary, 705 F.2d 638, 643-44 (2d Cir. 1983).

If the court remands the case to the Commissioner, it will do so under either Sentence 4 or Sentence 6 of 42 U.S.C. §

405(g). The reasons for choosing between these two remand types are poorly understood -- by this writer at least, and, I suspect, by many courts. The results are more clear, however: If the remand is pursuant to Sentence 6, then there is no judgment in the case and it must eventually return to district court following completion of proceedings on remand. If the remand is pursuant to Sentence 4, the case terminates immediately in a final judgment. Remand proceedings then take place, and if the plaintiff is dissatisfied with the outcome on remand she must file a new district court claim within 60 days after the remand determination becomes final. <u>See generally</u> <u>Shalala v. Schaefer</u>, 509 U.S. 292 (1993).

The distinction between Sentence 4 remands and Sentence 6 remands is important for two practical reasons. First, the judgment in a Sentence 4 remand starts the clock ticking on a plaintiff's application for attorney's fees under the Equal Access to Justice Act, 28 U.S.C. § 2412. That is, you must file your motion within 30 days after the judgment becomes final or lose your right to fees. If the remand is under Sentence 6, you can and, indeed, must wait until a judgment is eventually rendered in the case following completion of proceedings on remand.[3] Second, a Sentence 4 judgment is immediately appealable by either side to the court of appeals. <u>Forney v. Apfel</u>, 118 S.Ct. 1984 (1998). In a Sentence 6 case, nothing is appealable until the remand proceedings are concluded, the case has returned to district court, and a judgment has been entered.

Appeals

Final judgments in Social Security disability cases are appealable to the courts of appeals and, ultimately, to the U.S. Supreme Court. To appeal, a notice of appeal must be filed with the clerk of the district court (not the court of appeals) within 60 days of the district court's judgment. Thereafter, things move rather quickly. It is not uncommon for the case to be briefed, argued, and decided within six months of the filing of the notice of appeal.

On appeal, the Second Circuit performs a plenary review of the administrative record, focusing on the correctness, not of the district court's decision, but of the underlying determination of SSA. Vargas v. Sullivan, 898 F.2d 293, 296 (@d Cir. 1990). Or so, at least, the theory goes. In practice, the Second Circuit is likely to defer to the judgment of the district court unless something about the case particularly catches its attention. Since circuit court briefs are very time-consuming, it is good advice -- which I may some day follow myself -- not to undertake an appeal to the circuit unless your case presents a novel legal issue or involves unusually compelling facts.

1. A claimant in this situation might have recourse to a mandamus action under 28 U.S.C. § 1361. See Dietsch v. Schweiker, 700 F.2d 865 (2d Cir. 1983).

2. Interestingly, plaintiff can make the offer of new evidence for the first time even at the circuit court level. Tolany v. Heckler, 756 F.2d 268 (2d Cir. 1985). Apparently, as long as she shows good cause for not having presented the evidence to SSA, she need not excuse her failure to offer it to the district court.

3. On the other hand, in a Sentence 6 case, the plaintiff's attorney can probably recover fees for the remand proceedings themselves. See Sullivan v. Finkelstein, 496 U.S. 617 (1990).

UNITED STATES DISTRICT COURT
SOUTHERN DISTRICT OF NEW YORK

JULIO D________,

Plaintiff,

- against -

COMMISSIONER OF SOCIAL SECURITY,

Defendant.

COMPLAINT

97 Civ.

This is an action pursuant to 42 U.S.C. §§ 405(g) and 1383(c)(3) to review a final determination of the defendant Commissioner of Social Security ("the Commissioner") which denied plaintiff's applications for Social Security disability benefits and Supplemental Security Income ("SSI") benefits based upon disability.

Count I

1. Plaintiff, Julio D________, is a resident of New York County, New York. His Social Security account number is 123-45-6789.

2. Plaintiff filed applications for Social Security disability benefits and Supplemental Security Income based on disability on May 17, 1994 and October 24, 1994, respectively, alleging disability on account of cervical and lumbar spine injuries, depression, and visual impairment due to pterygia.

3. Plaintiff's claim was rejected by the Commissioner at the initial and reconsideration levels.

4. On June 1, 1995, a hearing on plaintiff's claim was held before Administrative Law Judge, James B. Reap. Thereafter, on September 25, 1995, ALJ Reap issued a decision finding that plaintiff was not disabled, even though he had severe exertional and non-exertional impairments, because he could still perform his past relevant work. The ALJ therefore denied plaintiff's claims for benefits. Judge Reap's decision became the final decision of the Commissioner when the Appeals Council declined review on January 17, 1997.

5. The Commissioner's decision was infected by errors of law and not supported by substantial evidence on the record as a whole. Among other things, the ALJ failed to accord proper weight to the findings and opinions of plaintiff's treating sources, failed to perform his duty to obtain from plaintiff's treating sources all medical evidence necessary to make an accurate determination of disability, as required by 42 U.S.C. § 423(d)(5)(B), and failed to call a vocational expert to clarify the impact of plaintiff's non-exertional impairments upon his occupational base.

6. In acting in the manner aforesaid, the Commissioner violated the Social Security Act and regulations promulgated thereunder.

7. Plaintiff has exhausted administrative remedies and this court has jurisdiction for judicial review pursuant to 42 U.S.C. §§ 405(g) and 1383(c)(3).

Count II

8. Plaintiff realleges the allegations set forth in paragraphs "1" through "7" hereof.

9. New and material evidence exists on the issue of plaintiff's disability and there was good cause for plaintiff's failure to incorporate it in the record of prior administrative proceedings.

WHEREFORE, plaintiff seeks judicial review of the Commissioner's decision and judgment for such relief as may be proper, including costs.

DATED: New York, New York
March 11, 1997

NEW YORK LEGAL ASSISTANCE GROUP
Attorneys for Plaintiff

By: ______________________________
James M. Baker
(JB-7115)
130 East 59th Street
New York, N.Y. 10022
212-750-0800

Attachment:

Action of Appeals Council on Request for Review,
January 17, 1997

NOTES

NOTES

7

OUTLINE OF ATTORNEY FEES IN SOCIAL SECURITY CASES

Victor Fusco

Scheine, Fusco, Brandenstein & Rada, PC
ATTORNEYS AT LAW

SOCIAL SECURITY DISABILITY DEPARTMENT
180 FROEHLICH FARM BLVD., PO BOX 307, WOODBURY, NY 11797-0307
516-496-0100 • 212-233-1457 • FAX: 516-496-2316
OTHER OFFICES: MANHATTAN, BRONX, HEMPSTEAD, COMMACK, MEDFORD

Outline of Attorney Fees in Social Security Cases

Victor Fusco, Esq.

1. Primer on Attorney Fees in Social Security Disability Cases
2. 42 U.S.C. 406 (b)
3. Equal Access to Justice Act
4. Regulations
5. Ruling SSR 82-89 (Use of Escrow)
6. Hallex Guidelines – Fee Petitions
7. Hallex Guidelines – Fee Agreements
8. Case Law:
   (a) Wells v Sullivan 2d. Cir 1990
   (b) Maier v Apfel SDNY 1998
9. Sample Administrative Level Fee Petition
10. Sample Equal Access to Justice Act Fee Petition
11. Sample 42 USC 406(b) Federal Court Fee Petition
12. Workers Compensation Offset Article and Exhibits

A Primer On Attorneys' Fees in Social Security Cases

Victor Fusco, Esq. & Aba Heiman, Esq.
of Scheine, Fusco, Brandenstein & Rada, P.C.
and the late Jill Boskey, Esq. CEDAR

I. APPLICABLE LAW

The Social Security Act specifically provides for attorneys fee awards for administrative level services at 42 USC 406(a), which in pertinent part reads:

The Commissioner may, by rule and regulation, prescribe the maximum fees which may be charged for services performed in connection with any claim before the Commissioner under this subchapter, and any agreement in violation of such rules and regulations shall be void, except as provided in paragraph (2) (A). Whenever the Commissioner, in any claim before him for benefits favorable to the claimant, he shall, if the connection with such claim, fix (in accordance with the regulations prescribed pursuant to the preceding sentence) a reasonable fee to compensate such attorney for the services performed by him in connection with such claim.

There are two methods of obtaining attorneys fees under the Social Security Act, the more simple method is the fee agreement, which is simply a written contract agreeing to accept a fee of 25% of the retroactive benefit or $4,000.00 whichever is less. 42 USC 406 (a) (2) (A)

The second method is the fee petition (Form SSA 1560) to which is appended a detailed listing of the work you actually performed, in chronological order (like a bill), it is submitted to SSA for approval.

Administrative Law Judges have authority to approve only up to a maximum of $5,000.00. Fee petitions in excess of $5,000.00 must be recommended to the Regional Chief Administrative law Judge. The Social Security Administration's broad authority to set rules and procedures for obtaining fees derives from 42 USC 406 (a) (1). Approvals of amounts in excess of $5,000.00 are the exception rather than the norm, although in Region II, attorneys are by and large given a very fair shake by the local OHA's and the Regional Office. No doubt, there are a few ALJ's who are considered "low-ballers," but most of them are very reasonable.

You need to decide if you are better off with a fee agreement, than you are with a fee petition. Some criteria:

1. Our advice is to never use a fee petition at the initial or reconsideration level. You can use a limited fee agreement if you are not sure how much work will pile up by the time the case reaches the hearing level, and desire to keep your options open. At the initial and reconsideration level the fee

adjudication is made by non-lawyers and the fees are unusually low, and rarely, if ever, even approach the full 25%. If you do use a limited agreement make sure it is clear that such is indeed what it is, otherwise you may wind up with ALJ's approving agreements that are void by their terms.

2. Don't use a fee agreement if you are relying upon ESCROW AS PART OF YOUR FEE.

3. Don't use a fee agreement if you will want to charge more than 25% because of offsets or other factors.

4. Do use a fee agreement if you have a concurrent SSI-Title II DIB case. 42 USC 406 (a) (2) (C) (i).

Caveat: always keep a running summary of your hours, in case the fee agreement is not approved and you are compelled to file a fee petition. If you haven't logged your time it will be difficult to prepare a fee petition.

Fee Petitions: experience has proven that a well detailed fee petition is the best tool to achieve a maximum fee. The judge most likely practiced law and has a good sense of what goes on in a law office. A good narrative description in chronological order of the services rendered, goes a long way to showing how you developed the case, and often will convince the judge that you deserve the fee you are asking for.

When requesting fees of over $5,000.00, it is our practice to submit a memo justifying in detail the reasons for the fee being sought. We generally discuss the complexity of the case, the nature of the work we did and the value of the claim to the claimant. It is only fair to give an adjudicator some basis for a substantial fee, that the adjudicator may be more than willing to award to you.

Be sure to send a copy of the fee petition to the claimant, preferably with an explanatory cover letter.

Fee Agreements: For claims determined or decided on or after July 1, 1991, the Social Security Administration (SSA) began approving representative fees using a new process, the **fee agreement** process, in cases in which certain conditions are met and no exceptions apply. In cases in which the conditions for the fee agreement process are not met, or an exception applies, SSA still utilize the fee petition process to approve representative fees.

The new process results from § 5106 of the Omnibus Budget Reconciliation Act of 1990, Public Law No. 101-508. That law amends §§ 206 (a) and 1631(d) (2) of the Social Security Act (the Act) to provide for the approval of representative fees using a fee agreement process under specified conditions.

It is important to recognize that the new law does not entirely replace the fee petition process. Representatives who intend to charge and collect a fee for services performed in proceedings before SSA must continue to petition SSA for approval of a fee when the fee agreement process does not apply. Therefore, SSA will have two alternative representative fees processes: the fee petition process and the fee agreement process under § 206(a) (2). If a claimant and a representative has submitted a fee agreement that meets the conditions set forth in the statute, and no exceptions apply, the decision maker must approve the agreement.

FEE AGREEMENT -- A fee agreement is a written statement signed by both the claimant and the representative specifying the fee the representative expects to charge and the claimant expects to pay for services the representative provides in pursing the claimant's benefits. Any wording which complies with the statutory conditions is acceptable.

The following conditions govern the fee agreement process:

- o The representative or the claimant files the agreement with SSA before the date they make a favorable decision on the claim. (ALJ will ask if attorney intends to file fee agreement).
- o The representative and the claimant both signed the agreement. (Must have original signatures).
- o The fee specified in the agreement does not exceed **25 percent of the claimant's past-due benefits** or **$4,000,** whichever is less. (for combined cases Title II and Title XVI 25% must be total of both).

NOTE: In concurrent claims, the 25% includes the combined past-due benefits of both titles. The $4,000 figure is the combined maximum they will approve for both titles. SSA will approve the lesser of the two.

- o The decision is favorable to the claimant.
- o The claim results in past-due benefits.

EXCEPTIONS -- Although the claimant and representative may have filed a fee agreement that otherwise meets the conditions for approval, SSA excepts or excludes the agreement from the process in the following situations:

- o The claimant appoints more than one representative associated in a firm, partnership, or legal corporation and all do not sign a single fee agreement;
- o The claimant appoints representatives who are not members of a single firm, partnership, or legal corporation;
- o The claimant discharges a representative, or a representative withdraws from the case, (and representative does not waive fee) before SSA decides the claim; or
- o The claimant has been declared legally incompetent and the claimant's legal guardian did not sign the fee agreement; we determine that the claimant is mentally incapable of managing his or her funds; or we are in the process of evaluating the claimant's mental capability. (If rep-payee signs agreement, fee agreement is O.K.)

NOTE: This exception to the agreement process does not apply when direct payment to the claimant is precluded based solely on a medical decision of disability because of drug addiction or alcoholism.

If the fee cannot be determined using the fee agreement process, and the representative intends to charge and collect a fee, the representative must file a fee petition.

APPROVAL -- When these conditions are met and none of the exceptions apply, the SSA decision maker must approve the fee agreement at the time he or she makes a favorable determination or decision. The **decision maker** at the initial and reconsideration levels of the administrative review process is the claims representative, claims authorizer, or reconsideration reviewer. At the hearing level, the decision maker is the Administrative Law Judge. At the request for review level, the decision maker is the Administrative Appeals Judge.

NOTICE OF APPROVAL OR DISAPPROVAL OF THE FEE AGREEMENT

SSA will send written notice about the determination made on the fee agreement to the claimant and representative if the decision on the claim is favorable to the claimant. The determination is limited, however, to whether the fee agreement does or does not meet the statutory conditions and is not otherwise excepted. SSA will neither approve nor disapprove any other part of the agreement between the claimant and representative.

SSA will not make a determination about the fee agreement and, therefore, will not send notice, if the decision on the claim is unfavorable.

If the decision maker disapproves the fee agreement, the notice will advise the claimant and the representative of the right to request administrative review. The claimant or the representative must file a request for administrative review within 15 days of receiving the notice of the determination made on the fee agreement.

NOTICE OF THE DETERMINATION OF THE AMOUNT OF THE FEE --

After SSA has approved the fee agreement and notified the claimant and representative, SSA will send another notice to the claimant, and copies to the representative and decision maker, which shows:

- o the amount of the past-due benefits;
- o the amount of the past-due benefits payable to the claimant;
- o the amount of the fee that the representative may charge and collect; and
- o an explanation that within 15 days of the date of receiving the notice, the claimant, the decision maker in the case, or the representative may ask SSA to review the amount of the fee

ADMINISTRATIVE REVIEW OF THE AMOUNT OF THE FEE

Note the differences between the fee petition process and the new fee agreement process on the last point above. SSA will review the amount of the fee if:

- o the claimant, an affected auxiliary beneficiary, or the **decision maker** submits a timely request to reduce the fee, or
- o the representative submits a timely request to increase the fee.

Generally, such protests should be filed where you believe SSA has miscalculated the benefits due claimant. More often than not it is the claimant who protests the fee, due a misunderstanding of the fee process. The usual objection concerns withheld amounts from auxiliaries, so at the time the agreement is entered into this should be carefully explained to the claimant.
The Social Security Administration's regulations in pertinent part provide as follows:

§404.1720 Fee for a representative's services.

(a) General. A representative may charge and receive a fee for his or her services as a representative only as provided in paragraph (b) of this section.

(b) Charging and receiving a fee. (1) the representative must file a written request with us before he or she may charge or receive a fee for his or her services.

(2) We decide the amount of the fee, if any, a representative may charge or receive.

(3) A representative shall not charge or receive any fee unless we have approved it, and he or she shall not charge or receive any fee that is more than the amount we approve. This rule applies whether the fee is charged to or received from you or from someone else.

(4) If the representative is an attorney and the claimant is entitled to past-due benefits, we will pay the authorized fee, or a part of the authorized fee directly to the attorney out of the past due benefits, subject to the limitations described in §404.1730(b)(1). If the representative is not an attorney, we assume no responsibility for the payment of any fee that we have authorized.

(c) Notice of fee determination. We shall mail to both you and your representative at your last known address a written notice of what we decide about the fee. We shall state in the notice -

> *(1) The amount of the fee that authorized;*
>
> *(2) How we made that decision;*
>
> *(3) That we are not responsible for paying the fee, except when we may pay an attorney from past due benefits; and*

(4) That within 30 days of the date of the notice, either you or your representative may request us to review the fee determination.

§404.1730 Payment of fees.

(a) Fees allowed by a Federal court. We will pay a representative who is an attorney, out of the claimant's past due benefits, the amount of fee allowed by a Federal Court in a proceeding under Title II of the Act. The payment we may to the attorney is subject to the limitations described in paragraph (b) (1) of this section.

(b) Fees we may authorize - (1) Attorneys. Except as provided in paragraph (c) of this section, if we make a determination or decision in favor of a claimant who was represented by an attorney, and as a result of the determination or decision past-due benefits are payable, we will pay the attorney out of the past-due benefits the smallest of -

> *(i) Twenty-five percent of the total of past-due benefits; or*
>
> *(ii) The amount of the fee that we set; or*
>
> *(iii) The amount agreed upon between the attorney and the claimant represented.*

The concept of fee amount regulation is most closely analogous to the Worker's Compensation system, where a board or commission or Administrative Law Judge or Examiner usually sets attorneys fees. However, there was a major difference. Workers Compensation proceedings are generally adversarial with two sides to the story. The ALJ (etc.) is in the middle. Here its Social Security who resists payment of benefits, and then once benefits are awarded, its the same agency that sets the attorney fee. It's like having an insurance company set your fee for beating them. Moreover, in Social Security, there is no lien against future benefits payable.

To make matters a bit more complicated, there is only one administrative level at which the attorneys fee is set by another attorney - the Administrative Law Judge.

In Social Security Claims and Procedures, Third Edition, by The Honorable Harvey McCormick, ALJ. (West Publishing Co., St. Paul, Minn. 1983), several basic points are set forth as a framework.

1. That the first amendment guarantees the right to be represented by

counsel in a civil proceeding is no comfort for most indigent claimants who can not prepay an attorney. (at page 386 - Vol. II)

2. ALJ's have an affirmative obligation to advise a claimant of the right to counsel on a contingency fee basis. (p. 382 - Vol. II).

3. As to attorneys fees, "Perhaps no other section of any law has caused more misunderstanding, mistrust and bad feeling between members of the Bar and HHS than the fee limitation provision..." (p. 391 - Vol. II).

Attorney fee issues get a bit more complex as cases find their way to Federal Court., Many cases are remanded, requiring services in two separate forums. Others are reversed outright with an award of benefits made by the court usually in the form of remand to compute benefits due.

This leads to the requirement that counsel file two fee petitions, one in Federal Court for work performed there and one before the Administration for work done at the agency level. The necessity for filing two fee petitions has been followed by virtually every Circuit. Under 42 USC 406, one feature remains quite clear: the attorneys fees are paid out of the claimant's money. This is, after all, the traditional "American Rule"

FEES IN FEDERAL COURT

There are two separate and distinct processes for obtaining fee awards in a federal court. One, the more recently enacted Equal Access to Justice Act, 28 USC 2412(d) (1)(A), provides that a court

"...shall award to a prevailing party... fees and other expenses. . .incurred by that party in any civil action. ..including proceedings for judicial review of agency action, brought by or against the United States... unless the court finds that the position of the United States was substantially justified or that special circumstances make an award unjust.

42 USC 406(b) relates to fees in Federal Court proceedings, independent of any fees payable under the Equal Access to Justice Act and states, in relevant part:

(b)(1) Whenever a court renders a judgment favorable to a claimant under this title who was represented before the Court by an attorney, the court may determine and allow as part of its judgment a reasonable fee for such representation, not in excess of 25 percent of the total past due benefits to which the claimant is entitled by reason of such judgment, and the Secretary may, notwithstanding the provisions of section 205(i), certify the amount of such fee for payment to such attorney out of, and not in addition to, the amount of such past due benefits.

20 CFR §404.1730 Payment of fees.

(a) Fees allowed by a Federal court. We will pay a representative who is an attorney, out of the claimant's past due benefits, the amount of fee allowed by a Federal Court in a proceeding under Title II of the Act. The payment we may to the attorney is subject to the limitations described in paragraph (b) (1) of this section.

Traditionally fees have been authorized under 42 USC 406 (b), which Congress in 1965, to promote the following policy considerations.

1) To provide an attorneys fee lien of sufficient enough amount to encourage attorneys to represent claimants.

2) To put a cap on the amount of lien to assure that excessive fees would

be impossible even if a fee adjudicator was overly generous. Dawson v. Finch 425 F. 2d 1192 (5th Cir. 1970) cert. den. 400 U.S. 830, 91 S. Ct. 60, 27 L. ED. 2d 60 rehearing denied. 400 U.S. 953, 91 S. CT. 233. 27 L. Ed. 2d 261.

3) To provide that fees should be regulated so as to avoid excessiveness, the theory being that a claimant in trouble might agree to anything to get help. (See generally S. Rep No. 404, 89th Cong., 1st Session 422 (1965) reptd. at 1965 U.S. Code Congress and Fed. News 2062.

However the traditional "American Rule" was being modified by many over 100 Federal "fee shifting" statutes. In 1981 The aforementioned Equal Access to Justice Act was enacted. The Equal Access to Justice Act, (5 U.S.C. P.L. 96-481, approved 10/21/81) provides that the purpose of the act is to encourage parties to defend against unreasonable Government action notwithstanding the expense involved. Congress specifically stated this law would be an exception to the "American Rule". (See Section 202(a), (b), (c)).

Section 204 of the original legislation included awards of fees to prevailing parties in Federal Court reviews of Social Security proceedings, as well as those of other federal agencies.

Under EAJA Section 204 the following limitations are applicable:

1. Costs may be awarded to a party who prevails against the U.S.

2. Unless expressly prohibited, a Court may award reasonable attorney fees to a prevailing part in any civil action against the U.S. 28 U.S.C. 2412(b) and a Court shall make such award, plus costs, unless:

   (a) The Government's position was substantially justified, or

   (b) Special circumstances make an award unjust.

3. The petition for fees under the EAJA must be filed within 30 days of "final judgement". 28 U.S.C. 2412 (d)(1)(B).

4. Any dilatory tactics by the prevailing party during the course of litigations may be taken into consideration in reducing the award.

5. The EAJA does not alter any other law shifting fees in actions against the Government.

6. Only a prevailing party with assets under one (now two) million dollars may apply for EAJA relief.

7. The current hourly rate is $125.00

It is safe to say that the various district courts do agree on one point: the EAJA enures to the benefit of the claimant. The Second Circuit dealt with this point in the case of Oguachuba v. Ins. 706 F.2d 93 (2nd Cir. 1983) wherein it was clearly held that an attorney has no standing under the EAJA to apply for fees for himself. Rather the petition must be brought in the name of the claimant and the award must benefit the

claimant, by reducing his or her outlay for attorney fees. Thus if the claimant has already paid the lawyer, (for example an hourly rate in a non SSD case) the award would go directly to the plaintiff.
an award unjust".

A number of cases have held that wherever appropriate or remotely feasible, an attorney must put in an EAJA application for his client. Taylor v. Heckler, 608 Fed. Supp. 1255, 1257 (D. NJ 1980); Losco v. Bowen, 638 F. Supp. 1262 (SDNY 1986). In Losco, Judge Ward contrasted EAJA fees with those payable 42 U.S.C. 406(b), noting: "the Court by no means intends to limit counsel in appeals from the Administration to an hourly benchmark of $75.00 per hour."

In 1985 a series of amendments to the EAJA went into effect, including an amendment repealing the sunset provision which caused the EAJA to expire in 1985. Trichillo v. Secretary of HHS, 647 F. Supp. 125 (NDNY 1986) (Upheld by the Second Circuit at 832 F.2d 743, holding cost of living increment applicable). The 1996 amendments raised the hourly to $125 from $75.

Although many federal courts, despite Wells v Bowen 907 F.2d 367 (2d Cir. 1990) *("Wells III")* do not honor the so-called "contingency fee" arrangements made between attorneys and claimants, the proscriptions in 42 USC 406(a) and (b) and 20 CFR 404.1720 obviously mandate contingency fees. What is not mandated is the amount of the fee. (Fees are contingent to the extent you must win to get them - though there are exceptions to this as well, and under Wells III, a fee of up to 25% of the past due benefits is considered by the Second Circuit to be reasonable in the majority of cases.)

Although many courts consider the 25% benchmark to be a reasonable fee in most cases because any depletion in the retroactive fund due claimant is statutorily limited, it is also true, to some extent, that the size of the award, in many, (not all) cases is not directly related to the attorney's efforts. The longer a case drags on, the bigger the retroactive award. Many cases are delayed because of a heavy calendar in the District Court. Others are delayed because of protracted litigation because of the Commissioner's intransigence. Certainly in the latter type of case, the more persevering the attorney, the greater fee he or she should be awarded. With an increasing backlog of cases, delay can be a significant factor in increasing the ultimate award of retroactive benefits.

The EAJA, on the other hand, limits the hourly rates payable as attorney fee awards. Contrast this with 42 USC 406(b) which limits the amount of a fee a court can set, to no more than 25% of the past due benefits. In contrast 42 USC 406(a) does not limit the Secretary's authority to set fees in excess of 25% of retroactive benefits.

What happens when the amount of the award under the EAJA exceeds the amount payable under 42 USC 406(b)? In Soto Valentin v. Heckler, 619 F. Supp. 627 (EDNY 1965), Judge Glasser held that the attorney keeps the larger of the two fees. In Weakley v. Bowen, 803 F.2d 575 (10th Cir. 1986) the Court approved an award of $5173.75 pursuant to the EAJA. Turning to the attorney's application under 42 USC 406(b), the Court noted that only $3042.25 was being withheld. The Court noted:

"Congress made clear in the 1985 re-enactment of EAJA that cases falling within the fee provision of the Social Security Act may also be subject to EAJA. To prevent double payment of fees for the same work

under both statutes, however, Congress directed that the smaller amount be given to the client, since the Social Security Act fee award reduces the client's recovery of past due benefits. See H.R. Rep. No. 120, 99th Cong. 1st Sess. 20 (1985), U.S. Code Cong. & Admin. News 1985, pp. 132, 148. Thus, the attorney will receive both the award under EAJA and the award under the Social Security Act, but will be required to pay the smaller amount to his client. At page 580 (emphasis ours)

See also Hawkins v. Heckler, 606 F. Supp. 1201 (D. Kan. 1985). There are some cases where the Courts have awarded $75.00 per hour, no matter what statute is involved. Of course, in such situations it really doesn't matter. The point to be stressed is that dual applications under both statutes do not result in double dipping by the attorney, since the EAJA award is only made to the prevailing party, not the lawyer.

In an earlier edition of this outline prepared for the New York State Bar Association, the late premier legal services litigator Jill Boskey, Esq., a prominent and well known practitioner in the field, staff attorney with MFY Legal Services, and founder of CEDAR,reviewed some of the requirements for filing EAJA petitions. We have again incorporated Jill's outline, with some updating:

OBTAINING FEES FOR REPRESENTATION OF A DISABILITY CLAIMANT UNDER THE EQUAL ACCESS TO JUSTICE ACT, 28 U.S.C. §2412.

I. BASIC REQUIREMENTS FOR AN EAJA FEE PETITION

A. Must file within 30 days of final judgment (judgment that is final is one which no longer appealable).

1. 90 days from entry of judgment

2. 30 days from entry of a stipulated settlement

3. See discussion infra at III, re cases that are or have been remanded.

B. Show that plaintiff is "eligible" to receive fees

1. Plaintiff must be a party

2. Plaintiff's net worth must not exceed $2,000,000 at the time civil action is filed.

3. Plaintiff's sworn affidavit, including affidavit filed with In Forma Pauperis petition, if any, shows "eligibility." Alternatively use attorney's affidavit.

C. State amount of fees and costs sought

1. Include itemized statement of actual time expended by attorney and/or expert witness

a. Contemporaneous time records specifying dates on which work performed, hours expended, nature of work performed, sworn to under oath. See New York State Association for Retarded Children v. Carey, 711 F.2d 1136 (2d Cir. 1983).

b. Amount of fee petition must be reasonable.

--"Average" amount of fees awarded in Social Security cases in 1989 was $3,000. See Commissioner, INS v. Jean, 110 S.Ct. 2316 (1990).

--Much higher fees have been awarded

*Carmel v. Bowen, 700 F. Supp. 794 (S.D.N.Y. 1988) (fees of $13,168.09 and costs of $3,168.09).

*Garcia v. Brown, 702 F. Supp. 409 (S.D.N.Y. 1988) (fees of $14,606.52 for 156.2 hours)

2. Explain rate at which fees are charged and basis for the computation of the rate.

a. Computation of rate for attorney time: $75 per hour plus cost of living increase based on increased in general CPI since 1981 enactment of EAJA. 42 U.S.C. §2412(d) (2) (A) (ii). See also Harris v. Sullivan, 968 F. 2d 263 (2d Cir. 1992) (use of general CPI); Trichillo v. Secretary of Health and Human Services, 823 F. 2d 702 (2d Cir. 1987) (upholding use of 1981 base). Rate increased to $125.00 an hour in 1996. With Cost of Living increases has recently been held to be $130.00 (Siconalfi, supra.)

--provide basis for CPI figure (e.g., Bureau of Labor Statistics: All Urban Consumers in New York / Northeastern New Jersey) Call 212-337-2400, Bureau of Labor Statistics

--list attorney's qualifications to show that "kind and quality of services furnished" are sufficient. 28 U.S.C. §2412 (d) (2) (A). (Attach resume or C.V.)

b. Computation of rate for expert witness time: no more than highest rate paid to expert witnesses by United States. 42 U.S.C. § 2412 (d) (2) (A) (i).

3. All time "reasonably expended" is compensable

a. Court may reduce award to the extent plaintiff unduly and unreasonably protracted resolution. 28 U.S.C. §§ 2412 (d) (1) (C), 2412 (d) (2) (D).

b. District Court has broad discretion to determine the reasonableness of a fee request. See Aston v. Secretary of Health and Human Services, 808 F. 2d 9 (2d Cir. 1986).

c. Attorney should use billing judgment as with a paying client, "writing off" excess time.

d. Fee should be awarded for all phases of the litigation if government's position is not substantially justified. See Smith by Smith v. Bowen, 867 F. 2d 731 (2d Cir. 1989); see also Trichillo V. Secretary of Health & Human Services, 823 F. 2d 702 (2d Cir. 1987).

e. Time spent on fee litigation is compensable. See Trichilo v. Secretary of Health and Human Services, 832 F. 2d 743 (2d Cir. 1987) substantially justified

f. Time spent on appeal settled without litigation is compensable. See Parks v. Bowen, 839 F.2d 44 (2d Cir. 1988).

g. Time expended before the agency on remand from court may be compensable. See Sullivan v.

Hudson, 109 S.Ct. 2248 (1989); See also Shalala v Schaefer, 113 S. Ct. 2625; 113 S.C. Rep 334 (1993)

4. "Expenses" compensable under EAJA include telephone, postage, travel, copying. See Aston v. Secretary of Health and Human Services, 808 F. 2d 9 (2d Cir. 1986). Computer research costs may also be compensable. See Carmel v. Bowen, 700 F. Supp. 794, 795 n.1 (S.D.N.Y. 1988). Paralegals awarded $75.00 (Siconalfi, supra.)

D. Allege that the position of the United States was not substantially justified

1. Position of the United States includes both the Agency's position in the administrative proceedings and the government's position in the civil action. 28 U.S.C. § 2412 (d) (B), 2412 (d) (2) (D). See also Smith by Smith v. Bowen, 867 F. 2d 731 (2d Cir. 1989); Eames v. Bowen, 864 F. 2d 251 (2d Cir. 1988); Trichillo v. Secretary of Health and Human Services, 823 F. 2d 702 (2d Cir. 1987).

2. To be substantially justified, the government's position must have a "reasonable basis both in law and fact" and must be justified "to a degree that could satisfy a reasonable person." Pierce v. Underwood, 487 U.S. 552, 108 S.Ct. 2541, 101 L. Ed.2d 490 (1988).

3. The burden of proving substantial justification is on the government. 28 U.S.C. § 2412 (d) (1) (A). See also Eames v. Bowen, 864 F. 2d 251 (2d Cir. 1988); Environmental Defense Fund v. Watt, 722 F. 2d 1081 (2d Cir. 1983).

E. Show that plaintiff is a prevailing party. To this issue, we must examine the holding of the U.S. Supreme Court, particularly Shalala v Schaefer, 113 S. Ct. 2625; 113 S.C. Rep 334 (1993). Until Schaefer a plaintiff was considered to be a prevailing party only when s/he won benefits. See McGill v. Secretary of Health & Human Services, 712 F. 2d 28 (2d Cir. 1983), cert. denied, 465 U.S. 1068, 104 S.Ct. 1420, 79 L.Ed 2d 745 (1984). And, traditionally, plaintiff could return to court after victory on remand to seek fees. See Green v. Bowen, 877 F. 2d 204 (2d Cir. 1989) (plaintiff was prevailing party when he won benefits before the Agency following stipulated dismissal of mandamus action). But all this changed with a series of Supreme Court Cases.

II. AND THEN THERE WERE FOUR! THE SUPREME COURT CHANGES THE NATURE OF SOCIAL SECURITY EAJA PRACTICE.

A.The Supreme Court on EAJA fees in Social Security cases

1. Sullivan v. Hudson, 490, U.S. 877, 109 S.Ct. 2248, 104 L.Ed2d 941 (1989): This was a groundbreaking case making EAJA attorneys fees available for representation of claimant during administrative proceedings on remand from the court, on the grounds that the subsequent administrative proceedings were intricately woven into the fabric of the federal court proceedings.

2. Sullivan v. Finkelstein, 496 U.S. 617, 110 S.Ct. 2658, 110 L.Ed.2d 563 (1990): Remands made under

sentence 4 of 42 U.S.C. §405 (g) are final, appealable judgments.

3. Melkonyan v. Sullivan, 501 U.S. ___, 111 S.Ct. 2157, 115 L.Ed.2d 78 (1991): Time to file EAJA petition does not run until final judgment is issued in the civil action (i.e., in court) and

a. The only kinds of remands permitted under 42 U.S.C. § 405 (g) are sentence 4 and sentence 6; and

b. Filing period for EAJA in sentence 4 remand begins after the final judgment affirming, modifying, or reversing is entered by the court and the appeal period has run; (i.e. immediately) and

c. Filing period for EAJA in sentence 6 remand begins after the postremand proceedings are completed the Secretary returns to court, the court enters a final judgment, and the appeal period runs; and

d. The Court's decision in Hudson is "not to the contrary"; and

e. Remands made under sentence 6 on motion by the Secretary before the Secretary has filed a response in the action are not implicated in the Melkonyan decision (Footnote 2).

B. Sentence 4 and Sentence 6 of 42 USC 405 (g)

1. Sentence 4 of 42 U.S.C. §405 (g) reads:

"The court shall have power to enter, upon the pleadings and transcript of the record, a judgment affirming, modifying, or reversing the decision of the Secretary, with or without remanding the cause for a rehearing.

2. Sentence 6 of 42 U.S.C. §405 (g):

"The court may, on motion of the Secretary made for good cause shown before he files his answer, remand the case to the Secretary for further action by the Secretary, and it may at any time order additional evidence to be taken before the Secretary, but only upon a showing that there is a new evidence which is material and that there is good cause for the failure to incorporate such evidence into the record in a prior proceeding; and the Secretary shall, after the case is remanded, and after hearing such additional evidence if so ordered, modify or affirm his findings of fact or his decision, or both, and shall file with the court any such additional and modified findings of fact and decision, and a transcript of the additional record and testimony upon which his action in modifying or affirming was based."

III. POST-MELKONYAN LITIGATION AND ISSUES.

A. Can fees ever be awarded in a case remanded "pursuant to § 405 (g) " before Melkonyan? (see also "B", infra)

1. Plaintiffs' positions:

a. Remand was sentence six

b. Court can and did retain jurisdiction in sentence 4 remand

c. Melkonyan should not be applied retroactively

2. Defendant's positions:

a. Remand was sentence four

b. Plaintiff's petition is untimely

c. Court cannot retain jurisdiction in sentence 4

d. "Remand" was voluntary dismissal

e. Melkonyan should be applied retroactively (?)

3. The Courts:

a. NO: Sargent v Sullivan, 941 F.2d 1207 (4th Cir. 1991)

b. YES (but remand in question found not to be final sentence 4 judgment): Welter v. Sullivan, 941 F 2d 674 (8th Cir. 1991)

c. In general, district courts outside the 5th Circuit attempt to award fees where applicable because no one could have known. See Sargent v. Sullivan, 941 F. 2d 1207 (4th Cir. 1991 (finds remand was neither sentence 4 nor sentence 6); see also Damato v. Sullivan, 945 F. 2d 982, 987 (7th Cir 1991) (finds remand was not sentence 4 but denies fees based on finding of substantial justification)

B. Can the court retain jurisdiction in a sentence 4 remand (whether remand was pre- and post-Melkonyan)?

1. Plaintiffs' position: Yes, under Hudson and Melkonyan.

2. Defendant's position: No, under Melkonyan

a. Remand was sentence four

b. Plaintiff's petition is untimely

c. Court cannot retain jurisdiction in sentence 4

d. "Remand" was voluntary dismissal

e. Melkonyan should be applied retroactively (?)

3. The Courts:

a. Yes Welter v. Sullivan, 941 F 2d 674 (8th Cir. 1991) (plaintiff is not a prevailing party at time of remand, so retention make sense); Hafner v. Sullivan, -- F. 2d -- (8th Cir. 1992) (1992 WL 188996 (8th Cir.)(further judicial review is virtual certainty when remand does not order payment of benefits); Gutierrez v. Sullivan, 953 F. 2d 579 (10th Cir. 1992) (recognizing subcategory of sentence 4 cases in which jurisdiction is retained consistent with Hudson);

b. NO (5th Circuit): Frizzel v. Sullivan, 937 F. 2d 254 (5th Cir. 1991); Luna v. U.S. Dept. of Health and Human Services, 948 F 2d 169 (5th Cir. 1991) (Not even when district court thought it had)

Supreme Court, 1993 Shalala v Schaefer, 113 S. Ct. 2625; 113 S.C. Rep 334 (1993). No More!

C. What kind of remand should be ordered in current cases where remand is sought pre-answer?

1. Plaintiffs' position: SENTENCE 6 (consistent with footnote 2 of Melkonyan)

2. Defendant's position: SENTENCE 4 (court should adopt Secretary's admission of error)

3. The Courts (two views, both from the Southern District of NY):

a.SENTENCE 6 Fernandez v. Sullivan, 91 Civ. 7659 (LMM), (October 22, 1992) (McKenna, J.) (S.D.N.Y.) (error admitted by Secretary establishes "good cause" for remand; court should not make a substantive ruling where parties agree that remand is appropriate)

b. SENTENCE 4 Jordan v. Sullivan, 785 F. Supp. 47 (S.D.N.Y. 1992 (Martin, J.) (court's vacatur of decision below based on admitted error reflects substantive ruling making remand sentence 4)

D. When does a party prevail in a sentence 4 remand?

1. Plaintiffs' position: AT TIME OF REMAND (not argued in many cases)

2. Defendant's position: AFTER DECISION ON REMAND (fee petition should be filed at time of remand and put in abeyance until conclusion of remand proceedings)

3. The Courts: Plaintiff prevails by obtaining remand Shalala v Schaefer, 113 S. Ct. 2625; 113 S.C. Rep 334 (1993). Court need not defer action on fee request.

All cases to the contrary were effectively overruled by Schaefer.

F. When are fees available for work on remand if plaintiff wins on remand and Secretary's position is not substantially justified?

1.Plaintiffs' position: ALL SENTENCE 6 REMANDS AND THOSE SENTENCE 4 REMANDS IN WHICH COURT RETAINS JURISDICTION (under Hudson, still seen as valid by Melkonyan Court)

2. Defendant's position: NEVER (under Melkonyan)

3. The Courts: Shalala v Schaefer, 113 S. Ct. 2625; 113 S.C. Rep 334 (1993) *"...We specifically noted in Melkonyan that Hudson was limited to a 'narrow class of qualifying administrative proceedings" where "the district court retains jurisdiction of the civil action" pending the completion of the administrative proceedings...We therefore do not consider the holding of Hudson binding as to sentence four remands that are ordered (as they should be) without retention of jurisdiction, or that are ordered with retention of jurisdiction that is challenged.."*
Or as stated in footnote 4: Hudson, remains good law for sentence six remands.

F. The Bottom Line.

It is rather apparent that the best course of action is to immediately file an Equal Access to Justice Act petition upon receipt of the court's decision. Obviously if the Court reverses the Government, you have prevailed and the action will be terminated unless the government appeals, which it is unlikely to do, unless the District Court opened up some new interpretation that the Social Security Administration can not live with. If you get your EAJA ready upon receipt of the Court's decision, it should be ready for filing by the time you get the actual judgment, usually a week or so later. Since you have presumably kept your time records, all that needs to be done is to have them typed up and annexed to an affidavit, along with a simple notice of motion, petition and a brief memo setting forth the basis of your request.

You simply can not go wrong by filing immediately. If you're found to be premature you can always resubmit later, and at least not be faced with the defense of untimeliness. If the case is remanded for further proceedings, the court will most likely be constrained to find it a sentence four remand, and thus your petition is also timely and should be filed. Even if later the court decides the remand was a sentence six, at worst it will defer considering your petition until later. If so, this opens up the possibility to amend your petition and add in the hours available under Sullivan v Hudson,for time spent on post remand administrative level services. The point is by filing immediately, you and your client can not lose! You only lose if you delay.

When we receive a favorable federal court decision in our office, all other activity stops until we get the EAJA filed. Under Taylor, (supra.) There arises a question of implied malpractice if one fails to act in this regard.

Moreover, true remands under sentence six, as described in Schaefer, tend to be the types of cases that in our office involve stipulated remands with the U.S. Attorneys Office, often for payment of benefits, sometimes for further proceedings. Under such circumstances, given the tremendous amount of cooperation and assistance given by the U.S. Attorneys it would be difficult to ask for EAJA, for obvious reasons.

42 USC 406

(a) Recognition of representatives; fees for representation before Commissioner of Social Security

(1) The Commissioner of Social Security may prescribe rules and regulations governing the recognition of agents or other persons, other than attorneys as hereinafter provided, representing claimants before the Commissioner of Social Security, and may require of such agents or other persons, before being recognized as representatives of claimants that they shall show that they are of good character and in good repute, possessed of the necessary qualifications to enable them to render such claimants valuable service, and otherwise competent to advise and assist such claimants in the presentation of their cases. An attorney in good standing who is admitted to practice before the highest court of the State, Territory, District, or insular possession of his residence or before the Supreme Court of the United States or the inferior Federal courts, shall be entitled to represent claimants before the Commissioner of Social Security. The Commissioner of Social Security may, after due notice and opportunity for hearing, suspend or prohibit from further practice before the Commissioner any such person, agent, or attorney who refuses to comply with the Commissioner's rules and regulations or who violates any provision of this section for which a penalty is prescribed. The Commissioner of Social Security may, by rule and regulation, prescribe the maximum fees which may be charged for services performed in connection with any claim before the Commissioner of Social Security under this subchapter, and any agreement in violation of such rules and regulations shall be void. Except as provided in paragraph (2)(A), whenever the Commissioner of Social Security, in any claim before the Commissioner for benefits under this subchapter, makes a determination favorable to the claimant, the Commissioner shall, if the claimant was represented by an attorney in connection with such claim, fix (in accordance with the regulations prescribed pursuant to the preceding sentence) a reasonable fee to compensate such attorney for the services performed by him in connection with such claim.

(2)(A) In the case of a claim of entitlement to past-due benefits under this subchapter, if—

(i) an agreement between the claimant and another person regarding any fee to be recovered by such person to compensate such person for services with respect to the claim is presented in writing to the Commissioner of Social Security prior to the time of the Commissioner's determination regarding the claim,

(ii) the fee specified in the agreement does not exceed the lesser of—

(I) 25 percent of the total amount of such past-due benefits (as determined before any applicable reduction under section 1320a-6(a) of this title), or

(II) $4,000, and

(iii) the determination is favorable to the claimant,

then the Commissioner of Social Security shall approve that agreement at the time of the favorable determination, and (subject to paragraph (3)) the fee specified in the agreement shall be the maximum fee. The Commissioner of Social Security may from time to time increase the dollar amount under clause (ii)(II) to the extent that the rate of increase in such amount, as determined over the period since January 1, 1991, does not at any time exceed the rate of increase in primary insurance amounts under section 415(i) of this title since such date. The Commissioner of Social Security shall publish any such increased amount in the Federal Register.

(B) For purposes of this subsection, the term "past-due benefits" excludes any benefits with respect to which payment has been continued pursuant to subsection (g) or (h) of section 423 of this title.

(C) In any case involving—

(i) an agreement described in subparagraph (A) with any person relating to both a claim of entitlement to past-due benefits under this subchapter and a claim of entitlement to past-due benefits under subchapter XVI of this chapter, and

(ii) a favorable determination made by the Commissioner of Social Security with respect to both such claims,

the Commissioner of Social Security may approve such agreement only if the total fee or fees specified in such agreement does not exceed, in the aggregate, the dollar amount in effect under subparagraph (A)(ii)(II).

(D) In the case of a claim with respect to which the Commissioner of Social Security has approved an agreement pursuant to subparagraph (A), the Commissioner of Social Security shall provide the claimant and the person representing the claimant a written notice of—

(i) the dollar amount of the past-due benefits (as determined before any applicable reduction under section 1320a-6(a) of this title) and the dollar amount of the past-due benefits payable to the claimant,

(ii) the dollar amount of the maximum fee which may be charged or recovered as determined under this paragraph, and

(iii) a description of the procedures for review under paragraph (3).

(3)(A) The Commissioner of Social Security shall provide by regulation for review of the amount which would otherwise be the maximum fee as determined under paragraph (2) if, within 15 days after receipt of the notice provided pursuant to paragraph (2)(D)—

(i) the claimant, or the administrative law judge or other adjudicator who made the favorable determination, submits a written request to the Commissioner of Social Security to reduce the maximum fee, or

(ii) the person representing the claimant submits a written request to the Commissioner of Social Security to increase the maximum fee.

Any such review shall be conducted after providing the claimant, the person representing the claimant, and the adjudicator with reasonable notice of such request and an opportunity to submit written information in favor of or in opposition to such request. The adjudicator may request the Commissioner of Social Security to reduce the maximum fee only on the basis of evidence of the failure of the person representing the claimant to represent adequately the claimant's interest or on the basis of evidence that the fee is clearly excessive for services rendered.

(B)(i) In the case of a request for review under subparagraph (A) by the claimant or by the person representing the claimant, such review shall be conducted by the administrative law judge who made the favorable determination or, if the Commissioner of Social Security determines that such administrative law judge is unavailable or if the determination was not made by an administrative law judge, such review shall be conducted by another person designated by the Commissioner of Social Security for such purpose.

(ii) In the case of a request by the adjudicator for review under subparagraph (A), the review shall be conducted by the Commissioner of Social Security or by an administrative law judge or other person (other than such adjudicator) who is designated by the Commissioner of Social Security.

(C) Upon completion of the review, the administrative law judge or other person conducting the review shall affirm or modify the amount which would otherwise be the maximum fee. Any such amount so affirmed or modified shall be considered the amount of the maximum fee which may be recovered under paragraph (2). The decision of the administrative law judge or other person conducting the review shall not be subject to further review.
(4)(A) Subject to subparagraph (B), if the claimant is determined to be entitled to past-due benefits under this subchapter and the person representing the claimant is an attorney, the Commissioner of Social Security shall, notwithstanding section 405(i) of this title, certify for payment out of such past-due benefits (as determined before any applicable reduction under section 1320a-6(a) of this title) to such attorney an amount equal to so much of the maximum fee as does not exceed 25 percent of such past-due benefits (as determined before any applicable reduction under section 1320a-6(a) of this title).
(B) The Commissioner of Social Security shall not in any case certify any amount for payment to the attorney pursuant to this paragraph before the expiration of the 15-day period referred to in paragraph (3)(A) or, in the case of any review conducted under paragraph (3), before the completion of such review.
(5) Any person who shall, with intent to defraud, in any manner willfully and knowingly deceive, mislead, or threaten any claimant or prospective claimant or beneficiary under this subchapter by word, circular, letter or advertisement, or who shall knowingly charge or collect directly or indirectly any fee in excess of the maximum fee, or make any agreement directly or indirectly to charge or collect any fee in excess of the maximum fee, prescribed by the Commissioner of Social Security shall be deemed guilty of a misdemeanor and, upon conviction thereof, shall for each offense be punished by a fine not exceeding $500 or by imprisonment not exceeding one year, or both.
(b) Attorney fees
(1)(A) Whenever a court renders a judgment favorable to a claimant under this subchapter who was represented before the court by an attorney, the court may determine and allow as part of its judgment a reasonable fee for such representation, not in excess of 25 percent of the total of the past-due benefits to which the claimant is entitled by reason of such judgment, and the Commissioner of Social Security may, notwithstanding the provisions of section 405(i) of this title, certify the amount of such fee for payment to such attorney out of, and not in addition to, the amount of such past-due benefits. In case of any such judgment, no other fee may be payable or certified for payment for such representation except as provided in this paragraph.
(B) For purposes of this paragraph—
(i) the term "past-due benefits" excludes any benefits with respect to which payment has been continued pursuant to subsection (g) or (h) of section 423 of this title, and
(ii) amounts of past-due benefits shall be determined before any applicable reduction under section 1320a-6(a) of this title.
(2) Any attorney who charges, demands, receives, or collects for services rendered in connection with proceedings before a court to which paragraph (1) of this subsection is applicable any amount in excess of that allowed by the court thereunder shall be guilty of a misdemeanor and upon conviction thereof shall be subject to a fine of not more than $500, or imprisonment for not more than one year, or both.
(c) Notification of options for obtaining attorneys
The Commissioner of Social Security shall notify each claimant in writing, together with the notice to such claimant of an adverse determination, of the options for obtaining attorneys to

represent individuals in presenting their cases before the Commissioner of Social Security. Such notification shall also advise the claimant of the availability to qualifying claimants of legal services organizations which provide legal services free of charge.

Equal Access to Justice Act

§ 2412. Costs and fees
Current through P.L. 105-41, approved 8-13-97

(a)(1) Except as otherwise specifically provided by statute, a judgment for costs, as enumerated in section 1920 of this title, but not including the fees and expenses of attorneys, may be awarded to the prevailing party in any civil action brought by or against the United States or any agency or any official of the United States acting in his or her official capacity in any court having jurisdiction of such action. A judgment for costs when taxed against the United States shall, in an amount established by statute, court rule, or order, be limited to reimbursing in whole or in part the prevailing party for the costs incurred by such party in the litigation.
(2) A judgment for costs, when awarded in favor of the United States in an action brought by the United States, may include an amount equal to the filing fee prescribed under section 1914(a) of this title. The preceding sentence shall not be construed as requiring the United States to pay any filing fee.
(b) Unless expressly prohibited by statute, a court may award reasonable fees and expenses of attorneys, in addition to the costs which may be awarded pursuant to subsection (a), to the prevailing party in any civil action brought by or against the United States or any agency or any official of the United States acting in his or her official capacity in any court having jurisdiction of such action. The United States shall be liable for such fees and expenses to the same extent that any other party would be liable under the common law or under the terms of any statute which specifically provides for such an award.
(c)(1) Any judgment against the United States or any agency and any official of the United States acting in his or her official capacity for costs pursuant to subsection (a) shall be paid as provided in sections 2414 and 2517 of this title and shall be in addition to any relief provided in the judgment.
(2) Any judgment against the United States or any agency and any official of the United States acting in his or her official capacity for fees and expenses of attorneys pursuant to subsection (b) shall be paid as provided in sections 2414 and 2517 of this title, except that if the basis for the award is a finding that the United States acted in bad faith, then the award shall be paid by any agency found to have acted in bad faith and shall be in addition to any relief provided in the judgment.
(d)(1)(A) Except as otherwise specifically provided by statute, a court shall award to a prevailing party other than the United States fees and other expenses, in addition to any costs awarded pursuant to subsection (a), incurred by that party in any civil action (other than cases sounding in tort), including proceedings for judicial review of agency action, brought by or against the United States in any court having jurisdiction of that action, unless the court finds that the position of the United States was substantially justified or that special circumstances make an award unjust.
(B) A party seeking an award of fees and other expenses shall, within thirty days of final judgment in the action, submit to the court an application for fees and other expenses which shows that the party is a prevailing party and is eligible to receive an award under this subsection, and the amount sought, including an itemized statement from any attorney or expert witness representing or appearing in behalf of the party stating the actual time expended and the rate at which fees and other expenses were computed. The party shall also allege that the position of the United States was not substantially justified. Whether or not the position of the

United States was substantially justified shall be determined on the basis of the record (including the record with respect to the action or failure to act by the agency upon which the civil action is based) which is made in the civil action for which fees and other expenses are sought.
(C) The court, in its discretion, may reduce the amount to be awarded pursuant to this subsection, or deny an award, to the extent that the prevailing party during the course of the proceedings engaged in conduct which unduly and unreasonably protracted the final resolution of the matter in controversy.
(D) If, in a civil action brought by the United States or a proceeding for judicial review of an adversary adjudication described in section 504(a)(4) of title 5, the demand by the United States is substantially in excess of the judgment finally obtained by the United States and is unreasonable when compared with such judgment, under the facts and circumstances of the case, the court shall award to the party the fees and other expenses related to defending against the excessive demand, unless the party has committed a willful violation of law or otherwise acted in bad faith, or special circumstances make an award unjust. Fees and expenses awarded under this subparagraph shall be paid only as a consequence of appropriations provided in advance.
(2) For the purposes of this subsection—
(A) "fees and other expenses" includes the reasonable expenses of expert witnesses, the reasonable cost of any study, analysis, engineering report, test, or project which is found by the court to be necessary for the preparation of the party's case, and reasonable attorney fees (The amount of fees awarded under this subsection shall be based upon prevailing market rates for the kind and quality of the services furnished, except that (i) no expert witness shall be compensated at a rate in excess of the highest rate of compensation for expert witnesses paid by the United States; and (ii) attorney fees shall not be awarded in excess of $125 per hour unless the court determines that an increase in the cost of living or a special factor, such as the limited availability of qualified attorneys for the proceedings involved, justifies a higher fee.);
(B) "party" means (i) an individual whose net worth did not exceed $2,000,000 at the time the civil action was filed, or (ii) any owner of an unincorporated business, or any partnership, corporation, association, unit of local government, or organization, the net worth of which did not exceed $7,000,000 at the time the civil action was filed, and which had not more than 500 employees at the time the civil action was filed; except that an organization described in section 501(c)(3) of the Internal Revenue Code of 1986 (26 U.S.C. 501(c)(3)) exempt from taxation under section 501(a) of such Code, or a cooperative association as defined in section 15(a) of the Agricultural Marketing Act (12 U.S.C. 1141j(a)), may be a party regardless of the net worth of such organization or cooperative association or for purposes of subsection (d)(1)(D), a small entity as defined in section 601 of Title 5;
(C) "United States" includes any agency and any official of the United States acting in his or her official capacity;
(D) "position of the United States" means, in addition to the position taken by the United States in the civil action, the action or failure to act by the agency upon which the civil action is based; except that fees and expenses may not be awarded to a party for any portion of the litigation in which the party has unreasonably protracted the proceedings;
(E) "civil action brought by or against the United States" includes an appeal by a party, other than the United States, from a decision of a contracting officer rendered pursuant to a disputes clause in a contract with the Government or pursuant to the Contract Disputes Act of 1978;
(F) "court" includes the United States Court of Federal Claims and the United States Court of Veterans Appeals;

(G) “final judgment” means a judgment that is final and not appealable, and includes an order of settlement;
(H) “prevailing party”, in the case of eminent domain proceedings, means a party who obtains a final judgment (other than by settlement), exclusive of interest, the amount of which is at least as close to the highest valuation of the property involved that is attested to at trial on behalf of the property owner as it is to the highest valuation of the property involved that is attested to at trial on behalf of the Government; and
(I) “demand” means the express demand of the United States which led to the adversary adjudication, but shall not include a recitation of the maximum statutory penalty (i) in the complaint, or (ii) elsewhere when accompanied by an express demand for a lesser amount.
(3) In awarding fees and other expenses under this subsection to a prevailing party in any action for judicial review of an adversary adjudication, as defined in subsection (b)(1)(C) of section 504 of title 5, United States Code, or an adversary adjudication subject to the Contract Disputes Act of 1978, the court shall include in that award fees and other expenses to the same extent authorized in subsection (a) of such section, unless the court finds that during such adversary adjudication the position of the United States was substantially justified, or that special circumstances make an award unjust.
(4) Fees and other expenses awarded under this subsection to a party shall be paid by any agency over which the party prevails from any funds made available to the agency by appropriation or otherwise.
[(5) Repealed. Pub.L. 104-66, Title I, § 1091(b), Dec. 21, 1995, 109 Stat. 722]
(e) The provisions of this section shall not apply to any costs, fees, and other expenses in connection with any proceeding to which section 7430 of the Internal Revenue Code of 1986 applies (determined without regard to subsections (b) and (f) of such section). Nothing in the preceding sentence shall prevent the awarding under subsection (a) of section 2412 of title 28, United States Code, of costs enumerated in section 1920 of such title (as in effect on October 1, 1981).
(f) If the United States appeals an award of costs or fees and other expenses made against the United States under this section and the award is affirmed in whole or in part, interest shall be paid on the amount of the award as affirmed. Such interest shall be computed at the rate determined under section 1961(a) of this title, and shall run from the date of the award through the day before the date of the mandate of affirmance.

Regulations Regarding Representation of Parties

Authority: Secs. 205(a), 206, and 702(a)(5) of the Social Security Act (42 U.S.C. 405(a), 406, and 902(a)(5)).
Source: 45 FR 52090, Aug. 5, 1980, unless otherwise noted; 58 FR 64883, 12/10/93; 61 FR 5939, 2/15/96
§ 404.1700 Introduction.
You may appoint someone to represent you in any of your dealings with us. This subpart explains, among other things-
(a) Who may be your representative and what his or her qualifications must be;
(b) How you appoint a representative;
(c) The payment of fees to a representative;
(d) Our rules that representatives must follow; and
(e) What happens to a representative who breaks the rules.

§ 404.1703 Definitions.
As used in this subpart-
Past-due benefits means the total amount of benefits payable under title II of the Act to all beneficiaries that has accumulated because of a favorable administrative or judicial determination or decision, up to but not including the month the determination or decision is made.

Representative means an attorney who meets all of the requirements of § 404.1705(a), or a person other than an attorney who meets all of the requirements of § 404.1705(b), and whom you appoint to represent you in dealings with us.

We, our, or us refers to the Social Security Administration.

You or your refers to any person claiming a right under the old-age, disability, dependents', or survivors' benefits program.

§ 404.1705 Who may be your representative.
(a) Attorney. You may appoint as your representative in dealings with us, any attorney in good standing who-
(1) Has the right to practice law before a court of a State, Territory, District, or island possession of the United States, or before the Supreme Court or a lower Federal court of the United States;
(2) Is not disqualified or suspended from acting as a representative in dealings with us; and
(3) Is not prohibited by any law from acting as a representative.
(b) Person other than attorney.

You may appoint any person who is not an attorney to be your representative in dealings with us if he or she-
(1) Is generally known to have a good character and reputation;
(2) Is capable of giving valuable help to you in connection with your claim;
(3) Is not disqualified or suspended from acting as a representative in dealings with us; and
(4) Is not prohibited by any law from acting as a representative.

§ 404.1706 Notification of options for obtaining attorney representation.

If you are not represented by an attorney and we make a determination or decision that is subject to the administrative review process provided under subpart J of this part and it does not grant all of the benefits or other relief you requested or it adversely affects any entitlement to benefits that we have established or may establish for you, we will include with the notice of that determination or decision information about your options for obtaining an attorney to represent you in dealing with us. We will also tell you that a legal services organization may provide you with legal representation free of charge if you satisfy the qualifying requirements applicable to that organization.[58 FR 64883, 12/10/93]

§ 404.1707 Appointing a representative.

We will recognize a person as your representative if the following things are done:

(a) You sign a written notice stating that you want the person to be your representative in dealings with us.

(b) That person signs the notice, agreeing to be your representative, if the person is not an attorney. An attorney does not have to sign a notice of appointment.

(c) The notice is filed at one of our offices if you have initially filed a claim or have requested reconsideration; with an administrative law judge if you requested a hearing; or with the Appeals Council if you have requested a review of the administrative law judge's decision.

§ 404.1710 Authority of a representative.

(a) What a representative may do.

Your representative may, on your behalf-

(1) Obtain information about your claim to the same extent that you are able to do;

(2) Submit evidence;

(3) Make statements about facts and law; and

(4) Make any request or give any notice about the proceedings before us.

(b) What a representative may not do.

A representative may not sign an application on behalf of a claimant for rights or benefits under title II of the Act unless authorized to do so under § 404.612.

§ 404.1715 Notice or request to a representative.

(a) We shall send your representative-

(1) Notice and a copy of any administrative action, determination, or decision; and

(2) Requests for information or evidence.

(b) A notice or request sent to your representative, will have the same force and effect as if it had been sent to you.

§ 404.1720 Fee for a representative's services.

(a) General.

A representative may charge and receive a fee for his or her services as a representative only as provided in paragraph (b) of this section.

(b) Charging and receiving a fee.

(1) The representative must file a written request with us before he or she may charge or receive a fee for his or her services.
(2) We decide the amount of the fee, if any, a representative may charge or receive.
(3) A representative shall not charge or receive any fee unless we have approved it, and he or she shall not charge or receive any fee that is more than the amount we approve. This rule applies whether the fee is charged to or received from you or from someone else.
(4) If the representative is an attorney and the claimant is entitled to past-due benefits, we will pay the authorized fee, or a part of the authorized fee, directly to the attorney out of the past-due benefits, subject to the limitations described in § 404.1730(b)(1). If the representative is not an attorney, we assume no responsibility for the payment of any fee that we have authorized.

(c) Notice of fee determination.
We shall mail to both you and your representative at your last known address a written notice of what we decide about the fee. We shall state in the notice-
(1) The amount of the fee that is authorized;
(2) How we made that decision;
(3) That we are not responsible for paying the fee, except when we may pay an attorney from past-due benefits; and
(4) That within 30 days of the date of the notice, either you or your representative may request us to review the fee determination.
(d) Review of fee determination

(1) Request filed on time. We will review the decision we made about a fee if either you or your representative files a written request for the review at one of our offices within 30 days after the date of the notice of the fee determination. Either you or your representative, whoever requests the review, shall mail a copy of the request to the other person. An authorized official of the Social Security Administration who did not take part in the fee determination being questioned will review the determination. This determination is not subject to further review. The official shall mail a written notice of the decision made on review both to you and to your representative at your last known address.
(2) Request not filed on time. (i) If you or your representative requests a review of the decision we made about a fee, but does so more than 30 days after the date of the notice of the fee determination, whoever makes the request shall state in writing why it was not filed within the 30-day period. We will review the determination if we decide that there was good cause for not filing the request on time.
(ii) Some examples of good cause follow:
(A) Either you or your representative was seriously ill and the illness prevented you or your representative from contacting us in person or in writing.
(B) There was a death or serious illness in your family or in the family of your representative.
(C) Material records were destroyed by fire or other accidental cause.
(D) We gave you or your representative incorrect or incomplete information about the right to request review.
(E) You or your representative did not timely receive notice of the fee determination.

(F) You or your representative sent the request to another government agency in good faith within the 30-day period, and the request did not reach us until after the period had ended.
(3) Payment of fees. We assume no responsibility for the payment of a fee based on a revised determination if the request for administrative review was not filed on time.

§ 404.1725 Request for approval of a fee.
(a) Filing a request.
In order for your representative to obtain approval of a fee for services he or she performed in dealings with us, he or she shall file a written request with one of our offices. This should be done after the proceedings in which he or she was a representative are completed. The request must contain-
(1) The dates the representative's services began and ended;
(2) A list of the services he or she gave and the amount of time he or she spent on each type of service;
(3) The amount of the fee he or she wants to charge for the services;
(4) The amount of fee the representative wants to request or charge for his or her services in the same matter before any State or Federal court;
(5) The amount of and a list of any expenses the representative incurred for which he or she has been paid or expects to be paid;
(6) A description of the special qualifications which enabled the representative, if he or she is not an attorney, to give valuable help in connection with your claim; and
(7) A statement showing that the representative sent a copy of the request for approval of a fee to you.
(b) Evaluating a request for approval of a fee.

(1) When we evaluate a representative's request for approval of a fee, we consider the purpose of the social security program, which is to provide a measure of economic security for the beneficiaries of the program, together with-
(i) The extent and type of services the representative performed;
(ii) The complexity of the case;
(iii) The level of skill and competence required of the representative in giving the services;
(iv) The amount of time the representative spent on the case;
(v) The results the representative achieved;
(vi) The level of review to which the claim was taken and the level of the review at which the representative became your representative; and
(vii) The amount of fee the representative requests for his or her services, including any amount authorized or requested before, but not including the amount of any expenses he or she incurred.
(2) Although we consider the amount of benefits, if any, that are payable, we do not base the amount of fee we authorize on the amount of the benefit alone, but on a consideration of all the factors listed in this section. The benefits payable in any claim are determined by specific provisions of law and are unrelated to the efforts of the representative. We may authorize a fee even if no benefits are payable.

§ 404.1728 Proceedings before a State or Federal court.
(a) Representation of a party in court proceedings.

We shall not consider any service the representative gave you in any proceeding before a State or Federal court to be services as a representative in dealings with us. However, if the representative also has given service to you in the same connection in any dealings with us, he or she must specify what, if any, portion of the fee he or she wants to charge is for services performed in dealings with us. If the representative charges any fee for those services, he or she must file the request and furnish all of the information required by § 404.1725.

(b) Attorney fee allowed by a Federal court.
If a Federal court in any proceeding under title II of the Act makes a judgment in favor of a claimant who was represented before the court by an attorney, and the court, under section 206(b) of the Act, allows to the attorney as part of its judgment a fee not in excess of 25 percent of the total of past-due benefits to which the claimant is entitled by reason of the judgment, we may pay the attorney the amount of the fee out of, but not in addition to, the amount of the past-due benefits payable. We will not certify for direct payment any other fee your representative may request.

§ 404.1730 Payment of fees.
(a) Fees allowed by a Federal court.
We will pay a representative who is an attorney, out of the claimant's past-due benefits, the amount of fee allowed by a Federal court in a proceeding under title II of the Act. The payment we make to the attorney is subject to the limitations described in paragraph (b)(1) of this section.

(b) Fees we may authorize
(1) Attorneys. Except as provided in paragraph (c) of this section, if we make a determination or decision in favor of a claimant who was represented by an attorney, and as a result of the determination or decision past-due benefits are payable, we will pay the attorney out of the past-due benefits the smallest of-
(i) Twenty-five percent of the total of the past-due benefits;
(ii) The amount of the fee that we set; or
(iii) The amount agreed upon between the attorney and the claimant represented.
(2) Persons other than attorneys. If the representative is not an attorney, we assume no responsibility for the payment of any fee that we have authorized. We will not deduct the fee from any benefits payable to the claimant represented.
(c) Time limit for filing request for approval of attorney fee.

(1) In order to receive direct payment of a fee from a claimant's past-due benefits, an attorney should file a request for approval of a fee, or written notice of the intent to file a request, at one of our offices within 60 days of the date the notice of the favorable determination is mailed.
(2) (i) If no request is filed within 60 days of the date the notice of the favorable determination is mailed, we will mail a written notice to the attorney and to the claimant, at their last known addresses. The notice will inform the attorney and the claimant that unless the attorney files, within 20 days from the date of the notice, a written request for approval of a fee under § 404.1725, or a written request for an extension of time, we will pay all the past-due benefits to the claimant.
(ii) The attorney must send the claimant a copy of any request made to us for an extension of time. If the request is not filed within 20 days of the date of the notice, or by the last day of any

extension we approved, we will pay all past-due benefits to the claimant. Any fee the attorney charges after that time must be approved by us, but the collection of any approved fee is a matter between the attorney and the claimant represented.

§ 404.1735 Services in a proceeding under title II of the Act.
Services provided a claimant in any dealing with us under title II of the Act consist of services performed for that claimant in connection with any claim he or she may have before the Commissioner of Social Security under title II of the Act. These services include any in connection with any asserted right a claimant may have calling for an initial or reconsidered determination by us, and a decision or action by an administrative law judge or by the Appeals Council.[62 FR 38448, 7/18/97]

§ 404.1740 Rules governing representatives.

(a) Purpose and scope.
(1) All attorneys or other persons acting on behalf of a party seeking a statutory right or benefit shall, in their dealings with us, faithfully execute their duties as agents and fiduciaries of a party. A representative shall provide competent assistance to the claimant and recognize the authority of the Agency to lawfully administer the process. The following provisions set forth certain affirmative duties and prohibited actions which shall govern the relationship between the representative and the Agency, including matters involving our administrative procedures and fee collections.
(2)All representatives shall be forthright in their dealings with us and with the claimant and shall comport themselves with due regard for the nonadversarial nature of the proceedings by complying with our rules and standards, which are intended to ensure orderly and fair presentation of evidence and argument.
(b) Affirmative duties
A representative shall, in conformity with the regulations setting forth our existing duties and responsibilities and those of claimants (see § 404.1512 in disability and blindness claims):
(1) Act with reasonable promptness to obtain the information and evidence that the claimant wants to submit in support of his or her claim, and forward the same to us for consideration as soon as practicable. In disability and blindness claims, this includes the obligations to assist the claimant in bringing to our attention everything that shows that the claimant is disabled or blind, and to assist the claimant in furnishing medical evidence that the claimant intends to personally provide and other evidence that we can use to reach conclusions about the claimant's medical impairment(s) and, if material to the determination of whether the claimant is blind or disabled, its effect upon the claimant's ability to work on a sustained basis, pursuant to § 404.1512(a);
(2) Assist the claimant in complying, as soons as practicable, with our requests for information or evidence at any stage of the administrative decisionmaking process in his or her claim. In disability and blindness claims, this includes the obligation pursuant to § 404.1512(c) to assist the claimant in providing, upon our request, evidence about:

(i) The claimant's age;
(ii) The claimant's education and training;
(iii) The claimant's work experience;
(iv) The claimant's daily activities both before and after the date the claimant alleges that he or she became disabled;

(v) The claimant's efforts to work; and

(vi) Any other factors showing how the claimant's impairment(s) affects his or her ability to work. In §§404.1560 through 404.1569, we discuss in more detail the evidence we need when we consider vocational factors; and

(3) Conduct his or her dealings in a manner that furthers the efficient, fair and orderly conduct of the administrative decisionsmaking process, including duties to:

(i) Provide competent representation to a claimant. Competent representation requires the knowledge, skill, thoroughness and preparation reasonably necessary for the representation. This includes knowing the significant issue(s) in a claim and having a working knowledge of the applicable provisions of the Social Security Act, as amended, the regulations and the Rulings; and

(ii) Act with reasonable diligence and promptness in representing a claimant. This includes providing prompt and responsive answers to requests from the Agency for information pertinent to processing of the claim.

(c) Prohibited Actions

A representative shall not:

(1) In any manner or by any means threaten, coerce, intimidate, deceive or knowingly mislead a claimant, or prospective claimant or beneficiary, regarding benefits or other rights under the Act;

(2) Knowingly charge, collect or retain, or make any arrangement to charge, collect or retain, from any source, directly or indirectly, any fee for representational services in violation of applicable law or regulation;

(3) Knowingly make or present, or participate in the making or presentation of, false or misleading oral or written statements, assertions or representations about a material fact or law concerning a matter within our jurisdiction;

(4) Through his or her own actions or omissions, unreasonably delay or cause to be delayed, without good cause (see § 404.911(b)), the processing of a claim at any stage of the administrative decisionsmkaing process;

(5) Divulge, without the claimant's consent, except as may be authorized by regulations prescribed by us or as otherwise provided by Federal law, any information we furnish or disclose about a claim or prospective claim;

(6) Attempt to influence, directly or indirectly, the outcome of a decision, determination or other administrative action by offering or granting a loan, gift, entertainment or anything of value to a presiding official, Agency employee or witness who is or may reasonably be expected to be involved in the administrative decisionmaking process, except as reimbursement for legitimately incurred expenses or lawful compensation for the services of an expert witness retained on a non-contingency basis to provide evidence; or

(7) Engage in actions or behavior prejudicial to the fair and orderly conduct of administrative proceedings, including but not limited to:

(i) Repeated absences from or persistent tardiness at scheduled proceedings without good cause (see § 404.911(b));

(ii) Willful behavior which has the effect of improperly disrupting proceedings or obstructing the adjudicative process; and

(iii) Threatening or intimidating language, gestures or actions directed at a presiding official, witness or Agency employee which results in a disruption of the orderly presentation and reception of evidence.

[63 FR 41404, 8/4/98]

TITLES II AND XVI—USE OF TRUST OR ESCROW ACCOUNTS IN COLLECTION OF ATTORNEY FEES

PURPOSE: To state the policy on the use of trust or escrow accounts in collecting attorney fees for representation before the Social Security Administration (SSA).

CITATIONS (AUTHORITY): Sections 206(a), 207, and 1631(d)(2) of the Social Security Act; Section 413(b) of the Black Lung Benefits Act (part B of title IV of the Federal Coal Mine Health and Safety Act of 1969, as amended); Regulations No. 4, sections 404.1720 through 404.1740; Regulations No. 10, sections 410.686b through 410.687a; Regulations No. 16, sections 416.1520 through 416.1540.

PERTINENT HISTORY: Legal organizations and individual attorneys have asked whether the use of trust or escrow accounts as a means of collecting attorney fees in connection with Social Security and black lung claims is consistent with the fee provisions of the law and regulations.

As a condition for undertaking representation, some attorneys solicit from Social Security or black lung claimants a deposit of money in a trust or escrow account as a means of assuring payment of the attorney's fees. The claimant may be asked to place funds into a trust or escrow account at the commencement of representation on a noncontingency fee basis, or in connection with a contingency fee agreement. In title XVI claims especially, some agreements may call for the claimant to deposit the first benefit check into a trust or escrow account pending approval of a fee by the Social Security Administration.

In regard to title II, title XVI, and black lung claims, the law provides that the Secretary may, by "rule and regulations, prescribe the maximum fees which may be charged" for services performed in connection with such claims, and that any agreement violating that rule or regulation would be void. The law also prohibits the charging or collecting of a fee, directly or indirectly, in excess of the maximum fee prescribed by the Secretary.

In certain cases the term "fees which may be charged" could be interpreted to include any amounts exacted by an attorney from a claimant's property, whether by way of a retainer, deposit in a trust or other escrow account, etc. If, however, the exaction is no more than security for the payment of a potential debt, it should not be considered a "fee." For example, a sum deposited under a trust or escrow agreement, which the claimant willingly entered into, could not legally be characterized as a "fee" if the agreement explicitly states that any money in excess of the fee authorized by SSA will be returned to the claimant when SSA approves a fee or when the claimant pays the attorney an amount SSA approves as a fee.

Applicable to title II, title XVI, and black lung benefits, the law provides that: "The right of any person to any future payment under this title shall not be transferable or assignable, at law or in equity . . ." This provision prohibits payment directly by SSA to a transferee or assignee of the claimant or someone else on his or her behalf. However, this provision does not preclude a claimant from using the benefits after receipt, any more than it precludes a claimant from using any other personal property as he or she sees fit. Thus, the placement of a claimant's funds (whether from benefit payments or other sources) into a trust or escrow account prior to and contingent upon SSA's authorization of a fee for the attorney's services is not a transfer or assignment within the meaning of the law.

Beyond these considerations, the fee provisions of the law that apply to title II and black lung claims differ significantly in one respect from the provisions applicable in title XVI claims. In title II and black lung cases, to assure that the claimant's attorney will be paid at least a part of the fee SSA approves, the law requires SSA to directly pay the attorney the authorized fee (up to a statutorily prescribed limit) out of the claimant's past-due benefits. In title XVI claims, there is no such statutory authority which could serve to encourage attorney representation. Thus, establishment of escrow and trust accounts, under agreements willingly entered into, is a mechanism that may encourage representation of claimants in title XVI claims, where otherwise the prospect of attorney representation would not exist.

As noted above, in title II and black lung claims, the law mandates that SSA will directly pay to an attorney the amount of the authorized fee (up to the prescribed limit) out of the claimant's past-due benefits. In cases where a title II or black lung claimant and his or her attorney have entered into a trust or escrow account agreement, the money deposited in the trust or escrow account may have been paid over to the attorney, in accordance with such agreement, after SSA's award of benefits to the claimant but before direct payment of the authorized fee out of past-due benefits. Were SSA to make direct payment to the attorney out of past-due benefits without taking into account the money paid to the attorney out of the trust or escrow account, it would be highly probable that the attorney would have "collected" a total fee in excess of the fee authorized by SSA, and thus find himself in violation of the fee provisions of the law and regulations. Therefore, while the law mandates direct payment of attorney fees in title II and black lung cases, that mandate need not be construed so rigidly as to force SSA to make a fee payment when it is known that that payment, when added to monies already collected, would place an attorney in violation of the law and SSA's own regulations.

POLICY STATEMENT: Consistent with Social Security law and regulations, an attorney may solicit from Social Security and black lung claimants whom he or she represents before SSA a deposit of money into a trust or escrow account as a means of assuring payment of the fee for services in connection with such representation, *provided that*

a. the claimant willingly entered into the trust or escrow agreement and willingly deposited the money in the trust or escrow account; and
b. none of the money in the account is paid over to the attorney unless and until SSA has authorized a fee for the attorney, and then only in an amount up to, but not exceeding, the authorized fee; and
c. any funds in the account in excess of the authorized fee will be refunded promptly to the claimant.

At the time the attorney petitions for a fee, the amount of money held in the trust or escrow account must be disclosed to SSA.

In title II and black lung cases, when the amount authorized by SSA as an attorney's fee is less than the total of (1) the money paid to the attorney from a trust or escrow account, and (2) the amount withheld from the claimant's past-due benefits for direct payment of the attorney's fee, SSA will reduce the amount of direct payment to the attorney by the amount that such total exceeds the authorized fee.

> EXAMPLE: If the authorized fee is $1000, but the combined total of escrow payments ($600) and withheld benefits ($600) is $1200, SSA will pay $400 directly to the attorney out of withheld benefits and will release the remainder of withheld benefits ($200) to the claimant.

If the total of withheld past-due benefits and money paid from a trust or escrow account is equal to or less than the amount of the authorized fee, there will be no reduction in the amount paid to the attorney from past-due benefits.

EFFECTIVE DATE: This policy is applicable to all claims or proceedings pending before SSA as of the publication of this policy statement. In any claim or proceeding where this policy was applied prior to the publication of this policy statement, such action will be deemed to have been taken properly and in accordance with interim procedures existing at that time.

DOCUMENTATION: A copy of the trust or escrow agreement or proof that any money from the trust or escrow account in excess of the authorized fee has been returned to the claimant must be provided to SSA upon request.

CROSS-REFERENCES: OHA Handbook, section 1-264(4); POMS sections GN 03920.001, GN 03920.070, GN 03970.005.

FROM HALLEX
Subject: Representative Fees
Chapter: I-1-200
I-1-200 TABLE OF CONTENTS

==

==

I-1-201 REPRESENTATIVES FEES -- GENERAL (Revised 02/93)

Citations: Social Security Act 206(a) and (b), 1631(d)(2), and 1872 Federal Mine Safety and Health Act of 1977, 42 U.S.C.
923, 936(a), and 957 20 CFR 404.1703, 404.1707, 404.1720-404.1735; 410.686b-410.686c; 416.1503, 416.1507, 416.1520-416.1535 42 CFR 498.10-498.13

A. Authority to Approve Fees

Sections 206(a) and 1631(d) of the Social Security Act (the Act) provide that the Secretary of Health and Human Services may prescribe the maximum fee that a representative may charge or collect from a claimant for services performed before the Secretary. Section 206(a) applies to all claims arising under title II of the Act as well as claims under the Federal Mine Safety and Health Act of 1977. Section 1631(d) applies to all claims arising under title XVI of the Act. The Office of the General Counsel (OGC) is currently assessing the authority of the Secretary to prescribe maximum fees in title XVIII cases. Pending issuance of the OGC opinion, any component processing title XVIII claims must contact the Special Counsel Staff before approving or requiring the submission of fee petitions in these cases.

1. The component or individual who issues a final favorable determination or decision or takes the last unfavorable action in a claim reviews the fee petition. For example, if an Administrative Law Judge (ALJ) issues a favorable decision which the claimant does not appeal and the Appeals Council does not review on its own motion, the ALJ reviews the fee petition and makes a fee determination. If the ALJ issues a partially favorable decision which the claimant appeals and the Appeals Council denies the request for review, the Attorney Fee Branch reviews the fee petition and makes a fee determination. We identify specific exceptions to this policy with Temporary Instructions (TIs).

2. If the ALJ with initial jurisdiction over the fee petition proposes to authorize a fee, or combination of fees, in excess of $5,000, the ALJ must refer the fee petition(s) to the Regional Chief ALJ (RCALJ) and recommend the amount of the fee(s) to be authorized. If the RCALJ with initial jurisdiction over the fee petition proposes to authorize a fee(s) in excess of $5,000, the RCALJ must refer the fee petition(s) to the Deputy Chief ALJ and recommend the amount of the fee(s) to be authorized. The RCALJ or Deputy Chief ALJ, as appropriate, will then review the recommendation and authorize the fee.

NOTE: In establishing whether the $5,000 limit applies, the determinative factor is the amount of the fee(s) which the ALJ proposes to authorize rather than the amount(s) the representative(s) requested.

NOTE: The $5,000 fee authorization limit imposed on ALJs does not apply to fee authorizations the Attorney Fee Branch processes.

3. If the ALJ with jurisdiction over the fee petition is unavailable for a period of 30 days or more, the Hearing Office Chief ALJ, subject to the $5,000 limit, must review the petition and make a fee determination or delegate that responsibility to another ALJ to avoid inordinate delays in processing fee petitions.

B. Requirement to File a Fee Petition (Also see HALLEX I-5-109, Representative Fee Approval Process.)

A representative must petition for approval to charge or collect any fee for services performed on behalf of an individual filing a claim under titles II and XVI of the Act and under the Federal Mine Safety and Health Act of 1977. The representative must file a petition whether the fee is paid by the claimant or a third party, or whether funds have been withheld to pay the fee. Similarly, it is not material whether the final decision is favorable or unfavorable.

EXCEPTION: Social Security Ruling 85-3 provides that a representative does not need to petition for approval to charge and collect a fee if a nonprofit organization or government agency will pay the fee and the claimant has no liability to pay any part of the fee.

C. Direct Payment of Fees to Attorney Representatives

The Act and implementing regulations provide for certification of direct payment of authorized fees to attorney representatives from withheld past-due benefits in title II claims. The statute does not authorize the Social Security Administration (SSA) to certify direct payment to non-attorney representatives or in title XVI claims. In title II claims in which the Secretary issues a favorable decision resulting in past-due benefits, the Act authorizes the Secretary to certify for direct payment to an attorney who performed services in connection with a favorably decided claim so much of the maximum fee as does not exceed 25 percent of such past-due benefits.

NOTE: The 25 percent of past due benefits withheld by SSA for payment of attorney fees concerns only the direct certification of payments to attorney representatives and is not a factor in determining a reasonable fee. Therefore, the fee authorizer does not need past-due benefit information to process a fee petition, and representatives should be reminded that fee petitions can be submitted and reviewed before past due benefit information is available.

I-1-210 APPOINTMENT OF REPRESENTATIVE(S)

Only the duly appointed representative(s) of a claimant may charge or collect a fee. A claimant may appoint more than one representative. A claimant must make all appointments in writing. (See I-1-110, Appointing a Representative.)

If a law firm or other entity is involved, only the duly appointed individual(s) in that firm or entity may file a fee petition and receive payment for services performed. Each duly appointed individual must file a separate fee petition for the services he or she performed. If an attorney who represented a claimant leaves the law firm, that attorney must still file a fee petition for the work he or she performed on the claim.

I-1-211 WAIVER OF FEE

If an attorney representative files a statement that he or she waives the right to charge a fee for services rendered, the fee authorizing staff at the hearing office or Appeals Council must notify the Office of Disability and International Operations (ODIO) or the Program Service Center (PSC), as appropriate. The hearing office provides notification by entering a statement into the "REMARKS" section of Form HA-5051 (Transmittal of Hearing Decision or Dismissal) directing that past-due benefits should not be withheld for the payment of an attorney's fee. The Appeals Council forwards the fee waiver statement to ODIO or the PSC using Form HA-505 (Transmittal by Office of Hearings and Appeals).

I-1-212 INFORMING REPRESENTATIVES OF FEE REGULATIONS

If the representative has not waived the right to charge and collect a fee in a written statement or on the record at the hearing, the fee authorizing staff must provide him or her with Form SSA-1560 (Petition to Obtain Approval of a Fee for Representing a Claimant Before the Social Security Administration). The staff may provide this form to the representative at any time during the pendency of the claim, or forward it to the representative with his or her copy of the final decision of the ALJ or AC.

The fee authorizing staff must also provide representatives with additional information about fee requests. For this purpose, the HO uses Form HA-533 (Notice to Representative at Hearing Level Regarding a Fee For Services). The AC developed and uses its own unnumbered form letter.

I-1-220 TIME LIMITS FOR FILING FEE PETITIONS

Neither the statute nor the regulations establish a time limit for filing a fee petition. If an attorney representative desires direct payment of a fee from past-due Title II benefits, however, 20 CFR 404.1730(c) provides time limits for filing a fee petition as set forth below.

A. Award Notice

After effectuating a favorable Title II decision in a case in which the claimant was represented, the Office of Disability and International Operations or the appropriate Program Service Center sends a copy of letter SSA-L937 (Social Security Information Notice) and a copy of the Award Notice to the claimant, the representative and the HO or the Appeals Council.

The SSA-L937 letter informs the claimant and the representative of the amount of benefits due and the amount withheld for the payment of an attorney fee. The letter also states that an attorney representative must file a fee petition within 60 days of the date of the Award Notice in order to receive direct payment of a fee from withheld benefits.

B. Sixty-day Diary

If the fee authorizer receives a copy of the Award Notice and does not have a pending fee petition, diary the file for 60 days from the date of the award. It is not necessary to send the attorney representative a 60-day letter because the Award Notice contains that information.

C. Twenty-day Notice

If the fee authorizer does not receive a fee petition or a written request for an extension of time to file within the 60-day period, send the attorney representative a notice that if we do not receive a fee petition within 20 days, the withheld benefits will be released to the claimant. It is not necessary to send such notice to a non-attorney representative because no funds are withheld to pay a fee. (See 20 CFR 404.1730(c)(2)(i).)

D. Releasing Withheld Benefits

If the fee authorizer does not receive a fee petition or has not granted an extension of time to file after the 20-day period has elapsed, inform the effectuating component by memorandum that no fee petition has been received and that the withheld funds must be released to the claimant.

I-1-230 PROCESSING FORM SSA-1560 (PETITION TO OBTAIN APPROVAL OF A FEE FOR REPRESENTING A CLAIMANT BEFORE THE SOCIAL SECURITY ADMINISTRATION) (REVISED 02/93)

Representatives should file Form SSA-1560 or a written statement providing the same information only when all services are completed.

NOTE: Fee authorizers generally will not accept supplemental fee petitions unless the representative has performed additional services after the initial fee authorization.

A. Upon receipt of a Form SSA-1560 or a written statement providing the same information [see 20 CFR 404.1725(a) and 416.1525(a)], the fee authorizing staff must take the following actions:

1. Date stamp the form or statement and associate it with the HO or the Appeals file.
2. Determine whether the individual who filed the fee petition was duly appointed the claimant's representative on the Form SSA-1696 (Appointment of Representative) or other written document. (See I-1-110, Appointing a Representative.)

If the individual who filed the fee petition was not duly appointed by the claimant, the fee authorizing staff will return the fee petition to the individual with a written explanation that only a claimant's duly appointed representative may charge and collect a fee.

3. Determine that the petition specifies the amount of the fee which the representative wants to charge. [20 CFR 404.1725(a)(3) and 416.1525(a)(3)]. The fee authorizing staff must return any petition which does not show a dollar amount.

NOTE: The fee authorizer must not attempt to convert a percentage amount to a dollar amount. Past-due title II benefits may be subject to offsets such as worker's compensation or overpayments. The fee authorizer should not speculate whether the representative is requesting a percentage of the past-due benefits before or after the offset is/was applied.

4. Confirm that the fee request shows that the representative sent a copy of the fee request to the claimant. If the representative did not do so, return the petition to the representative with a notice that the representative did not follow the procedures in 20 CFR 404.1725(a)(7).
5. Diary the case for 30 days from the date of the fee petition for receipt of any comments from the claimant, unless the claimant's comments have been submitted with the fee petition, e.g., claimant has signed the Form SSA-1560 indicating agreement with the requested fee.

B. After the expiration of the 30-day diary period, the fee authorizer with jurisdiction over the fee petition must review the petition pursuant to the regulatory criteria (See I-1-240, Evaluating

Fee Petitions) and make a fee determination, subject to the $5,000 limit. (See I-1-201 A., Authority to Approve Fees.)

I-1-240 EVALUATING FEE PETITIONS

The regulations do not specify maximum fees; rather, they prescribe criteria for evaluating fee petitions and determining reasonable fees for representatives [20 CFR 404.1725(b) and 416.1525(b)].

A. Criteria for Evaluating Fee Petitions

When evaluating fee petitions, the fee authorizer must consider the purpose of the Social Security program; namely, to provide a measure of economic security for program beneficiaries, together with—

- the extent and type of services performed;
- the complexity of the case;
- the level of skill and competence required in providing the services;
- the amount of time spent on the case;
- the results achieved by the representative;
- the level of review to which the claim was taken and the level of review at which the representation began; and,
- the amount of the fee requested.

B. Excluded Activities

In evaluating the amount of time a representative spent on the case, the fee authorizer must exclude any time claimed for:

1. Preparing the fee petition or any other activities related to charging or collecting a fee, such as status inquiries, and
2. Any services the representative performed before a state or federal court.

EXCEPTION: Acquiescence Ruling 87-1(6), Webb v. Richardson, applies to fee authorizations in the Sixth Circuit (Michigan, Ohio, Tennessee and Kentucky).

C. Expenses

The representative's expenses are not considered part of the fee for services. The representative must look to the claimant for reimbursement of any expenses. 20 CFR 404.1725(b)(1)(vii) and 416.1525(b)(1)(vii).

I-1-245 AUTHORIZATION TO CHARGE AND RECEIVE A FEE

A. Form HA-L530 (Authorization to Charge and Receive a Fee)

To prepare Form HA-L530:

1. Fill in the identifying information at the top of the form; i.e., date, claimant's name, wage earner's name (if different from the claimant's name), wage earner's Social Security number, type of claim, name and address of the claimant, and the names of auxiliary beneficiaries (if the representative has included the names of the claimant's dependents on the fee request).
2. Indicate the fee authorized in the section beginning, "You are hereby authorized...."
3. In the section beginning, "NOTE: IF EITHER YOU OR THE CLAIMANT DISAGREES....," fill in the Regional Chief ALJ's (RCALJ's) name and the Regional Office address if the fee authorizer is an ALJ, or the name of the Deputy Chair of the Appeals Council and the AC address if the fee authorizer was the Attorney Fee Branch.

NOTE: Enter the name and address of the RCALJ in the Region where the case was heard.

4. Check the appropriate block in the section beginning "The paragraph or paragraphs checked below ..." as follows:

a. First block:

Check the first block if it can be determined that all of the authorized fees will be paid directly to the attorney representative out of funds withheld from the claimant's past-due benefits, and insert the name and address of the office which processed the award; i.e., Office of Disability and International Operations (ODIO) or the appropriate Program Service Center (PSC), in case the attorney wishes to obtain information as to the status of the fee authorization.

For those cases processed in ODIO, by the Office of Disability Operations, the staff should type in the following address:

Office of Disability and International Operations
Division of Appealed Claims
P.O. Box 17295
Baltimore, Maryland 21235

NOTE: If the attorney requests the status of his or her payment after the fee has been authorized, tell him or her to write to ODIO or the appropriate PSC at the address provided.

b. Second block:

Check the second block if it can be determined that the amount withheld is less than the authorized fee.

c. Third block:

Check the third block if no funds have been withheld; i.e., the claimant is not entitled to any past-due benefits, the representative is not an attorney, or the claim is for Supplemental Security Income.

d. Last block:

Check the last block if it is necessary to add an additional or special paragraph(s) to the authorization; i.e., when the authorized fee is less than what was requested.

NOTE: If the additional information that the fee authorizer must add is too lengthy for the available space on the HA-L530, use a continuation sheet as an attachment.

B. Sample Paragraphs

The following sample paragraphs may be appropriate:

1. Auxiliary Beneficiaries:

"The approved fee is for all services performed for the claimant and auxiliary beneficiaries."

2. Out-of-Pocket Expenses:

"We do not consider out-of-pocket expenses when we authorize a fee; therefore, you must seek reimbursement from the claimant."

3. Retainer Fee Paid by Claimant:

a. If the retainer fee is less than the authorized fee and there are withheld benefits:

"Since the claimant previously paid you a retainer fee of $*** for your services which you are holding in an escrow account, the remaining balance of $*** will be sent to you out of the funds withheld from the claimant's past-due benefits."

b. If the retainer fee is less than the authorized fee and there are no withheld benefits:

"The claimant previously paid $*** towards your fee which you are holding in an escrow account; therefore, the balance remaining for your services is $***. You should look to the claimant for payment of the balance."

c. If the retainer fee exceeds the authorized fee:

"The claimant previously paid $*** towards your fee which you are holding in an escrow account. Because this amount exceeds the amount of the fee you are authorized to collect, you must refund $*** to the claimant."

4. Concurrent Title II and Title XVI Cases:

"The fee approved is for all services performed in connection with both claims."

C. Distribution of Form HA-L530

The fee authorizing staff will distribute the Form HA-L530 as follows:

1. Claim File Copy

• For allowances:

Mail the claim file copy of Form HA-L530, Form SSA-1129 or other appropriate benefit information notice (if available), and the claim file copy of Form SSA-1560 to the effectuating component, using a route slip (Form HA-505).

• For denials:

Mail the claim file copy of Form HA-L530 and the claim file copy of Form SSA-1560 to the office or component having the claim file, using a route slip (Form HA-505).

2. Mail the representative's copy (original) to the representative.

3. Mail the claimant's copy to the claimant.

4. Place a copy of Form HA-L530, Form SSA-1560, the benefit information (if available), and the route slip to the effectuating component in the HO or Appeals file.

I-1-246 DISAPPROVAL OF A FEE REQUEST

If the fee authorizer decides not to authorize a fee, the authorizing staff must issue an order of disapproval, using Form HA-515 (Hearing Order) if the authorizer is an ALJ, or Form HA-517 (Order of Appeals Council) if the authorizer is the Attorney Fee Branch. The order of disapproval must include a rationale for the action.

A. Administrative Review Notice

The order must provide notice to the representative that he or she may request an administrative review of the order of disapproval and that the request must be made within 30 days of the date of the order. (See I-1-250, Administrative Reviews.)

B. Distribution

The fee authorizing staff will distribute the order in the same way as the HA-L530. (See I-1-245 C., Distribution of Form HA-L530.)

I-1-250 ADMINISTRATIVE REVIEWS

The regulations at 20 CFR 404.1720(d) and 416.1520(d) afford both the representative and the claimant the right to request administrative review of the initial fee authorization. A fee authorization made after an administrative review is not subject to further administrative or judicial review. (See 20 CFR 404.903(f) and 416.1403(a)(6).)

A. Delegation of Authority

If an ALJ made the initial fee authorization, the RCALJ in the Region where the case was heard has the authority to conduct the administrative review.

If the RCALJ set the initial fee, either as the presiding ALJ or on a recommendation from a presiding ALJ (See I-1-201 A., Authority to Approve Fees), the Deputy Chief ALJ has the authority to conduct the administrative review.

If the Deputy Chief ALJ set the initial fee either as the presiding ALJ or on recommendation from an RCALJ (See I-1-201 A., Authority to Approve Fees), the Chief ALJ has authority to conduct the administrative review.
If the Attorney Fee Branch made the initial fee authorization, the Deputy Chair of the Appeals Council has the authority to conduct the administrative review.
B. Procedures on Review
1. When a request for administrative review is received, the hearing office, Regional Office or Attorney Fee Branch staff will provide the reviewing official with the following:
• a copy of the decision;
• a copy of the exhibit list;
• a copy of the cassette envelope;
• a copy of the award notice or other benefit information;
• the fee petition;
• the fee authorization; and
• any other documents or information that might be helpful in performing the administrative review.
2. The RCALJ, Deputy Chief ALJ, the Chief ALJ or the Deputy Chair of the AC, as appropriate, will take the following actions in conducting an administrative review:
• Determine whether the claimant or the representative filed the administrative review request within 30 days of the original fee authorization, or has established good cause for not filing the request timely. Examples of good cause are provided at 20 CFR 404.1720(d)(2) and 416.1520(d)(2).
If the request is untimely and good cause is not found, notify the representative and the claimant that the prior fee authorization is final and not subject to further review.
• If the representative filed a request for administrative review and did not send a copy to the claimant, return the request to the representative with a notice that the representative did not follow the procedures in 20 CFR 404.1720(d)(1) and 416.1520(d)(1).
If the claimant filed the request for administrative review and did not send a copy to the representative, send the representative a copy of the request.
• If the representative is an attorney and there are withheld past-due Title II benefits, send a memorandum to the effectuating component advising them not to release any of the withheld benefits until the administrative review is completed.
• If the administrative review results in a reduction or increase of the authorized fee, send a letter to the representative and the claimant giving the reasons for the change, and prepare and distribute a new Form HA-L530 showing the new amount. [See Section I-1-245, Authorization to Charge and Receive a Fee.]
If the administrative review does not change the amount of the authorized fee, send a letter to the representative and claimant giving the reasons for the determination.
• If past-due benefits were withheld, send a copy of the letter or the new Form HA-L530 to the effectuating component.

I-1-260 EVIDENCE OR ALLEGATIONS OF VIOLATIONS OF LAW

If the hearing office or AC has evidence or receives allegations of violations of the statute or regulations pertaining to the charging or collecting of fees, the HO or AC staff must refer the matter by memorandum to the Special Counsel Staff (SCS), and provide complete documentation of the incident or actions in question. Take the following actions to refer the case:

1. Prepare a brief memorandum for signature of the HO Chief ALJ or the Deputy Chair of the AC describing the alleged violation and summarizing the facts of the case.
2. Assemble existing evidence pertaining to the alleged violation including:
• copies of any available files. Because the claim file may already be with another component, indicate in the referral what action has been taken to locate the claim file and what arrangements have been made to have it forwarded to SCS;
• documents or statements from the claimant(s) or other persons alleging fee violations;
• originals or copies of bills, receipts, cancelled; checks or money orders; and
• copies of fee agreements.
3. Indicate whether the HO or AC has received other complaints concerning the representative.

I-1-270 EQUAL ACCESS TO JUSTICE ACT

The Equal Access to Justice Act (EAJA), 5 U.S.C. 504, 28 U.S.C. 2412, authorizes an attorney to obtain reimbursement of expenses incurred (e.g., legal fees, expert witness fees, etc.) in the course of representing a litigant in a court action and certain administrative proceedings involving a government agency. The EAJA stipulates that reimbursement of legal fees and other expenses apply only to proceedings in which the party prevails against the agency, provided the court finds that the position of the government was not substantially justified.

The EAJA also specifically provides that when a representative receives fees for the same work under both section 206(b) of the Social Security Act and EAJA, the representative must refund to the claimant the amount of the smaller fee. If a representative is known or suspected to have collected fees under both statutes, but did not refund the smaller fee to the claimant, the representative may be in violation of section 206(b)(2) of the Social Security Act. (See I-1-260, Evidence or Allegation of Violations of Law.)

The United States Supreme Court in the case of Sullivan v. Hudson, 109 S.Ct. 2248 (1989), held that when a court orders a remand of a Social Security case to the Secretary and retains continuing jurisdiction pending the Secretary's decision on a claimant's right to benefits, the remand proceedings are an integral part of the civil action. Thus, fees under EAJA for representational services during proceedings before SSA on remand are available subject to other limitations in the EAJA.

HALLEX INSTRUCTIONS

I-5-109 SUBJECT: OBRA 1990—REPRESENTATIVE FEE APPROVAL PROCESS

I. Purpose

The purpose of this Temporary Instruction (TI) is to convey the policy and procedures we have developed to implement § 5106(a) of the Omnibus Budget Reconciliation Act of 1990 (OBRA 1990), Pub.L. No. 101-508.

II. Introduction

This TI includes changes in the representative fee approval process resulting from § 5106(a) of OBRA 1990. Effective with claims decided on or after July 1, 1991, the Social Security Administration (SSA) has two methods of approving representative's fees:

1. the fee petition process described in HALLEX I-1-200 et seq.; and
2. the fee agreement process described in these instructions.

Unless a representative submits a fee agreement (see III. A. below for definition), we will assume that he or she will file a fee petition or waive a fee. If a representative elects the fee agreement process but the agreement does not meet the conditions described in IV. A. 1. or an exception in IV. A. 2. applies, the representative must file a fee petition if he or she wants to charge and collect a fee.

III. Definitions

A. Fee Agreement

A fee agreement is a written statement signed by the claimant and his or her representative specifying the fee the representative expects to charge and collect, and the claimant expects to pay, for services the representative provides in pursuing the claimant's benefit rights in proceedings before SSA. A fee agreement submitted to SSA may remain in effect throughout the administrative appeals process of a claim(s), and during the administrative proceedings following a court remand.

A fee agreement may contain a provision that limits its application to services through a specific level of the administrative appeals process. For example, the provision may state "This agreement remains in effect only through the initial Administrative Law Judge (ALJ) hearing." Such a provision would provide, in essence, for a two-tiered fee structure:

• if the claim is decided favorably at or below the level of the initial ALJ hearing, the fee would be the lesser of 25 percent of past-due benefits, or $4,000; but

• if the claim progresses beyond that level, the representative would request a fee through the fee petition process.

The decision maker will be able to readily ascertain, at the time of the favorable decision, which tier of the fee structure applies, and will either approve or disapprove the fee agreement, based on the current level of appeal.

B. Decision Maker

1. Hearing Level: the ALJ.
2. Request for Review Level: the Administrative Appeals Judge (AAJ).

NOTE: All future references in this transmittal to "request for review level" include administrative proceedings before the Appeals Council following a court remand.

C. Processing Centers (PCs)
PCs are the six Program Service Centers and the Office of Disability and International Operations.

IV. Policy
A. Fee Agreement
1. Conditions
The following statutory conditions must be met for the representative to obtain SSA's approval to charge and collect a fee under the fee agreement process.
a. The representative or the claimant files the agreement with SSA before the date we make a favorable decision on the claim.
b. The representative and the claimant both signed the fee agreement.
c. The fee specified in the agreement does not exceed 25 percent of the claimant's past-due benefits or $4,000, whichever is less.
NOTE: In concurrent claims, the 25 percent includes the combined past-due benefits of both titles, and the $4,000 figure is the combined maximum we will approve for both titles under the fee agreement process. We will approve the lesser of the two (i.e., 25 percent of the total past-due benefits or $4,000).
NOTE: Agreements that specify a minimum fee do not meet the statutory conditions for approval under the fee agreement process (e.g., the representative's fee will be 25 percent of past-due benefits or $4,000, whichever is less, except that if 25 percent of past-due benefits does not exceed $1,250, the representative's fee will be $1,250).
d. Our decision is favorable to the claimant.
e. The claim results in past-due benefits.
2. Exceptions to the Fee Agreement Process
The agreement is excepted from the fee agreement process in the following situations:
a. The claimant appoints more than one representative associated in a firm, partnership, or legal corporation and all do not sign a single fee agreement;
b. The claimant appoints representatives who are not members of a single firm, partnership, or legal corporation;
c. The claimant discharges a representative or a representative withdraws from the case before SSA decides the claim, and the representative did not waive his or her fee;
d. The claimant has been declared legally incompetent and the claimant's legal guardian did not sign the fee agreement; or we determine that the claimant is mentally incapable of managing his or her funds, or we are in the process of evaluating the claimant's mental capability, and the person who is responsible for the care of the claimant did not sign the fee agreement.
NOTE: This exception to the fee agreement process is not required when direct payment of title XVI benefits to the claimant is precluded based solely on a medical decision of disability because of drug addiction or alcoholism.
3. Approval
The decision maker must approve the fee agreement, at the time he or she makes a favorable decision on the claim if the fee agreement meets the conditions listed in section IV. A. 1. above

and none of the exceptions in section IV. A. 2. apply. The decision maker will approve the agreement subject to the condition that the favorable decision will result in past-due benefits.
NOTE: The decision maker's approval or disapproval of a fee agreement is limited to whether the agreement meets the statutory conditions and is not otherwise excepted.

4. Notice

When the decision on the claim is favorable, we will mail to the claimant and the representative, with the decision, a separate written notice of the determination on the fee agreement.

The notice will advise the parties of the right to request administrative review if the decision maker has disapproved the fee agreement. The claimant or the representative must file a request for administrative review within 15 days of receiving the notice of the determination made on the fee agreement.

NOTE: Information concerning the right to request administrative review of the actual fee amount determined under an approved fee agreement will be included in the notice issued by the effectuating component. This notice will contain information concerning the right to request administrative review of the amount of the fee within 15 days of receiving the notice.

If the decision on the claim is unfavorable, the decision maker will not make a determination about the fee agreement and, therefore, will not send notice.

B. Administrative Review

When SSA has approved a fee under the fee petition process, follow the instructions in HALLEX I-1-25O. Our policy on administrative review under the fee agreement process follows. The instructions for processing administrative reviews are in sections VII. and VIII. of this TI.

Under the fee agreement process, there are two separate and distinct administrative review processes: the review of the determination disapproving a fee agreement; and the review of the amount of the fee determined under a fee agreement. The timeframe for requesting an administrative review under either review process is 15 days from the date of receipt of the respective notice. Because the claimant and representative can request review under either review process, it is possible for the claimant and representative to file two requests for administrative review: the first when he or she receives notice of the disapproval of the fee agreement; and the second when we have reversed the determination made on the fee agreement, set a fee amount under the agreement, and the claimant or representative objects to the amount of the fee.

1. Request for Administrative Review of the Disapproval of the Fee Agreement

a. Filing the Request

We will review the determination made on the fee agreement if the claimant or the representative submits a request for administrative review to one of SSA's offices within 15 days of receiving the disapproval notice.

b. Reviewing Official

The following officials are delegated the authority to conduct administrative review of the disapproval of the fee agreement (regardless of who requests administrative review).

• Hearing Level—the Regional Chief ALJ.

NOTE: If the decision maker was the Regional Chief ALJ (RCALJ), the reviewing official is the Deputy Chief ALJ or the Chief ALJ.

• Request for Review Level—the Deputy Chair, Appeals Council.

NOTE: If the decision maker was the Deputy Chair, Appeals Council, the reviewing official is the Chair, Appeals Council.

c. Informing the Parties

The delegated reviewing official (reviewing official) must notify the decision maker and all parties of the request for administrative review, and afford them 15 days to submit written information responding to the request.

d. Review of the Disapproval of the Fee Agreement

The reviewing official will consider the fee agreement, the disapproval of the fee agreement, the request for administrative review, along with any additional information provided, and affirm or reverse the decision maker's determination on the fee agreement.

e. Notice of Determination on Administrative Review

The reviewing official must mail a written notice of the determination made on administrative review to the claimant and the representative at their last known addresses. The reviewing official must also mail a copy of the notice to the decision maker.

The notice will advise the parties that the determination is not subject to further review.

2. Request for Administrative Review of the Amount of the Fee Under the Fee Agreement Process

a. Filing the Request

We will review the determination made on the amount of a fee under the fee agreement process if the claimant, an affected auxiliary beneficiary(ies), i.e., one who has benefited from the representative's services to the claimant who appointed the representative and who will share in payment of the fee (hereafter, affected auxiliary), or the decision maker submits a timely request to reduce the fee; or the representative (including any co-representative or co-counsel who signed the agreement) submits a timely request to increase the fee. The request must be filed at one of SSA's offices within 15 days of receiving the notice of the amount of the fee.

• Claimant, Affected Auxiliary, or Representative Request

A claimant, affected auxiliary, or representative has an unqualified right to request administrative review.

• Decision Maker Request

A decision maker may request administrative review only when there is prima facie evidence that the representative did not represent the claimant's interest adequately, or that a fee is clearly excessive in light of the services provided.

NOTE: Prima facie evidence means good and sufficient evidence which, standing alone and unexplained, establishes a given fact.

b. Reviewing Official

The following officials are delegated the authority to conduct administrative review of the fee amount determined under the fee agreement.

• Hearing Level

If the claimant, an affected auxiliary, or the representative requests administrative review, the reviewing official is the ALJ.

If the ALJ requests administrative review, the reviewing official is the RCALJ. If the RCALJ requests administrative review, the reviewing official is the Deputy Chief ALJ or the Chief ALJ.

• Request for Review Level

If the claimant, an affected auxiliary, or the representative requests administrative review, the reviewing official is the Attorney Fee Officer in the Attorney Fee Branch (AFB).

If the AAJ requests administrative review, the reviewing official is the Deputy Chair, Appeals Council. If the Deputy Chair, Appeals Council, requests administrative review, the reviewing official is the Chair, Appeals Council.

c. Informing the Parties

The reviewing official must notify all other parties of the request for administrative review, including the decision maker, if appropriate, and afford them 15 days to submit written information responding to the request.

d. Review of the Determination of the Amount of the Fee

When the fee agreement meets the conditions for approval and is not otherwise excepted, the reviewing official will defer to the written fee agreement as the expression of the intentions of the parties. Generally, parties expect to be held to the terms of their agreement. However, the reviewing official will intervene and set a reasonable fee, either affirming, lowering, or raising the original fee, when, through a request for administrative review:

• the claimant, an affected auxiliary, or the representative expresses dissatisfaction with the fee; or

• the decision maker has shown that either the representative did not represent the claimant's interest adequately or the fee is clearly excessive in light of the services provided.

The review mechanism enables the Secretary to redress situations in which the fee set under the agreement does not represent reasonable compensation for the services provided in the case. It does not compel changes to the fee set under the agreement.

e. Review of the Determination of the Amount of the Fee in Concurrent Titles II and XVI Claims or When There Are One or More Affected Title II Auxiliaries or Both

The reviewing official must consider the total fee for all services when reviewing a request for administrative review of the determination of the amount of the fee. In concurrent claims involving a common issue, e.g., disability, this means considering the fee amounts based on the past-due benefits resulting from both the titles II and XVI claims. In title II claims involving one or more auxiliaries, this means considering the fee amount based on the past-due benefits of the primary claimant and any affected auxiliary.

When a party requests administrative review and SSA has not determined the total fee under the agreement, the reviewing official must:

• ask the effectuating component to expeditiously make a fee determination, notify all parties, and send a copy of the fee determination to the reviewing official;

• notify the parties that he or she cannot work on the request until SSA determines the total fee; and

• defer conducting the review until receiving notice of the outstanding fee amount(s).

EXAMPLE:

In a concurrent claims situation favorably decided at the hearing level, the claimant timely requests administrative review of the title II fee amount, which is less than $4,000. The field office (FO) has not yet determined and sent notice of the title XVI fee. The hearing assistant (HA) contacts the FO and asks that they determine the title XVI fee, notify the claimant and representative of the fee, and send the ALJ a copy of the notice. At the same time, the ALJ notifies the claimant and representative when acknowledging receipt that she will conduct the review once the FO has determined the title XVI fee. The HA then diaries the request for receipt of the title XVI notice.

f. Notice of Determination on Administrative Review

The reviewing official must mail a written notice of the determination made on administrative review to the claimant, affected auxiliaries (except those who reside with the claimant), and the representative at their last known addresses.

The reviewing official must also mail a copy of the notice to the decision maker when the decision maker requested review or commented on the review.

The notice will advise the parties that the determination is not subject to further review.

V. Hearing Office Procedures

A. When the Fee Agreement Process Applies

A fee agreement timely submitted in connection with a claim favorably decided at the hearing level on or after July 1, 1991, must be considered under the fee agreement process.

B. Receipt of a Fee Agreement

On receiving a fee agreement, hearing office (HO) support staff will:

1. Date stamp the fee agreement, and associate it with the claim(s) file;
2. Ensure the file contains Form SSA-1696-U4 (Appointment of Representative) or other notice of appointment (see HALLEX I-1-111, Documenting Appointment of Representative, if none is in file); and
3. Annotate the Form SSA-1128 (Representative Involved) (see Exhibit 1) with pertinent information, and staple it to the outside lower right of the claim file.

C. Favorable (or Partially Favorable) Decision

1. When making a favorable or partially favorable decision, the ALJ will:

a. Approve or disapprove the fee agreement.

NOTE: The ALJ's approval or disapproval of a fee agreement is limited to whether the agreement meets the statutory conditions and is not otherwise excepted.

b. Record the determination about the fee agreement by signing the Form HA-515-U6 (ORDER) (see Exhibit 3 or 4, as appropriate).

c. If the ALJ approves the fee agreement but believes a request for administrative review of the amount of the fee may be appropriate (see IV. B. 2. a.), inform the HO staff to diary the HO file for a copy of the letter which notifies the claimant about the fee amount set under the fee agreement.

2. When the ALJ makes a favorable or partially favorable decision, the HO staff will:

a. Retain a copy of the fee agreement and the order approving or disapproving the agreement in the HO file.

b. Mail the order with the decision and distribute copies of the order with copies of the decision. If the HO has already released the decision, mail the order separately. If the ALJ disapproves the fee agreement, enclose a Form SSA-1560-U4 (Petition to Obtain Approval of a Fee for Representing a Claimant Before the Social Security Administration) with the representative's copy of the decision and order. (See HALLEX I-1-212, Informing Representatives of Fee Regulations.)

c. Ensure that the claim(s) file contains the original copy of the fee agreement and a copy of the order. In concurrent titles II and XVI claims, place the original copy of the fee agreement and a copy of the order in the title II file, and copies in the title XVI file.

d. Maintain a list of the claims in which the ALJ has asked to see a copy of the letter notifying the claimant about the fee amount set under the fee agreement.

e. On receiving the letter that notifies the claimant about the fee amount, determine whether the ALJ asked to see it. If so, immediately give the letter and the HO file to the ALJ so that he or she can decide whether to request administrative review of the fee amount.

D. Other Than Favorable Decision

The ALJ will make a determination on a fee agreement only when the ALJ favorably or partially favorably decides the claim.

E. ALJ Requests Administrative Review of the Fee Amount

If the ALJ requests administrative review, he or she must send the written request and copies of all pertinent materials to the RCALJ and send a copy to the AFB (see Exhibit 5).

The ALJ must file the request within 15 days of the Office of Hearings and Appeals (OHA) receiving the notice of the fee amount and explain in the request why the ALJ believes there is prima facie evidence that the representative did not represent the claimant's interest adequately or that the fee is clearly excessive in light of the services provided.

NOTE: It is extremely important to timely send a copy of a request to the AFB to prevent a premature release of title II past-due benefits to the attorney, if one is involved.

VI. Appeals Council Procedures

A. When the Fee Agreement Process Applies

A fee agreement timely submitted in connection with a claim favorably decided at the request for review level on or after July 1, 1991, must be considered under the fee agreement process.

B. Docket and Files Branch Actions

1. If the Docket and Files Branch (DFB) receives the fee agreement enclosed with a request for review, proceed as shown in HALLEX I-3-071, Docket and Files Procedures, and date stamp the fee agreement.

2. If the DFB receives the fee agreement without a request for review, date stamp the fee agreement and determine the location of the claim(s) file.

a. If the claim(s) file is in the Office of Appellate Operations (OAO), send the fee agreement to the appropriate OAO branch, i.e., the Program Review Branch, or the Retirement and Survivors Insurance, Health Insurance, and Supplemental Security Income Staff.

b. If the claim(s) file is not in OAO, send the fee agreement to the AFB.

C. OAO Branch Actions

1. On receiving a fee agreement from DFB, the OAO branch will:

a. Associate it with the claim(s) file;

b. Ensure the file contains Form SSA-1696-U4 (Appointment of Representative) or other notice of appointment (see HALLEX I-3-085, Branch Screening for Other Reasons, if none is in file); and

c. Annotate the Form SSA-1128 (Representative Involved) (see Exhibit 1) with pertinent information, and staple it to the outside lower right of the claim(s) file.

2. On receiving the claim(s) file, Fee Agreement Recommendation, and the unsigned Appeals Council Order from the AFB (see VI. E. below), the OAO branch will place the Fee Agreement Recommendation in the appeals file with the OAO working papers and associate the order with the decision.

If the AFB makes a fee agreement recommendation after the Appeals Council has issued a favorable or partially favorable decision, annotate the appeals file accordingly, and forward the fee agreement to the appropriate AAJ.

D. Analyst Actions When Recommending a Favorable (or Partially Favorable) Decision

When recommending that the Appeals Council issue a favorable decision, the Hearings and Appeals analyst (analyst) will route the claim(s) file and the fee agreement to the AFB for their necessary action.

NOTE: If the analyst is recommending that the AAJ remand for additional proceedings to evaluate the claimant's mental capability, or the record shows that the claimant has been declared legally incompetent, the analyst must so advise the AFB.

E. AFB—Responsibilities

1. Making a Fee Agreement Recommendation

When the analyst recommends a favorable or partially favorable decision (see D. above), he or she will send the fee agreement and the claim(s) file to the AFB. The AFB will:
a. Determine whether the fee agreement meets the conditions in IV. A. 1. and whether any of the exceptions in IV. A. 2. apply and complete the Fee Agreement Recommendation form (see Exhibit 2).
b. Prepare the appropriate Appeals Council Order (see Exhibit 3 or 4) for the signature of the AAJ.
c. Return the claim(s) file with the fee agreement, the completed Fee Agreement Recommendation form, and the Appeals Council Order to the appropriate OAO branch.
2. AFB Receives Fee Agreement After Appeals Council Issued Favorable Decision
If the DFB forwards a fee agreement in a case in which the Appeals Council issued a favorable or partially favorable decision and the claim(s) file is already with a PC or FO for effectuation of the decision, determine whether the fee agreement was presented to SSA before or after the date of the favorable decision.
a. If the fee agreement was presented to SSA before the date of the favorable decision, the AFB will:
• Determine whether the fee agreement meets the conditions in IV. A. 1.
• If the agreement meets these conditions, telephone a claims authorizer or reconsideration reviewer in the PC, or a claims representative in the FO, where the claim(s) file is located.
• Ask the individual to review the claim(s) file to determine whether any of the exceptions in IV. A. 2. applies.
• Proceed with 1. above.
b. If the fee agreement was presented to SSA after the date of the favorable decision, the AFB will:
• Recommend that the AAJ disapprove the fee agreement by completing a Fee Agreement Recommendation form.
• Prepare an Appeals Council Order (see Exhibit 4).
• Send the Fee Agreement Recommendation and order to the AAJ through the OAO branch that previously handled the request for review.
3. Appeals Council Requested Copy of the Notice of the Amount of the Fee
PCs send the notice of the amount of the fee to the AFB. Therefore, if an AAJ has requested a copy of the notice (see F. below), the AFB will:
a. Maintain a list of such requests by the name and Social Security number (SSN) of each claimant with an annotation of the AAJ's name.
b. On receiving a notice, determine whether an AAJ asked to see it. If so, immediately send the notice and appeals file to the AAJ, so that he or she can decide whether to request administrative review.
4. Receipt of Request for Administrative Review
The AFB is designated to receive the original request for administrative review filed by claimants and representatives and to receive a copy of the request filed by a decision maker.
a. When the AFB receives an original request for administrative review, it will:
• Date stamp the request.
• Call the PC to advise PC staff of the pending request when SSA is withholding title II or Part B black lung benefits for possible direct payment to an attorney representative. Give the PC the name and SSN of the claimant.
NOTE: Each PC will designate its primary and alternate contacts.

• Acknowledge receipt of the request.
• Route the request to the reviewing official.

b. When the AFB receives a copy of a request for administrative review, it will call the PC as shown in a., second bullet, above.

F. AAJ Actions

1. When making a favorable or partially favorable decision, the AAJ will:

a. Approve or disapprove the fee agreement.

NOTE: The AAJ's approval or disapproval of a fee agreement is limited to whether the fee agreement meets the statutory conditions and is not otherwise excepted.

b. Sign the Appeals Council Order prepared by the AFB, if he or she agrees with the recommendation.

c. If the AAJ approves the fee agreement but believes a request for administrative review of the amount of the fee may be appropriate (see IV. B. 2. a.), inform the AFB that he or she wants a copy of the letter which notifies the claimant about the fee amount set under the fee agreement.

NOTE: The AAJ will make a determination on a fee agreement only when the Appeals Council decides the claim favorably or partially favorably.

2. If the AAJ requests administrative review, he or she must send the written request and copies of all pertinent materials to the Deputy Chair, Appeals Council, and send a copy to the AFB (see Exhibit 5). The AAJ must file the request within 15 days of OHA receiving the notice of the fee amount and explain in the request why the AAJ believes there is prima facie evidence that the representative did not represent the claimant's interest adequately or that the fee is clearly excessive in light of the services provided.

NOTE: It is extremely important to timely send a copy of a request to the AFB to prevent a premature release of title II past-due benefits to the attorney if one is involved.

G. Appeals Technician—Actions on Favorable or Partially Favorable Decision Involving a Fee Agreement

When the Appeals Council makes a favorable or partially favorable decision, the appeals technician will:

1. Retain a copy of the fee agreement and the order approving or disapproving the agreement in the appeals file.

2. Mail the order with the decision and distribute copies of the order with copies of the decision. If the AAJ disapproves the fee agreement, enclose a Form SSA-1560-U4 (Petition to Obtain Approval of a Fee for Representing a Claimant Before the Social Security Administration) with the representative's copy of the decision and order. (See HALLEX I-1-212, Informing Representatives of Fee Regulations and I-3-822, Release of Files—Fully or Partially Favorable Decision.)

3. Ensure that the claim(s) file contains the original copy of the fee agreement and a copy of the order. In concurrent titles II and XVI claims, place the original copy of the fee agreement and a copy of the order in the title II file, and copies in the title XVI file.

VII. Administrative Review of the Disapproval of the Fee Agreement (Hearing and Request for Review Levels)

Follow the five-step review process, below, when reviewing a determination made on the fee agreement.

A. Establish Authority to Conduct Administrative Review

Determine whether you have authority (see IV. B. 1. b.) to act on the request for administrative review.

1. If you have the authority to conduct administrative review, secure the HO file (or appeals file in OAO) and proceed with steps B. through E.
2. If you do not have the authority, acknowledge receipt, (see C. 1. a. below), advising the requester that you are referring the request to the individual delegated the authority to conduct the review, and forward the request as indicated.
NOTE: If the requester did not request administrative review through the AFB, call the AFB at (703) 305-0113 to advise them of the request.
B. Examine the File and Request for Administrative Review
Examine the HO file (or appeals file in OAO) and the request for administrative review in order to:
1. Identify:
• all parties (i.e., the claimant, or the individual whom we recognize as having the authority to sign the fee agreement on the claimant's behalf, and representative(s));
• the fee agreement; and
• the determination.
2. Screen the request for administrative review for:
• timely filing;
• by a proper party; and
• the need for action on any other issue(s) raised, e.g., the claimant objects to a date established for disability, or a date of birth determination.
3. Initiate Any Necessary Development
Obtain an explanation, if the requester did not provide a reason(s), for late filing. You may also wish to contact the other parties concerning the explanation. You may modify the letter described in C. 1. a. below, which acknowledges receipt of the request for administrative review, to ask for additional information. Ask for a response within 15 days, and diary the case for 30 days. If you do not receive an explanation at the end of 30 days, proceed to 4. below.
4. Act on Late Filing or Filing by Improper Party
If the request was not timely filed and you do not find good cause for the late filing based on the explanation (examples of good cause are provided at 20 CFR §§ 404.1720(d)(2)(ii) and 416.1520(d)(2)(ii)) or the request was not filed by a proper party, prepare a letter telling the requester:
a. The reason(s) for deciding that he or she did not show good cause; or
b. That he or she is not a proper party; and
c. That we will not act on the request for administrative review of the determination for that reason.
Send copies to the other party(ies) and the decision maker.
C. Provide Notice of the Request for Administrative Review
1. Timely Filed Request
a. Prepare a letter telling the requesting party that we:
• received his or her request;
• are notifying the other party(ies) and the decision maker; and
• are giving the other party(ies) and the decision maker the opportunity to comment or submit additional information.
b. Prepare letters informing the other party(ies) and the decision maker:
• of the request for administrative review; and
• that they may, within 15 days, comment in writing and submit relevant information.

Enclose a copy of the request for administrative review.
Send the letters and enclosures and diary the case for 30 days.
2. Late Filing—Good Cause Shown
If the requester submits the reason(s) for late filing with the request for administrative review, and you find good cause for the late filing, prepare a brief explanation of the good cause finding to include in the letters described in 1. above.
D. Review the Fee Agreement Disapproval
1. Follow-up for any additional information you previously requested but have not received. Advise the party that if we do not receive it within 15 days, we will make our determination on the request for administrative review based on the information in file. Re-diary the case for 30 days. Once the diary expires, proceed to 2. and 3. below.
2. Consider the following:
a. Were the conditions for approving the fee agreement met at the time the decision maker made the favorable decision? (See IV. A. 1.)
b. Did any of the exceptions to the fee agreement process apply at the time the decision maker made the favorable decision or, if later, disapproved the fee agreement? (See IV. A. 2.)
EXAMPLE:
The representative filed the fee agreement with an SSA office on January 7. An ALJ, in another SSA office, made a favorable decision on January 13. On January 17, SSA began evaluating the claimant's mental capability. Subsequently, the ALJ received and disapproved the fee agreement. The reviewing official must affirm the disapproval. The fee agreement met all of the statutory conditions for approval and none of the exceptions applied when the decision maker favorably decided the claim; however, one of the exceptions applied when the decision maker received and disapproved the agreement.
3. If the fee agreement met all of the conditions in IV. A. 1., and none of the exceptions in IV. A. 2. applied, the reviewing official must reverse the previous disapproval determination and approve the fee agreement.
E. Issue Notice of the Determination Made on Administrative Review
1. Prepare a letter to the requester which includes:
a. A response to the issue(s) raised.
b. An explanation of whether we affirmed or reversed the previous disapproval determination made on the fee agreement.
NOTE: If you affirm the previous disapproval, remind the representative that he or she must request approval of any fee the representative wants to charge and collect (see HALLEX I-2-212, Informing Representatives of Fee Regulations).
c. A statement that the determination made on administrative review is not subject to further review.
d. A statement that you are sending copies of the determination to the party(ies) and decision maker named.
2. Send copies of the determination to the other party(ies) and decision maker, as IV. B. 1. e. requires.
3. Place a copy of the determination in the Regional Office (RO) or HO file (or appeals file in OAO).
4. Send the determination to the PC and or FO which is effectuating the favorable decision on the claim(s).

5. For assessment purposes, send a copy of the fee agreement, request for administrative review, any development associated with the request, and the determination to:
OHA, Division of Policy, Planning and Evaluation
Planning and Evaluation Branch
Suite 1606 Skyline
5107 Leesburg Pike
Falls Church, VA 22041-3255

VIII. Administrative Review of the Amount of the Fee Under the Fee Agreement (Hearing and Request for Review Levels)

Follow the nine-step review process, below, when reviewing the amount of the fee under the fee agreement.

A. Establish Authority to Conduct Administrative Review

Determine whether you have authority (see IV. B. 2. b.) to act on the request for administrative review.

1. If you have the authority to conduct administrative review, secure the HO file (or appeals file in OAO) and proceed with steps B. through I.
2. If you do not have the authority, acknowledge receipt, advising the requester that you are referring the request to the individual delegated the authority to conduct the review, and forward the request as indicated.

NOTE: If the requester did not request administrative review through the AFB, call the AFB at (703) 305-0113 to advise them of the request.

B. Examine the File and Request for Administrative Review

Examine the HO file (or appeals file in OAO) and the request for administrative review in order to:

1. Identify:

• All parties (i.e., the claimant or the individual whom we recognize as having the authority to sign the fee agreement on the claimant's behalf; an affected auxiliary; the representative(s); and the decision maker);
• the fee agreement;
• the determination of the fee amount; and
• the issues to be resolved.

2. Screen the request for administrative review for:

• timely filing;
• by a proper party; and
• the need for action on any other issue(s) raised.

EXAMPLE:
The claimant objects to the calculation of the past-due benefits amount based on an adjustment in his or her workers' compensation. The claimant did not contact the effectuating component, but included the objection in his request for administrative review. Consider such an objection an implied request for reconsideration of the initial determination of the past-due benefits amount and forward that request to the effectuating component.

3. Consider the Test a Decision Maker Must Meet

When a decision maker requested administrative review, decide whether prima facie evidence shows either that the representative did not represent the claimant's interest adequately or the fee is clearly excessive in light of the services provided.

EXAMPLES:

• The representative delayed the claim(s) by procedural missteps or by repeatedly requesting extensions of time to submit readily available information or evidence.
• We were ready to issue a favorable decision when we received a claimant's appointment of representative and fee agreement. The $3,700 fee which resulted under the approved agreement is clearly excessive for the time it took the representative to interview the claimant, complete an appointment of representative and a fee agreement, and submit them.
a. If you recognize prima facie evidence showing inadequate representation or a clearly excessive fee, proceed to 4.
b. If you do not recognize prima facie evidence showing inadequate representation or a clearly excessive fee, and there is no clear clerical error, send a letter telling the decision maker that:
• you did not find prima facie evidence of inadequate representation or a clearly excessive fee;
• SSA will not review the determination further; and
• the previous determination of the amount the representative may charge for his or her work in the case is final.
Send copies of the letter to the other parties.
c. If you do not recognize prima facie evidence, but there is a clear clerical error involved, send a letter telling the decision maker that:
• you did not find prima facie evidence of inadequate representation or a clearly excessive fee;
• SSA will not review the determination further; and
• you are notifying the effectuating component that a clear clerical error has been made and that you request that it release a corrective notice(s) which includes new administrative review rights. Send copies of this letter to the other parties and notify the effectuating component(s) of the need for corrective action.
4. Initiate Any Necessary Development
a. Obtain an explanation if the requester, other than a decision maker, did not provide a reason(s) for late filing. You may also wish to contact the other parties concerning the explanation. You may modify the letter described in VIII. C. 1. a. below, which acknowledges receipt of the request for administrative review, to ask for additional information. Ask for a response within 15 days, and diary the case for 30 days. If you do not receive an explanation at the end of 30 days, proceed to 5. below.
b. Determine if you need the claim(s) file. If the party requesting review has objected to the calculation of the fee under the agreement or the amount of the past-due benefits, or there is an apparent error in the calculation shown in the claimant's notice of the fee amount, request the claim(s) file and ask the PC or the FO to include the following when forwarding the file:
• completed Form SSA-1129-U3 (Attorney Fee Case—Past-due Benefit Summary) in title II cases;
• completed Form SSA-1834 (Worksheet for Proration of Withheld Benefits Attorney Fee Case) when there are one or more affected auxiliaries; and/or
• Supplemental Security Income Display (SSID), with the complete computation history, or the manually completed computation form in a title XVI claim.
If an unusual situation is involved or the reviewing official anticipates difficulty following the computation, also request a brief narrative explanation from the benefit authorizer or claims representative.
c. Ascertain whether SSA has determined the total fee for all services under the fee agreement when the request involves concurrent titles II and XVI claims involving a common issue, or one

or more delayed affected auxiliaries (see IV. B. 2. e.). If SSA has not determined the total fee, then:

• telephone the effectuating component (an inquiries specialist in the PC or an operations supervisor in the FO) and ask that they expeditiously make a fee determination, notify all parties, and send a copy of the fee determination to you;

• notify the parties when you acknowledge receipt that you cannot conduct the review until SSA determines the total fee; and

• diary the request for 30 days, unless the effectuating component indicates that outstanding development will require a longer diary period, to await notice of the fee determination. If you have not received notice of the outstanding fee at the end of the diary period, send a written follow-up to the module branch chief in the PC or the office manager in the FO.

5. Act on Late Filing or Filing by Improper Party

If the request was not timely filed and you do not find good cause for the late filing based on the explanation (examples of good cause are provided at 20 CFR §§ 404.1720(d)(2)(ii) and 416.1520(d)(2)(ii)) or the request was not filed by a proper party, prepare a letter telling the requester:

a. The reason(s) for deciding that he or she did not show good cause; or

b. That he or she is not a proper party; and

c. That we will not act on the request for administrative review of the determination for that reason.

Send copies of the letter to the other parties.

NOTE: If a decision maker does not request administrative review timely, the reviewing official will not review the determination, unless the decision maker submits, with the request, information that establishes good cause for late filing.

C. Provide Notice of the Request for Administrative Review

1. Timely Filed Request

a. Prepare a letter telling the requesting party that we:

• received his or her request;

• are notifying the other parties;

• are giving the other parties the opportunity to comment or submit additional information; and

• if appropriate, will not conduct the review until SSA has determined the total fee under the fee agreement.

b. Prepare letters informing the other parties:

• who requested administrative review;

• that they may, within 15 days, comment in writing and submit relevant information; and

• if appropriate, we will not conduct the review until SSA has determined the total fee under the fee agreement.

Enclose copies of the request for administrative review. Because of Privacy Act considerations, do not reveal the:

• claimant's mailing address when sending a copy of a letter addressed to the claimant, or the claimant's request for administrative review, to a party other than that claimant's representative or the decision maker.

• auxiliary beneficiary's mailing address when sending a copy of a letter addressed to the beneficiary, or the beneficiary's request for administrative review, to a party other than that beneficiary's representative or the decision maker.

This means the address must be covered before photocopying or completely blocked out before mailing.
Send the letters and enclosures and diary the case for 30 days.
2. Late Filing—Good Cause Shown
If the requester submits the reason(s) for late filing with the request for administrative review, and you find good cause for the late filing, prepare a brief explanation of the good cause finding to include in the letters described in 1. above.
D. Examine the Claim(s) File When Received
1. Ensure that you properly identified all parties to the administrative review.
2. Follow-up for any additional information you requested but have not received. Advise the party that if we do not receive it within 15 days, we will make our determination on the request for administrative review based on the information in file. Re-diary the case for 30 days. Once the diary expires, proceed with E. below.
E. Review the Fee Agreement Approval
1. If not considered previously under VII.:
—Were the conditions for approving the fee agreement met at the time the decision maker made the favorable decision? (See IV. A. 1.)
—Did any of the exceptions to the fee agreement process apply at the time the decision maker made the favorable decision or, if later, approved the fee agreement? (See IV. A. 2.)
a. If the decision maker's approval determination was incorrect, proceed to 2. below.
b. If the decision maker's approval determination was correct, proceed to F. below.
NOTE: The reviewing official will include in the notice of the administrative review determination (I. below) a response to any issue(s) raised concerning the approval of the fee agreement.
2. If the reviewing official believes the decision maker's approval determination was incorrect, he or she will:
a. Prepare a letter to the parties explaining that he or she plans to disapprove the fee agreement and why; and tell the parties that they may, within 15 days, comment in writing and submit relevant information. (The reviewing official may include this explanation in the acknowledgment letter.)
b. Diary, or re-diary, the case for 30 days.
c. When the diary period expires or, if earlier, when all parties have commented, the reviewing official will decide whether the decision maker's approval determination was correct, considering the fee agreement, comments, and relevant information received.
3. If the reviewing official determines that the fee agreement was incorrectly approved, he or she will proceed as described in VII. E. above. In addition:
a. Advise the representative that he or she must request approval of any fee he or she wants to charge and collect (see HALLEX I-1-212, Informing Representatives of Fee Regulations). Enclose a Form SSA-1560-U4 (Petition to Obtain Approval of a Fee for Representing a Claimant Before the Social Security Administration) for that purpose.
b. In a title II or Part B black lung case involving an attorney representative, advise the attorney that he or she must request approval of the fee, or file a written notice of the intent to do so, within 60 days in order to receive direct payment from past-due benefits withheld (see HALLEX I-1-220, Time Limits for Filing Fee Petitions).
F. Consider the Amount of the Fee Under the Terms of the Agreement

1. If necessary, consider whether SSA determined the amount of the fee under the agreement correctly.
a. The reviewing official will recalculate, or request the PC or FO to recalculate, the amount of the fee when:
• A party disagrees with the calculation; or
• There appears to be an error considering the $4,000 limit, the percentage specified in the agreement, and any other terms in the fee agreement.
b. The claim(s) file(s) should contain the payment history and fee amount worksheets when the reviewing official receives it. If these documents are not in file and the reviewing official believes a recalculation or confirmation of the amounts determined is necessary, he or she will refer the file(s) to the appropriate component (PC or FO) and ask for a recalculation or confirmation and a brief narrative explanation. Diary, or re-diary, the case for 30 days.
NOTE: Refer to section GN T03920.001C. of the Program Operations Manual System (POMS) for the definition of past-due benefits.
2. Determine whether the approved fee agreement includes terms for modifying the amount of the fee within the 25 percent and $4,000 limits, or whether there is an arithmetic error in SSA's computation of the fee amount. The reviewing official will check the fee amount to determine if SSA correctly determined the amount of the fee under the agreement and if:
a. SSA correctly determined the fee, proceed to 3. below.
b. SSA incorrectly determined the fee, then:
• correctly determine the fee under the terms of the agreement;
• notify all parties of that fee amount;
• provide the parties 15 days to comment;
• if the amount of the fee can be modified in a manner consistent with the party's request, and no party objects during the comment period, modify the amount of the fee without evaluating the representative's services and the circumstances, as set out below; and proceed to I. below.
• if the amount of the subsequently determined fee is inconsistent with the party's request or a party objected during the comment period, proceed to 3. below.
EXAMPLE:
SSA set a fee of $1,500, which is 25 percent of past-due benefits. The claimant timely filed a request for administrative review, stating that she owes no more than $1,000. The fee agreement provided for a fee of the lesser of 25 percent or $4,000 and further stated that, if SSA favorably decided the claim below the Appeals Council level, the fee would not exceed $1,000. SSA favorably decided the claim on the claimant's request for hearing. The reviewing official notifies the parties that the correct fee under the terms of the agreement is $1,000. The representative did not comment on the request for administrative review. The reviewing official will modify the fee to the correct amount, $1,000, in accordance with the agreement's terms.
3. Consider the following factors to assess whether the fee determined under the fee agreement process is reasonable and to decide whether to affirm or modify a fee and, if so, to what extent.
• The expectation of the parties when they entered into the fee agreement, as expressed in the written agreement filed with SSA.
• The successful results the representative achieved.
• The amount the representative requested for his or her services, including any amount authorized or requested before but not including the amount of any expenses incurred.
• The level of administrative review to which the claim was taken and the level at which the claimant retained the representative.

• The complexity of the case.
• The extent and type of services provided.
• The level of skill and competence required of the representative in providing the services.
• The amount of time the representative spent on the case.

G. Request an Explanation of Services and Time Spent

1. If the reviewing official expects to assess whether the fee determined under the fee agreement is reasonable, ask the representative to submit a written explanation detailing his or her services and the amount of time spent on the case, if he or she has not already done so, and to send copies of the written explanation to the other parties. The reviewing official must send a copy of the request to the other parties.

NOTE: A Form SSA-1560-U4 (Petition to Obtain Approval of a Fee for Representing a Claimant Before the Social Security Administration) may be used for this purpose.

2. When examination of the claim(s) file reveals a concurrent titles II and XVI case involving a common issue and the representative's services led to a favorable decision in both programs, the reviewing official will ask the representative for an explanation which addresses services in connection with both the titles II and XVI claims, i.e., services that were unique to one as well as services that are common to both (see Social Security Ruling 83-27).

NOTE: In cases described in B. 4. c. above, the reviewing official must inform the parties that he or she will review the total fee under the fee agreement and consider the services the representative provided in connection with both claims.

3. The reviewing official must ensure that all parties received copies of the representative's explanation and afford them the opportunity to submit written comments within 15 days of receipt of this notice.

H. Consider Whether the Fee Is Reasonable

Because the factors the reviewing official considers are qualitative as well as quantitative, he or she will use the factors shown in F. 3. to first determine the range within which a fee would be considered reasonable.

1. The reviewing official will affirm the fee amount if he or she determines that the fee originally determined under the fee agreement process, or subsequently determined under F. 2. above, falls within the range considered reasonable for the services provided.

2. The reviewing official will modify the fee if he or she determines that the fee originally determined under the fee agreement process, or subsequently determined under F. 2. above, does not fall within the range considered reasonable for the services provided. He or she must determine a reasonable fee based on evaluation of the factors listed in F. 3.

NOTE: The reviewing official has the same authority to approve specific fee amounts as indicated in HALLEX I-1-201 A.

EXAMPLES:

• The ALJ concludes that a reasonable fee for the case would be between $3,000 and $3,500. The fee originally determined under the fee agreement process is $3,490, and there has been no change in the amount of the past-due benefits or past-due benefits payable. The ALJ affirms the fee amount.
• The ALJ concludes that a reasonable fee for the case would be between $4,500 and $5,000. The fee originally determined under the fee agreement process is $4,000. The ALJ has the authority to approve a fee up to and including $5,000 (see HALLEX I-1-201 A.).
• The claimant's past-due benefits are $800 because of his receipt of workers' compensation benefits. The fee determined under the fee agreement process is $200. The representative timely

requested administrative review, stating that the $200 fee is unreasonable compensation for the services she performed. The claimant did not respond to the notice of the request for administrative review. The ALJ concludes, considering the factors contained in F. 3. above, that a reasonable range for the representative's services would be $900 to $1400. The ALJ modified the originally determined fee to $1200, which is a fee within the reasonable range.

• The fee originally determined under the fee agreement process was $4,000. The claimant timely requested administrative review, stating that 25 percent of his past-due benefits payable was $2,250. SSA had revised its determination of the past-due benefits payable because his receipt of workers' compensation required a reduction; however, the reduction occurred immediately after release of the notice of the fee amount. The representative responded to the notice of the request for administrative review, stating that $4,000 was an entirely reasonable fee for his services. The Attorney Fee Officer concluded, considering the factors contained in F. 3. above, that a reasonable range for the representative's services would be $2,000 to $2,500. The Attorney Fee Officer modified the originally determined fee, based on the most recent past-due benefits computation, to $2,250, which is a fee within the reasonable range.

NOTE: Although increases and decreases in the amount of past-due benefits or past-due benefits payable usually do not affect the amount of the fee under the fee agreement process, if a party requests administrative review, SSA determines the fee under the fee agreement process when it notifies the parties of the amount of the fee after administrative review.

I. Issuing Notice of the Administrative Review Determination

1. Prepare a letter to the requester which includes:

a. The authority for administrative review:

—For title II cases, § 206(a)(3) of the Social Security Act, as amended;

—For title XVI only, or concurrent titles II and XVI cases, §§ 206(a)(3) and 1631(d)(2) of the Social Security Act, as amended; or

—For Part B black lung cases, § 413(b) of the Federal Mine Safety and Health Act and § 206(a)(3) of the Social Security Act, as amended.

NOTE: The regulations generally cited as authority for administrative review of fees determined under the fee petition process do not apply to fees determined under the fee agreement process.

b. A response to the issue(s) raised.

c. A statement as to whether we affirmed or modified the amount of the fee and our reason(s) for doing so.

d. The amount of the fee we determined on review.

e. A statement that the determination is not subject to further review, pursuant to:

—For title II cases, § 206(a)(3)(C) of the Social Security Act, as amended.

—For title XVI only, or concurrent titles II and XVI cases, §§ 206(a)(3)(C) and 1631(d)(2)(A) of the Social Security Act, as amended.

—For Part B black lung cases, § 413(b) of the Federal Mine Safety and Health Act and § 206(a)(3)(C) of the Social Security Act, as amended.

f. A statement that you are sending copies of the determination to the parties named.

2. Send copies of the determination to the other parties, as IV. B. 2. e. requires. (See C. 1. b. above for Privacy Act considerations.)

3. Place a copy of the determination in the RO or HO file (or appeals file in OAO).

4. Send the determination and the claim(s) file to the component(s) which effectuated the favorable decision.

5. For assessment purposes, send a copy of the fee agreement, the notice of the original fee determination, the request for administrative review, any development associated with the request, and the review determination to:

OHA, Division of Policy, Planning and Evaluation
Planning and Evaluation Branch
Suite 1606 Skyline
5107 Leesburg Pike
Falls Church, VA 22041-3255

IX. Inquiries

HO personnel should call the RO. RO personnel should call the Division of Field Practices and Procedures in the Office of the Chief Administrative Law Judge (OCALJ) on (703) 305-0022. OAO personnel should refer questions through their branch chief to the Acting Deputy Director's Office on 305-0106. OAO will follow the procedures in HALLEX I-3-113, Referral to Division of Policy, Planning and Evaluation (DPP.E), when referring an inquiry to the Office of Management, Division of Policy and Planning (OM/DP.P—formerly OPPE).

Questions that cannot be answered by personnel in OCALJ or the Acting Deputy Director's Office should be referred to OM/DPP.

EXHIBIT 1

TABLE

TABULAR OR GRAPHIC MATERIAL SET FORTH AT THIS POINT IS NOT DISPLAYABLE

EXHIBIT 2

Claimant's Name ____________________
Claim Number _________________________
Representative's Name ____________________

FEE AGREEMENT RECOMMENDATION

I reviewed the fee agreement.

□ The fee agreement meets the conditions for approval, and none of the exceptions apply.
□ The fee agreement does not meet the condition(s) for approval because:
□ The Social Security Administration did not receive the written fee agreement before making the favorable decision.
□ The claimant and his or her representative(s) did not all sign the fee agreement.
□ It sets a fee that is more than the lesser of 25 percent of the past-due benefits or $4,000.
□ The fee agreement is excepted from the process because the following exception(s) applies:
□ The claimant appointed more than one representative associated in a firm, partnership, or legal corporation and all did not sign a single fee agreement.
□ The claimant appointed representatives who are not members of a single firm, partnership, or legal corporation.
□ The claimant discharged a representative, or a representative withdrew from the case, before the claim was decided.
□ The claimant has been declared legally incompetent and the claimant's legal guardian did not sign the fee agreement; or we determined that the claimant is mentally incapable of managing his or her funds, or we are in the process of evaluating the claimant's mental capability, and the person who is responsible for the care of the claimant did not sign the fee agreement.

I prepared for the signature of the AAJ, an Appeals Council Order based on the above.

____

Signature

____

Date

EXHIBIT 3

ALJ OR AAJ APPROVES THE FEE AGREEMENT

LANGUAGE FOR THE HA-515-U6 OR HA-517-U9

I approve the fee agreement between the claimant and his or her representative subject to the condition that the claim results in past-due benefits.

My determination is limited to whether the fee agreement meets the statutory conditions for approval and is not otherwise excepted. I neither approve nor disapprove any other aspect of the fee agreement.

____

Signature

____

Title

____

Date

EXHIBIT 4

ALJ OR AAJ DISAPPROVES THE FEE AGREEMENT

LANGUAGE FOR THE HA-515-U6 OR HA-517-U9

I do not approve the fee agreement between the claimant and his or her representative because:

[Only include those that apply]

☐ The Social Security Administration did not receive the written agreement before I decided the claim.

☐ The claimant and his or her representative(s) did not all sign the fee agreement.

☐ The fee agreement sets a fee that is more than the lesser of 25 percent of the past-due benefits or $4,000.

☐ The claimant appointed more than one representative from a firm, partnership, or legal corporation and all representatives did not sign a single fee agreement.

☐ The claimant appointed representatives who are not members of a single firm, partnership, or legal corporation.

☐ The claimant discharged a representative, or a representative withdrew from the case, before I decided the claim.

☐ The claimant has been declared legally incompetent and the claimant's legal guardian did not sign the fee agreement; or we have determined that the claimant is mentally incapable of managing his or her funds, or we are in the process of evaluating the claimant's mental capability, and the person who is responsible for the care of the claimant did not sign the fee agreement.

Because I do not approve the fee agreement for the reason(s) indicated above, the claimant's representative must file a fee petition if he or she wants to charge and collect a fee. I have enclosed with the representative's copy a Form SSA-1560 (Petition to Obtain Approval of a Fee for Representing a Claimant Before the Social Security Administration) which may be used for this purpose.

HOW TO ASK US TO REVIEW THE DETERMINATION ON THE FEE AGREEMENT

You or your representative can ask us to review the determination on the fee agreement. If you decide to ask us for a review, write us within 15 days from the day you get this order. Tell us that you disagree and give your reasons. Send your request to this address:
Social Security Administration
Office of Hearings and Appeals
Attorney Fee Branch
5107 Leesburg Pike
Falls Church, VA 22041-3255
Your representative also has 15 days to write us if he or she does not agree with the determination on the fee agreement.
You should include the social security number(s) shown on this order on any papers you send us.

____
Signature

____
Title

____
Date

EXHIBIT 5

MEMORANDUM TO: Regional Chief, Deputy Chief, or Chief ALJ or Deputy Chair, or Chair, Appeals Council
REGARDING: _____ - _______ - _______,
FROM: _________________________
SUBJECT: Request for Administrative Review of Fee Based on an Approved Fee Agreement—ACTION

I approved the fee agreement between ____________________ and _________________________.

I ask for a reduction of the fee which would otherwise result under the agreement because, I believe, there is prima facie evidence which shows that:
☐ ___________________________________ did not represent the claimant's interest adequately.
☐ the fee is clearly excessive in light of the services provided.
My reasons follow.

____
Attachment(s) ☐ Yes ☐ No
cc: ______________________________________, ??
____, ??
Attorney Fee Branch, OAO, OHA

ATTACHMENT 1

QUESTIONS AND ANSWERS FEE AGREEMENT PROCESS

Use of the Fee Agreement Process

1. Can a non-attorney representative use the fee agreement process?
Yes. However, the Social Security Administration (SSA) will not withhold the fee from past-due benefits. The representative must collect the fee from the claimant. The fee agreement process did not change the direct payment provision.
2. Can a representative use the fee agreement process in a supplemental security income (title XVI) case?

Yes. However, SSA does not withhold money from past-due title XVI benefits even if the representative is an attorney. As stated above, the fee agreement process did not change the direct payment provision.

3. Can the fee agreement process be used in title XVI claims which involve an interim assistance agreement?

Yes.

Appointment of Representative

4. Can a representative combine the appointment of representative and fee agreement into one statement?

Yes. If the claimant appoints a representative, he or she must do so in writing, using either a Form SSA-1696-U4 (Appointment of Representative) or an equivalent statement. The fee agreement can contain a statement appointing the representative; however, for the purposes of uniformity and ease of reference, we encourage, but do not require, the representative to file an SSA-1696-U4 in all cases (see HALLEX I-1-110, Appointing the Representative).

5. If the Form SSA-1696-U4 is in file, must the representative(s) named in this form also sign the fee agreement?

Yes. If a claimant appoints a representative(s) by signing an SSA-1696-U4, or equivalent statement, and also enters into a fee agreement with the representative(s), the appointed representative(s) must sign a single fee agreement.

6. On the Form SSA-1696-U4, can an individual accept the appointment on behalf of a firm, e.g., John Smith for Jane Doe's Office?

No. SSA recognizes the appointment of individuals, not firms. Therefore, if a claimant appoints a firm or corporation, and the representative accepts on behalf of the firm, SSA recognizes that representative in his or her individual capacity. The claimant may, of course, appoint more than one representative.

7. Should an Administrative Law Judge (ALJ) or Administrative Appeals Judge (AAJ) approve a fee agreement which is made with a law firm and or corporation rather than with an individual representative if the Form SSA-1696-U4 meets SSA's guidelines?

If the individual who signs the fee agreement for a firm or a corporation is the appointed representative, the ALJ or AAJ must approve the fee agreement if all the other conditions are met and none of the exceptions apply. If someone other than the appointed representative signs the fee agreement on behalf of a firm or a corporation, the ALJ or AAJ must disapprove the fee agreement because the appointed representative did not sign the fee agreement.

8. If a representative and claimant both signed the Form SSA-1696-U4 and the fee agreement, should the ALJ or AAJ approve the fee agreement if a paralegal in the appointed representative's firm actually attended the hearing?

Yes. An appointed representative may receive assistance from other individuals in the firm. In such a situation, SSA assumes that the paralegal is working under the direct supervision of the appointed representative who remains ultimately responsible for the claimant's case.

Fee Agreements—General

9. Can a hearing office (HO) create its own fee agreement form and require representatives to use it?

No. The statute does not require the use of particular language. Therefore, representatives may craft their own fee agreements and decision makers must approve an agreement if the statutory conditions of the fee agreement process are met and no exceptions apply.

10. Can a representative amend an existing fee agreement to comply with the requirements of the fee agreement process?
Yes. In such a situation, the ALJ or AAJ must base his or her determination on whether the amended fee agreement meets the conditions of the fee agreement process and none of the exceptions apply at the time the favorable decision is made.
11. If the file contains several fee agreements, which one should the ALJ or AAJ act on?
The ALJ or AAJ acts on the most recently negotiated fee agreement received by SSA before the date of the favorable decision.
12. Before making the fee agreement determination, can the ALJ or AAJ inquire as to the number of hours spent on the claim or the services provided?
No. The number of hours spent on a claim and services provided are not conditions for approval of a fee agreement. Therefore, the ALJ or AAJ cannot request this information in making a determination on the fee agreement.

Evaluating A Fee Agreement

13. If the ALJ or AAJ receives a fee agreement before the date of the decision which he or she clearly cannot approve, should he or she disapprove it immediately or wait until issuing the decision?
The ALJ or AAJ should not approve or disapprove an agreement unless and until he or she is issuing a favorable decision.
14. The statute says that the adjudicator (hereinafter, decision maker) must approve the agreement at the time the decision maker makes a favorable decision. Can this mean at the time the ALJ gives instructions to the decision writer?
No. It is the Office of Hearings and Appeals' (OHA's) longstanding policy that a decision is made at the time the ALJ signs it and the HO dates and mails the decision.
15. In evaluating a fee agreement, what should the ALJ or AAJ look for in determining whether to approve the agreement?
The ALJ or the AAJ must:
• review the SSA-1696-U4 or equivalent statement to determine who is the appointed representative(s);
• ascertain that the individual(s) who signed the fee agreement is in fact the claimant's appointed representative(s);
• review the provisions in the fee agreement to ascertain whether the agreement meets all of the statutory conditions of the fee agreement process; and
• compare the information in the fee agreement, the SSA-1696-U4 or equivalent statement, and the file to determine whether any exceptions apply.

Provisions in Fee Agreements

16. Should an ALJ or AAJ approve a fee agreement that contains a provision that the claimant will pay a minimum fee?
No. Agreements that specify a minimum fee do not meet the statutory conditions for approval under the fee agreement process. For example, assume that a fee agreement provides that if SSA favorably decides the claim, the representative's fee will be 25 percent of the past-due benefits or $4,000, whichever is less, except that if 25 percent of the past-due benefits does not exceed $1,250, the claimant will pay a fee of $1,250. In this case, the fee agreement does not conform to the conditions of the statute because the claimant has not in fact agreed to pay a fee which is the lesser of 25 percent or $4,000. In some cases (which cannot be known until SSA calculates the

amount of past-due benefits), the claimant would have to pay a fee greater than 25 percent of the past-due benefits, contrary to the provisions of the statute.

17. Should an ALJ or AAJ approve a fee agreement that contains a provision that a representative has a right to seek review of the amount that would otherwise be the maximum fee under the fee agreement provision in § 206(a)(2) of the Social Security Act (the Act), as amended?

Yes. The right to seek such review is provided for in § 206(a)(3) of the Act, as amended. A fee agreement containing such a provision states no more than what is in the statute, and must be approved if it otherwise meets the statutory conditions and no exceptions apply.

18. Should an ALJ or AAJ approve a fee agreement that contains a provision that the fee does not include any out-of-pocket expenses, e.g., costs to get copies of doctors' or hospitals' reports, state sales tax, etc.?

Yes. Out-of-pocket expenses are extra expenses the representative incurs and are not considered part of the fee which SSA authorizes under the statute and regulations.

19. Should an ALJ or AAJ approve a fee agreement if it contains a provision that the representative may request administrative review of the amount of the fee if the past-due benefits do not exceed a certain amount? For example, assume a fee agreement provides that if SSA favorably decides the claim, the representative's fee will be 25 percent of the past-due benefits or $4,000, whichever is less, except if the past-due benefits do not exceed $1,250, the representative may seek administrative review of the amount that would otherwise be the maximum fee under § 206(a)(2) of the Act.

Yes. Although this provision may appear to indicate a minimum fee, it merely indicates the representative's intent to request administrative review if a desired fee is not realized. This provision is not contrary to the provisions of the statute.

20. Should an ALJ or AAJ approve a fee agreement that contains a provision that if 25 percent of the past-due benefits is more than $4,000, the representative will receive a fee of $4,000 and retain the right to petition for an additional fee?

No. The fee agreement and fee petition processes are alternative, not interchangeable, methods of approving representative fees.

21. Should an ALJ approve a fee agreement that contains a provision which specifies that the agreement applies only to services with respect to the claim through a specific level of the administrative review process, e.g., the initial ALJ hearing level?

Yes. OHA interprets provisions like these to provide, in essence, for a two-tiered fee structure. In the example above, the fee structure is as follows:

- if the claim is decided favorably at or below the level of the initial ALJ hearing, the fee would be the lesser of 25 percent of past-due benefits or $4,000; but
- if the claim progresses beyond that level, the representative would request a fee through the fee petition process.

The ALJ will be able to readily ascertain, at the time of the favorable decision, which tier of the fee structure applies. If the applicable clause is the first one, i.e., the lesser of 25 percent of past-due benefits or $4,000, the requirement of § 206(a)(2)(A)(ii) of the Act is satisfied and the ALJ could approve the agreement. However, if the second clause applies, e.g., the ALJ issues a favorable decision following a remand by the Appeals Council, § 206(a)(2)(A)(ii) of the Act would not be satisfied and the ALJ would disapprove the fee agreement. The representative would then have to petition for approval of any fee. In either situation, the fee so determined would compensate the representative for all services for which a fee could be paid under § 206(a) of the Act, i.e., all administrative services.

If an ALJ previously disapproved a fee agreement because it contained the subject provision and the claimant or representative timely requests administrative review, the reviewing official will reverse the determination made on the fee agreement if the other requirements of § 206(a)(2)(A) are met and none of the exceptions apply.

NOTE: The term "initial ALJ hearing" refers to all actions at the request for hearing level. Once the ALJ issues a decision and the claim proceeds to the Appeals Council level, the second clause of the provision described above applies.

22. Should an ALJ or AAJ approve a fee agreement that contains a provision which states that if SSA favorably decides the claim, a third party will pay the representative a fee equal to the lesser of 25 percent of the past-due benefits or $4,000 and the claimant will not incur any financial liability?

Yes. If the fee agreement meets all of the other conditions of § 206(a)(2) and none of the exceptions apply, the ALJ or AAJ must approve the fee agreement.

23. Should an ALJ or AAJ approve a fee agreement, signed by the claimant and the representative, when the agreement provides that, if another person referred the case, the representative may share his or her fee with the referring or forwarding person?

Yes. If the claimant appointed one representative and the claimant and the representative both signed the agreement, the ALJ or AAJ should approve the agreement if all of the other conditions of § 206(a)(2) are met and no exceptions apply. A referring attorney or non-attorney, who is not the claimant's appointed representative, need not also sign the fee agreement.

Exceptions

24. If a claimant had two representatives but the first representative waived his or her fee, does exception a. in IV.A.2. of HALLEX TI 5-109 still apply?

No. Because the first representative waived his or her fee, this exception does not apply. Neither does exception c. of the same section.

The purpose of these two exceptions is to avoid a situation in which a decision maker might inadvertently approve the fee agreement of both representatives and authorize each representative to collect the maximum amount allowed by the statute. Once one of the representatives waives his or her fee, the situation mentioned above is no longer at issue.

25. Should an ALJ or AAJ disapprove a fee agreement because the claimant has been found to have a mental impairment?

SSA's intent is to exclude from the fee agreement process those situations in which an adult claimant may be mentally incapable of entering into a valid contract. It is up to the ALJ or AAJ to decide on this issue. If the ALJ or AAJ believes that the claimant's mental impairment is such that he or she was mentally incapable of entering into a valid contract, then the ALJ or AAJ must except the fee agreement from the process.

If the ALJ or AAJ approves the fee agreement, SSA will assume that he or she considered the exception and decided that the claimant was mentally capable of entering into a valid contract. The exception does not pertain to fee agreements signed by a court appointed representative or a person who is responsible for the care of the claimant, including a relative.

Representative's Signature or Lack Thereof

26. Can representatives use stamped or photocopied signatures in lieu of original signatures?

Yes. Representatives may use stamped or photocopied signatures in lieu of an actual signature. Representatives may also submit a copy of the original fee agreement.

27. Can an ALJ or AAJ disapprove a fee agreement because the representative's signature is illegible?

No. However, if there is a question about the identity of the representative, the ALJ or AAJ may contact the representative for clarification.

28. If the ALJ or AAJ is prepared to issue a favorable decision, and discovers that the agreement is otherwise in accord with the statute, but that the claimant or representative failed to sign it, should the ALJ or AAJ delay issuing the decision until the representative can correct the omission?

No. The ALJ or AAJ must approve or disapprove the agreement as it stands at the time he or she is making the favorable decision on the claim. In this case, the ALJ must disapprove the agreement.

Post-Decision

29. What should the ALJ or AAJ do if a representative calls to state that he or she received the decision but did not receive a copy of the fee agreement determination?

If the ALJ or AAJ acted on the fee agreement, send the representative another copy of the determination. If the ALJ or AAJ did not make a fee agreement determination, he or she must review the fee agreement, make his or her determination, and send a copy to the claimant, the representative, and the processing center (PC) and or the FO.

30. If the ALJ or AAJ did not make a fee agreement determination on a fee agreement that was in file when he or she made the favorable decision, does the representative now have to file a fee petition?

No. The ALJ or AAJ must issue an order either approving or disapproving the fee agreement. If the PC or FO receives a favorable decision with an unprocessed fee agreement in file, they will contact the ALJ or AAJ to request a fee agreement determination. If the HO or Appeals Council notes the omission on its own, it must obtain a determination from the ALJ or AAJ and forward the determination to the PC and or the FO.

Post-Fee Agreement Determination

31. What should the HO tell a representative who calls and states that although the ALJ approved the fee agreement, the representative received an award letter which advises him or her to file a fee petition?

The HO must advise the representative that the PC used an incorrect notice. The HO will instruct the representative to send a copy of the award notice and fee agreement approval to the PC and request that they process the fee agreement pursuant to the instructions in GN T03920.001 ff. of the POMS (Program Operations Manual System).

32. If an ALJ or AAJ disapproved a fee agreement because it contained a provision that the agreement applied only to a certain level of the administrative appeals process, should he or she now issue an amended fee agreement determination?

No. SSA will not revise the disapproval determination on such a fee agreement absent a pending request for administrative review. In such a case the representative must petition for approval of a fee.

33. When a fee petition and a fee agreement are in file, which one does SSA honor?

The fee agreement and the fee petition processes are not interchangeable. Therefore, which instrument SSA honors will depend on the situation.

If the ALJ or AAJ approved the fee agreement and the representative subsequently filed a fee petition, either on his or her own initiative or in response to an erroneous notice from the PC, the ALJ or AAJ will not act on the fee petition. The HO or Appeals Council staff must advise the representative that SSA will not process the fee petition because SSA is authorizing a fee based on the fee agreement.

If the ALJ or AAJ disapproved the fee agreement and the representative filed a fee petition in response to the disapproval notice which directs the representative to petition for a fee if he or she wishes to charge and collect a fee, the ALJ or Attorney Fee Branch (AFB) must process the fee petition.

If the ALJ or AAJ approved the fee agreement, SSA sent proper notice of the fee amount and the right to request administrative review, and the representative then filed a fee petition in response to the notice of the fee amount, asking for a higher fee than that shown in the notice, the ALJ or AFB will not process the fee petition as such. If a fee petition is filed within the 15-day period for administrative review, the ALJ or AFB will consider it a timely filed request for administrative review of the amount of the fee under the fee agreement and process it under the administrative review procedures.

Miscellaneous

34. At what point can a representative pay funds held in a trust or escrow account to himself or herself under the fee agreement process?

When the representative receives notice of the authorized fee amount under the fee agreement.

35. If the representative submits a contingency fee agreement, i.e., an agreement in which the representative will charge and collect a fee only if SSA favorably decides the claim and receives no fee if SSA's decision is unfavorable, and SSA's decision is unfavorable, can the representative then file a fee petition?

No. The fee agreement process did not change the way SSA treats contingency fee agreements. If the claimant and the representative entered into a contingency contract, as described above, SSA will honor it.

36. If the Appeals Council vacates a favorable hearing decision on own motion review and remands the case to an ALJ for further proceedings, will it also vacate the ALJ's determination on the fee agreement?

Yes.

37. Can a PC reverse an ALJ or AAJ's fee agreement determination?

No.

38. Is the Form SSA-1128 (Representative Involved) only required in a fee agreement case?

No. The Form SSA-1128 is required in all cases in which a representative is involved, regardless of whether it is a fee agreement or fee petition case. It is very important that HO or Appeals Council staff, as appropriate, complete this form and attach it to the file anytime the claimant is represented. A correctly annotated Form SSA-1128 alerts staff within OHA, the PCs, and FOs of the representation and prevents processing errors.

ATTACHMENT 2

QUESTION AND ANSWERS ADMINISTRATIVE REVIEW PROCESS

GENERAL

1. How does a party to the fee agreement know where to file a request for administrative review?

When the Administrative Law Judge (ALJ) or Administrative Appeals Judge (AAJ) disapproves a fee agreement or the processing center (PC) or field office (FO) notifies the claimant, any affected auxiliary, the representative, and decision maker of the amount of the fee, they also inform the parties of where to send a written request for administrative review.

2. What development is needed in cases in which a claimant, affected auxiliary, or representative does not request administrative review timely?

The reviewing official must secure a written explanation of why the request was not filed within the 15-day period, if the original request for administrative review does not include an explanation. The reviewing official may afford another party or parties an opportunity to comment on the explanation given for late filing if the reviewing official believes the other party or parties may have knowledge of the situation.

Example: The claimant requests administrative review on July 15. He explains that he did not receive the notice, dated May 30, until June 30. The reviewing official enclosed a copy of the claimant's explanation in the letter informing the representative of the request for administrative review. The representative responded with a copy of his office records, showing that he had discussed the May 30 notice with the claimant, who indicated that he also had his notice, during a 15 minute telephone call on June 5. The reviewing official then determined that the claimant had not shown good cause and included his findings in the final letter to the parties.

3. Are the follow-up procedures when reviewing a fee agreement disapproval (VII. D. 1.) applicable when reviewing the timeliness issue (VII. B. 3.)?

No. The letter requesting good cause information must explain that if nothing is submitted within the noticed timeframe, we will assume that the requester has nothing to submit and the reviewing official will proceed with his or her action.

4. When addressing the 15-day time period to request administrative review, do we assume receipt of relevant notices within 5 days of the date on the notice, in the absence of contrary evidence?

Yes.

5. Is an affected auxiliary a proper party to file a request for administrative review on the fee agreement's disapproval, as he or she is permitted to file a request for administrative review of the fee amount? Can you provide an example of an "improper" party for purposes of requesting administrative review?

The only parties who may request administrative review of the disapproval of a fee agreement are the individuals who signed the agreement, i.e., the claimant and the representative(s). The only parties who may request administrative review of the fee amount are the claimant, any affected auxiliary, the representative(s), and the decision maker.

Example of an improper party: a claims representative (CR) files a request for administrative review of the fee amount, and he or she was not the decision maker.

6. Who has jurisdiction to conduct administrative review of the disapproval of the fee agreement at the initial and reconsideration levels?

In all cases favorably decided below the hearing level, responsibility for conducting administrative review is the same under both the fee agreement and the fee petition processes. In the Program Service Centers the reviewer is the Special Case Review Analyst, Security and Integrity Section. In the Office of Disability Operations the reviewer is the Disability Specialist, Division of Appealed Claims, and in the Office of International Operations the reviewer is the Reconsideration Reviewer.

7. Can a CR request administrative review of the amount of the fee under the fee agreement?

If the CR is the decision maker, he or she may request reduction of the amount of the fee under the agreement but only when prima facie evidence shows:

• the representative did not represent the claimant's interest adequately; or
• the fee is clearly excessive in light of the services provided.

8. What information must the hearing offices (HOs) or Appeals Council retain in their files in the event a request for administrative review is filed?

The HOs and Appeals Council must keep a copy of the following documents:
• the appointment of the representative;
• the fee agreement;
• the fee agreement determination; and
• the notice of the fee amount, if applicable.

When a request for administrative review is filed, the Regional Office, HO, or the Appeals Council must also keep a copy of the following documents:
• the request for administrative review;
• any development associated with the request for administrative review; and
• the determination made on administrative review.

9. Who has authority to conduct an administrative review of the disapproval of the fee agreement at the request for review level if the Deputy Chair, Appeals Council, was the decision maker?

The Chair, Appeals Council, is the reviewing official in such a situation.

10. Who has authority to conduct an administrative review of the amount of a fee if the ALJ or AAJ, as the decision maker, requests administrative review, as does the claimant and or representative?

The reviewing official in such a situation is the Regional Chief Administrative Law Judge (RCALJ) or Deputy Chair, Appeals Council, respectively. The RCALJ or Deputy Chair issues a single determination on all the issues raised in the requests for administrative review.

11. Regarding the above, if the reviewing official will not act on the decision maker's request because it was untimely, who then acts on the claimant's and or representative's request for administrative review?

The RCALJ or Deputy Chair, Appeals Council, acts on the requests. He or she issues a single determination resolving all the issues raised by the requests for administrative review.

12. Who has authority to conduct an administrative review of the fee amount requested by an ALJ who decided the case while in travel status?

Determining the authority to conduct administrative review requested by a visiting ALJ is the same as determining the authority to conduct administrative review in a fee petition case (see HALLEX I-1-250 A., Delegation of Authority). Therefore, the RCALJ in the Region where the case was heard has the authority to conduct the administrative review.

Administrative Review of the Disapproval of the Fee Agreement

13. What authority do we cite in a notice advising the parties that the determination is not subject to further review?

Sections 206(a) and 1631(d) of the Social Security Act, as amended, do not specifically provide for administrative review of the disapproval of a fee agreement. We decided that such review is appropriate. We will amend the regulations to provide for administrative review of a disapproval of a fee agreement. Until that time, do not include an authority citation in the notice.

14. If an ALJ or AAJ disapproves a fee agreement because the representative did not sign it, can the representative request administrative review of the disapproval and submit a signed fee agreement?

The reviewing official must base the determination on administrative review on whether the fee agreement met the conditions of the fee agreement process and none of the exceptions applied at the time the ALJ or AAJ issued the favorable decision or, if later, at the time the ALJ or AAJ disapproved the fee agreement. Therefore, in the above scenario, although the representative has a right to request administrative review, the reviewing official will not reverse the fee agreement determination. The fee agreement did not meet a condition of the fee agreement process at the time the ALJ or AAJ issued the decision.

15. If the reviewing official affirms the disapproval of a fee agreement, should he or she remind the representative that the representative must request approval of any fee he or she wants to collect?

Yes.

Administrative Review of the Amount of the Fee Under the Fee Agreement

16. Will we modify a fee solely because an affected auxiliary objects to his or her sharing in the payment of the fee?

No. SSA does not modify a fee solely because an affected auxiliary considers unfair his or her sharing in payment of the approved fee (see Hopkins v. Cohen, 390 U.S. 530 (1968), reproduced as Social Security Ruling 68-61c (C.E. 1968)).

17. When reviewing the amount of the fee under the terms of a properly approved agreement, SSA assumes that the past-due benefits amount on which the fee is based was correctly calculated; however, if the requester has questioned or disagreed with the calculation of the amount of the past-due benefits and the central or sole issue on administrative review is this calculation, what action is appropriate?

When the requester (claimant, affected auxiliary, or representative) has disagreed with the amount of the past-due benefits on which the fee under the agreement is based, the reviewing official must also consider the request for administrative review an appeal, or a request to reopen and revise, the determination or decision of the past-due benefits amount.

Example: The representative timely requested administrative review. She stated that SSA had incorrectly computed the title II past-due benefits amount, and, therefore, the fee under the agreement, as worker's compensation offset was incorrectly applied. The reviewing official referred her request, filed during the appeals period, to the PC, who subsequently issued a reconsideration determination affirming the initial determination of the past-due benefits. Upon return of the claim(s) file, the reviewing official proceeded with the administrative review.

18. When one of the parties has requested administrative review of the amount of the fee, when will the reviewing official set a "reasonable fee" in a fee agreement case?

When the fee agreement meets the conditions for approval and is not otherwise excepted, the reviewing official will defer to the written fee agreement as the expression of the intentions of the parties. Generally, parties expect to be held to the terms of their agreement. However, the reviewing official will intervene and set a reasonable fee, either affirming, lowering, or raising the original fee, when, through a request for administrative review:

• the claimant, an affected auxiliary, or the representative expresses dissatisfaction with the fee that results under the agreement; or

• the decision maker has presented prima facie evidence showing that either the representative did not represent the claimant's interest adequately or the fee is clearly excessive for the services provided.

The review mechanism enables the Secretary to redress situations in which the fee set under the agreement does not represent reasonable compensation for the services provided in the case. It does not compel changes to the fee set under the agreement. (See VIII. H.)

19. Section IV. B. 2. indicates that a decision maker must present prima facie evidence that the representative did not represent the claimant's interest adequately or the fee is clearly excessive in light of the services provided in order to have the fee amount modified. What evidence must

the claimant, affected auxiliary, or representative, requesting administrative review, present to have the amount of the fee modified?

If a claimant, affected auxiliary, or representative expresses dissatisfaction with the amount of a fee by filing a timely request for administrative review, the reviewing official must decide whether the fee determined under the fee agreement process reasonably reflects the value of the services provided.

20. If a representative requests review of the fee amount under an agreement and the ALJ decides to increase the fee amount, can the ALJ authorize more than $5,000?

No. Currently, ALJs are delegated the authority to approve a fee "up to and including $5,000" (HALLEX I-1-201 A. 2.). The fee agreement process did not change this policy. Therefore, if the ALJ believes a fee in excess of $5,000 is reasonable, the ALJ must refer the request, with a recommendation, to the RCALJ.

Scheine Fusco Brandenstein & Rada, P.C.
ATTORNEYS AT LAW

SOCIAL SECURITY DISABILITY DEPARTMENT
180 FROEHLICH FARM BLVD., PO BOX 307, WOODBURY, NY 11797-0307
516-496-0100 • 212-233-1457 • FAX:516-496-2316

OTHER OFFICES: MANHATTAN, BRONX, HEMPSTEAD, COMMACK, MEDFORD

Expedited Attorney Fee retainer agreement

The parties, in view of the recent amendments to the Social Security Act, particularly as pertain to attorneys fees, hereby agree as follows:

1. Attorney agrees to represent claimant through the hearing level, under the expedited attorney fee process. If further proceedings are necessary the expedited attorney fee process will not apply unless a further retainer agreement under the expedited process is completed.

2. Through the hearing level of adjudication, Attorney agrees to represent claimant on a contingency fee basis and will accept the lesser of 25% of all retroactive benefits on all beneficiaries on the wage earner's account who become entitled to payments by reason of any successful result in this Social Security Disability Claim or $4000.00 whichever is less.

3. In the event of a favorable decision at the hearing level, the Attorney will not be required to submit an itemized fee petition, but instead will utilize the expedited attorney fee process provided by the amended section 206 (a) of the Social Security Act 42 USC 406 (a).

4. Client is responsible for all costs, expenses and disbursements incurred in the prosecution of this claim.

5. A copy of this agreement shall be filed with the Office of Hearings and Appeals pursuant to 42 USC 406(a) as amended, which provides that the Social Security Administration be notified of such agreement prior to the issuance of a favorable decision.

Social Security Number upon which claim is based:	Date of this Retainer:
Print Client Name:	Client Signature:
Print Attorney Name:	Attorney Signature:

SS-RET-1 T:\RETAINER\EXPEDITE.HV2

Scheine Fusco Brandenstein & Rada, P.C.
Attorneys at Law

SOCIAL SECURITY DISABILITY DEPARTMENT
180 FROEHLICH FARM BLVD., PO BOX 307, WOODBURY, NY 11797-0307
516-496-0100 • 212-233-1457 • FAX: 516-496-2316

OTHER OFFICES: MANHATTAN, BRONX, HEMPSTEAD, COMMACK, MEDFORD

Expedited Attorney Fee Agreement Pursuant to 42 U.S.C. 406 (a) Valid through Reconsideration only

The parties, in view of the recent amendments to the Social Security Act, particularly as pertain to attorneys fees, hereby revise and amend their retainer agreement as follows:

1. Attorney agrees to represent claimant through the ***RECONSIDERATION*** level. If further proceedings are necessary beyond the RECONSIDERATION level, the underlying retainer agreement dated_______________ will apply unless a further expedited retainer agreement will be used. This shall be at the option of the attorney.

2. Attorney agrees to represent claimant through the reconsideration level on a contingency fee basis and will accept as his/her fee the lesser of (a) 25% of all retroactive benefits on all beneficiaries on the wage earner's account who become entitled to payments by reason of any successful result in this Social Security Disability Claim or (b) $4000.00 maximum.

3. Attorney will not be required to submit an itemized fee petition, but instead will utilize the expedited attorney fee process provided by the amended section 206 (a) of the Social Security Act 42 USC 406 (a).

4. All other provisions, as to client's responsibility for all costs, expenses and disbursements incurred in the prosecution of this claim, remain in effect, as set forth in the underlying retainer agreement dated:

_______________________________.

5. A copy of this agreement shall be filed with the Social Security Admnistration and a copy shall be filed with the Social Security District Office pursuant to 42 USC 406(a) as amended, which provides that the Social Security Administration be notified of such agreement prior to the issuance of a favorable decision.

Dated: ___________________________

Social Security Number upon which claim is based:

____

Print Name of Client:___________________

Client's signature:____________________

Print Name of Attorney: ________________

Attorney's signature:___________________

SFBR # ______________

Dale WELLS, William Hlywa, Plaintiffs-Appellants,
v.
Louis W. SULLIVAN, M.D., Secretary of Health and Human Services, Defendant-Appellee,
Appeal of John S. HOGG.
Nos. 1034, 1035, Dockets 89-6244, 89-6246.
United States Court of Appeals,
Second Circuit.
Argued March 19, 1990.
Decided June 29, 1990.

OPINION
LEAD GEORGE C. PRATT, Circuit Judge:
For the second time these two social security cases are on appeal on issues of attorney's fees. In the first appeal, Wells v. Bowen, 855 F.2d 37 (2d Cir.1988) (Wells I), we held that an attorney may apply for and be awarded fees under both the Equal Access to Justice Act (EAJA), 28 U.S.C. § 2412(d), and the Social Security Act (SSA), 42 U.S.C. § 406(b), and we remanded for a determination of a reasonable fee under § 406(b). Now, John S. Hogg, plaintiffs' attorney, appeals from a further order of the United States District Court for the Northern District of New York, Howard G. Munson, Chief Judge, that fixed the amounts of attorney's fees to be allowed. Hogg claims that the awards were unreasonable because they were based on lodestar calculations made by the district court in derogation of contingent fee arrangements with his clients.

In Wells I, decided before the Supreme Court's recent opinion in Venegas v. Mitchell, 495 U.S. 82, 110 S.Ct. 1679, 109 L.Ed.2d 74 (1990), we mentioned in passing that we did not "believe that the contingency percentage embodied in any given attorney-client contract should be treated by the court as presumptively 'reasonable' for purposes of 42 U.S.C. § 406(b)." 855 F.2d at 45. In doing so, however, we did not examine in any detail the problems surrounding contingent fee agreements in relation to social security fee awards. Now, prompted by the Supreme Court's analysis in Venegas, and the well reasoned positions that the sixth and seventh circuits have adopted, see McGuire v. Sullivan, 873 F.2d 974 (7th Cir.1989); Rodriguez v. Bowen, 865 F.2d 739 (6th Cir.1989), we address the problem in greater detail.

BACKGROUND

After attorney Hogg had litigated and won past due payments for Dale Wells and William Hlywa, who had been wrongly denied benefits by the Social Security Administration, he applied for attorney's fees under the EAJA and also under the SSA. Initially, the district court refused to award "dual fees" and granted attorney's fees only under the EAJA. On the earlier appeal, we held that awards under both statutes are permitted, provided the attorney retains only the larger award and remits the smaller to the claimant, and we remanded the cases for determination of the fees to be awarded under the SSA. Wells I, 855 F.2d at 48.

[WELLS V SULLIVAN 907 F.2d 367(1990)][On remand, Hogg submitted requests for fees based on his contingent fee agreements with the claimants. He requested $4,725.00, 14% of the past due benefits won for Wells, and $7,244.75, 25% of the past due benefits won for Hlywa. Neither claimant objected to the fee requests. Nevertheless, the district court ignored the contingency agreements, and instead awarded fees according to its own determination based on lodestar calculations. It fixed Hogg's fee at $3,843.45 in Wells's case, and $5,756.40 in Hlywa's case. Hogg now appeals these fee awards on the grounds that the district court erred by ignoring the contingent fee arrangements, by incorrectly applying the lodestar method, and by setting an unreasonably low enhancement rate. Finding his arguments convincing on the first ground, we need not address the other two.

DISCUSSION

SSA provides that a court may award an attorney who has represented a successful claimant in a social security case "a reasonable fee * * * not in excess of 25% of the total of the past due benefits to which the claimant is entitled." 42 U.S.C. § 406(b). Section 406(b) does not prohibit contingent fee agreements; at the same time, it gives no guidance as to how a court should treat them in determining a "reasonable fee". Until recently, case law also has provided us with little guidance on the subject. Now, however, relying on Venegas, on the insights provided by the sixth and seventh circuits, and on certain policy considerations, we feel we can define more fully how contingent fee arrangements in successful social security cases should be treated.

A. Venegas v. Mitchell and § 406(b)

In Venegas, a prevailing civil rights plaintiff sought to prevent his former attorney from collecting a contingent fee in an amount substantially larger than the fee awarded for the case by the district court under 42 U.S.C. § 1988. 495 U.S. 82, 110 S.Ct. 1679, 109 L.Ed.2d 74 (1990). Venegas argued that the § 1988 fee award, to be paid by the defendant, precluded his attorney from collecting a larger fee from him under their private contingency agreement.

The Court held, however, that § 1988 does not invalidate contingent fee agreements between successful civil rights plaintiffs and their attorneys. It examined the language, purpose, and intent of § 1988 and found that a civil rights plaintiff was entitled to enter into a contingent fee arrangement with his attorney even though § 1988 contemplated that the district court would award a reasonable fee, and even though the contingent fee exceeded the court's award. Id. at 1683.

In upholding the validity of the private agreement the Court placed great importance upon freely negotiated contracts and indicated that, absent fraud or overreaching, courts must enforce such private contingency fee agreements, which are, after all, embodiments of the intentions and wishes of the parties. See id. at 1683-84. Three points of the Court's analysis are significant. First, although the language of § 1988 provides that a "court * * * may allow the prevailing party * * * a reasonable attorney's fee" to be paid by the defendant, the Court found that there was nothing "on its face [to] prevent the plaintiff from promising an attorney a percentage" of the judgment. Id. at 1682.

Second, the purpose of § 1988 fees is to "enable civil rights plaintiffs to employ reasonably competent lawyers without cost to themselves if they prevail." Id. Depriving plaintiffs of the option of entering contingent fee agreements "would not further § 1988's general purpose of enabling such plaintiffs * * * to secure competent counsel" or counsel of their choice in vindicating important constitutional rights. Id. at 1684.

Finally, according to the Court, the legislative history of § 1988 indicates that there was no intent to abrogate the freedom of a civil rights plaintiff to enter a fee contract. Attorney's fees are awarded to a prevailing plaintiff under § 1988 as part of the costs of the action, and this is done even though the plaintiff may have had the financial resources to pay an attorney. "We have [always] therefore accepted, at least implicitly,[WELLS V SULLIVAN 907 F.2d 367(1990)] that statutory awards of fees can coexist with private fee arrangements." Id. at 1683. Further, the Court pointed out, because it is the plaintiff's right to settle, waive, or negotiate the underlying civil rights cause of action with his opponent, it would be inconsistent to find that a plaintiff cannot do the same with his lawyer in regard to fees. Otherwise, plaintiffs would be placed "in the peculiar position of being more free to negotiate with their adversaries than with their own attorneys." Id.

In sum, according to the Court, contingent fee arrangements are not prohibited by § 1988 but coexist with it and further its purpose of ensuring adequate representation for civil rights plaintiffs. See id. at 1684.

This analysis applies equally well to § 406(b), and, we believe, justifies a similar result. First, we consider the language of the statute. Section 406(b) is not, of course, a fee-shifting statute, as is § 1988. It is directed not at the fee to be paid by the defendant to the plaintiff, but at the fee to be paid by the plaintiff to his own attorney, and the section permits the court to determine the amount of "a reasonable fee for * * * representation", provided the amount does not exceed 25% of the past due benefits. 42 U.S.C. § 406(b)(1). Just as with § 1988, however, nothing on the face of this statute prevents the plaintiff from promising the attorney a percentage. Second, the purpose of § 1988 in civil rights cases--to enable plaintiffs to obtain competent representation by ensuring adequate compensation to their attorneys--is implicitly recognized as a valid factor in social security cases; § 406(b) seeks only to regulate the contingent fees favorably to the plaintiff by limiting the contingency to 25%, and favorably to the attorney by permitting payment directly from the government out of the plaintiff's award. See Sen.Rep. No. 404, 1965 U.S.Code Cong. & Ad.News, 1943, 2062. Neither the statute itself nor its legislative history displays any intent to invalidate all contingent fee arrangements. On the contrary, congress intended only to limit such agreements to a maximum of 25%. Further, to deny social security claimants the option of entering contingent fee arrangements would tend to defeat the general remedial purpose of the statute by unnecessarily restricting claimants' options in securing adequate counsel or counsel of their choice. Thus, just as a civil rights plaintiff may, without offending the purpose of § 1988, contract to pay his attorney more than the amount of the fee shifted to the defendant, so a social security plaintiff may normally contract up to the maximum allowed by statute, without offending § 406(b).

Finally, the Court's concern for a client's freedom to contract with his own attorney in the § 1988 context carries corresponding weight in social security cases. As in § 1988 situations, the underlying social security claim in § 406(b) cases belongs to the claimant, who is free to waive or assert it; yet, unless he is able to enter a contingent fee agreement, he would not be free to negotiate a fee with his attorney within the statutory limit. Thus, as the Court held under § 1988, it would be inconsistent to allow claimants more power to determine their dealings with their adversary, the Social Security Administration, than they have with their own attorneys.
We conclude, therefore, that § 406(b) does not invalidate all contingent fee arrangements--it merely sets their upper limit--and because such arrangements effectuate congress's objective of securing adequate representation for social security claimants, a requested fee based on a contingent fee arrangement should be enforced unless the court finds it to be unreasonable.

B. Lessons from Other Circuits

We can benefit from the wisdom of the sixth and seventh circuits which have extensively analyzed the problem of contingent fees in social security cases. See McGuire v. Sullivan, 873 F.2d 974 (7th Cir.1989); Rodriguez v. Bowen, 865 F.2d 739 (6th Cir.1989); In re Horenstein, 810 F.2d 73 (6th Cir.1986); McKittrick v. Gardner, 378 F.2d 872 (7th Cir.1967). From their discussions, a few important principles can be discerned.

First, enhancements for the risk of nonpayment are appropriate considerations [WELLS V SULLIVAN 907 F.2d 367(1990)], in determining § 406(b) fees. See, e.g., McKittrick, 378 F.2d at 875 (contingency enhancement is of highest importance under § 406(b) in availability of adequate representation). In the absence of a fixed-fee agreement, payment for an attorney in a social security case is inevitably uncertain, and any reasonable fee award must take account of that risk. Indeed, we, too, have recognized that contingency risks are "necessary factors" in determining reasonable fees under § 406(b). Wells I, 855 F.2d at 45.

Second, the traditional lodestar method, borrowed from fee-shifting contexts, is not appropriate for evaluating a reasonable fee to be paid by the client in a social security case where there is a contingent fee agreement. See McGuire, 873 F.2d at 980; Rodriguez, 865 F.2d at 743-44. In fee-shifting cases, courts must carefully scrutinize the awards to ensure they are reasonable not only to the plaintiff who benefits, but also to the defendant who must pay the fee. Thus, in determining a "reasonable fee" to be shifted to the defendant, courts have looked to the lodestar method, which necessarily emphasizes the calculation of a reasonable rate of compensation for the number of hours reasonably worked. See Wells I, 855 F.2d at 43; see also, Blum v. Stenson, 465 U.S. 886, 898, 104 S.Ct. 1541, 1548, 79 L.Ed.2d 891 (1984); McGuire, 873 F.2d at 980.

However, since there is no shifting of fees under § 406(b), courts need not be Solomon-like arbiters of "reasonableness" between the opposing interests of prevailing plaintiffs and losing defendants. See McGuire, 873 F.2d at 979. Rather, because a successful social security claimant evaluates and pays his own attorney, a court's primary focus should be on the reasonableness of the contingency agreement in the context of the particular case; and the best indicator of the "reasonableness" of a contingency fee in a social security case is the contingency percentage actually negotiated between the attorney and client, not an hourly rate determined under lodestar calculations.

Third, because § 406(b) requires the district court to review the reasonableness of any requested fee, contingent fee agreements cannot simply be adopted as per se reasonable in all social security cases. Wells I, 855 F.2d at 45-46; see McGuire, 873 F.2d at 979. We must recognize, however, that a contingency agreement is the freely negotiated expression both of a claimant's willingness to pay more than a particular hourly rate to secure effective representation, and of an attorney's willingness to take the case despite the risk of nonpayment. See Rodriguez, 865 F.2d at 746; Wells I, 855 F.2d at 45. Therefore, we ought normally to give the same deference to these agreements as we would to any contract embodying the intent of the parties. See McGuire, 873 F.2d at 981; Rodriguez, 865 F.2d at 746.

Based on these principles, we hold that where there is a contingency fee agreement in a successful social security case, the district court's determination of a reasonable fee under § 406(b) must begin with the agreement, and the district court may reduce the amount called for by the contingency agreement only when it finds the amount to be unreasonable. McGuire, 873 F.2d at 981; see Rodriguez, 865 F.2d at 746.

C. Policy Considerations
This approach will assist social security claimants to obtain effective representation. Many claimants are indigent or are on low or fixed incomes and cannot afford to retain counsel at fixed hourly rates, see McKittrick, 378 F.2d at 875 ("Most of the disability claimants have no other resources for the payment of fees."), yet they are willing to pay a portion of any recovery they may receive in return for successful representation. Ignoring reasonable contingent fee agreements or automatically reducing them would impair claimants' ability to secure representation. See McGuire, 873 F.2d at 980.

Moreover, many attorneys are unwilling to accept the risk of nonpayment without a guaranteed contingency percentage of the recovery. See id. at 980; Wells I, 855 F.2d at 45; Coup v. Heckler, 834 F.2d 313, 325 (3d Cir.1987) ("Undue rigidity in limiting attorneys in contingent fee situations to hourly rates * * * may have that unfortunate[WELLS V SULLIVAN 907 F.2d 367(1990)] consequence."). Thus, accepting reasonable contingency agreements as the basis for a § 406(b) social security fee provides a critical incentive for able attorneys to practice in the social security field and increases the likelihood that a claimant can find an attorney sufficiently committed and skilled to litigate successfully against the government. See McGuire, 873 F.2d at 980.

This approach also relieves the courts, which "are sometimes spending almost as much time reviewing and setting fees as they are in dealing with the merits of the benefits determination."

Rodriguez, 865 F.2d at 746; see also Hensley v. Eckerhart, 461 U.S. 424, 437, 103 S.Ct. 1933, 1941, 76 L.Ed.2d 40 (1983) ("A request for attorney's fees should not result in a second major litigation."). In each case where the contingent fee is found to be reasonable, based on a general assessment of the fee in relation to the nature of the litigation, the need for complicated lodestar calculations, expert evidence, and protracted litigation vanishes.

Finally, accepting reasonable contingency agreements substantially reduces the anomalous role of the Social Security Administration in first denying benefits to a claimant, and then after losing the case, posing as a protector of the plaintiff, but spending more time and money in order to reduce the fees to be paid to the claimant's attorney. The Social Security Administration may make fee recommendations, but it is prevented from routinely opposing requested fees based on contingency agreements. See Wells I, 855 F.2d at 47.

D. Reasonable Contingency Agreements and Hogg's Fees

When a contingent fee has been agreed to by the parties, the district court must determine whether the fee is reasonable. It must give due deference to the intent of the parties, but it ought not blindly approve every fee request made pursuant to a contingent agreement. While the court need not make mathematical calculations, it should, of course, determine whether the contingency percentage is within the 25% cap; it should also consider whether there has been fraud or overreaching in making the agreement, and whether the requested amount is so large as to be a windfall to the attorney. See McGuire, 873 F.2d at 981; Rodriguez, 865 F.2d at 746; see also Wells I, 855 F.2d at 43-44. Should the district court find that the agreement provides an unreasonable fee under the circumstances, the court may reduce the fee provided it states the reasons for and the amounts of the deductions. See Wells I, 855 F.2d at 43.

In this case, based on the contingent fee arrangements with his clients, Hogg requested the maximum fee of 25% of the total past due benefits won for Hlywa, and a fee of 14% of the past due benefits won for Wells. The district court did not determine that the contingent fees were unreasonable, yet it awarded amounts less than those agreed to. We now reverse the awards and remand these cases to the district court for an appropriate determination of the reasonableness of the fees giving proper deference to the agreements of the parties.

Reversed and remanded.

Richard MAIER, Plaintiff,

v.

Kenneth S. APFEL, Commissioner of Social Security, Defendant.

No. 95 Civ. 9264(JGK).

United States District Court, S.D. New York.

July 17, 1998.

Charles E. Binder, Richard Nager, Binder and Binder, New York City, for plaintiff.

Mary Jo White, United States Attorney, for the Southern District of New York by Susan D. Baird, Assistant United States Attorney, New York City, for defendant.

OPINION AND ORDER

KOELTL, J.

In an Opinion and Order dated September 5, 1997, this Court determined that the decision of the Commissioner of Social Security[1] ("Commissioner") denying Social Security Disability Benefits to the plaintiff, Richard Maier, was not supported by substantial evidence. See Maier v. Chater, No. 95 Civ. 9264, 1997 WL 570938, at *9 (S.D.N.Y. Sept.5, 1997). The Court remanded the case to the Commissioner for the calculation and payment of benefits.

The plaintiff's counsel has now filed a motion for attorney's fees under both: (1) the Equal Access to Justice Act ("EAJA"), 28 U.S.C. § 2412(d), and (2) the Social Security Act, 42 U.S.C. § 406(b).

First, the plaintiff's counsel seeks $5,485.36 under the Equal Access to Justice Act. That fee is calculated at the rate of $138.87 per hour for 39.5 hours of time. The Commissioner does not oppose that application and concedes that it is reasonable. That application is granted.

The plaintiff's counsel also seeks an award of 25% of the past due benefits that have been awarded to the plaintiff. This award is sought on the basis of a contingency agreement between plaintiff and the plaintiff's counsel. The plaintiff and his counsel entered into such an agreement prior to the plaintiff's application for disability benefits, and again after the denial of those benefits by the Commissioner and prior to the institution of the action for review of the Administrative Law Judge's decision in this Court. The agreements provided in substantial part that the plaintiff would pay to his counsel 25% of the past due benefits awarded. While the plaintiff agreed to pay $170 in costs, the plaintiff would not have to pay fees after the District Court litigation if the plaintiff was unsuccessful in recovering past due benefits.

The Commissioner has calculated that 25% of the amount of past due benefits in this case amounts to $17,317.50. The parties agree that the plaintiff is entitled to the

1. On September 29, 1997, Kenneth S. Apfel was sworn in as Commissioner of Social Security. Pursuant to Rule 25(d) of the Federal Rules of Civil Procedure, he is automatically substituted as the defendant in this case.

lesser award under the EAJA or the Social Security Act so that his counsel would not be paid both awards. See Wells v. Bowen, 855 F.2d 37, 42 (2d Cir.1988) ("Wells I"). The Commissioner points out that, given the number of hours expended by the plaintiff's counsel, the award under the Social Security Act would amount to an hourly fee of $438.42 which the Commissioner describes as excessive and unreasonable. The Commissioner therefore objects to an award of $17,317.50 as an unreasonable deduction from the past due benefits otherwise due the plaintiff.

For the reasons explained below, the application for attorney's fees under the Social Security Act in the amount of 25 of past due benefits, or $17,317.50, is approved. I.

The Social Security Act provides that a court may award an attorney who has represented a successful claimant in a social security case "a reasonable fee . . . not in excess of 25 percent of the total of the past-due benefits to which the claimant is entitled. . . ." 42 U.S.C. § 406(b). The Court of Appeals for the Second Circuit has explained the standards to be applied to a request for attorney's fees under the Social Security Act based on a contingent fee agreement. See Wells v. Sullivan, 907 F.2d 367 (2d Cir.1990) ("Wells II"). In Wells II, the Court of Appeals noted that the lodestar method of calculating a fee based on the hours expended and reasonable rates for those hours "is not appropriate for evaluating a reasonable fee to be paid by the client in a social security case where there is a contingent fee agreement." Wells II, 907 F.2d at 371. The Court of Appeals further explained:

> [S]ince there is no shifting of fees under § 406(b), courts need not be Solomon-like arbiters of "reasonableness" between the opposing interests of prevailing plaintiffs and losing defendants. . . . Rather, because a successful social security claimant evaluates and pays his own attorney, a court's primary focus should be on the reasonableness of the contingency agreement in the context of a particular case; and the best indicator of the "reasonableness" of a contingency fee in a social security case is the contingency percentage actually negotiated between the attorney and client, not an hourly rate determined under lodestar calculations.

Wells II, 907 F.2d at 371. The Court of Appeals then set forth what a Court should consider when determining whether a fee is reasonable:

> [The Court] must give due deference to the intent of the parties, but it ought not blindly approve every fee request made pursuant to a contingent agreement. While the court need not make mathematical calculations, it should, of course, determine whether the contingency percentage is within the 25% cap; it should also consider whether there has been fraud or overreaching in making the agreement, and whether the requested amount is so large as to be a windfall to the attorney.

Id. at 372.

Applying these standards in this case, the requested fee is reasonable and should be awarded. Since the contingent fee agreement called for a fee of 25% if the plaintiff was successful in his appeal, the fee is plainly within the 25% cap in the statute. Further, the Commissioner does not assert that there was any fraud or overreaching in this case and there is no basis for such an allegation. The fee agreement was entered into at the outset of the application process when there was no guarantee as to how the application would be decided. The agreement was reaffirmed after the application had been denied in the administrative proceedings and prior to the filing of the case in this Court, when the plaintiff faced the very difficult process of overturning a decision by an Administrative Law Judge which was required to be affirmed if there was substantial evidence to support it. In addition, the plaintiff was an educated former police officer. Indeed, in the course of this litigation over fees the plaintiff submitted a letter reaffirming his 25% contingency fee agreement with his counsel and expressing his thanks and appreciation to his counsel on the successful prosecution of his appeal.

Finally, it cannot be said that the award is so large as to constitute a windfall for the plaintiff's counsel. The contingent fee in this case reflected the substantial risk involved in the case. In addition to the deferential standard of review that the plaintiff had to overcome, the plaintiff was faced with a substantial administrative record to present to the Court. This included the records of three treating physicians and an independent medical consultant. The case was complex and the amount of time that was expended was, from the Court's observation, spent very efficiently and understated the amount of hours that could reasonably have been spent on the case. The plaintiff's counsel should not be penalized for working efficiently on the case as compared to other attorneys who might have taken longer to perform the same work and whose corresponding hourly rate would be lower due to their lack of experience and productivity. The Commissioner also notes that an associate rather than a partner at Binder & Binder worked the majority of the hours that attorneys at the firm spent on the case. While the Commissioner appears to concede the extensive relevant experience of the partner in charge of this case, he questions the associate's experience. However, the work was efficiently done because it was supervised by the partner and the work product produced by the attorneys together was persuasive and economically produced.

In sum, the plaintiff's counsel reached a successful result in a difficult case in which it could have received nothing. The plaintiff freely negotiated the contract and remains satisfied with that contract even in the face of paying this award to his counsel. Accordingly, having independently reviewed the fees, the Court finds them reasonable. See also Reyes v. Secretary of Health and Human Servs., 807 F.Supp. 293, 297 (S.D.N.Y.1992); James. v. Sullivan, No. CIV-88-1320E, 1990 WL 139326 (W.D.N.Y. Sept.17, 1990).

CONCLUSION

1. The plaintiff's motion for attorney's fees under the EAJA is granted in the amount of $5,485.36 to be paid by the Government to the plaintiff.

2. The plaintiff's motion for attorney's fees under the Social Security Act is granted in the amount of $17,317.50 to be paid to the plaintiff's attorneys from the amount of the past due benefits otherwise due to the plaintiff.

SO ORDERED.

Sample Fee Petition at Administrative Level

- Cover Letter to ALJ
- Cover Letter to Claimant
- SSA 1560
- Itemization

Scheine, Fusco, Brandenstein & Rada, P.C.
ATTORNEYS AT LAW

SSD-FILE

SOCIAL SECURITY DISABILITY DEPARTMENT
180 FROEHLICH FARM BLVD., PO BOX 307, WOODBURY, NY 11797-0307
516-496-0100 • 212-233-1457 • FAX:516-496-2316

OTHER OFFICES: MANHATTAN, BRONX, HEMPSTEAD, COMMACK, MEDFORD

October 27, 1995

Honorable Joyce Krutick Barlow
U.S. Administrative Law Judge
Office of Hearings and Appeals
Social Security Administration
18 Rector Street, 10th Floor
Newark, NJ 07102

Re: Joseph F.

Dear Judge Barlow:

Enclosed for your examination and adjudication are:

1. Copies of our fee petition requesting your approval of a fee in the amount of $5,000.00 for our services rendered to the above-named claimant.
2. A copy of our explanatory cover letter to the claimant.

Assuming our fee request is approved, a balance of $704.00 from the total withholding of $5,704.00 will be due the claimant.

Thank you for your courtesy herein.

Respectfully submitted,

SCHEINE, FUSCO, BRANDENSTEIN & RADA, P.C.

By:______________________________
JOHN ANTONOWICZ, ESQ.

JA/ar
encs.
cc: client

Scheine Fusco Brandenstein & Rada, P.C.
Attorneys at Law

SSD-FILE

SOCIAL SECURITY DISABILITY DEPARTMENT
180 FROEHLICH FARM BLVD., PO BOX 307, WOODBURY, NY 11797-0307
516-496-0100 • 212-233-1457 • FAX:516-496-2316

OTHER OFFICES: MANHATTAN, BRONX, HEMPSTEAD, COMMACK, MEDFORD

October 27, 1995

Re: Your Social Security Case
Attorneys Fee Petition
SFBR#: S95-0092/S5C

Dear Mr. F

Enclosed please find: (1) A copy of our attorneys fee petition, and (2) a copy of our accompanying letter to the Honorable Joyce Krutick Barlow, U.S. Administrative Law Judge.

We are requesting approval of an attorneys fee in the amount of $5,000.00 for professional services rendered in connection with your claim for Social Security Disability Benefits.

You have already, no doubt, received and reviewed your Social Security Notice of Award dated August 27, 1995 and Notices of Award outlining your family member's benefits dated August 27, 1995. According to the information received from the Social Security Administration, there has been withheld the sum of $5,704.00 from past due benefits on your account, in anticipation of direct payment of the attorney fee.

Because our fee request does not exceed the amount already withheld, it will not be necessary for you to pay us any money directly out of your own pocket towards attorneys fees. In the event approval is given to the amount we have requested, the Social Security Administration will send the fee to us directly, barring any inadvertent errors.

Since the fee we have requested is less than the total amount withheld, and assuming Social Security approves the fee in the amount we have requested, you can expect to receive a refund of the difference between the total attorney fee withholding of $5,704.00, and the actual amount requested, $5,000.00. This refund will be in the amount of $704.00, and will be paid to you by the Social Security Administration at the same time it sends us our check for the approved fee. Please understand that <u>we</u> do not send you this refund, Social Security does, and you will not receive it until the Agency gets around to sending out these checks.

The fee request does not include case expenses or disbursements.

Please bear in mind that the fee we have requested is not necessarily binding upon the Administrative Law Judge, who will make an independent evaluation of our services and approve what is believed to be a reasonable fee. In the event we believe the fee fixed does not reasonably compensate us for the services rendered, the law does give us the right to request an increment by filing an application with the Chief Administrative Law Judge. Should you desire to comment about the fee we have requested, you may write to Judge Joyce Krutick Barlow within 20 days of this letter. Please send a copy of any comments to this office.

We thought we should advise you that in the event Social Security reduces the fee to an amount less than an attorney has requested, they will immediately refund to the claimant all of the remaining retroactive benefits. Then if the attorney decides to appeal the fee and Social Security increases it, Social Security directs the claimant to pay the increase. Therefore, when you receive the fee authorization, if you note a reduction in the fee, you should put aside the difference between the amount approved and the amount originally requested by this office when you get your withholding refunded by Social Security.

We will let you know whether or not we intend to appeal any reduction in the attorneys' fee within 30 days of our receipt of an authorization. It is necessary that we advise you of this because unfortunately it has become increasingly necessary to file appeals of attorney fee authorizations which have not kept pace with the increases in the cost of doing business. We thought you would rather know this in advance than be put into a position where you had to pay out moneys which you had already earmarked for other expenses.

We are pleased that your claim was favorably resolved. It was the personal pleasure of the undersigned to have participated in your case. If there are any questions, please contact this office.

Very truly yours,

SCHEINE, FUSCO, BRANDENSTEIN & RADA, P.C.

By:____________________________
JOHN ANTONOWICZ, ESQ.

encs.: copy of ltr. to ALJ
SSA 1560
fee petition
cc: Judge Barlow

PETITION TO OBTAIN APPROVAL OF A FEE FOR REPRESENTING A CLAIMANT BEFORE THE SOCIAL SECURITY ADMINISTRATION

IMPORTANT INFORMATION ON REVERSE SIDE

PAPERWORK/PRIVACY ACT NOTICE: Your response to this request is voluntary, but the Social Security Administration may not approve any fee unless it receives the information this form requests. The Administration will use the information to determine a fair value for services you rendered to the claimant named below, as provided in section 206 of the Social Security Act (42 U.S.C. 406).

I request approval to charge a fee of → Fee $ 5000.00 (Show the dollar amount)

for services performed as the representative of → Mr. Mrs. Ms. Joseph F.

My Services Began: 2 / 10 / 95 (Month Day Year)

Type(s) of claim(s): Title II DIB

My Services Ended: 10 / 27 / 95

Enter the name and the Social Security number of the person on whose Social Security record the claim is based.
Joseph F xxx / xx / xxxx

1.	Itemize on a separate page or pages the services you rendered before the Social Security Administration (SSA). List each meeting, conference, item of correspondence, telephone call, and other activity in which you engaged, such as research, preparation of a brief, attendance at a hearing, travel, etc., related to your services as representative in this case. Attach to this petition the list showing the dates, the descriptions of each service, the actual time spent in each, and the total hours.		
2.	Have you and your client entered into a fee agreement for services before SSA? If "yes," please specify the amount on which you agreed, or attach a copy of the agreement to this petition. 25% of retro or ☐ See attached	☒ YES	☐ NO
3.	(a) Have you received, or do you expect to receive, any payment toward your fee from any source other than from funds which SSA may be withholding for fee payment?	☐ YES	☒ NO
	(b) Do you currently hold in a trust or escrow account any amount of money you received toward payment of your fee?	☐ YES	☒ NO
	If "yes" to either or both of the above, please specify the source(s) and the amount(s). Source: ______ $ ______ Source: ______ $ ______ **Note:** If you receive payment(s) after submitting this petition, but before SSA approves a fee, you have an affirmative duty to notify the SSA office to which you are sending this petition.		
4.	Have you received, or do you expect to receive, reimbursement for expenses you incurred? If "yes," please itemize your expenses and the amounts on a separate page.	☐ YES	☒ NO
5.	Did you render any services relating to this matter before any State or Federal court? If "yes," what fee did you or will you charge for services in connection with the court proceeding? $ ______ Please attach a copy of the court order if the court has approved a fee.	☐ YES	☒ NO

I certify that the information above, and on the attachment(s), is true and correct to the best of my knowledge and belief. I also certify that I have furnished a copy of this petition and the attachment(s) to the person(s) for whom I performed the services. I understand that failure to comply with Social Security laws and regulations pertaining to representation may result in suspension or disqualification from practice before SSA, the imposition of criminal penalties, or both.

Signature of Representative	Date	Address (include Zip Code)
[signature]	10-27-95	PO Box 307 Woodbury NY 11797

Firm with which associated, if any	Telephone No. and Area Code
SCHEINE, FUSCO, BRANDENSTEIN & RADA P.C.	(516) 481-4981

[Note: The following is optional. However, SSA can consider your fee petition more promptly if your client knows and already agrees with the amount you are requesting.]

I understand that I do not have to sign this petition or request. It is my right to disagree with the amount of the fee requested or any information given, and to ask more questions about the information given in this request (as explained on the reverse side of this form). I have marked my choice below.

☒ I agree with the $ 5000 fee which my representative is asking to charge and collect. By signing this request, I am not giving up my right to disagree later with the total fee amount the Social Security Administration authorizes my representative to charge and collect.

OR

☐ I do not agree with the requested fee or other information given here, or I need more time. I understand I must call, visit, or write to SSA within 20 days if I have questions or if I disagree with the fee requested or any information shown (as explained on the reverse sides of this form).

Signature of Claimant	Date
Joseph F.	10/30/95
Address (include Zip Code)	**Telephone No. and Area Code**
9 My Street, MYTOWN, NJ	201-XXX-XXXX

FILE COPY

FEE PETITION

CLIENT	LAW FIRM
JOSEPH F	SCHEINE, FUSCO, BRANDENSTEIN & RADA, P.C. 180 Froehlich Farm Boulevard P.O. Box 307 Woodbury, New York 11797-0307 Tel. (516) 496-0100

DATE	SERVICES RENDERED/WORK PERFORMED	HOURS
02/10/95	Initial telephone inquiry by claimant. Basic facts elicited, case screened. First mutually convenient appointment arranged for the client to visit us at our office location most convenient for client. Phone call from Glenn Faber, Esq., to advise of referral of the claimant to our office. Letter to client to confirm date, time, and place of appointment. Advised of information that would be needed at appointment and enclosed directions to our office.	1/2
02/23/95	Initial consultation with client and John Antonowicz, Esq., in our New York City office. Ascertained all salient details of claim; age, education; work experience; nature of medical impairment; subjective complaints; restrictions on daily and social activities; names, addresses, dates of treatment of all treating sources. Treatment rendered; medications and response thereto. Ascertained procedural status of the claim. Reviewed all papers claimant had brought. Explained meaning of "disability" for Social Security purposes; discussed claimant's burden of proof; medical vocational guidelines effect on the claim. Explained attorney fee provisions of the Social Security Act, and our own office policy and procedures. Had claimant execute all necessary forms to enable us to undertake representation; i.e., retainer agreement; medical releases, SSA-1696. Phone call to Newark Superintendent of Schools re: client's school records. Phone call to St. Cecilia's Roman Catholic Church re: obtaining copies of client's school records.	1 1/2

Date	Description	Time
02/27/95	File was assembled for client. File memorandum dictated and transcribed. File indexed and cross indexed, docket control card completed, appropriate recall dates input into manual docket control, and complete entry of file made.	3/4
03/04/95	Letter to Dr. Cary Glastein requesting a detailed medical report on claimant's condition. Explained in detail the requirements for Social Security purposes. Enclosed pertinent listings and RFC forms to be completed.	
	Letter to Dr. Peter Rutan requesting a detailed medical report on claimant's condition. Explained in detail the requirements for Social Security purposes. Enclosed pertinent listings and RFC forms to be completed.	
	Letter to Dr. John Huddad requesting copies of the claimant's records. Medical Authorization attached.	
	Letter to Dr. Howard Taylor requesting copies of the claimant's records. Medical Authorization attached.	
	Letter to SSA-OHA, advising of our representation of the claimant, enclosing form SSA-1696, and requesting copy of the claimant's PIA determination, earnings record.	1 3/4
03/06/95	Letter and authorization to New York State Workers' Compensation Board requesting access to claimant's file so we might extract medical evidence. We had not represented claimant in the past in his WC claim although he had just retained us to handle that case as well.	1/3
03/07/95	Letter to Glenn Faber, Esq., who had recommended client, thanking for recommendation, requesting any available medical evidence.	
	Copied client's original documents. Letter to client enclosing all original documents that were brought to initial consultation.	1/2

2

03/10/95	Receive and review correspondence, via fax, from Dr. Haddad, re: our request for evidence.	1/6
03/13/95	Receive and review correspondence from client re: medical status, enclosing check for anticipated medical expenses.	1/6
03/14/95	Letter to Dr. Haddad enclosing Physical Capacities forms to be completed.	
	Receive and review in detail evidence from Dr. Taylor.	1/2
03/16/95	Received postcard verification of proof of service of certified mail to SSA-DO. Filed same, annotating file copy of the original outgoing correspondence. Removed item from follow up diary.	1/12
03/20/95	Phone call from client re: case status and medical expenses.	1/6
03/22/95	Receive reply letter from Dr. Taylor regarding our request for client's medical data.	
	Letter to client regarding contents of reply from Dr. Taylor and advising procedure required to obtain information requested.	1/3
03/31/95	Letter to Glenn Faber, Esq., again requesting copies of any available medical evidence.	
	Follow up request to Dr. Glastein again requesting medical evidence on client's condition. Copies of prior correspondence attached.	
	Follow up request to Dr. Rutan again requesting medical evidence on client's condition. Copies of prior correspondence attached.	3/4
04/04/95	Receive and review in detail medical evidence from the file of Glenn Faber, Esq.	3/4
04/06/95	Phone call to the office of Dr. Rutan to discuss case, left message with service.	
	Phone call to the office of Dr. Glastein to discuss case, left message with service.	1/4

04/11/95	Receive and review in detail evidence from Dr. Taylor and Chilton Memorial Hospital.	
	Receive reply letter from Dr. Rutan regarding our request for client's medical data.	
	Letter to client regarding contents of reply from Dr. Rutan and advising procedure required to obtain information requested.	
	Letter to SSA-OHA enclosing medical evidence from Dr. Taylor & Chilton Memorial Hospital.	1
04/17/95	Receive and review correspondence from client with payment to cover cost of obtaining medical data (received check).	
	Letter with check to Dr. Rutan to cover cost of obtaining client's medical data.	
	Letter with check to Dr. Taylor to cover cost of obtaining client's medical data.	1/2
04/18/95	Letter to St. Cecilia's Roman Catholic Church, requesting copies of client's school records. Authorization attached.	
	Letter to SSA-OHA enclosing medical evidence from four treating sources: Dr. Rutan, Dr. Taylor, Dr. Gilson and Elmhurst Hospital.	
	Receive reply letter from Dr. Glastein (Shore Orthopaedic Group) regarding our request for client's medical data.	
	Letter to client regarding contents of reply from Dr. Glastein and advising procedure required to obtain information requested.	1 1/2
04/19/95	Receive and review in detail evidence from Dr. Santomauro.	
	Letter to SSA-OHA enclosing medical evidence from Dr. Santomauro (Sleeptech).	1/3
04/21/95	Review file, gave direction.	1/6
04/25/95	Receive and review correspondence from Dr. Haddad re: our request for evidence.	
	Receive and review in detail evidence from St. Cecilia's Roman Catholic Church.	1/3

4

04/26/95	Receive and review in detail evidence from Dr. Haddad.	
	Phone call to client to discuss medical expenses.	1/3
04/27/95	Letter with check to Shore Orthopaedic Group to cover cost of obtaining client's medical data.	
	Letter to client re: medical expenses.	
	Phone call from Office of Hearings and Appeals to schedule hearing date. Review diary, check for calendar conflicts, make sure prep date is arranged, if not already confirmed. Assure exhibits have been requested, if not already done so. Review file to see what medical evidence requests are still outstanding so that follow-up correspondence or call would be made. Allocate enough time for attorney to prepare for Hearing and enough time for attorney to handle Hearing, including reasonable delays, waiting, etc. Clear attorney calendar.	1
05/01/95	Letter to client advising of date of hearing and appointment for pre-hearing conference. Other details in preparation of hearing discussed.	
	Received postcard verification of proof of service of certified mail to SSA-OHA. Filed same, annotating file copy of the original outgoing correspondence. Removed item from follow up diary.	1/3
05/04/95	Receipt and review of Notice of Hearing. Examine Notice of Hearing for issues contained therein. Review diary for any conflicts. Review diary for ample time to prepare client and for attorney's own self-preparation. Enter into Hearing diary. (Manual and computerized).	1/4
05/05/95	Received postcard verification of proof of service of certified mail to SSA-OHA. Filed same, annotating file copy of the original outgoing correspondence. Removed item from follow up diary.	1/12

5

05/08/95	Receive and review in detail additional evidence from the file of Glenn Faber, Esq. Visit to Office of Hearings and Appeals located in Newark, New Jersey. Requested exhibit file. Examined and copied entire exhibit file. Travel time round trip. Assembly of a duplicate exhibit file and attached index tabs for easy access to exhibits at hearing. Attorney's complete reading, review and study of exhibit file and preparation of a detailed comprehensive abstract of the exhibit file. Prehearing review and study of all medical documentation, comparison of contents of our file to that of OHA's exhibit file. Select all medicals that OHA did not already have & prepare documentation for submission to Administrative Law Judge. Letter to the Honorable Joyce Barlow enclosing medical evidence from seven treating sources.	7 1/2
05/15/95	Receive and review in detail evidence from Dr. Glastein. Letter to Dr. Glastein thanking for report, requesting RFC chart to be completed and returned. Letter to Judge Barlow enclosing evidence from Dr. Glastein.	3/4
05/17/95	Visit to New York State Workers' Compensation Board located in Brooklyn. Requisitioned client's Workers' Compensation folder. Reviewed and examined Workers' Compensation file. Made copies of medical evidence on Board operated machine. Issued check to Workers' Compensation Board to pay for copies made on Board Machine on this file. (Including travel time two ways).	4 1/2

6

05/19/95	Phone call from client re: work activity. Review all medical evidence obtained from Workers' Compensation Board file. Letter to ALJ Barlow enclosing medical evidence from Riverview Medical Center. Letter to Dr. Noah Gilson requesting copies of the claimant's records and completion of RFC forms. Explained in detail the requirements for Social Security purposes and the client's medical history. Medical Authorization attached.	2
05/22/95	Receive and review in detail evidence from Dr. Rutan. Received postcard verification of proof of service of certified mail to SSA-OHA. Filed same, annotating file copy of the original outgoing correspondence. Removed item from follow up diary.	1/3
05/30/95	Receive reply letter from Dr. Gilson regarding our request for client's medical data. Letter to SSA-1696, advising this claim and requesting any medicals.	1/3
05/30/95	Prehearing conference with client. Reviewed the facts of the claim. Instructed client on how to give testimony, listening to questions, answering directly, etc. Explained hearing procedures. Discussed role of various participants at Social Security hearing.	2
05/31/95	Complete and thorough review of our entire file. Review of all meds received to date. Prehearing conference with client. Reviewed the facts of the claim. Instructed client on how to give testimony, listening to questions, answering directly, etc. Explained hearing procedures. Discussed role of various participants at SS hearing. Phone call to Dr. Glastein re: our request for evidence.	1 3/4

6/01/95	Travel to Hearing Office located in Newark, New Jersey. Prehearing review of exhibit file. Waiting time. Hearing before Administrative Law Judge Barlow. Travel from hearing location.	4
06/05/95	Received postcard verification of proof of service of certified mail to SSA-OHA. Filed same, annotating file copy of the original outgoing correspondence. Removed item from follow up diary.	1/12
06/09/95	Received postcard verification of proof of service of certified mail to Filed same, annotating file copy of the original outgoing correspondence. Removed item from follow up diary.	1/12
06/14/95	Receive and review in detail evidence from Dr. Glastein (RFC forms).	1/6
06/19/95	Received postcard verification of proof of service of certified mail to SSA-OHA. Filed same, annotating file copy of the original outgoing correspondence. Removed item from follow up diary.	1/12
06/30/95	Receive and review decision of ALJ Barlow granting benefits to client.	1/6
07/17/95	Careful analysis of decision and file. Detailed letter to client, four pages, explaining how SSA would process the decision. Explained date of onset, date of entitlement, benefits due, waiting period, Award Certificate, SSA processing time, Medicare rights, attorney fee process, future benefit rights and obligations.	
	Letter to ALJ Barlow constituting Notice of Intent to file a fee petition as required by regulations. Copies to DO, ODIO and client.	1
07/20/95	Receive and review in detail evidence from Dr. Gilson.	n/c
08/28/95	Receive and review from SSA-ODIO, award notices for claimant and all auxiliaries. Reviewed all pertinent dates and amounts contained therein including Workers' Compensation offset calculations.	1/3
	Compensible Hours (Time for which fee is sought)......................................	38

UNITED STATES DISTRICT COURT
EASTERN DISTRICT OF NEW YORK
--x

SS #

Plaintiff,

NOTICE OF MOTION
CV-95-2817 NG

-against-

KENNETH APFEL as
Commissioner of Social Security,

Defendant.
--x

PLEASE TAKE NOTICE that on April 2, 1999, at 9:30 AM, or as soon thereafter as counsel can be heard, that the undersigned, attorney for the plaintiff herein, shall move before the Honorable NINA GERSHON, United States District Judge for the Eastern District of New York at the Federal Courthouse located at 225 Cadman Plaza East, Brooklyn, New York, for an order pursuant to 42 USC 406(b), fixing a fee to plaintiff's attorneys for services rendered to plaintiff in this action and in Civil Action 93 CV 1004 (Dearie, J) (AUSA Stanley Alpert)

There is annexed a memorandum of the law, affirmation of services rendered and supporting documentation.

Dated: Woodbury, New York
January 6, 1999

Respectfully submitted,
Scheine, Fusco, Brandenstein & Rada, P.C.
Attorneys for the Plaintiff,
180 Froehlich Farm Boulevard
Post Office Box 307
Woodbury, New York 11797-0307
Tel: (516) 496-0100

BY:______________________________
MICHELLE F. STRUM, ESQ.
Telephone 516-496-0100 Ext.: 4265

TO: Linda Marino, Assisant
United States Attorney for the Eastern District of New York
1 Pierrepont Plaza
Brooklyn, New York 11201

Sample Equal Access to Justice Act Fee Petition

- Cover Letter to Assistant US Attorney
- Notice of Filing
- Petition by client
- Memo of Law/Affirmation
- Affidavit of Services Rendered

Scheine, Fusco, Brandenstein & Rada, P.C.
ATTORNEYS AT LAW

SOCIAL SECURITY DISABILITY DEPARTMENT
180 FROEHLICH FARM BLVD., PO BOX 307, WOODBURY, NY 11797-0307
516-496-0100 • 212-233-1457 • FAX: 516-496-2316
OTHER OFFICES: MANHATTAN, BRONX, HEMPSTEAD, COMMACK, MEDFORD

January 21, 1999

Paul Kaufman
Assistant United States Attorney
Eastern District of New York
147 Pierrepont Street
Brooklyn, New York 11201

Dear Mr. Kaufman:

Enclosed are two copies of our notice of filing a petition under the Equal Access to Justice Act. One copy is for you and one copy is for your client.

We will withhold motions for sixty days during which time I am hopeful we can resolve the issue. If after sixty days we can not, we will agree to a motion schedule and file our respective papers at that time.

Please note that to comply with the statute we are filing the original with the court on January 21, 1999.

Please call the undersigned, or if I am not available, call Victor Fusco, to discuss this matter.

Thank you for your kind courtesy and cooperation herein.

Very truly yours,
SCHEINE, FUSCO, BRANDENSTEIN & RADA, P.C.,

BY:____________________________
MARC A. GRODSKY, ESQ.

OUR TWENTIETH ANNIVERSARY 1978-1998

UNITED STATES DISTRICT COURT
EASTERN DISTRICT OF NEW YORK
---X

Plaintiff,

versus

CIVIL ACTION
No. CV-97-5431
(GERSHON, J.)

HON. KENNETH S. APFEL, as
COMMISSIONER OF SOCIAL SECURITY

Defendant.
---X

NOTICE OF FILING OF PETITION FOR ALLOWANCE OF
COUNSEL FEES UNDER THE EQUAL ACCESS TO JUSTICE ACT

PLAINTIFF, DELIA A , by her attorney, MARC A. GRODSKY, ESQ., herewith gives notice of filing her petition under the Equal Access to Justice Act for an award of counsel fees in the amount of $3,913.75, as and for services and costs in connection with the above entitled action, pursuant to Section 204, Subsection 2412(b) of the Equal Access to Justice Act. The parties will follow Judge Gershon's standard motion procedure in the event this claim can not be otherwise resolved between them.

There is annexed hereto a formal petition, an affirmation of petitioner's attorney with an itemization of services rendered to the petitioner, a memo of law and supporting documentation.

Dated: Woodbury, New York
January 21, 1999

Respectfully submitted,
SCHEINE, FUSCO, BRANDENSTEIN & RADA, P.C.
180 Froehlich Farm Boulevard
Post Office Box 307
Woodbury, NY 11797-0307
Tel: 516-496-0100 / 212-233-1457

By:______________________________
MARC A. GRODSKY, ESQ. (MG-2898)

TO: Paul Kaufman
Assistant United States Attorney
Eastern District of New York

UNITED STATES DISTRICT COURT
EASTERN DISTRICT OF NEW YORK
---X

DELIA A ,
SSN:

Plaintiff,

versus

CIVIL ACTION
No. 97-CV-5431
(GERSHON, J.)

HON. KENNETH S. APFEL, as
COMMISSIONER OF SOCIAL SECURITY

Defendant.

---X

PETITION FOR ALLOWANCE
OF COUNSEL FEES UNDER THE
EQUAL ACCESS TO JUSTICE ACT

PLAINTIFF, DELIA A , by her attorney, MARC A. GRODSKY, ESQ., herewith petitions the Court for an allowance of counsel fees in the amount of $3,913.75, as and for services and costs in connection with the above entitled action, pursuant to Section 204, Subsection 2412(b) of the Equal Access to Justice Act, 28 U.S.C. 2412, on the grounds that petitioner is an individual who has a net worth which did not exceed the sum of one million Dollars at the time the civil action was filed, and, further that plaintiff was the prevailing party, and is eligible to receive an award of fees, and, further that the position of the government in this case was substantially unjustified as demonstrated by the Court's reversal of the Administrative determinations denying petitioner Social Security Benefits.

- continued -

In support of this petition, there is annexed hereto an affirmation of petitioner's attorney with an itemization of services rendered to the petitioner.

Dated: Woodbury, New York
January 20, 1999

Respectfully submitted,
SCHEINE, FUSCO, BRANDENSTEIN & RADA, P.C.
180 Froehlich Farm Boulevard
Post Office Box 307
Woodbury, NY 11797-0307
Tel: 516-496-0100 / 212-233-1457

By:______________________________
MARC A. GRODSKY, ESQ. (MG-2898)

TO:
Paul Kaufman
Assistant United States Attorney
Eastern District of New York
Civil Division
147 Pierrepont Street
Brooklyn, New York 11201

UNITED STATES DISTRICT COURT
EASTERN DISTRICT OF NEW YORK
-----------------------------------X

DELIA A.
SSN:

Plaintiff,

-against-

KENNETH S. APFEL as
COMMISSIONER OF SOCIAL SECURITY

Defendant.
-----------------------------------X

Civil Action
No. 97-CV-5431
(GERSHON, J.)

AFFIRMATION OF COUNSEL IN SUPPORT OF PETITION FOR FEES UNDER EQUAL ACCESS TO JUSTICE ACT

In support of plaintiff, Delia A. s, petition for counsel fees under the Equal Access To Justice Act, MARC A. GRODSKY, ESQ., declares as follows:

1. I am an attorney at law duly licensed to practice law in the States of New York and New Jersey, and in the Southern and Eastern Districts of New York. I am admitted to the United States Court of Appeals for the Second Circuit and the District of New Jersey. My co-counsel was Victor Fusco, an attorney since 1976, a member of the Bar of the State of New York, and the Southern and Eastern Districts of New York, the United States Court of Appeals and the United States Supreme Court. He is past president of the New York Social Security Bar Association and current president of the National Organization of Social Security Claimants' Representatives.

2. Annexed herewith is an itemization of services rendered to plaintiff demonstrating that my firm devoted 27.5

attorney hours in the prosecution of this case in the Federal Court. We also devoted 2.25 para-professional hours, and these have been treated as a "cost" calculated at $75.00 per hour as suggested by Siconolfi v. Apfel, 1998 WL 827433 (E.D.N.Y.) Docket No. 97 CV 4694 (Johnson, J.).

3. We commenced prosecution of this action on August 22, 1997 when we received the decision of the Appeals Council declining to assert jurisdiction over the claim.

4. Delia A   , our client and the plaintiff herein, now seeks an award of fees under the Equal Access To Justice Act in connection with recompense for fees to which counsel will become entitled, by reason of a favorable Federal Court decision in the captioned Social Security Disability case, and the ensuing fees which shall result to counsel under Section 42 U.S.C. 406(b).

5. The Equal Access to Justice Act applies to Social Security cases where "a party prevails" against the government, and the position taken by the government in the litigation is not substantially justified. Berman v. Schweiker, 713 F.2d 1290, 1295 (7th Cir., 1983); McGill v. Secretary of Health and Human Services, 712 F.2d 28 (2nd Cir., 1983); Ocasio v. Schweiker, 540 F.Supp. 1320, 1323 (SD-NY, 1982). Congress has recently reauthorized the Equal Access To Justice Act. The changes from the original bill are not of consequence to the application made herein.

6. In the case of McGill v. Secretary of Health and Human Services, 712 F.2d, 28, 30 (2nd Circuit, 1983), the Court held that where a Federal Court reverses a decision of the Secretary of Health and Human Services, then there is a prima facie

evidence that plaintiff is a prevailing party, and the government's position was not substantially justified. The Second Circuit noted that even "counsel for the Secretary conceded at oral argument that a plaintiff who is awarded disability benefits by the Court would be eligible for attorney's fees under the Equal Access To Justice Act," Id. at 30. A plaintiff also prevails by obtaining a remand according to Shalala v Schaefer, 113 S. Ct. 2625; 113 S.C. Rep 334 (1993). Therefore, plaintiff is a prevailing party and the government's position is not justified. The government bears the burden of showing its position was substantially justified Environmental Defense Fund v. Watt, 722 F.2d 1081, 1085 (2nd Circuit, 1983).

7. An attorney for a Social Security claimant has an affirmative obligation to file a fee petition under the Equal Access to Justice Act, where benefits have been obtained. See: Taylor v. Heckler, 608 F.Supp 1255 (DC-NJ 1985) at 1256-7. "If '1this avenue of recovery is available to counsel, it is incumbent upon counsel to pursue it or justify the failure to do so. Otherwise, the net award to claimant may be unnecessarily reduced." Accord: Wells v. Bowen, 855 F.2d 37, 42. (2d Circuit 1988).

8. Your affirmant declares that based upon his office's investigation and discussion with Delia A , that she, the plaintiff, is a party with assets of less than one million dollars. Indeed, substantially less than one million dollars, as will be brought out by a perusal of the Administrative record upon which this claim originally rested.

9. Counsel intends to file a petition for approval of

a fee with this Court once a Social Security Award Certificate is issued. Section 206(b), 42 U.S.C. 406(b) of the Social Security Act provides that this Court may award a fee in an amount equivalent up to, but not exceeding twenty-five (25%) percent of the claimant's past due benefits for services rendered to the plaintiff before this Court. Since it will be no less than three to four months before the Award Certificate is issued, and possibly much longer if auxiliary awards need to be computed, counsel cannot file his 42 U.S.C. 406(b) petition at a point in time contemporaneous with the filing of an <u>Equal Access to Justice Act</u> fee petition, which must be filed within thirty (30) days.

10. Counsel's services were contingent. Plaintiff paid basic expenses: filing fees, process fees. Other than reimbursement for expenses no monies have been paid to counsel.

11. Under the case holdings in <u>Guthrie v. Schweiker</u>, 718 F.2d 104, (4th Circuit, 1983), and <u>Oguachuba v. Immigration and Naturalization Service</u>, 706 F.2d 93, 97-98 (2nd Circuit 1983), the Equal Access fee award enures to plaintiff to recompense him for amounts he will be required to pay his attorney under 42 U.S.C. 406(b). The purpose of the <u>Equal Access To Justice Act</u> is to <u>reduce</u> (not totally eliminate) the economic imbalance between the government and an individual claimant. An award of attorney's fees pursuant to the <u>Equal Access To Justice Act</u> provides the incentive necessary to enable persons (as opposed to attorneys) such as plaintiff to pursue benefits they legally deserve.

12. The <u>Equal Access To Justice Act</u> fee petition can compensate petitioner only for services counsel rendered in Federal

Court, unless this case was remanded to the Secretary for further proceedings pursuant. Sullivan v. Hudson, 490 U.S. 877; 109 S.Ct. 2248; 104 L.Ed. 294 (1989). Such is not the case here.

13. Appended hereto is an itemization of services rendered in this case which is documented by counsel's file. This itemization includes only services before this Court. The affidavit is based on **contemporaneous time records** (first handwritten and then transferred to computer) per New York State Association for Retarded Children v. Carey, 711 F.2d 1136,1148 (2nd Circuit, 1983).

14. As documented on the attached affidavit, our firm devoted 27.5 attorney hours to this case. The Equal Access To Justice Act provides for counsel fees to be fixed at a rate of $125.00 per hour subject to upward adjustment to reflect increases in the cost of living. In Siconolfi v Apfel, supra, decided November 23, 1998, Judge Johson of the Eastern District of New York determined that with cost of living adjustemnts, the current adjusted rate under EAJA is actually $130.00 perhour.

In addition, compensable costs included $150.00 in filing fees to the Clerk of the Court and $20.00 (rounded) in certified mailing fees to the United States Attorney for the Eastern District, the Attorney General of the United States and the Commissioner of Social Security.

15. The time spent pursuing relief under EAJA is also compensable; Commissioner of INS v. Jean, 110 S.Ct. 2316, 496 U.S. 154; 110 L.Ed.2d 134; 58 USLW 4701; 20 ELR 20910; CCH UIR P15,427A (1990). "Expenses" compensable under EAJA include telephone,

postage, travel, copying. See Aston v. Secretary of Health and Human Services, 808 F. 2d 9 (2d Cir. 1986). Computer research costs may also be compensable. See Carmel v. Bowen, 700 F. Supp. 794, 795 n.1 (S.D.N.Y. 1988). We have not billed for research expenses or telephone or routine mailing of papers.

16. We have therefore calculated our EAJA request as follows:

attorney 27.5 hrs at $130.00	$ 3,575.00
paralegal 2.25 hrs at $75.00	$ 168.75
filing fees	$ 150.00
certified mail	$ 20.00
total	$ 3,913.75

WHEREFORE, it is respectfully requested that this Court fix an award in the amount of $3,913.75, (to include costs) under the Equal Access To Justice Act.

Dated: Woodbury, New York
January 20, 1999

SCHEINE, FUSCO, BRANDENSTEIN & RADA, P.C.
180 FROEHLICH FARM BLVD.
WOODBURY, NY 11797
Main line 516-496-0100 - NYC line 212-233 1457
Fax line 516-496-2316

BY: ______________________________
MARC A. GRODSKY, ESQ. (2898)

CC: Paul Kaufman
Assistant United States Attorney
Attorney for Defendant
Eastern District of New York
Civil Division
147 Pierrepont Street
Brooklyn, New York 11201

UNITED STATES DISTRICT COURT
EASTERN DISTRICT OF NEW YORK
---X

DELIA A ,
SSN:

Plaintiff,

-against-

KENNETH APFEL as
COMMISSIONER OF SOCIAL SECURITY

Defendant.

---X

CIVIL ACTION
No. 97-CV-5431
(GERSHON, J.)

AFFIRMATION OF SERVICES

STATE OF NEW YORK)
) ss.:
COUNTY OF NASSAU)

MARC A. GRODSKY, ESQ. an attorney duly licensed to practice in the State of New York, hereby affirms as follows:

1. He is a member of the bar of this Court as well the Southern District of New York, the District of New Jersey, the Court of Appeals for the Second Circuit, the United States Court of International Trade and the Bars of the State of New York and the State of New Jersey. This affirmation is made with the knowledge that the Court shall rely upon it in assessing and fixing attorney's fees either under 42 §406(b), or under the Equal Access to Justice Act, or both.

3. The following persons worked on this case:

MG = MARC A. GRODSKY, ESQ., attorney of record
VF = VICTOR FUSCO, ESQ., supervisory attorney
MS = MICHELLE F. STRUM, ESQ., administraive attorney
RS = ROSALIE SANTACROCE, paralegal
CH = CAROL HUGGARD, paralegal

For clarity, we have designated services by non attorneys by using *italics*, in the itemization which appears below.

4. Herein follows a detailed itemization of services rendered in connection with the above entitled case. This itemization is based upon contemporaneous records kept as the work progressed and contained in our file. The following recitation represents a true and accurate depiction of the services rendered, and work performed as a result of our representation of the plaintiff in this matter.

5. The services rendered are herein described as follows:

DATE	SERVICES RENDERED	BY	PARA	TIME
8/22/97	Receipt of Appeals Council's Final Administrative determination dated: 8/19/97.	MS		1/12
8/26/97	Review of Appeals Council's Final Administrative determination dated: 8/19/97 and review of file. Victor Fusco also reviewed with him.	MS VF	1	
9/19/97	Prepared detailed 3-page letter to client re: further rights and remedies following Appeals Council denial. Explained all about Federal cases, remand, reveral, affirmance, substantial evidence rule, attorney fees, EAJA, time frames.			
	Preparation of complaint in Civil Action against U.S. Social Security Administration for judicial review of a final decision of the SSA. Preparation of Summons. Preparation of Civil Cover Sheet.	MS		1 3/4

9/22/97	Visited Eastern District of New York-Uniondale clerk's office to file summons and complaint.	MG		1	
10/3/97	Receipt and review of scheduling order from J. Gershon.	MG			1/6
10/7/97	Service on U.S. Attorney General, Eastern District U.S. Attorney and Social Secuirty Administration of copies of summons and complaint.		*CH*	1	
11/1/97	Return Service of Process to the Court.		*CH*		1/4
12/22/97	Receipt and docketing of administrative transcript.	MG			1/6
1/20/98	Receipt and review of Answer from U.S. Attorney.	MG			1/4
3/16/98	Receipt of check from client.	MG			1/12
3/28/98	Phone call to U.S. Atty regardng status of government's brief. Advised new U.S. Attorney is Paul Kaufman. Brief has been mailed.	MG			1/4
3/30/98	Receipt and review of motion and brief from gov't.	MG		1	1/4
4/1/98	In office research: [1] our index card file [2] our memo file [3] West Social Security Law Reporter [4] Commerce Clearing House Unemployment Ins. Reporter with Social Security [5] SS Law [6] SS Regs [7] SS Rulings [8] LEXIS research. Research case law. Research medical literature. Study of Administrative Transcript. Abstract and outline relevant portions of Administrative transcript in preparation for brief.	MG		4	3/4

4/2/98	Composition and drafting of brief on computer. Further study of record. Further legal research.	MG	5	1/2
4/6/98	Review first draft of memo. Edited, corrected; revised; further annotated.	MG	1	1/4
4/6/98	VF reviewed draft of memo. Made suggestions, edited, corrected; revised; further annotated. Return to MG for corrections.	VF	1	3/4
4/8/98	Review second draft of memo. Edited, corrected; revised.	MG	1	
4/8/98	Review second draft of memo. Edited, corrected; revised. Return to MG for correections.	VF		2/3
4/8/98	Review third draft of memo. Edited, corrected; revised.	MG		2/3
4/8/98	Review fourth draft of memo. Edited, corrected; revised.	MG		1/2
4/8/98	Review fifth draft of memo. Edited, corrected; revised.	MG		1/2
4/8/98	Review fifth draft of memo. Edited, corrected; revised. Return to MG for final corrections.	VF		1/3
4/8/98	Review final draft of memo. Edited, corrected; revised.	MG		1/2
4/8/98	Prepare table of contents and table of authorities.	MG	1	1/4
4/13/98	Prepared final draft for service and filing. Served Clerk of the Court and Assistant US Attorney with copies of memo of law and notice of motion.	*RS*	1	
12/9/98	Phone call with Paul Kaufman Regarding oral argument scheduling.	MG		1/12
12/11/98	Receipt of letter from Paul Kaufman confirming oral argument date.	MG		1/12
12/29/98	Preparation for oral argument. Review of briefs, administrative record. Tabs on record, notes for argument.	MG	3	

4

12/30/98	Travel to and from EDNY-Brooklyn. Appearance at oral argument. Discussion with Paul Kaufman post-decision.	MG	4	
1/4/98	Receipt and review of decision of J. Gershon.	MG		1/12
1/15/98	Preparation of EAJA memo, affidavit, petition.	MG	2	1/2
		Total Attorney time	27	1/2
		Total Paralegal time	2	1/4

The Equal Access To Justice Act provides for counsel fees to be fixed at a rate of $125.00 per hour subject to upward adjustment to reflect increases in the cost of living. No upward adjustment is being requested. The correct adjusted rate per Siconolfi v. Apfel, 1998 WL 827433 (E.D.N.Y.) Docket No. 97 CV 4694 (Johnson, S.). dated 11/23/98 is $130.00 per hour. Please note that we are not billing additional amounts for photocopies, telephone calls, regular mail postage or Lexis computer research fees, although such expenditures have been held compensable. We are not seeking any upward adjustment in the hourly rate other than the cost of living increase recommended by Judge Stirling Johnson in the Siconolfi case.

We request compensation for 27.5 hours at $130.00 for a total of $3,575.00 towards fees.

In addition, compensable costs (all figures, other than filing fees, are rounded to the next lowest dollar) include $150.00 in filing fees to the Clerk of the Court, and $20.00 (rounded) in certified mail (process service) fees to the United States

Attorney, Social Security Administration, and U.S. Attorney General and additional postage and certified mail as the case progressed.

We are also requesting $168.75 for 2.25 hours of para-professional time at $75.00 per hour (per Siconolfi). Total recoverable expenses sought amount to $338.75.

The total award under the Equal Access to Justice Act being sought is $ 3,575.00 ($338.75 + $ 3,575.00 = $ 3,913.75).

WHEREFORE, it is respectfully requested that this Court fix an award in the amount of $3,913.75 under the Equal Access To Justice Act. Counsel should be directed to maintain this amount in escrow until such time as the Court rules on a subsequent fee request to be made under 42 USC 406(b). At that point Counsel will determine which of the two fee awards should be reimbursed to the plaintiff.

Dated: Woodbury, New York
January 19, 1999

Respectfully submitted,
SCHEINE, FUSCO, BRANDENSTEIN & RADA, P.C.
180 Froehlich Farm Blvd.,
P.O. Box 307
Woodbury, NY 11797-0307
516-496-0100

BY: ______________________________
MARC A. GRODSKY, ESQ.
Attorney for Plaintiff

TO:
Paul Kaufman, Asst. U.S. Attorney
Eastern District of New York
Civil Division
147 Pierrepont Street
Brooklyn, New York 11201

6

UNITED STATES DISTRICT COURT
EASTERN DISTRICT OF NEW YORK

DOMINICK
ss#

Plaintiff,

95 CIV 2817 (NG)

-against-

KENNETH APFEL, in his capacity as
THE COMMISSIONER OF THE
SOCIAL SECURITY ADMINISTRATION

Defendant.

MEMORANDUM IN SUPPORT OF REQUEST FOR COUNSEL FEE AWARD PURSUANT TO 42 U.S.C. 406(b)

MICHELLE F. STRUM, ESQ., the attorney of record in the above-captioned case, herewith petitions this Court to approve statutory attorney's fees, under 42 U.S.C. 406(b) in the amount of $19,375.00 for services rendered to the plaintiff, DOMINICK F in the above matter, as well as in a related predecessor matter, 93 CIV 1004 (Dearie, J.).[1]

[1] Unlike the Equal Access to Justice Act, a 406(b) fee, only becomes an issue if and when the claimant receives benefits. One might argue that if we want a fee for the work we did before Judge Dearie, we should file a petition with Judge Dearie in Civil Action 93 Civ 1004. However, it makes little sense to encumber the courts with additional motions. In the interest of judicial economy, we are asking the last judge to rule on this case, Judge Gershon, to fix our fee. While there may have been two civil actions, there was only one case, i.e., one claim for disability, based on one single application. If Judge Gershon instructs us to make a separate application before Judge Dearie, we will follow the Court's directive.

This requested fee is a contingency fee. Counsel and plaintiff agreed upon a contingent fee of twenty five percent of plaintiff's past due benefits if we were successful in this case. The total amount withheld by the Commissioner of Social Security, is $26,991.50 as demonstrated by Award Certificates dated July 12, 1998 for Wife: Theresa, Daughter: Allisa, and Son: Jospeh, and the Award Certificate dated April 1, 1997 for the plaintiff, wage earner.

The fee requested is actually less than the agreed upon amount, and is based on an hourly rate of $250.00 per hour multiplied by 77 3/4 compensable attorney hours devoted to the claim in the Federal Court civil actions.

We previously documented our time to the Ccurt in an Civil Action 95-2817 (Gershon) in an affirmation by MICHELLE F. STRUM, ESQ., dated December 12, 1996, submitted in connection with our petition under the Equal Access to Justice Act (EAJA.) (Copy annexed). This 42 USC 406 (b) claim is also premised upon that previously submitted itemization a copy of which is appended hereto, together with a supplemental affirmation, showing an additional 40 hours attorney time and 12 hours of para professional time as compensable services in connection with the predecessor action. We do recognize that the time spent in preparing a fee application for 42 U.S.C. 406 (b) fees, is not compensable time, and therefore it has not been included. The fee requested is based only on attorney time expenditures. The paralegal time is included for informational purposes.

The parties stipulated to, and this Court made an award under the Equal Access to Justice Act, in the amount of

$4,200.00. The EAJA award money ordinarily enures to the benefit of the plaintiff, and offsets the fee award under 42 U.S.C. 406(b). Counsel may compromise and accept a reduced amount under the Equal Access to Justice Act, rather than risk having his client awarded nothing by a court, should the issue be litigated. Such "stipulation" does not by implication automatically apply tot he vlauation of services under 42 USC 406 (b). Otherwise, counsel might be discouraged from and penalized for any and every attempt to settle an Equal Access to Justice Act petition on an amicable basis.

Because the time devoted to preparing the EAJA petition was spent in an effort to collect additional moneys for the claimant, it has been held compensable. Commissioner, Immigration and Naturalization Service, Et. Al., v. Jean, 496 U.S. 154; 110 S. Ct. 2316; 110 L.Ed. 2d 134 (1990). Lee and Ft. Stueben Co., Inc v Johnson and von Raab, 799 F.2d 31, at 39 (3rd Cir. 1986); Flanders v Shalala, 91 Civ 337 (Northern District, June 29, 1994) 1994 [U.S. Dist. Lexis 9189] , and has therefore been included.

We believe the $250.00 hourly rate herein requested is eminently reasonable. In 1990, over seven years ago in the case of Mara v. Sullivan, 734 F.Supp. 642 (S.D.N.Y. 1990), Judge Sweet ruled that $200.00 was at the time considered a reasonable hourly rate in a Social Security case, for experienced Social Security disability practitioners. More recently, in Maier v. Appel, 1998 WL 401536 (SDNY 1998) 95 Civ 9264 JGK, Judge John Koeltl of the Soutdhern District of New York held that a resulting hourly rate of $438.42 per hour was not "excessive and unreasonable" as the

Commissioner of Social Security had contended. The Court considered is the fact that Social Security attorneys work on a contingency fee basis and followed the reasoning in <u>Wells v. Sullivan</u>, 907 F. 2d 367 (2nd Cir 1990), "<u>Wells II</u>." Noting that in the first decision by the Second Circuit in <u>Wells v. Bowen</u>, 855 F.2d 37 (2d Cir. 1988) the Circuit originally looked to the contingency nature of representation and felt it should be "factored in" to the ultimate attorney's fee. In <u>Wells v. Sullivan</u>,907 F.2d 367, (2d Cir. 1990) the Second Circuit basically ruled that Social Security Disability Benefits Cases are contingency fee cases and that a contingent fee of 25 percent is not unreasonable in most cases.

In this case, we are not asking for the full 25 percent of plaintiff's past due benefits ($26,991.50) for Federal Court level services. We are asking for a reasonable contingent hourly rate of $250.00 per hour. We might point out that if this granted, the EAJA award, presently being held in escrow, will enure to the benefit of the claimant.

The record will reflect that we devoted extensive time to Mr. Filocomo's case at the administrative levels. We do reserve the right to apply to the Social Security Administration for approval of a fee for the services we rendered before the Social Security Administration, under 42 U.S.C. 406(a) which grants to the Commissioner the sole authority to approve fees for services rendered before the Commissioner.

We respectfully suggest to the court that we have done everything possible to protect Dominick F rights, including taking the case to Federal Court twice, and obtaining an award under the Equal Access to Justice Act for him. Under these circumstances, we believe the fee requested is eminently reasonable and we beg the court's approval of same.

Dated: Woodbury, New York
January 5, 199

Respectfully submitted,
SCHEINE, FUSCO, BRANDENSTEIN & RADA, P.C.

BY: ______________________
Michelle F. Strum, Esq.

TO: LINDA MARINO, ESQ.
Asst. U.S. Attorney for
Eastern District of New York
1 Pierrepont Plaza, 14th Fl.
(Civil Division)
Brooklyn, NY 11201

TO:

Brooklyn, NY

UNITED STATES DISTRICT COURT
EASTERN DISTRICT OF NEW YORK

DOMINICK
SS#

Plaintiff,

-against-

95 CV 2817 NG

Shirley Chater,
as COMMISSIONER OF THE SOCIAL SECURITY ADMINISTRATION

Defendant.

AFFIRMATION OF SERVICES

STATE OF NEW YORK)
) ss.:
COUNTY OF NASSAU)

MICHELLE F. STRUM, ESQ., an attorney duly licensed to practice in the State of New York, hereby affirms as follows:

I. She is a member of the bar of this Court as well the Southern District of New York, the District of New Jersey and the bars of the States of New York and New Jersey.

II. This affirmation is made with the knowledge that the Court shall rely upon it in assessing and fixing attorney's fees either under 42 §406(b), or under the Equal Access to Justice Act, or both.

III. Herein follows a detailed itemization of services rendered in connection with the above entitled case. This itemization is based upon contemporaneous records kept as the work progressed and contained in our file. The following recitation represents a true and accurate depiction of the services rendered, and work performed as a result of our representation of the plaintiff in this matter.

IV. The persons who worked on this case are:

1. Michelle F. Strum, Esq. Attorney of Record (MFS)

2. Rosalie Santacroce, Certified Paralegal (RS) who was assigned to me until recently due to sick leave

3. Victor Fusco, Esq. (VF) Senior member of the firm, firm's managing attornye and supervising attorney of the Social Security Department, who provided guidance and assistance as shown below.

4. Lenny Solicito, (LS) a certified paralegal who runs our word processing department.

5. John E. Antonwicz, (JA) an attorney with the firm who formerly was a staff attorney for the Social Security Administration's Office of Hearing and Appeals, and provided guidance as documented.

6. Aba Heiman, (AH) a member sof the firm, and former Claims Representative for the Social Security Administration who also provided guidance as shown.

7. Janet Bunde, (JB) firm's bookeeper.

8. Claire Stein (CS) another senior paralegal, who assited as shown, and typed edits to the final draft of the brief.

V. The services rendered are herein described as follows:

date	Services Rendered - Work Performed	Atty	Para	Hrs	Min
06-02-95	Review Appeals Council decision affirming ALJ denial	MFS			1/6
06-07-95	Tel disc with claimant re further appeal, he to decide	MFS			1/12
06-08-95	Reviewed and discussed case with Victor Fusco, John Atonowicz and Aba Heiman, re: merits of further appeal	MFS			1/2
06-19-95	Review letter from clt confirming he wants to appeal to Federal Court again	MFS			1/12
06-29-95	Review of file. Review all prior procedural decisions for appropriate dates. Prepared complaint; summons; covers; cover sheet.	MFS		1	

06-30-95	Prepared pleadings per attorney instructions		RS	1	
06-30-95	Reviewed completed complaint and accompanying paperwork, had appropriate copies made, and readied for filing with the court.	MFS			1/3
07-06-95	Prepared check for Court Clerk - filing fees		JB		1/12
	Letter to client requesting remittance of filing fee for	MFS			1/12
	USDC and advising status.		RS		1/6
07-14-95	Visited EDNY Uniondale clerks office to file summons and complaint, plus travel two ways	MFS			3/4
07-17-95	Receive and record reimbursement from client for filing fees and recorded same		JB		1/4
07-25-95	Receive and review letter from client enclosing medical evidence	MFS			1/6
07-28-95	Receive and review letter from client enclosing medical evidence.	MFS			1/6
07-31-95	Receive and review letter from client enclosing medical evidence.	MFS			1/6
07-21-95	Visited Office of the United States Attorney for the Eastern District of New York in Brooklyn to effectuate personal service of summons and complaint. No travel time charged, already there on other business.	MFS			1/2
08-01-95	Receive and review correspondence from Judge Ross, scheduling order, annotated file, diary.	MFS			1/4
08-04-95	Dictation	MFS			1/6
	Ltr. to U.S. Attorney General advising the institution of a Civil Action on behalf of our client for a judicial review of a final decision of the SSA, sent certified mail return receipt requested Ltr. to Comm'r of SSA advising the insitution of a Civil Action on behalf of our client for a judicial review of a final decision of the SSA, sent certified mail return receipt requested		RS		1/2
08-11-95	Receive and review letter from client enclosing medical evidence from Dr. Paul	MFS			1/6
08-17-95	Receive and review letter from client enclosing additional medical evidence.	MFS			1/6
09-20-95	Receive and review letter from client enclosing medical evidence from Dr. Paul	MFS			1/6
10-20-95	Receive and review correspondence from US Atty enclosing transcript pages 214-375. Read same.	MFS		1	
12-11-95	Receive and scan revised transcript (375 pages) Combination of two prior transcripts we had rec'vd. Nothing new.	MFS			1/2
10-31-95	Receive and review correspondence from client enclosing doctors note.	MFS			1/6
11-06-95	Receive and review letter from client enclosing varies items of medical evidence from various doctors, review all reports	MFS			1/3
11-13-95	Receive and review correspondence from client enclosing doctors note.	MFS			1/6

12-19-95	Receive and review correspondence from client enclosing doctors note.	MFS			1/6
01-08-96	Receive and review letter from client enclosing varies items of medical evidence from various doctors, review all reports	MFS			1/3
01-22-96	Receive and review letter from client enclosing medical evidence	MFS			1/6
02-15-96	Receive and review correspondence from AUSA, ie: ANSWER	MFS			1/6
02-16-96	Review file, review pleadings, scheduling order. Attorney conference: MFS and V. Fusco each reviewed file, and discussed the case in depth including problems in proving the case, ie: Date last insured issue, lack of treatment during relevant periods, recommendations made for brief, only MFS time charged.	MFS		1	1/4
02-20-96	Receive and review letter from client enclosing medical evidence from Dr. Wolpin.	MFS			1/6
02-28-96	Client called to ascertain case status. File pulled and client advised. Memorandum to the file		RS		1/6
03-04-96	Receive and review correspondence from client, questions about his case.	MFS			1/12
03-06-96	Review file for proofs of service per diary entry.	MFS			1/12
	Letter to clerk of the court enclosing proofs of service on all parties.		RS		1/4
03-13-96	Review file per diary entry.	MFS			1/6
03-18-96	Received postcard verification of proof of service of certified mail to US District Court. Filed same, annotating file copy of the original outgoing correspondence. Removed item from follow up diary.		RS		1/12
04-13-96	Review file per diary entry.		RS		1/6
07-12-96	Telephone discussion with Linda Marino AUSA, re scheduling of motions	MFS			1/6
07-17-96	Receive, review, sign and return stipulation of scheduling to AUSA	MFS			1/6
07-18-96	Receive and review correspondence from client enclosing doctors note.	MFS			1/6
07-22-96	Study of Administrative Transcript Abstract and outline relevant portions of Administrative transcript in preparation for brief.	MFS		4	
07-26-96	Work on brief; Researching cases; Research regulations in 20 CFR; Research SSA Rulings. Review med evidence in trascript. Study of rationale of the ALJ's decision to ascertain compliance with the requirements of the Courts and Secretary for the ALJ's consideration of the treating physician rule and all the material evidence.	MFS		2	1/4
07-29-96	Continued working on brief	MFS		1	1/4

08-06-96	Continued work on brief. Comparison of the exhibits and testimony with the decision for material omissions and accurate reporting of the evidence. Handwritten drafting of the brief.	MFS		3	
08-12-96	Receive and review US Atty motion papers annd memo of law, review work drafted to date to ensure all issues raised by US atty were dealt with. Continued andwritten drafting of the brief.	MFS		2	1/4
08-15-96	Continued work on brief. Weighing the material evidence for stress in argument. Continued handwritten drafting of the brief.	MFS		1	3/4
08-20-96	Complete first handwritten draft of memo gave to typing service	MFS		1	1/3
08-21-96	Type brief for MFS		LS	4	1/4
08-23-9	Review, edit and revise first typed draft of memo	MFS		1	
08-26-96	Continued to revise first draft. Review, edit and revise draft of memo; Review all notes on relevant law, annotate first draft of memo by pluggin in citations to relevant cases, rulings, regulatiuons where appropriate.	MFS		2	1/2
08-27-96	Typed revised memo		LS	1	1/2
08-27-96	Reviewing the draft of the brief, with changes for accuracy of effectiveness of presentation. Revise, correct, edit, proof & typo 2nd draft.	VF		1	
08-28-96	Typed revisions		LS	1	
08-28-96	Proof-read final draft, assemble appeal and sign off. Notice of motion, letter, prepared.	MFS			1/3
08-29-96	Copies made, readied for filing, mailed out to US Atty, sent certified mail return receipt requested. US Atty to file all copies with the Ct.		RS		1/4
08-29-96	Two page letter to client enclosing copy of memo and explaining case status, procedures.	MFS			1/2
09-03-96	Receive and review letter from client enclosing medical evidence.	MFS			1/12
09-09-96	Receive and review letter from client enclosing medical evidence from Dr. Braaf.	MFS			1/12
09-12-96	Received postcard verification of proof of service of certified mail to US ATTY. Filed same, annotating file copy of the original outgoing correspondence. Removed item from follow up diary.		RS		1/12
09-20-96	Receive and review faxed reply brief and attachment from US Atty	MFS		1	
09-25-96	Receive and review correspondence from US Atty - hard copy of memo	MFS			NTC
11-18-96	Receive and review decision from Judge Ross	MFS			1/2
11-27-96	Receive and review final order from the clerk	MFS			1/12
12-11-96	Prepare Motion for award under Equal Access to Justice Act, and supporting documents, hand drafted.	MFS		3	
12-12-96	Type up motion, memo, attachments		CES	2	

12-12-96	Review memo, affidavit, motion, review court rules, prepare notice of filing, prepare corrrespondence to US Atty. Mail Originals to US Atty.	MFS	1	
12-13-96	Visit EDNY, file EAJA Petition with the Court	VF		2/3

Totals	para-professional	11	3/4
	Attorney	37	3/4

Dated: Woodbury, New York
December 12, 1996

Michelle F. Strum, Esq.

Sworn to before me this 12 day of December 1996

UNITED STATES DISTRICT COURT
EASTERN DISTRICT OF NEW YORK

DOMINICK
SS#

Plaintiff,

-against-

US DEPT OF HHS

Defendant.

93 CV 1004
Judge Dearie

AFFIRMATION OF SERVICES

STATE OF NEW YORK)
) ss.:
COUNTY OF NASSAU)

MICHELLE F. STRUM, ESQ., an attorney duly licensed to practice in the State of New York, hereby affirms as follows:

I. She is a member of the bar of this Court as well the Southern District of New York, the District of New Jersey and the bars of the States of New York and New Jersey.

II. This affirmation is made with the knowledge that the Court shall rely upon it in assessing and fixing attorney's fees either under 42 §406(b), or under the Equal Access to Justice Act, or both.

III. Herein follows a detailed itemization of services rendered in connection with the above entitled case. This itemization is based upon contemporaneous records kept as the work progressed and contained in our file. The following recitation represents a true and accurate depiction of the services rendered, and work performed as a result of our representation of the plaintiff in this matter.

IV. The persons who worked on this case are:

1. Michelle F. Strum, Esq. Attorney of Record (MFS)

2. Victor Fusco, Esq. (VF) Senior member of the firm, firm's managing attornye and supervising attorney of the Social Security Department, who provided guidance and assistance as shown below.

3. Lenny Solicito, (LS) a certified paralegal who runs our word processing department.

4. Aba Heiman, (AH) a member of the firm, and former Claims Representative for the Social Security Administration who also provided guidance as shown.

5. Claire Stein (CS) another senior paralegal, who assisted as shown.

V. The services rendered are herein described as follows:

93 CV 1004	Dominick Filocomo v. HHS			
date	Services rendered work completed	By Atty	Para	
02-11-93	Review of Appeals Council's Final Administrative determination. Aba Heiman and Victor Fusco discussed claim and merits of going to Federal Court	VF AH		1/2
02-24-93	Further review of file re: going up to USDC, call to claimant to discuss,	AH		1/2
02-25-93	Review of file for relevant dates to dictate pleadings, VF dictated complaint and instructions for accompanying papers	VF		1/2
03-01-93	Received and reviewed letter from client confirming our proceeding with appeal and enclosing filing fee, recorded same.		CS	1/6
03-08-93	Prepared complaint; summons; covers; cover sheet. Check for Clerk		CS	1

03-09-93	Visited Eastern District of New York- Uniondale clerks office to file summons and complaint. Travel from Hempstead 2 ways	MFS			1/2
03-19-93	Courtesy letter to U.S. Attorney, Eastern District, Civil Division, advising we recently instituted a Civil Action against the U.S. Dept. of HHS for a judicial review of a final decision of the SSA. cc: regional atty for SSA. Ltr. to U.S. Attorney General advising the institution of a Civil Action on behalf of our client for a judicial review of a final decision of the SSA. copies of summons and complaint enclosed, certified mail - return receipt requested. Ltr. to Commissioner of SSA advising the institution of a Civil Action on behalf of our client for a judicial review of a final decision of the SSA certified mail - return receipt requested		CS	1	
04-01-93	Received postcard verifications of proof of service of certified mail to general and Social Security Administration. Filed same, annotating file copy of the original outgoing correspondence. Removed item from follow up diary		CS		1/12
04-20-93	Visited Office of the United States Attorney for the Eastern District of New York to effectuate personal service of summons and complaint. Travel 2 way from our NYC office	MFS		1	

06-14-93	Client called to ascertain case status. File pulled and client advised.		CS		1/6
07-21-93	Receive and review correspondence from clt re: case status		CS		1/12
11/2/93	Read entire administrative transcript. Review of ALJ decision, tab and underline and clip pertinent areas or error. Compare ALJ recitation of the evidence to our copies of the exhibits. Comparison of the exhibits and testimony with the decision for material omissions and accurate reporting of the evidence. Organizing the evidence for patterns sufficient to constitute generalities and conclusions.	MFS		6	
11-03-93	Research, case law, rulings, regulations, our prior brief bank, Long hand drafting of memorandum of law.	MFS		5	
11-04-93	Organizing the material. Study of rationale of the ALJ's decision to ascertain compliance with the requirements of the Courts and Secretary for the ALJ's consideration of the treating physician rule and all the material evidence. Further drafting. Gave to LS for first draft	MFS		4	
11-05-93	Typed Brief from MFS longhand		LS	5	

11-08-93	Review first draft of memo. Extensive revision of brief to shorten it, while not losing salient arguments proofread; made necessary corrections. Corrected typos, checked cites.Review all notes on relevant law, annotate first draft of memo by plugging in citations to relevant cases, rulings, regulations where appropriate. Return for a second draft	MFS		3	3/4
11-09-93	Typed revised brief		LS	3	1/2
11-11-93	VF reviewed final draft and ok'd for submission.	VF			1/3
11-11-93	MFS reviewed final draft dictated notice of motion and instructions for number of copies and filing	MFS			3/4
11-12-93	Prepared copies of brief and notices of motion and readied for filing, typed correspondence		CS	1	
11-12-93	Reviewed all assembled documents, signed off. Letter to Court. Sent to Assistant United States Attorney via Fed Ex, detailed letter to client with copy of papers and explanation fop court procedures	MFS			1/2
12/08/93	Received and reviewed letter from Assistant United States Attorney dated 12/8 to Judge Dearie	MFS			1/12
12/17/93	Received and reviewed Court endorsement of Mr Alperts 12-7 letter asking for additional time	MFS			1/12
01/10/94	Received and reviewed government memo and studied in contrast to our memo and the record and the cases we cited.	VF MFS		1	3/4

01/11/94	Continued to review government brief, check out all cases cited herein we didn't already know, additional; research and prepared reply letter brief on computer	MFS	4	
01/12/94	Review, edit, revise and prepare final draft of reply	VF	1	1/2
01-20-94	Attorney's pre-argument preparation: review abstracts and file memorandums; review copies of exhibits; review of medical texts in point; review pertinent Social Security rulings, regulations, listings, grids, etc. Outline all of arguments in large print with reference to the record and briefs. Practice moot argument with Victor Fusco as AUSA and Aba Heiman as the judge	MFS VF AH	3	
01-21-94	Travel to Brooklyn Federal Court. Argue Motion before Judge Dearie, return Trip.	MFS	3	
03-14-94	Received and reviewed Judge Dearie's decision remanding. Tel discussion with claimant re further proceedings	MFS		1/4
	total attorney time		40	
	total non attorney		12	

Dated: Woodbury, New York
January

Michelle F. Strum, Esq.

Sworn to before me this 6 day of January

S92-0051 | MFS

Social Security Administration
Office of Disability and
International Operations
PO Box 17295
Baltimore, Maryland 21241

Refer to: S2HA141

Michelle F Strum
Attorney at Law
PO Box 307
Woodbury NY 11797-0307

Dear Ms. Strum:

This refers to the claim for disability insurance benefits of and family.

We are withholding $26,991.50 representing 25 percent of past-due benefits in anticipation of direct payment of an authorized attorney's fee. We are writing at this time to determine whether you have petitioned the U.S. District Court and/or the Social Security Administration for a fee.

Please write to Social Security Administration, Office of Disability and International Operations, Division I, Special Appeals Examining Section 1, PO Box 17295, Baltimore, Maryland 21241, to let us know whether you have or will petition for a fee. If you like, you may fax your response to (410) 966-1998.

If you have been authorized by the court or SSA to receive a fee in this case, please send us a copy of that authorization. If you do not intend to petition for a fee, your written statement expressly waiving your fee is necessary before we can release the withheld benefits to the claimant.

W Burnell Hurt
Director

0103 M7

Social Security Administration
Retirement, Survivors, and Disability Insurance
Notice of Award

Office of Disability and
International Operations
1500 Woodlawn Drive
Baltimore, Maryland 21241
Date: April 1, 1997
Claim Number:

We are writing to let you know that you are entitled to monthly disability benefits from Social Security beginning March 1990.

What We Will Pay

- Your first check is for $980.00.
- This is the money you are due through March 1997.
- After the first check, you will receive $980.00 on or about the third of each month.

Your Benefits

The following chart shows your benefit amount(s) before any deductions or rounding. The amount you actually receive may differ from your full benefit amount. When we figure how much to pay you, we must deduct certain amounts, such as Medicare premiums and workers' compensation offset. We must also round down to the nearest dollar.

Beginning Date	Benefit Amount	Reason
March 1990	$ 817.10	Entitlement began
December 1990	$ 861.20	Cost-of-living adjustment
December 1991	$ 893.00	Cost-of-living adjustment
December 1992	$ 919.70	Cost-of-living adjustment
December 1993	$ 943.60	Cost-of-living adjustment
December 1994	$ 970.00	Cost-of-living adjustment
December 1995	$ 995.20	Cost-of-living adjustment
December 1996	$ 1024.00	Cost-of-living adjustment

SEE NEXT PAGE

The Date You Became Disabled

On November 17, 1996 the United States District Court decided that your period of disability began May 26, 1982. The law provides that benefit payments can begin no more than 12 months prior to the date you filed your application. Since you filed your application on March 14, 1991, your benefit payments will begin March 1990 which is the earliest month of entitlement under the law.

Information About Medicare

You are entitled to hospital insurance under Medicare beginning March 1992.

You are entitled to medical insurance under Medicare beginning March 1997.

We charge a monthly premium for your medical insurance. The rates are shown below:

Amount	Beginning Date
$ 43.80	March 1997

We are taking medical insurance premiums due through April 1997 out of the check you will receive around April 3, 1997. These premiums total $87.60. We will deduct medical insurance premiums 1 month in advance.

We will send your Medicare card in about 4 weeks. You should take this card with you when you need medical care. If you need medical care before you receive the card, use this letter as proof that you are covered by Medicare.

If you do not want medical insurance, please complete the enclosed card and return it to us in the envelope we have provided. You will need to do this by the date shown on the card. If you decide you do not want the insurance, we will return any premiums that you have paid.

We did not give you earlier medical insurance because we did not process it timely. If you want to have these benefits earlier, you can choose medical insurance benefits beginning March 1992. If you want this benefit to start earlier, you must do the following things within 30 days after the date of this notice:

- tell us in writing that you want medical insurance benefits beginning March 1992;
- pay us $2,401.20. (this covers premiums due from March 1992 through February 1997); or,

SEE NEXT PAGE

• tell us we can withhold this amount from the check.

If you want the benefits beginning March 1992 but find it hard to pay the premium amount in a lump sum, ask us about other ways to pay the money.

Information About Lawyer's or Representative's Fees

Your lawyer may ask the court to approve a fee no larger than 25 percent of past due benefits. Past due benefits are those payable through October 1996, the month before the court's decision. For this reason, we are withholding $18,332.50.

After the court sets the fee, we will let you and the lawyer know how much of this money will be used to pay the fee. We will send any remainder to you.

Other Social Security Benefits

The benefits described in this letter are the only ones you can receive from Social Security. If you think that you might qualify for another kind of Social Security benefit in the future, you will have to file another application.

Your Responsibilities

The decisions we made on your claim are based on information you gave us. If this information changes, it could affect your benefits. For this reason, it is important that you report changes to us right away. We have enclosed a pamphlet, "When You Get Social Security Disability Benefits... What You Need To Know." It will tell you what must be reported and how to report. Be sure to read the parts of the pamphlet which explain what to do if you go to work or if your health improves.

Things To Remember

Doctors and other trained staff found that you are disabled under our rules. However, we must review all disability cases. Therefore, we will review your case in 5 to 7 years. We will send you a letter before we start the review. Based on that review, your benefits will continue if you are still disabled, but will end if you are no longer disabled.

SEE NEXT PAGE

Do You Disagree With The Decision?

You are entitled to benefits because of a decision made by the United States District Court.

We already told you about your right to appeal the decision made by the Unites States District Court. If you feel any action we are taking to carry out the decision is wrong, you also have the right to appeal that part of your case.

You have 60 days to ask for an appeal.

The 60 days start the day after you receive this letter.

You will have to have a good reason for waiting more than 60 days to ask for an appeal.

We are sending a copy of this letter to your lawyer.

If You Have Any Questions

If you have any questions, you may call us toll-free at 1-800-772-1213, or call your local Social Security office at 1-718-951-1005. We can answer most questions over the phone. You can also write or visit any Social Security office. The office that serves your area is located at:

SSA BRANCH OFFICE
KINGS PLAZA
4123 AVENUE U
BROOKLYN,NY 11234

If you do call or visit an office, please have this letter with you. It will help us answer your questions. Also, if you plan to visit an office, you may call ahead to make an appointment. This will help us serve you more quickly when you arrive at the office.

W Burnell Hurt
W. Burnell Hurt
Director

Enclosure(s):
Form HCFA-2690
Envelope
SSA Pub No 05-10153

Social Security Administration M7

Retirement, Survivors, and Disability Insurance

Notice of Award

Office of Disability and
International Operations
1500 Woodlawn Drive
Baltimore, Maryland 21241
Date: July 12. 1998
Claim Number:

We are writing to let you know that you are entitled to monthly child's benefits from Social Security beginning April 1992.

Your Benefits

You will receive a check for $2,982.00. This is the money you are due through April 1997.

The following chart shows your benefit amount(s) before any deductions or rounding. The amount you actually receive may differ from your full benefit amount. When we figure how much to pay you, we must deduct certain amounts, such as Medicare premiums and workers' compensation offset. We must also round down to the nearest dollar.

Beginning Date	Benefit Amount	Reason
March 1990	$ 136.20	Entitlement began
December 1990	$ 143.60	Cost-of-living adjustment
December 1991	$ 148.90	Cost-of-living adjustment

We raised the monthly benefit beginning July 1994 because we stopped paying another person on this record.

Information About Lawyer's or Representative's Fees

Since an attorney represented the person on whose Social Security record your claim was filed, the attorney's services assisted all claimants on this account to become entitled to benefits. For this reason, we must withhold 25 percent of all past-due benefits, $994.00, toward payment of the attorney's fee. Section 206(a) of the Social Security Act requires an attorney to obtain authorization from the Social Security Administration before a fee may be charged for services. This section of the law also provides that up to 25 percent of the claimant's past-due benefits can be used toward the payment of such fee.

When the amount of the fee is determined, the authorized fee

SEE NEXT PAGE

will be paid directly to the attorney from the withheld benefits. If the amount of the authorized fee is less than the total amount withheld from all beneficiaries, it will be paid proportionally from withheld benefits. Any of the amount withheld from your benefits not needed for payment of the authorized fee will be sent to you.

The benefits described in this letter are the only ones you can receive from Social Security. If you think that you might qualify for another kind of Social Security benefit in the future, you will have to file another application.

Do You Disagree With The Decision?

If you think we are wrong, you have the right to appeal. We will correct mistakes. We will look at any new facts you have. Then a person who did not make the first decision will decide your case again.

- You have 60 days to ask for an appeal.
- The 60 days start the day after you get this letter.
- You will have to have a good reason for waiting more than 60 days to ask for an appeal.
- You have to ask for an appeal in writing. We will ask you to sign a form SSA-561-U2, called "Request for Reconsideration". Contact one of our offices if you want help.

If You Have Any Questions

If you have any questions, call us at 1-800-772-1213. We can answer most questions over the phone. If you prefer to visit one of our offices, please check the local telephone directory for the office nearest you. Or call us and we can give you the office address. Please have this letter with you if you call or visit an office. It will help us answer your questions.

W. Burnell Hurt
Director

M7

Social Security Administration
Retirement, Survivors, and Disability Insurance
Notice of Award

Office of Disability and
International Operations
1500 Woodlawn Drive
Baltimore, Maryland 21241
Date: July 12, 1998
Claim Number:

Joseph

We are writing to let you know that you are entitled to monthly child's benefits from Social Security beginning March 1990.

What We Will Pay

You will receive a check for $15,867.75. This is the money you are due through June 1996.

Your Benefits

The following chart shows your benefit amount(s) before any deductions or rounding. The amount you actually receive may differ from your full benefit amount. When we figure how much to pay you, we must deduct certain amounts, such as Medicare premiums and workers' compensation offset. We must also round down to the nearest dollar.

Beginning Date		Benefit Amount	Reason
March 1990	$	136.20	Entitlement began
December 1990	$	143.60	Cost-of-living adjustment
December 1991	$	148.90	Cost-of-living adjustment
July 1992	$	223.40	Benefits to another person began or ended
December 1992	$	230.10	Cost-of-living adjustment
December 1993	$	236.00	Cost-of-living adjustment
July 1994	$	471.20	Benefits to another person began or ended
December 1994	$	485.00	Cost-of-living adjustment
December 1995	$	497.60	Cost-of-living adjustment

We raised the monthly benefit beginning July 1992 because we stopped paying another person on this record.

We stopped your benefits because you are no longer a full-time elementary or high school student.

SEE NEXT PAGE

INFORMATION ABOUT WORK AND EARNINGS

The monthly earnings test applies only to 1 year. That year is the first year a beneficiary has a non-work month after entitlement to Social Security benefits. Our records show that you had or will have at least one non-work month in 1990. Therefore, we will pay benefits for years after that based on annual work and earnings.

THE BASIS FOR OUR DECISION

Based on the information given to us, you were born on July 8, 1978.

OTHER SOCIAL SECURITY BENEFITS

The benefits described in this letter are the only ones you can receive from Social Security. If you think that you might qualify for another kind of Social Security benefit in the future, you will have to file another application.

Information About Lawyer's or Representative's Fees

Since an attorney represented the person on whose Social Security record your claim was filed, the attorney's services assisted all claimants on this account to become entitled to benefits. For this reason, we must withhold 25 percent of all past-due benefits, $5289.25, toward payment of the attorney's fee. Section 206(a) of the Social Security Act requires an attorney to obtain authorization from the Social Security Administration before a fee may be charged for services. This section of the law also provides that up to 25 percent of the claimant's past-due benefits can be used toward the payment of such fee.

When the amount of the fee is determined, the authorized fee will be paid directly to the attorney from the withheld benefits. If the amount of the authorized fee is less than the total amount withheld from all beneficiaries, it will be paid proportionally from withheld benefits. Any of the amount withheld from your benefits not needed for payment of the authorized fee will be sent to you.

We are sending a copy of this letter to your lawyer.

Your Responsibilities

Your benefits are based on the information you gave us. If this information changes, it could affect your benefits. For this reason, it is important that you report changes to us right away.

We have enclosed a pamphlet, "When You Get Social Security Retirement or Survivors Benefits... What You Need to Know." It tells you what must be reported and how to report. Please be

SEE NEXT PAGE

sure to read that part of the pamphlet which explains how work could change your payments.

Do You Disagree With The Decision?

If you think we are wrong, you have the right to appeal. We will correct mistakes. We will look at any new facts you have. Then a person who did not make the first decision will decide your case again.

- You have 60 days to ask for an appeal.
- The 60 days start the day after you get this letter.
- You will have to have a good reason for waiting more than 60 days to ask for an appeal.
- You have to ask for an appeal in writing. We will ask you to sign a form SSA-561-U2, called "Request for Reconsideration". Contact one of our offices if you want help.

If You Have Any Questions

If you have any questions, call us at 1-800-772-1213. We can answer most questions over the phone. If you prefer to visit one of our offices, please check the local telephone directory for the office nearest you. Or call us and we can give you the office address. Please have this letter with you if you call or visit an office. It will help us answer your questions.

W Burnell Hurt

W. Burnell Hurt
Director

M7

Social Security Administration
Retirement, Survivors, and Disability Insurance
Notice of Award

Office of Disability and
International Operations
1500 Woodlawn Drive
Baltimore, Maryland 21241
Date: July 12, 1998
Claim Number:

Theresa

We are writing to let you know that you are entitled to monthly wife's benefits from Social Security beginning March 1990.

What We Will Pay

You will receive a check for $7,127.25. This is the money you are due through June 1994.

Your Benefits

The following chart shows your benefit amount(s) before any deductions or rounding. The amount you actually receive may differ from your full benefit amount. When we figure how much to pay you, we must deduct certain amounts, such as Medicare premiums and workers' compensation offset. We must also round down to the nearest dollar.

Beginning Date	Benefit Amount	Reason
March 1990	$ 136.20	Entitlement began
December 1990	$ 143.60	Cost-of-living adjustment
December 1991	$ 148.90	Cost-of-living adjustment
July 1992	$ 223.40	Benefits to another person began or ended
December 1992	$ 230.10	Cost-of-living adjustment
December 1993	$ 236.00	Cost-of-living adjustment

We raised the monthly benefit beginning July 1992 because we stopped paying another person on this record.

To be entitled to benefits as wife, you must be taking care of a child who is entitled to benefits on Social Security record. And, that child must be under age 16 or disabled.

SEE NEXT PAGE

INFORMATION ABOUT WORK AND EARNINGS

The monthly earnings test applies only to 1 year. That year is the first year a beneficiary has a non-work month after entitlement to Social Security benefits. Our records show that you had or will have at least one non-work month in 1990. Therefore, we will pay benefits for years after that based on annual work and earnings.

OTHER SOCIAL SECURITY BENEFITS

The benefits described in this letter are the only ones you can receive from Social Security. If you think that you might qualify for another kind of Social Security benefit in the future, you will have to file another application.

Information About Lawyer's or Representative's Fees

Since an attorney represented the person on whose Social Security record your claim was filed, the attorney's services assisted all claimants on this account to become entitled to benefits. For this reason, we must withhold 25 percent of all past-due benefits, $2375.75, toward payment of the attorney's fee. Section 206(a) of the Social Security Act requires an attorney to obtain authorization from the Social Security Administration before a fee may be charged for services. This section of the law also provides that up to 25 percent of the claimant's past-due benefits can be used toward the payment of such fee.

When the amount of the fee is determined, the authorized fee will be paid directly to the attorney from the withheld benefits. If the amount of the authorized fee is less than the total amount withheld from all beneficiaries, it will be paid proportionally from withheld benefits. Any of the amount withheld from your benefits not needed for payment of the authorized fee will be sent to you.

We are sending a copy of this letter to your lawyer.

Your Responsibilities

Your benefits are based on the information you gave us. If this information changes, it could affect your benefits. For this reason, it is important that you report changes to us right away.

We have enclosed a pamphlet, "When You Get Social Security Retirement or Survivors Benefits... What You Need to Know." It tells you what must be reported and how to report. Please be sure to read that part of the pamphlet which explains how work could change your payments.

SEE NEXT PAGE

Do You Disagree With The Decision?

If you think we are wrong, you have the right to appeal. We will correct mistakes. We will look at any new facts you have. Then a person who did not make the first decision will decide your case again.

- You have 60 days to ask for an appeal.
- The 60 days start the day after you get this letter.
- You will have to have a good reason for waiting more than 60 days to ask for an appeal.
- You have to ask for an appeal in writing. We will ask you to sign a form SSA-561-U2, called "Request for Reconsideration". Contact one of our offices if you want help.

SEE NEXT PAGE

If You Have Any Questions

If you have any questions, call us at 1-800-772-1213. We can answer most questions over the phone. If you prefer to visit one of our offices, please check the local telephone directory for the office nearest you. Or call us and we can give you the office address. Please have this letter with you if you call or visit an office. It will help us answer your questions.

W Burnell Hurt

W. Burnell Hurt
Director

UNITED STATES DISTRICT COURT
EASTERN DISTRICT OF NEW YORK

DOMINICK

Plaintiff, 95-CIV-2817 (NG)

-against-

KENNETH APFEL
as COMMISSIONER OF SOCIAL SECURITY

Defendant.

Affidavit of Service

State of New York }
County of Nassau }

I, , being duly sworn, say: I am not a party to the action, an over 19 years of age and reside at PORT JEFFERSON, NY

That on JANUARY ~~6~~ 12TH 1999, I served the within NOTICE OF MOTION AND PETITION FOR COUNSEL FEES PURSUANT TO 42 USC 406(B) upon LINDA MARINO, ESQ, of the United States Attorney's Office for the Eastern District of New York, Civil Division, 14th Floor, 1 Pierrepont Plaza, Brooklyn, NY 11201 and upon 124 Indiana Avenue, BNrooklyn, NY 11234-6907, by depositing true copies thereof, each in a post-paid wrapper, in an official depository under the exclusive care and custody of the U.S. Postal Service, within New York State, at Woodbury New York

Sworn to before me on this 12TH day of January 1999

Victor Fusco
NOTARY PUBLIC, STATE OF NEW YORK
QUALIFIED IN COUNTY OF NASSAU
REG. # 02FU 4626260
COMMISSION EXPIRES APRIL 30, 2000

Scheine, Fusco, Brandenstein & Rada, PC
ATTORNEYS AT LAW

SOCIAL SECURITY DISABILITY DEPARTMENT
180 FROEHLICH FARM BLVD., PO BOX 307, WOODBURY, NY 11797-0307
516-496-0100 • 212-233-1457 • FAX: 516-496-2316
OTHER OFFICES: MANHATTAN, BRONX, HEMPSTEAD, COMMACK, MEDFORD

Workers' Compensation Offsets

A Guide for New York State Practitioners

Victor Fusco

It is well settled that the Social Security Administration must look to state Workers' Compensation law in deciding whether to apply offset provisions. Hodge v. Shalala, 27 F. 3rd 430 (Ninth Circuit, 1994); Sciarotta v. Bowen, 837 F.2d 135 (3rd Cir. 1988); Black v. Schweiker, 670 F.2d 108 (9th Cir. 1992); Swain v Schweiker, 676 F.2d 543, 546, (11th Cir.), cert. denied, 459 U.S. 991 (1982); Davidson v. Sullivan, 942 F.2d 90 (1st Cir. 1991); Grant v. Weinberger, 482 F.2d 1290 (6th Cir. 1973); Iglinsky v Richardson, 433 F.2d. 405 (5th Cir.1970).

An individual who receives both Social Security Disability benefits (SSD) and Workers' Compensation benefits (WC) is entitled to receive up to 80% of their former highest income between the two benefits. See: 42 U.S.C. §424a (a); 20 CFR §404.408; SSR 72-37c; Richardson v. Belcher, 404 U.S. 78, 92 S.Ct. 254. The Social Security Administration (SSA) will compute the highest annual income based on whatever method is most favorable to the claimant. (See 42 U.S.C. § 415).[1]

Very detailed regulations and illustrations regarding the application of the WC offset may be found at 20 C.F.R. 404.408.

To calculate the offset you must have copy of a certified SS earnings record, or at least a benefits estimate - to calculate an approximation.

80% of the highest former earnings is designated as the "ACEH" on the earnings record. You can check the ACEH by using the highest year in the five years prior to the onset of disability or, if the highest year did not occur within the five years prior to onset, you may use an average of the highest five **consecutive** years over the lifetime. If you are using this "high-five" method, simply add up the years and divide by five for the average. Take either that average or the high one-year in the last five (whichever is higher) and divide by 12 for the "high-monthly wage," then multiply that by .80. The result should equal that which SSA reports as the ACEH, i.e., 80% of the highest monthly wage.

[1] Offset does not apply in states with plans which provide that WC benefits will be reduced by any amount payable as SSD, if the state's plan was enacted prior to February 18, 1981, 42 U.S.C. §424a(d).

For example, assume that our client became disabled in 1996. His highest year of earnings from 1991-1995 was $36,000. Let's assume he earned $40,000 in 1985, but his average earnings during the five years surrounding 1985 was less than $36,000. Therefore, $36,000.00 is the figure you would use to calculate the ACEH. $36,000 divided by 12 equals $3,000. Multiply that by .80 for an ACEH of $2,400. Between SSD and WC this person can not receive more than $2,400.00 total monthly benefits.

If you do not have a Certified Earnings Record, you can still compute the ACEH from a benefits estimate or a SEQY (a summary strip of earnings).

Next, determine (from the benefits estimate or earnings record) the **PIA** or "Primary Insured Amount," i.e. the monthly benefit payable to the claimant at the time he/she is found disabled, (before offsets are imposed). This benefit rate (PIA) is subject to possible reduction due to offset and will also be increased to account for cost of living adjustments. These cost of living increases are not subject to offset.

Also look at the FMAX (Family Maximum Benefit) - the amount payable to the wage earner's family (only if there are eligible auxiliary beneficiaries). In low PIA cases, the FMAX and PIA are often the same amount, in which case there are no benefits available to pay eligible family members. Generally, eligible auxiliaries are entitled to 50% of the wage earner's benefit. Therefore, the FMAX will ordinarily equal 150% of the PIA. Children are ordinarily entitled while under age 18 and also from 18 until 19 if still in high school. If a child graduates after age 18, but before age 19, benefits are payable until the month of high school graduation. (For a complete discussion of child's (and mother's) benefits see 42 U.S.C. §402(d)).

Once we know the **ACEH**, we simply subtract the amount of the monthly WC benefit. **Caveat:** you must translate the weekly WC benefits into monthly figures. If the amount remaining after this calculation is **more** than the PIA (or FMAX in appropriate cases) then there is no offset. If the amount remaining is less, we calculate the amount of offset.

Example 1. Assume the claimant receives $400.00 per week WC. One method of ascertaining the monthly rate is to multiply the $400.00 weekly rate x 52, which equals $20,800.00, and divide that by 12, yielding monthly WC of $1,733.00 (rounded). Assume that the wage earner's monthly SSD benefit (PIA) in this particular case is $1,000.00 and that the family benefit is an additional $500.00, for an FMAX of $1,500.00. Deduct the $1,733.00 monthly WC from the ACEH of $2,400.00. The resulting amount is $667.00. As the claimant would have been entitled to receive $1,000.00 before offset, the claimant's benefits will be reduced by $333.00. The auxiliary benefit will be totally reduced to $0.00.

This claimant cannot get more than $667.00 in total Social Security benefits, rather than the full $1,500.00 FMAX benefit. Offset is always applied first to auxiliary beneficiaries.

If there's a 4% cost of living adjustment (COLA), the amount of the COLA is based on the total SSD benefits before offset so that an additional $60.00 (4% of $1,500.00) would be payable in this case. Thus, the wage earner's benefit would be increased by $40.00 to $707.00 and the children would now receive $20.00 per month.

Obtaining Earnings Records

Earnings records come in several forms. The "**SEQY**" is simply a strip summary of the claimant's earnings. It does not tell you the benefit amounts, but has sufficient data to determine the impact of offset. It will also provide clues as to whether the earnings history may create "offset" issues or "date last insured" problems.

Another tool, the **Benefits Estimate** is obtained by mailing a completed form **SSA-7004** to SSA, Data Operations Center, PO Box 7004, Wilkes Barre, PA 18767-7004. The form is available from your District Office, or through Tele-service. If you want the estimate sent to your own office include an authorization signed by the claimant so permitting. Complete this form as accurately as possible since what you will receive is an **estimate and only that.** While the estimates are rather close to the final figures, since they are partly based on unverified information provided by the claimant, they are never 100% accurate. If the claimant has already filed a claim for SSD, you can't get this estimate.

The most common and easily utilized tool is the **Certified Earnings Record** such as is found in most ALJ hearing exhibit files. The **MBR** (Master Benefits Record) has even more information.

In cases where you are retained after an SSD application has been filed, make a Freedom of Information Act request to the District Office for a copy of the Certified Earnings Record. Stay on top of the District Office (DO) to get this data. These requests are often ignored. The DO may aver that once the DIB claim is in process, the earnings record comes off the system and you can't get it until the hearing level. (Don't believe it, press the issue).

It behooves counsel to obtain some type of earnings record, immediately upon being retained, in any type of case where the SSD may have an impact, or be impacted. We recommend that every PI practitioner or WC attorney obtain at least a benefits estimate as part of the initial set-up of the case. If you contemplate prosecuting an SSD case, it is wise to try to obtain one or have the client obtain one, even prior to your being retained.

My firm gets them on all of our cases, including PI and WC even if an SSD claim is not on the immediate horizon. The estimate alerts us to which potential SSD cases will be more lucrative and enables us to compute WC offset before ever filing an application. It enables you to give better advice to your client, and to ensure their expectations are reasonable.

Workers' Compensation Information

Practitioners can sign up SSD cases before the application is filed or at any point in the administrative process. At whatever stage the case comes in, when setting up the initial appointment, caution your client to bring all WC decisions or records of payment, or have your Workers' Compensation file handy. Upon set-up of your SSD file, submit these decisions to SSA. You can submit "copies" even though the DO "insists" on originals. At the hearing level, make them an exhibit if possible. You want to place SSA on notice that the claimant is receiving WC and the amounts thereof. This may prevent an embarrassing overpayment later. (If there is an overpayment, guess who'll get blamed...you!).

Problems and Pitfalls

You can **never** presume to know the effect of WC offset, nor can you guess at the PIA or FMAX by simply finding out what the claimant earned in the most recent employment. You must elicit a very detailed work history, particularly if no earnings record is available. Don't merely inquire into job duties and physical demands and skills required. Ask about salary levels, longevity in the job position, periods of layoff and unemployment. A claimant's lifetime earning pattern is an important clue, if not to the value of the case, at least to the urgency of getting a formal earnings statement from SSA. (You can also purchase computer programs that will figure out PIA amounts from an accurate earnings history or from a SEQY. National Technical Information Services at 703-487-4650, sells a program called "ANY PIA" for about $60.00, or you can go to the internet http:\\www.ssa.gov and choose "compute your own benefit." (I've never been able to actually do this, nor have I been able to download SSA's form from their website, although they say is can be done.)

Your client may recently have held a very high paying job, but may have only worked in that job for the last year or so. Prior to that time, the client may have had sporadic employment, non-covered employment, or lower paying jobs in another field. The primary benefit amount may be very low. There probably will be no offset if the PIA is low, because the ACEH, based on most recent employment, may be quite high.

Another client may be injured on a recent job that paid much less than what they made in the past. In states that have compensation schemes that do not utilize an "Annual Average Weekly Wage," such individual's WC will be based on the salary on that most recent job and may be very low. This claimant may have a high ACEH based on prior years' employment, but low WC payments based on most recent work, and, as a result, may also not be impacted by offset.

Example 2. Mr. Smith earned $48,000 in 1996, but only $15,000 in 1997 because he lost his higher-paying job and was forced to take a lower-paying job. (Let's assume a PIA of $1200 and FMAX of $1800). He was injured on the $15,000.00 job in early 1997. In most jurisdictions, WC benefits will not be more than 2/3 of his salary or $192.00 per week (or $826.12 per month). Obviously, with an ACEH of $3,200.00 per month, WC of $826.12 would not cause an offset. ACEH of $3200.00 - $826.12 = $2,373.88, which is greater than the PIA of $1200 and greater than the FMAX of $1800.00, so <u>no offset applies</u>.

Example 3. In contrast, let us assume Mr. Jones begins a new job with a $48,000 rate of pay on January 1, 1998. Prior to that time, he never made more than $15,000. During his second week of employment at his new job, he suffers a disabling injury. In New York his Average Weekly Wage would be based on the wages paid on the new job (utilizing the payroll of a similar worker to find the reasonable value of services in this current employment).[2]

Since Mr. Jones worked only two weeks at the new salary, his SS earnings record for all practical purposes will be based on his prior earnings that never exceeded $15,000 per year.

---

[2] Some states may simply fix a reasonable value of the services based upon the salary level in that particular line of work. Practitioners in states that utilize State Average Weekly Wage must adjust their calculations accordingly. Every state is different and every SS practitioner should read their state's statutes on the methods of computing WC benefit rates.

In New York, Mr. Jones would be entitled to maximum weekly WC of $400.00 or $1,733.33 per month. For SSD purposes, his ACEH is based upon the highest full year's salary of $15,000.00 from 1997.

Take the $15,000.00 and divide it by 12 for an average monthly wage of $1,250.00, 80% of which is $1,000.00 per month.

Thus, between WC and SSD, Mr. Jones cannot receive more than $1,000.00 per month. However, he is already receiving $1,733.33 per month in WC benefits, and thus, his benefits (and his family's benefits) would be totally offset.

There can be many variations between these two examples. Therefore, it behooves the practitioner to look at the earnings record and the current WC benefits and to remember:

(1) Don't assume that a currently high-wage earner will have a high ACEH.

(2) Don't assume that someone who is currently a low wage earner will have a low ACEH.

(3) If there are gaps or erratic salary patterns, review the earnings record with your client to verify that it is accurate. Only then can you explain the ramifications to the client.

In my office, after we review a benefits estimate or earnings record, we send a letter to each client in which we explain the impact of WC benefits on his SSD benefits, if applicable. We send this as early in the case as possible.[3]

Forms of Compensation Awards, Impact on Offsets

In New York as in most states, several types of benefits are payable. Temporary total benefits, temporary partial benefits, permanent total benefits and permanent partial benefits, and permanent partial benefits on a "schedule."

The vast majority of work place injuries involve minor injuries to extremity, such as a broken foot, arm, hand, or occupational repetitive strain injuries to the wrist or elbow or injuries of that type. "Schedule loss" awards computed by medically measuring the percentage loss of use of the extremity and paying the claimant a flat schedule of benefits commensurate with such loss. The claimant can receive the award even if there is never a day lost from work.

New York provides on-going payments during periods of disability. Knowing the maximum WC rate is $400 or 2/3 of the AWW under $600, even if you only have a SEQY and can figure the ACEH, and

---

[3] Once you know how to compute the offset and what documents you need to do it, you would think that it would be a relatively clear cut and simple thing to do. Unfortunately, no!

WC procedures and forms differ from state to state. If you think it's difficult for the practitioner, pity the SSA Benefits Analysts who need to be familiar with fifty variants on the theme with each state's law having different ways of explaining what benefits are payable and each state providing for benefits in a slightly different way. It is essential that you have some grasp on your state's basic WC terminology even if you never handle a WC case.

have no other information other than the fact your client is receiving WC, you can at least deduct the maximum WC rate from the ACEH, to get an idea of whether offset will be an issue.

It is important to know if the WC benefits (be they for total or partial disability) are time limited in scope. In New York, for example, permanent partial (or total) disability benefits can be paid without time limitation in non-schedule cases. What's confusing is that the time-limited benefits in schedule cases are also considered "permanent partial disability benefits." If a client getting SSD has a schedule loss award, which causes offset, the client must be advised that when the schedule runs out his SSD can be increased because the offset will no longer be applicable.

Some limited claims are resolved on a "period of disability." If the claimant fully recovers, the case is closed with no further awards. Some cases are closed with no further casusally related disability even though the claimant may be disabled from other causes and still eligible for SSD.

Where a claimant is permanently disabled from a non scheduable condition, and cannot work at all or can work but with a permanent reduction in earning capacity, the case is generally resolved on what is called a **permanent disability "classification" (PPD or PTD)**. Generally, non-schedulable injuries to include cardiac, lung, brain, spinal injuries, and injuries that would ordinarily be schedulable, except that the claimant remains symptomatic with a probable need for continuing medical care. (i.e. development of chronic osteomyelitis in the leg, or perhaps develops a chronically unstable knee, etc.)

Such **classified** claimant may be given a permanent disability rating, such as a "50% causally related disability," and an appropriate permanent WC rate is fixed, based upon the proportional percentage of what is 2/3rds of the AWW. If benefits will be paid forever, and the claimant is offset, that offset will be applied through age 65 when the disability benefits are automatically converted into retirement benefits to which offset does not apply.

Medical benefits are paid directly to the health care provider by the insurance carrier and the amounts paid for medical care are not delineated in the awards made by the board or Commission, nor considered part of the "award."

Whenever there is a decision awarding WC benefits, a writing will ordinarily be issued by the Workers Compensation Board. Carriers are periodically required to issue statements of the benefits paid to date and those being paid into the future (C-8). SSA accepts such writings as prima facie evidence of the amounts being paid to the claimant.

However, SSA often confuses schedule loss claims, which have a finite payout of benefits, with permanent partial disability claims, which may be characterized by ongoing "pension" type payments. If SSA mistakenly presumes that a schedule award is permanent payment, they may continue to offset a claimant who is no longer subject to offset. There is a wide body of regulatory material permitting SSA to treat the schedule loss payments as periodic payments for as long as they are paid. LUMP SUM dispositions of non-schedule cases create additional problems with respect to offsets.

Checking the Notice of Award

It is incumbent upon the practitioner to carefully review the offset computations, and other issues, in every SSD Notice of Award to ascertain whether the claimant's benefits are being properly maximized.

1. Ascertain as early in the claim as you can, whether there was any protective filing which would enable the claimant to receive benefits earlier than one year prior to the date the "formal" application was filed.

2. Was there a prior application filed within a year of the current one, which should be reopened automatically?

3. Was there a prior application within four years, which should have, been reopened on the basis of new and material evidence?

4. Did the claimant have a prior period of disability within five years of the current period, so as to preclude the imposition of any waiting period?

5. Does SS indicate that a Workers' Compensation offset has been applied? If so, you immediately must test SSA's calculations.

6. Does the Notice of Award fail to recognize that the claimant is getting Workers' Compensation? If no offset would apply anyway, no harm's been done. However, if benefits were over-paid because SSA overlooked the WC awards and failed to compute the offset, you'd better immediately advise your client and take affirmative steps to correct the mistake, so your client isn't hit with an even larger overpayment in the future.

7. Make sure your client has applied for auxiliary benefits, and realize it may take several months longer to get the awards for the auxiliaries. These have to be checked, too.

Realize that if the WC offset calculation is wrong, the amount withheld and payable to you as your fee may also be wrong. If, in a Fee Petition case, you fail to check the Award Certificate, you may be misled into requesting a much lower fee than you deserve. If it is a Fee Agreement case and you don't appeal the offset and the fee, SSA may not honor your request for an increased fee when it finally issues a correct award letter on the grounds that you didn't appeal the fee in time. My firm protectively appeals any unclear Award Certificate containing a WC offset.

By the same token, if you fail to submit WC information while the claim is pending and a claimant is over-paid, you may need to return a proportionate part of your fee, if not by command from SSA, most certainly by your local bar association grievance committee. If you have a deal with your client that your fee will not exceed 25% of past-due benefits and SSA over-calculates the past due benefits, you have a moral obligation to refund a proportionate part of benefits which were overpaid for your fee.

Worse, you may have a very angry client, who may say "you're my lawyer, you should've known this would happen and you should've taken care of it . . ." It should be your practice to check for the latest

WC awards every time you review the file, if it is your own office's WC case. If it is not, any time you communicate with your client, ask him/her (or the attorney handling the WC case) to update you as to the status of the WC case and to send you any recent decision(s) or payment verifications from the carrier.

As you receive these documents, immediately file them with the DO as a protective measure. If you have continually supplied SSA with verification of the WC rates, and nevertheless there still results an overpayment, it will certainly be without fault on the part of you or the claimant. That should make it somewhat easier to obtain a waiver of any overpayment that might occur in the future, because of a failure by SSA to properly calculate the offset.

Reimbursement to Employer

Where a company or municipality pays salary or "sick pay" to an employee who is out of work due to an on the job injury, there may be an award of WC made payable for the period of disability. Ordinarily it will be made payable to the employer. P.O.M.S. § DI-11501.045 (E) provides that such benefits are **not offsetable** in most circumstances.

Lump Sum Settlements

A lump sum settlement (LSS) is generally calculated as a "commutation" of several years of benefits in one lump sum. In some states, lump sum awards, like schedule loss awards, are typically "allocated." (However, in New York, courts have held that the "allocation" is solely for purposes of calculations the Board may need to make for Special Funds purposes) Billigmeier v. Cress Dry Wall, 174 AD 2d 903, 571 NYS2d 600; affirmed 79 NY 2d 994, 584 NYS2d 435. Billigmeier held that because a settlement was a lifetime settlement of claimant's rights, a subsequent comp carrier on a later case could not offset its benefits by an amount equal to an allocation on the prior case lump sum. The argument that Social Security should likewise consider a New York Lump Sum allocation to be a one time payout to be allocated over a sperson's lifetime failed both in the Eastern District and in the Second Circuit Court of Appeals.

If a claimant receives weekly WC of $300.00, a carrier might offer a "5 year lump" of benefits totaling $78,000.00. Assume that, after fees, claimant nets $70,000. SSA will simply treat the $70,000 as a continued payment over the next 4 1/2 years. See: **SSR 87-20c and 87-21c** and **20 CFR § 404.408**

To minimize the effect of offset in a LSS, in states that "allocate," like New York, you may allocate the payout over more years at a lower rate. Once we've agreed to the LSS dollar figure of $78,000.00, the carrier often does not care how the LSS is allocated for adjudicative purposes, nor does the Board. **(However, SSA will not give credence to revised lump sum agreements, which usually occur when a claimant complains that the lawyer screwed up and cost him Social Security Disability Benefits, by not allocating properly).** SSA will accept an "allocation" provided the board or commission sets it forth in the original LSS order or decision. **CAVEAT**: Get it right the first time; SSA is loath to honor an **amended LSS decision**.

Assuming the case is settled at the WC Board on June 1, 1999, and allocated at $300 a week. The LSS would ordinarily run out around January of 2004(as SSA gives a credit for the attorneys' fees). If the

WC B allocates the lump sum settlement at the weekly WC rate of $100.00 (avoiding offset), that lump sum settlement would run out some 15 years down the road, rather than five years later. To determine the highest possible allocation that does not run into offset, you must know the claimant's ACEH. Adjusting the potential lump sum settlement to maximize your client's benefits may entail working with another attorney who may be handling the claimant's WC case and who hasn't a clue as to what you are talking about.[4] Some practitioners have reported great difficulty in securing language to prorate the settlement.[5]

Unfortunately, the reallocation method does not work in all states, and under tremendous pressure from labor and the claimants bar, SSA has withdrawn proposed new rules that would have eliminated the ability to creatively maximize benefits by utilizing WC lump sums.

Using Your Social Security Savvy To Negotiate Compensation Rates

In our opinion, it is generally better to initially maximize WC rates to the highest extent possible, even if it means the SSD will be offset.[6] A claimant who is classified permanent partial may get WC payments for life. In contrast, there is always a possibility that SSD can be terminated. The statute requires most SSD claims are reviewed every three years. Secondly, since WC LSS's ordinarily are predicated on the weekly benefit rate, if you agree to reduce a compensation rate any more than you have to, you may be jeopardizing the value of a potential lump sum settlement for the client.

Also, if you must compromise a permanent WC rate, you may want to do it based on how offset will affect the PIA, not the FMAX, as kids do grow up! Be sure to inform your client as to what you are doing!

Third Party Settlements - Reverse Offsets!

Where a claimant is entitled to pursue WC plus a secondary cause of action against a third-party, when the third-party case is settled, the WC carrier will have a lien for benefits it may have paid. When that lien is re-paid, it is as if the claimant did not receive any Workers' Compensation at all to the extent of the repayment. SSA regulations provide for elimination (retroactively) of the entire offset, as provided for by Social Security's own internal rule found at P.O.M.S. DI 11501.041 (D).

Often the claimant will also have "deficiency compensation" into the future, which means that all compensation benefits will stop until claimant "consumes" the dollar for dollar value of the third party settlement. SSA can not impose offset until the deficiency is used up and the claimant's compensation benefits are reinstated.

---

[4] However, Hodge v. Shalala, 27 F. 3rd 430 (Ninth Circuit, 1994), held that in **Oregon** cases (only) an LSS is a substitute for periodic payments and represents a stream of lost future wages intended to provide wage replacement for a worker's loss of earning capacity, and that although they must be offset when they overlap SSD, the offset amount should be allocated to age 65. The logic of this decision is when disability claimant reaches age 65, the benefits become retirement benefits and are no longer subject to offset. The Hodge decision became Acquiescence Ruling 95-2(9).

[5] Unfortunately, the reallocation method does not work in all states, and under tremendous pressure from labor and the claimants bar, SSA has withdrawn proposed new rules that would have eliminated the ability to creatively maximize benefits by utilizing WC lump sums.

[6] This may not be true where there are third party cases with liens, LTD cases or other considerations.

New York practitioners need to deal with the implications caused by the case of Kelly v. State Insurance Fund, 60 N.Y. 2d 131, 468 N.Y.S. 2d 850, (1983). In essence, often times a claimant will be relieved of payment of the existing compensation lien in return for not enforcing their rights under Kelley, which might, in certain circumstances require the comp carrier to throw in fresh money to pay for the privilege of being released from further obligation to pay the claimant. Without carefully constricted language in the stipulation of settlement, Social Security will never understand what has been done, and will not release the claimant from the offset for the retroactive period because they will not understand that consideration has actually been given by the claimant in the form of paying for the waive by relieving the carrier of an obligation to make payment to the claimant.

If the claimant's SSD benefits had been offset during this period, an application could be made to reverse and remove the offset. To satisfy the technical requirements of the P.O.M.S. DI 11501.045 (D) the application should include:

1. Copies of any agreements and stipulations between the parties, including the WC carrier.

2. Copy of the Board decision finding deficiency compensation exists, and that payments have been suspended.

3. A copy of the check paid to the carrier to pay-off the lien.

It may take SSA some time to remove the offset, but if you stay on top of them, they will. Sounds simple enough, doesn't it!

By now you should have learned that because we are talking about Social Security law, nothing is simple, despite what they write on the fee authorizations.

Scheine, Fusco, Brandenstein & Rada, P.C.
ATTORNEYS AT LAW

SOCIAL SECURITY DISABILITY DEPARTMENT
180 FROEHLICH FARM BLVD., PO BOX 307, WOODBURY, NY 11797-0307
516-496-0100 • 212-233-1457 • FAX:516-496-2316

OTHER OFFICES: MANHATTAN, BRONX, HEMPSTEAD, COMMACK, MEDFORD

To the Social Security Administration

My Account Number is:____________________ ______

My name is:______________________________________

Gentlemen:

I, hereby authorize you to release to my attorneys, SCHEINE, FUSCO, BRANDENSTEIN & RADA, P.C. the following:

☐ Benefits estimate form

☐ Copy of Master benefits record

☐ Copy of certified earnings record

☐ Summary Strip of earnings

☐ Other__________________________________ ______________________

for the following reason(s):

☐ So they may advise me of my potential benefits under the Social Security Act;

☐ So that they can compute and advise me of any offsets which may apply toward my Workers' Compensation case;

☐ So that they may assist me with my estate planning;

☐ So that they may anticipate the collateral source rule in connection with my personal injury case;

☐ So that they may compute offsets in connection with long-term disability benefits which I received from a private carrier;

☐ I am presently receiving Workers' Compensation. Before I pursue a claim for Social Security disability benefits, I want to know the extent to which I may be offset;

☐ Other____

Dated:______________________ Signature: ________________________________

Sworn to me before me this _________ day of,____________________ 19_____.

______________________________ Seal:
Notary Public

SOCIAL SECURITY ADMINISTRATION

Form Approved
OMB No. 0960-0466 ☐ SP

Request for Earnings and Benefit Estimate Statement

To receive a free statement of your earnings covered by Social Security and your estimated future benefits, all you need to do is fill out this form. Please print or type your answers. When you have completed the form, fold it and mail it to us.

1. Name shown on your Social Security card:

   ______________________ ______
   First Name — Middle Initial

   ____
   Last Name Only

2. Your Social Security number as shown on your card:

   ☐☐☐-☐☐-☐☐☐☐

3. Your date of birth ______ ______ ______
   Month — Day — Year

4. Other Social Security numbers you have used:

   ☐☐☐-☐☐-☐☐☐☐
   ☐☐☐-☐☐-☐☐☐☐

5. Your sex: ☐ Male ☐ Female

6. Other names you have used *(including a maiden name)*:

   ____
   ____

7. Show your actual earnings for last year and your estimated earnings for this year. Include only wages and/or net self-employment income covered by Social Security.

   A. Last year's actual earnings: *(Dollars Only)*

   $ ☐☐☐,☐☐☐.0 0

   B. This year's estimated earnings: *(Dollars Only)*

   $ ☐☐☐,☐☐☐.0 0

8. Show the age at which you plan to retire:

   6 5 *(Show only one age)*

9. Below, show the average yearly amount you think you will earn between now and when you plan to retire. We will add your estimate of future earnings to those earnings already on our records to give you the best possible estimate.

   Enter a yearly average, not your total future lifetime earnings. Only show earnings covered by Social Security. Do not add cost-of-living, performance or scheduled pay increases or bonuses. The reason for this is that we estimate retirement benefits in today's dollars, but adjust them to account for average wage growth in the national economy.

   However, if you expect to earn significantly more or less in the future due to promotions, job changes, part-time work, or an absence from the work force, enter the amount in today's dollars that most closely reflects your future average yearly earnings.

   Most people should enter the same amount they are earning now (the amount in 7B).

   Future average yearly earnings: *(Dollars Only)*

   $ ☐☐☐,☐☐☐.0 0

10. Address where you want us to send the statement.

    V. Fusco, Esq. File #
    Name

    P. O. Box 307
    Street Address (Include Apt. No., P.O. Box, or Rural Route)

    Woodbury, NY 11797-0307
    City — State — Zip Code

11. ☐ Please check this box if you want to get your statement in Spanish instead of English.

I am asking for information about my own Social Security record or the record of a person I am authorized to represent. I understand that if I deliberately request information under false pretenses I may be guilty of a federal crime and could be fined and/or imprisoned. I authorize you to use a contractor to send the statement of earnings and benefit estimates to the person named in item 10.

Please sign your name (Do not print)

Signature ______________________

Date ______ c/o attorney 516-496-0100
(Area Code) Daytime Telephone No.

Form SSA-7004-SM (2-93) Destroy Prior Editions

```
***  REC 0098035 0080505 H5DB11E0 bDWA  ICWIRE          (R-XPR.)  ***
$                                *RAAUIJAZ RUEVHHV2744 0340000-UUUU--RUSAXPR.
NH NAME        JOSEPH L                                   SN:                PG 001+

INPUT          02/03/98  OHA HEMPSTEAD NY                 DO:X70  UN:AMT    MOD:
RUN DATE       02/03/98  V:10/29/97      CO:  /           XR SN:
CONTROL                034 241  CC:D  BLK:X               SV:NN             DESK:
EVENT          EARNINGS RECORD-PIA DETERMINATION
TID            BENEFIT ESTIMATE
               CAUTION: INFORMATIONAL ONLY
REMARKS        ACE     3159.20   FULLY INSURED RIB   A CLAIM STATUS
               ACEH     3159.20 H BASE IS 1 YR   NO 37-50 QC
ID INFO        REQ NAME:        REQ SEX:M    REQ DOB:09/14/51 A
DATES          DO:09/26/96   DENT:03/97
NH MISC        AX:ES  PC:1   BIC:A
INS STAT       DISABILITY:  EXCL REQ QC:23   EXCL HAS:40
               NON-EXCL REQ QC:23   NON-EXCL HAS:40    DIS DLI:12/01


NH NAME        JOSEPH L                                   SN:                PG 002+

INPUT          02/03/98  OHA HEMPSTEAD NY                 DO:X70  UN:AMT    MOD:
               DISABILITY TEST: 20/40 MET    20/40 NON-EX MET
TOT COV        SSA QC
                WAGE QC AFTER 1946:  99   WAGE QC AFTER 1950:  99
                SE QC:NONE   AG QC:NONE
TOT EARN       SSA
                TOT AFTER 1936:      672332.54
                TOT AFTER 1950:      672332.54
COMPUTATIONAL YEARLY EARNINGS
MAX    AMT YR QC    REGULAR     U INDEXED     WIDOWS     U RAILROAD  RQSM DMW  SA

 7800      68 NCCC    853.80       3639.92
           69 #NNC    387.25       1560.73
           70 CCCC   3819.24      14664.87
           71 CCCC   6665.77      24370.27
```

```
NH NAME     JOSEPH L [redacted]                              [redacted]  PG 003+

INPUT        02/03/98  OHA HEMPSTEAD NY                  DO:X70  UN:AMT   MOD:
 9000        72 CCCC    7421.85        24712.65
10800        73 CCCC    8457.17        26501.77
13200        74 CCCC    9792.41        28964.17
14100        75 CCCC   10213.93        28110.20
15300        76 CCCC   12681.67 H      32648.90
16500        77 CCCC   13345.16 L      32414.40
17700  250  78 CCCC   14928.57 H      33592.77
22900  260  79 CCCC   14757.94        30537.43
25900  290  80 CCCC   15274.47        28994.59
29700  310  81 CCCC   18743.57 L      32325.76
32400  340  82 CCCC   20508.33 H      33523.77
35700  370  83 CCCC   22396.18 H      34909.11
37800  390  84 CCCC   23673.72 H      34851.69
```

```
IH NAME     JOSEPH L [redacted]                           SN:[redacted]  PG 004+

INPUT        02/03/98  OHA HEMPSTEAD NY                  DO:X70  UN:AMT   MOD:
39600 410 85 CCCC    27529.74 H     38872.23
42000 440 86 CCCC    27944.23 H     38320.11
43800 460 87 CCCC    32040.85 H     41303.71
45000 470 88 CCCC    33035.52 H     40586.98
48000 500 89 CCCC    41119.76 H     48595.09
51300 520 90 CCCC    42691.82 H     48225.34
53400 540 91 CCCC    41012.98 H     44664.45
55500 570 92 CCCC    41380.85 H     42856.91
57600 590 93 CCCC    47391.80 H     48663.75
60600 620 94 CCCC    44489.77 H     44489.77
61200 630 95 CCCC    45925.04 H     45925.04
62700 640 96 CCCC    43849.15 H     43849.15
65400 670 97 NNNN
```

– Hi 1 yr

47391.80
divided by 12 =
3949. x
.80
3159

```
H NAME     JOSEPH L [redacted]                            SN:[redacted]  PG 005

NPUT        02/03/98  OHA HEMPSTEAD NY                   DO:X70  UN:AMT   MOD:
8400 700 98 NNNN
OMP DATA   DI  - COMP TYPE:NS 78 DIS EX                   AIME:$3336.00
           EFF DATE:01/97  PIA:$1236.60  PIFC:L  FAM MAX:$1854.90
           EFF DATE:12/97  PIA:$1262.50  PIFC:L  FAM MAX:$1893.80
           START BASE YEAR/START DATE:1951   LAST BASE YEAR/CLOSE DATE:1996
           DIVIDEND: $760618.93   DM:228  DOY:4  YOC:27  I/Y:

N
```

Your Personal Earnings and Benefit Estimate Statement
from the SOCIAL SECURITY ADMINISTRATION

October 22, 1998

C/O SCHEINE FUSCO ET AL
SS DIV FILE PO BOX 390
WOODBURY, NY 11797-0390

A Message from the Commissioner

We are pleased to send you the Personal Earnings and Benefit Estimate Statement you requested. We hope it will help you to better understand the Social Security program and what it means to you and your family. The statement shows the estimated amount of benefits, under current law, that you and your family may be eligible for now and in the future. It also lists the earnings that your employers (or you, if you're self-employed) have reported to Social Security. We hope you will use this information along with other information you may have about your savings, pensions and investments to help you plan for a secure financial future.

Remember, Social Security can be an important part of your financial future whether you're young or old, male or female, single or married. It can help you when you need it most by paying you benefits when you retire or if you become severely disabled. Social Security also can help support your family when you die.

Some people are concerned that Social Security won't be there in the future. The program has changed in the past to meet the demands of the times, and it must do so again. Today we are working to resolve long-range financing issues and to ensure that future generations of Americans can count on the same financial protections from Social Security as past generations did.

ACE:
65400 ÷ 12 = 5450 x .8 = 4360

Kenneth S. Apfel
Commissioner of Social Security

PIA 1455
(MAX Cat) 150% = 2182.

No offset will apply
Standing A Ann

The Facts You Gave Us

Your Name	Diane
Your Social Security Number	
Your Date of Birth	03/ /1958
1997 Earnings	Over $65,400
1998 Earnings	Over $68,400
Your Estimated Future Average Yearly Earnings	Over $68,400
Age You Plan To Stop Working	65
Other Social Security Numbers You've Used	None

Your Social Security Earnings

On page 4, we explain more about covered earnings and Social Security and Medicare taxes. The following chart shows your reported earnings. It may not show some or all of your earnings from last year because they are not yet recorded. This year's earnings will not be reported to us until next year.

If your own records do not agree with the earnings amounts shown, please contact us right away. If possible, have your W-2 or tax return for those years available.

	Social Security			Medicare		
Years	Maximum Taxable Earnings	Your Reported Earnings	Estimated Taxes You Paid	Maximum Taxable Earnings	Your Reported Earnings	Estimated Taxes You Paid
1937-50	$3,000	$ 0	$ 0			
1951	3,600	0	0			
1952	3,600	0	0			
1953	3,600	0	0			
1954	3,600	0	0			
1955	4,200	0	0			
1956	4,200	0	0			
1957	4,200	0	0			
1958	4,200	0	0	Medicare did not start until 1966.		
1959	4,800	0	0			
1960	4,800	0	0			
1961	4,800	0	0			
1962	4,800	0	0			
1963	4,800	0	0			
1964	4,800	0	0			
1965	4,800	0	0			
1966	6,600	0	0	$6,600	$ 0	$ 0
1967	6,600	0	0	6,600	0	0
1968	7,800	0	0	7,800	0	0
1969	7,800	0	0	7,800	0	0
1970	7,800	0	0	7,800	0	0
1971	7,800	0	0	7,800	0	0
1972	9,000	0	0	9,000	0	0
1973	10,800	0	0	10,800	0	0
1974	13,200	256	12	13,200	256	2
1975	14,100	1,205	59	14,100	1,205	10
1976	15,300	1,115	55	15,300	1,115	10
1977	16,500	0	0	16,500	0	0
1978	17,700	0	0	17,700	0	0
1979	22,900	0	0	22,900	0	0
1980	25,900	0	0	25,900	0	0
1981	29,700	0	0	29,700	0	0
1982	32,400	2,028	109	32,400	2,028	26
1983	35,700	17,793	960	35,700	17,793	231
1984	37,800	22,370	1,208	37,800	22,370	290
1985	39,600	26,334	1,501	39,600	26,334	355
1986	42,000	32,652	1,861	42,000	32,652	473
1987	43,800	39,227	2,235	43,800	39,227	568
1988	45,000	38,043	2,305	45,000	38,043	551
1989	48,000	45,032	2,728	48,000	45,032	652
1990	51,300	50,960	3,159	51,300	50,960	738
1991	53,400	53,400	3,310	125,000	54,006	783
1992	55,500	55,500	3,441	130,200	60,009	870
1993	57,600	57,600	3,571	135,000	62,320	903
1994	60,600	60,600	3,757	No Limit	64,358	933
1995	61,200	61,200	3,794	No Limit	66,811	968
1996	62,700	62,700	3,887	No Limit	68,561	994
1997	65,400	65,400	4,054	No Limit	73,182	1,061
1998	68,400			No Limit		
Total estimated Social Security taxes paid			$ 42,006	**Total estimated Medicare taxes paid**	$	10,418

2

Your Estimated Social Security Benefits

Your work under Social Security helps you and your family to qualify for benefit payments. The kinds of benefits you might get are described below. For each benefit, you need a certain number of work credits (see page 5). Once you have enough credits, your benefit amount depends on your average earnings over your working lifetime. We used the earnings in the chart on page 2 to figure your credits and estimate your benefits. We included any 1997 and 1998 earnings and any estimated future earnings you told us about.

Retirement Benefits

To get Social Security retirement benefits, you need 40 credits of work. That is also how many you need for Medicare at age 65. Your record shows that you have enough credits.

On page 5, we explain about different ages when you can retire. If you worked at your present rate up to each retirement age, your monthly amount would be about:

At age 65 (reduced benefit) . . . . $ 1,420
At full-retirement age (66 and 8 months) . . . . $ 1,600
At age 70 . . . . $ 2,040

Disability Benefits

On page 6, we tell you about disability benefits. If you become disabled right now, you need 20 credits to qualify for benefits. You had to earn these credits in the last 10 years. Your record shows that you have earned enough credits within the right time.

Right now, your monthly disability amount would be about . . . . $ 1,455

Family Benefits

If you get retirement or disability benefits, your spouse and young children may also qualify for benefits. See page 6 for more information about family benefits.

Survivor Benefits

If you die, certain members of your family may qualify for survivor benefits on your record. See page 6 for an explanation of who may qualify.

If you die right now, you need 18 credits for your survivors to get benefits. Your record shows you have enough. If they met all other requirements, monthly benefit amounts would be about:

For your child . . . . $ 1,140
For your spouse who is caring for your child . . . . $ 1,140
When your spouse reaches full-retirement age . . . . $ 1,525
For all your family members, if others also qualify (more children, for example) . . . . $ 2,675

We may also be able to pay your spouse or children a one-time death benefit of $255.

Medicare

Medicare hospital and medical insurance is a two-part benefit program that helps protect you from the high costs of medical care. Hospital insurance benefits (Part A) help pay the cost when you are in the hospital and for certain kinds of follow-up care. Medical insurance benefits (Part B) help pay the costs of doctors' services.

If you have enough work credits, you may qualify for Medicare hospital insurance at age 65, even if you are still working. You may qualify before age 65 if you are disabled or have permanent kidney failure. Your spouse may also qualify for hospital insurance at 65 on your record.

Almost anyone who is 65 or older or who qualifies for Medicare hospital insurance can enroll for medical insurance. You must pay a monthly premium for it.

For More Information or To Correct Your Record

After you read this statement, if you have questions, want to apply for benefits or want to request a Statement in Spanish, please call 1-800-772-1213* or visit our Website at www.ssa.gov/mystatement. If you are reporting missing or wrong earnings, have your W-2 or tax return for those years available, if possible. This Statement is just an estimate of your potential benefits. You do not qualify for Social Security or Medicare until you apply and meet all the requirements. Meanwhile, your record is updated each year and you can request a new statement to make sure it stays correct.

Your Social Security Earnings

On page 4, we explain more about covered earnings and Social Security and Medicare taxes. The following chart shows your reported earnings. It may not show some or all of your earnings from last year because they are not yet recorded. This year's earnings will not be reported to us until next year.

If your own records do not agree with the earnings amounts shown, please contact us right away. If possible, have your W-2 or tax return for those years available.

	Social Security			Medicare		
Years	Maximum Taxable Earnings	Your Reported Earnings	Estimated Taxes You Paid	Maximum Taxable Earnings	Your Reported Earnings	Estimated Taxes You Paid
1937-50	$3,000	$ 0	$ 0			
1951	3,600	0	0			
1952	3,600	0	0			
1953	3,600	0	0			
1954	3,600	0	0			
1955	4,200	0	0			
1956	4,200	0	0			
1957	4,200	0	0			
1958	4,200	0	0		Medicare did not start until 1966.	
1959	4,800	0	0			
1960	4,800	0	0			
1961	4,800	473	14			
1962	4,800	700	21			
1963	4,800	2,322	84			
1964	4,800	3,228	117			
1965	4,800	3,438	124			
1966	6,600	3,725	143	$6,600	$ 3,725	$ 13
1967	6,600	4,211	164	6,600	4,211	21
1968	7,800	4,713	179	7,800	4,713	28
1969	7,800	5,065	212	7,800	5,065	30
1970	7,800	6,684	280	7,800	6,684	40
1971	7,800	7,398	340	7,800	7,398	44
1972	9,000	8,090	372	9,000	8,090	48
1973	10,800	8,539	414	10,800	8,539	85
1974	13,200	9,123	451	13,200	9,123	82
1975	14,100	0	0	14,100	0	0
1976	15,300	2,162	107	15,300	2,162	19
1977	16,500	7,842	388	16,500	7,842	70
1978	17,700	8,908	449	17,700	8,908	89
1979	22,900	9,577	486	22,900	9,577	100
1980	25,900	11,294	573	25,900	11,294	118
1981	29,700	12,002	642	29,700	12,002	156
1982	32,400	13,034	703	32,400	13,034	169
1983	35,700	13,766	743	35,700	13,766	178
1984	37,800	15,114	816	37,800	15,114	196
1985	39,600	17,010	969	39,600	17,010	229
1986	42,000	17,937	1,022	42,000	17,937	260
1987	43,800	20,677	1,178	43,800	20,677	299
1988	45,000	22,340	1,353	45,000	22,340	323
1989	48,000	23,537	1,426	48,000	23,537	341
1990	51,300	25,244	1,565	51,300	25,244	366
1991	53,400	27,549	1,708	125,000	27,549	399
1992	55,500	19,682	1,220	130,200	19,682	285
1993	57,600	14,248	883	135,000	14,248	206
1994	60,600	12,995	805	No Limit	12,995	188
1995	61,200	14,259	884	No Limit	14,259	206
1996	62,700	18,943	1,174	No Limit	18,943	274
1997	65,400	20,306	1,259	No Limit	20,306	294
1998	68,400			No Limit		
Total estimated Social Security taxes paid			$ 23,268	**Total estimated Medicare taxes paid**		$ 5,156

Your Estimated Social Security Benefits

Your work under Social Security helps you and your family to qualify for benefit payments. The kinds of benefits you might get are described below. For each benefit, you need a certain number of work credits (see page 5). Once you have enough credits, your benefit amount depends on your average earnings over your working lifetime. We used the earnings in the chart on page 2 to figure your credits and estimate your benefits. We included any 1997 and 1998 earnings and any estimated future earnings you told us about.

Retirement Benefits

To get Social Security retirement benefits, you need 40 credits of work. That is also how many you need for Medicare at age 65. Your record shows that you have enough credits.

On page 5, we explain about different ages when you can retire. If you worked at your present rate up to each retirement age, your monthly amount would be about:

At age 65 (reduced benefit)	$ 910
At full-retirement age (66 years of age)	$ 980
At age 70	$ 1,325

Disability Benefits

On page 6, we tell you about disability benefits. If you become disabled right now, you need 33 credits to qualify for disability benefits. You had to earn 20 of these credits in the last 10 years. Your record shows that you have earned enough credits within the right time.

Right now, your monthly disability amount would be about . . . . . $ 940

1591 - 940 = 651 Comp Annual before offset

1393 - 940 = 453 " " " "

Family Benefits

If you get retirement or disability benefits, your spouse and young children may also qualify for benefits. See page 6 for more information about family benefits.

Survivor Benefits

If you die, certain members of your family may qualify for survivor benefits on your record. See page 6 for an explanation of who may qualify.

If you die right now, you need 33 credits for your survivors to get benefits. Your record shows you have enough. If they met all other requirements, monthly benefit amounts would be about:

For your child	$ 710
For your spouse who is caring for your child	$ 710
When your spouse reaches full-retirement age	$ 950
For all your family members, if others also qualify (more children, for example)	$ 1,745

We may also be able to pay your spouse or children a one-time death benefit of $255.

Medicare

Medicare hospital and medical insurance is a two-part benefit program that helps protect you from the high costs of medical care. Hospital insurance benefits (Part A) help pay the cost when you are in the hospital and for certain kinds of follow-up care. Medical insurance benefits (Part B) help pay the costs of doctors' services.

If you have enough work credits, you may qualify for Medicare hospital insurance at age 65, even if you are still working. You may qualify before age 65 if you are disabled or have permanent kidney failure. Your spouse may also qualify for hospital insurance at 65 on your record.

Almost anyone who is 65 or older or who qualifies for Medicare hospital insurance can enroll for medical insurance. You must pay a monthly premium for it.

For More Information or To Correct Your Record

After you read this statement, if you have questions, want to apply for benefits or want to request a Statement in Spanish, please call 1-800-772-1213* or visit our Website at www.ssa.gov/mystatement. If you are reporting missing or wrong earnings, have your W-2 or tax return for those years available, if possible. This Statement is just an estimate of your potential benefits. You do not qualify for Social Security or Medicare until you apply and meet all the requirements. Meanwhile, your record is updated each year and you can request a new statement to make sure it stays correct.

*Social Security treats all calls confidentially--whether they are made to our toll-free number or to one of our local offices. But we also want to be sure that you receive accurate and courteous service. That is why we have a second Social Security representative listen to some incoming and outgoing telephone calls.

Your Social Security Earnings

On page 4, we explain more about covered earnings and Social Security and Medicare taxes. The following chart shows your reported earnings. It may not show some or all of your earnings from last year because they are not yet recorded. This year's earnings will not be reported to us until next year.

If your own records do not agree with the earnings amounts shown, please contact us right away. If possible, have your W-2 or tax return for those years available.

	Social Security			Medicare		
Years	Maximum Taxable Earnings	Your Reported Earnings	Estimated Taxes You Paid	Maximum Taxable Earnings	Your Reported Earnings	Estimated Taxes You Paid
1937-50	$3,000	$ 0	$ 0			
1951	3,600	0	0			
1952	3,600	0	0			
1953	3,600	0	0			
1954	3,600	0	0			
1955	4,200	0	0			
1956	4,200	103	2			
1957	4,200	100	2			
1958	4,200	0	0		Medicare did not start until 1966.	
1959	4,800	174	4			
1960	4,800	516	15			
1961	4,800	921	27			
1962	4,800	1,040	32			
1963	4,800	0	0			
1964	4,800	0	0			
1965	4,800	0	0			
1966	6,600	0	0	$6,600	$ 0	$ 0
1967	6,600	0	0	6,600	0	0
1968	7,800	0	0	7,800	0	0
1969	7,800	0	0	7,800	0	0
1970	7,800	0	0	7,800	0	0
1971	7,800	0	0	7,800	0	0
1972	9,000	0	0	9,000	0	0
1973	10,800	0	0	10,800	0	0
1974	13,200	0	0	13,200	0	0
1975	14,100	0	0	14,100	0	0
1976	15,300	0	0	15,300	0	0
1977	16,500	0	0	16,500	0	0
1978	17,700	0	0	17,700	0	0
1979	22,900	0	0	22,900	0	0
1980	25,900	0	0	25,900	0	0
1981	29,700	563	30	29,700	563	7
1982	32,400	6,673	360	32,400	6,673	86
1983	35,700	13,324	719	35,700	13,324	173
1984	37,800	14,175	765	37,800	14,175	184
1985	39,600	405	23	39,600	405	5
1986	42,000	0	0	42,000	0	0
1987	43,800	0	0	43,800	0	0
1988	45,000	3,382	204	45,000	3,382	49
1989	48,000	14,497	878	48,000	14,646	212
1990	51,300	23,887	1,481	51,300	23,887	346
1991	53,400	25,844	1,602	125,000	25,844	374
1992	55,500	26,791	1,661	130,200	26,791	388
1993	57,600	26,899	1,667	135,000	26,899	390
1994	60,600	26,935	1,669	No Limit	26,935	390
1995	61,200	22,498	1,394	No Limit	22,498	326
1996	62,700	16,499	1,022	No Limit	16,499	239
1997	65,400	17,874	1,108	No Limit	17,874	259
1998	68,400			No Limit		
				Total estimated Medicare taxes paid	$	3,428

Your Social Security Earnings

On page 4, we explain more about covered earnings and Social Security and Medicare taxes. The following chart shows your reported earnings. It may not show some or all of your earnings from last year because they are not yet recorded. This year's earnings will not be reported to us until next year.

If your own records do not agree with the earnings amounts shown, please contact us right away. If possible, have your W-2 or tax return for those years available.

	Social Security			Medicare		
Years	Maximum Taxable Earnings	Your Reported Earnings	Estimated Taxes You Paid	Maximum Taxable Earnings	Your Reported Earnings	Estimated Taxes You Paid
1937-50	$3,000	$ 0	$ 0	Medicare did not start until 1966.		
1951	3,600	0	0			
1952	3,600	0	0			
1953	3,600	0	0			
1954	3,600	0	0			
1955	4,200	0	0			
1956	4,200	0	0			
1957	4,200	0	0			
1958	4,200	0	0			
1959	4,800	0	0			
1960	4,800	0	0			
1961	4,800	0	0			
1962	4,800	0	0			
1963	4,800	0	0			
1964	4,800	0	0			
1965	4,800	0	0			
1966	6,600	0	0	$6,600	$ 0	$ 0
1967	6,600	0	0	6,600	0	0
1968	7,800	0	0	7,800	0	0
1969	7,800	0	0	7,800	0	0
1970	7,800	0	0	7,800	0	0
1971	7,800	0	0	7,800	0	0
1972	9,000	0	0	9,000	0	0
1973	10,800	0	0	10,800	0	0
1974	13,200	0	0	13,200	0	0
1975	14,100	0	0	14,100	0	0
1976	15,300	0	0	15,300	0	0
1977	16,500	0	0	16,500	0	0
1978	17,700	0	0	17,700	0	0
1979	22,900	0	0	22,900	0	0
1980	25,900	0	0	25,900	0	0
1981	29,700	28	1	29,700	28	0
1982	32,400	7,550	407	32,400	7,550	98
1983	35,700	14,783	798	35,700	14,783	192
1984	37,800	2,135	115	37,800	2,135	27
1985	39,600	0	0	39,600	0	0
1986	42,000	0	0	42,000	0	0
1987	43,800	1,492	85	43,800	1,492	21
1988	45,000	4,247	257	45,000	4,247	61
1989	48,000	10,975	665	48,000	10,975	159
1990	51,300	6,020	373	51,300	6,020	87
1991	53,400	31,171	1,932	125,000	31,171	451
1992	55,500	5,856	363	130,200	5,856	84
1993	57,600	0	0	135,000	0	0
1994	60,600	241	14	No Limit	241	3
1995	61,200	6,831	423	No Limit	6,831	99
1996	62,700	5,428	336	No Limit	5,428	78
1997	65,400	3,254	201	No Limit	3,254	47
1998	68,400			No Limit		
Total estimated Social Security taxes paid			$ 5,970	**Total estimated Medicare taxes paid**		$ 1,407

2

Your Social Security Earnings

On page 4, we explain more about covered earnings and Social Security and Medicare taxes. The following chart shows your reported earnings. It may not show some or all of your earnings from last year because they are not yet recorded. This year's earnings will not be reported to us until next year.

If your own records do not agree with the earnings amounts shown, please contact us right away. If possible, have your W-2 or tax return for those years available.

	Social Security			Medicare		
Years	Maximum Taxable Earnings	Your Reported Earnings	Estimated Taxes You Paid	Maximum Taxable Earnings	Your Reported Earnings	Estimated Taxes You Paid
1937-50	$3.000	$ 0	$ 0	Medicare did not start until 1966.		
1951	3.600	0	0			
1952	3.600	0	0			
1953	3.600	0	0			
1954	3.600	0	0			
1955	4.200	0	0			
1956	4.200	0	0			
1957	4.200	0	0			
1958	4.200	0	0			
1959	4.800	0	0			
1960	4.800	0	0			
1961	4.800	0	0			
1962	4.800	0	0			
1963	4.800	0	0			
1964	4.800	0	0			
1965	4.800	0	0			
1966	6.600	0	0	$6.600	$ 0	$ 0
1967	6.600	0	0	6.600	0	0
1968	7.800	0	0	7.800	0	0
1969	7.800	622	26	7.800	622	3
1970	7.800	3.137	131	7.800	3.137	18
1971	7.800	2.960	136	7.800	2.960	17
1972	9.000	3.093	142	9.000	3.093	18
1973	10.800	4.849	235	10.800	4.849	48
1974	13.200	10.156	502	13.200	10.156	91
1975	14.100	11.464	567	14.100	11.464	103
1976	15.300	8.540	422	15.300	8.540	76
1977	16.500	11.530	570	16.500	11.530	103
1978	17.700	14.308	722	17.700	14.308	143
1979	22.900	0	0	22.900	0	0
1980	25.900	0	0	25.900	0	0
1981	29.700	2.227	119	29.700	2.227	28
1982	32.400	18.722	1.011	32.400	18.722	243
1983	35.700	18.479	997	35.700	18.479	240
1984	37.800	10.050	542	37.800	10.050	130
1985	39.600	0	0	39.600	0	0
1986	42.000	5.076	289	42.000	5.076	73
1987	43.800	0	0	43.800	0	0
1988	45.000	13.354	809	45.000	13.354	193
1989	48.000	30.625	1.855	48.000	30.625	444
1990	51.300	31.897	1.977	51.300	31.897	462
1991	53.400	36,061	2.235	125.000	36.061	522
1992	55.500	38,218	2.369	130.200	38.218	554
1993	57.600	39.003	2,418	135.000	39.003	565
1994	60.600	41.524	2.574	No Limit	41.524	602
1995	61.200	28.295	1.754	No Limit	28.295	410
1996	62.700	323	20	No Limit	323	4
1997	65.400	9.063	561	No Limit	9.063	131
1998	68.400			No Limit		
Total estimated Social Security taxes paid			$ 22.983	Total estimated Medicare taxes paid		$ 5.221

Your Personal Earnings and Benefit Estimate Statement
from the SOCIAL SECURITY ADMINISTRATION

November 6, 1998

C/O SCHEINE FUSCO ET AL
SS DIV FILE
PO BOX 307
WOODBURY, NY 11797-0307

A Message from the Commissioner

We are pleased to send you the Personal Earnings and Benefit Estimate Statement you requested. We hope it will help you to better understand the Social Security program and what it means to you and your family. The statement shows the estimated amount of benefits, under current law, that you and your family may be eligible for now and in the future. It also lists the earnings that your employers (or you, if you're self-employed) have reported to Social Security. We hope you will use this information along with other information you may have about your savings, pensions and investments to help you plan for a secure financial future.

Remember, Social Security can be an important part of your financial future whether you're young or old, male or female, single or married. It can help you when you need it most by paying you benefits when you retire or if you become severely disabled. Social Security also can help support your family when you die.

Some people are concerned that Social Security won't be there in the future. The program has changed in the past to meet the demands of the times, and it must do so again. Today we are working to resolve long-range financing issues and to ensure that future generations of Americans can count on the same financial protections from Social Security as past generations did.

Kenneth S. Apfel
Commissioner of Social Security

The Facts You Gave Us

Your Name	
Your Social Security Number	
Your Date of Birth	
1997 Earnings	$26,000
1998 Earnings	$26,000
Your Estimated Future Average Yearly Earnings	$26,000
Age You Plan To Stop Working	65
Other Social Security Numbers You've Used	None

Your Social Security Earnings

On page 4, we explain more about covered earnings and Social Security and Medicare taxes. The following chart shows your reported earnings. It may not show some or all of your earnings from last year because they are not yet recorded. This year's earnings will not be reported to us until next year.

If your own records do not agree with the earnings amounts shown, please contact us right away. If possible, have your W-2 or tax return for those years available.

	Social Security			Medicare		
Years	Maximum Taxable Earnings	Your Reported Earnings	Estimated Taxes You Paid	Maximum Taxable Earnings	Your Reported Earnings	Estimated Taxes You Paid
1937-50	$3,000	$ 0	$ 0			
1951	3,600	0	0			
1952	3,600	0	0			
1953	3,600	0	0			
1954	3,600	0	0			
1955	4,200	0	0			
1956	4,200	0	0			
1957	4,200	0	0			
1958	4.200	0	0	Medicare did not start until 1966.		
1959	4,800	0	0			
1960	4,800	0	0			
1961	4,800	0	0			
1962	4,800	0	0			
1963	4,800	0	0			
1964	4,800	0	0			
1965	4,800	0	0			
1966	6,600	0	0	$6,600	$ 0	$ 0
1967	6,600	0	0	6,600	0	0
1968	7,800	0	0	7,800	0	0
1969	7,800	0	0	7,800	0	0
1970	7,800	0	0	7,800	0	0
1971	7,800	0	0	7,800	0	0
1972	9,000	34	1	9,000	34	0
1973	10,800	84	4	10,800	84	0
1974	13,200	3.019	149	13,200	3,019	27
1975	14,100	7.728	382	14,100	7,728	69
1976	15,300	8.685	429	15,300	8,685	78
1977	16,500	10.584	523	16,500	10.584	95
1978	17,700	13.195	666	17,700	13.195	131
1979	22,900	12.877	654	22,900	12.877	135
1980	25,900	14.286	725	25,900	14,286	150
1981	29,700	16,123	862	29,700	16,123	209
1982	32,400	19,087	1,030	32,400	19,087	248
1983	35,700	17.431	941	35,700	17,431	226
1984	37,800	19,102	1,031	37,800	19,102	248
1985	39,600	19.875	1,132	39,600	19,875	268
1986	42,000	23.321	1.329	42,000	23,321	338
1987	43,800	20,543	1,170	43,800	20,543	297
1988	45,000	24,787	1.502	45,000	24,787	359
1989	48,000	26,486	1,605	48,000	26,486	384
1990	51,300	28,900	1,791	51,300	28.900	419
1991	53,400	30,636	1.899	125,000	30,636	444
1992	55,500	24,657	1.528	130,200	24,657	357
1993	57,600	0	0	135,000	0	0
1994	60,600	3,190	197	No Limit	3,190	46
1995	61,200	1,177	72	No Limit	1,177	17
1996	62,700	18,531	1,148	No Limit	18,531	268
1997	65,400	14,238	882	No Limit	14,238	206
1998	68,400			No Limit		
Total estimated Social Security taxes paid			$ 21,652	**Total estimated Medicare taxes paid**		$ 5,019

Your Estimated Social Security Benefits

Your work under Social Security helps you and your family to qualify for benefit payments. The kinds of benefits you might get are described below. For each benefit, you need a certain number of work credits (see page 5). Once you have enough credits, your benefit amount depends on your average earnings over your working lifetime. We used the earnings in the chart on page 2 to figure your credits and estimate your benefits. We included any 1997 and 1998 earnings and any estimated future earnings you told us about.

Retirement Benefits

To get Social Security retirement benefits, you need 40 credits of work. That is also how many you need for Medicare at age 65. Your record shows that you have enough credits.

On page 5, we explain about different ages when you can retire. If you worked at your present rate up to each retirement age, your monthly amount would be about:

At age 65 (reduced benefit) .... $ 945
At full-retirement age (66 and 4 months) .... $ 1,035
At age 70 .... $ 1,340

Disability Benefits

On page 6, we tell you about disability benefits. If you become disabled right now, you need 20 credits to qualify for disability benefits. You had to earn 20 of these credits in the last 10 years. Your record shows that you have earned enough credits within the right time.

Right now, your monthly disability amount would be about .... $ 1,115

Family Benefits

If you get retirement or disability benefits, your spouse and young children may also qualify for benefits. See page 6 for more information about family benefits.

Survivor Benefits

If you die, certain members of your family may qualify for survivor benefits on your record. See page 6 for an explanation of who may qualify.

If you die right now, you need 20 credits for your survivors to get benefits. Your record shows you have enough. If they met all other requirements, monthly benefit amounts would be about:

For your child .... $ 840
For your spouse who is caring for your child .... $ 840
When your spouse reaches full-retirement age .... $ 1,125
For all your family members, if others also qualify (more children, for example) .... $ 1,975

We may also be able to pay your spouse or children a one-time death benefit of $255.

Medicare

Medicare hospital and medical insurance is a two-part benefit program that helps protect you from the high costs of medical care. Hospital insurance benefits (Part A) help pay the cost when you are in the hospital and for certain kinds of follow-up care. Medical insurance benefits (Part B) help pay the costs of doctors' services.

If you have enough work credits, you may qualify for Medicare hospital insurance at age 65, even if you are still working. You may qualify before age 65 if you are disabled or have permanent kidney failure. Your spouse may also qualify for hospital insurance at 65 on your record.

Almost anyone who is 65 or older or who qualifies for Medicare hospital insurance can enroll for medical insurance. You must pay a monthly premium for it.

For More Information or To Correct Your Record

After you read this statement, if you have questions, want to apply for benefits or want to request a Statement in Spanish, please call 1-800-772-1213* or visit our Website at www.ssa.gov/mystatement. If you are reporting missing or wrong earnings, have your W-2 or tax return for those years available, if possible. This Statement is just an estimate of your potential benefits. You do not qualify for Social Security or Medicare until you apply and meet all the requirements. Meanwhile, your record is updated each year and you can request a new statement to make sure it stays correct.

*Social Security treats all calls confidentially--whether they are made to our toll-free number or to one of our local offices. But we also want to be sure that you receive accurate and courteous service. That is why we have a second Social Security representative listen to some incoming and outgoing telephone calls.

w/8-1:00

Your Personal Earnings and Benefit Estimate Statement
from the SOCIAL SECURITY ADMINISTRATION

November 6, 1998

C/O SCHEINE FUSCO ET AL
SS DIV FILE
PO BOX 390
WOODBURY, NY 11797-0390

A Message from the Commissioner

We are pleased to send you the Personal Earnings and Benefit Estimate Statement you requested. We hope it will help you to better understand the Social Security program and what it means to you and your family. The statement shows the estimated amount of benefits, under current law, that you and your family may be eligible for now and in the future. It also lists the earnings that your employers (or you, if you're self-employed) have reported to Social Security. We hope you will use this information along with other information you may have about your savings, pensions and investments to help you plan for a secure financial future.

Remember, Social Security can be an important part of your financial future whether you're young or old, male or female, single or married. It can help you when you need it most by paying you benefits when you retire or if you become severely disabled. Social Security also can help support your family when you die.

Some people are concerned that Social Security won't be there in the future. The program has changed in the past to meet the demands of the times, and it must do so again. Today we are working to resolve long-range financing issues and to ensure that future generations of Americans can count on the same financial protections from Social Security as past generations did.

Kenneth S. Apfel

Kenneth S. Apfel
Commissioner of Social Security

The Facts You Gave Us

Your Name	
Your Social Security Number	
Your Date of Birth	05/16/1967
1997 Earnings	None
1998 Earnings	$20,000
Your Estimated Future Average Yearly Earnings	$20,000
Age You Plan To Stop Working	65
Other Social Security Numbers You've Used	None

Your Social Security Earnings

On page 4, we explain more about covered earnings and Social Security and Medicare taxes. The following chart shows your reported earnings. It may not show some or all of your earnings from last year because they are not yet recorded. This year's earnings will not be reported to us until next year.

If your own records do not agree with the earnings amounts shown, please contact us right away. If possible, have your W-2 or tax return for those years available.

	Social Security			Medicare		
Years	Maximum Taxable Earnings	Your Reported Earnings	Estimated Taxes You Paid	Maximum Taxable Earnings	Your Reported Earnings	Estimated Taxes You Paid
1937-50	$3,000	$ 0	$ 0			
1951	3,600	0	0			
1952	3,600	0	0			
1953	3,600	0	0			
1954	3,600	0	0			
1955	4,200	0	0			
1956	4,200	0	0			
1957	4,200	0	0			
1958	4,200	0	0		Medicare did not start	
1959	4,800	0	0		until 1966.	
1960	4,800	0	0			
1961	4,800	0	0			
1962	4,800	0	0			
1963	4,800	0	0			
1964	4,800	0	0			
1965	4,800	0	0			
1966	6,600	0	0	$6,600	$ 0	$ 0
1967	6,600	0	0	6,600	0	0
1968	7,800	0	0	7,800	0	0
1969	7,800	0	0	7,800	0	0
1970	7,800	0	0	7,800	0	0
1971	7,800	0	0	7,800	0	0
1972	9,000	0	0	9,000	0	0
1973	10,800	0	0	10,800	0	0
1974	13,200	0	0	13,200	0	0
1975	14,100	0	0	14,100	0	0
1976	15,300	0	0	15,300	0	0
1977	16,500	0	0	16,500	0	0
1978	17,700	0	0	17,700	0	0
1979	22,900	0	0	22,900	0	0
1980	25,900	0	0	25,900	0	0
1981	29,700	0	0	29,700	0	0
1982	32,400	0	0	32,400	0	0
1983	35,700	0	0	35,700	0	0
1984	37,800	0	0	37,800	0	0
1985	39,600	0	0	39,600	0	0
1986	42,000	0	0	42,000	0	0
1987	43,800	0	0	43,800	0	0
1988	45,000	0	0	45,000	0	0
1989	48,000	0	0	48,000	0	0
1990	51,300	0	0	51,300	0	0
1991	53,400	0	0	125,000	0	0
1992	55,500	0	0	130,200	0	0
1993	57,600	4,829	299	135,000	4,829	70
1994	60,600	3,126	193	No Limit	3,126	45
1995	61,200	6,410	397	No Limit	6,410	92
1996	62,700	5,123	317	No Limit	5,123	74
1997	65,400	14,060	871	No Limit	14,060	203
1998	68,400			No Limit		
Total estimated Social Security taxes paid			$ 2,077	**Total estimated Medicare taxes paid**		$ 484

2

Your Estimated Social Security Benefits

Your work under Social Security helps you and your family to qualify for benefit payments. The kinds of benefits you might get are described below. For each benefit, you need a certain number of work credits (see page 5). Once you have enough credits, your benefit amount depends on your average earnings over your working lifetime. We used the earnings in the chart on page 2 to figure your credits and estimate your benefits. We included any 1997 and 1998 earnings and any estimated future earnings you told us about.

Retirement Benefits

To get Social Security retirement benefits, you need 40 credits of work. That is also how many you need for Medicare at age 65. Your record shows that you have at least 24 credits.

Because you do not have enough credits yet to get retirement benefits, we are not giving you a benefit estimate now. If you work in the future and earn enough credits to qualify, we will give you an estimate then.

Disability Benefits

On page 6, we tell you about disability benefits. If you become disabled right now, you need 20 credits to qualify for benefits. You had to earn these credits in the last 10 years. Your record shows that you have earned enough credits within the right time.

Right now, your monthly disability amount would be about .... $ 320

Family Benefits

If you get retirement or disability benefits, your spouse and young children may also qualify for benefits. See page 6 for more information about family benefits.

Survivor Benefits

If you die, certain members of your family may qualify for survivor benefits on your record. See page 6 for an explanation of who may qualify.

If you die right now, you need 9 credits for your survivors to get benefits. Your record shows you have enough. If they met all other requirements, monthly benefit amounts would be about:

For your child	$ 435
For your spouse who is caring for your child	$ 435
When your spouse reaches full-retirement age	$ 580
For all your family members, if others also qualify (more children, for example)	$ 875

We may also be able to pay your spouse or children a one-time death benefit of $255.

Medicare

Medicare hospital and medical insurance is a two-part benefit program that helps protect you from the high costs of medical care. Hospital insurance benefits (Part A) help pay the cost when you are in the hospital and for certain kinds of follow-up care. Medical insurance benefits (Part B) help pay the costs of doctors' services.

If you have enough work credits, you may qualify for Medicare hospital insurance at age 65, even if you are still working. You may qualify before age 65 if you are disabled or have permanent kidney failure. Your spouse may also qualify for hospital insurance at 65 on your record.

Almost anyone who is 65 or older or who qualifies for Medicare hospital insurance can enroll for medical insurance. You must pay a monthly premium for it.

For More Information or To Correct Your Record

After you read this statement, if you have questions, want to apply for benefits or want to request a Statement in Spanish, please call 1-800-772-1213* or visit our Website at www.ssa.gov/mystatement. If you are reporting missing or wrong earnings, have your W-2 or tax return for those years available, if possible. This Statement is just an estimate of your potential benefits. You do not qualify for Social Security or Medicare until you apply and meet all the requirements. Meanwhile, your record is updated each year and you can request a new statement to make sure it stays correct.

*Social Security treats all calls confidentially--whether they are made to our toll-free number or to one of our local offices. But we also want to be sure that you receive accurate and courteous service. That is why we have a second Social Security representative listen to some incoming and outgoing telephone calls.

3

date: 1/20/99 T:\vfsfrms\lssrecom

Lump sum settlement memo - from: VICTOR FUSCO, ESQ. to: MITCHELL G. SCHUMAN

RE: William J. [redacted] file # 597-0434/MFS clt age or d/o/b: 1/

Age

W97-078

Please review Workers' Compensation file for possible lump sum settlement.

☐ We looked at before, but file was premature for LSS
☐ Claimant refused in the past (before SS award)
☐ Claimant wanted to wait for result of SSD claim
☐ We recommended awaiting results of SSD which is now resolved (for source of income)

Please note: ☐ classified at: $______ ☐ not classified, latest rate: $ 378 TR

☐ claimant is single/divorced ☒ claimant is married ☐ has K 1121 children

2/99

☐ Total eligible auxiliaries in Social Security Disability claim:______

Source of Income	☐ clt working, earns $	clt working at ☐ RE ☐ No RE
clt job title	Courier – Fed Ex	☐ savings: $
☐ spouse: $	occuptn: Disabled	☐ spouse NOT working
☐ alimony		☐ rents
☐ pensions	☐ Insurance/LTD	See needle note 32 on LTD status
☐ royalties	☐ other	Kemper

☐ Social Security Disability awarded as of 10/5/98 retro to 11/97

☐ Monthly benefit W/E $ 1360 (PIA) Family: $ 2148 Fmax

Claimant ☐ is offset ☒ NOT offset at current rate ☒ NOT offset at any rate

Auxiliaries ☒ Offset ☐ NOT offset at current rate ☐ NOT offset at any rate

To compute max WC clt can get before wage earners benefits are offset:		To compute max WC clt can get before family benefits are offset:	
ACEH	H: Yr 1993 53352÷12.80%=3556	ACEH	3556
- PIA	1360	-FMX	2148
=	2196	=	1408
x 12 =	26361	x 12	16896
÷ 52	507	÷ 52	324

Recommendation: LSS allocated at: $ 400

Note the most LSS can be allocated at before offset applies is: $______

File can not be LSS ☐ Self Insured won't LSS ☐ Open Issues ☐ No income ☐ Premature

Completed by (circle): VF JA MR AH MFS MG John Infranca Gregg Scaglione Nick Parisi Eileen Geraghty Carol Baker

Scheine, Fusco, Brandenstein & Rada, P.C.
ATTORNEYS AT LAW

180 Froehlich Farm Blvd., Woodbury, NY 11797-2923
516-496-0100 • Fax:516-496-2316

Other Offices: Manhattan, Bronx, Hempstead, Commack, Medford

August 15, 1998

SOCIAL SECURITY ADMINISTRATION
OFFICE OF DISABILITY AND
INTERNATIONAL OPERATIONS
1500 WOODLAWN DR
BALTIMORE MD 21241

SOCIAL SECURITY ADMINISTRATION
DISTRICT OFFICE
75 OAK ST
PATCHOGUE NY 11772

Re: William [redacted]
[redacted] Coram, NY 11727
SS#: [redacted]
SFBR File #: S97-0439 / MFS
Social Security Disability Claim

Sirs:

We are in receipt of a fully favorable Administrative Law Judge decision dated July 17, 1998.

Enclosed please find copies of all relevant Workers' Compensation decisions as follows: 5-21-98; 11-21-97 and 9-19-97

We also enclose a C-8 record of payments issued by the carrier dated 6-1-98.

Please note that Workers' Compensation payments continue at the rate of $378.00, per week ($1,638.00 monthly).

Kindly note that we are also representing the claimant in the Workers' Compensation case, so if you need further information, please feel free to contact us. (Our W97-0780 & W96-0047).

Very truly yours,
SCHEINE, FUSCO, BRANDENSTEIN & RADA, P.C.

By: ______________________
MICHELLE F. STRUM, ESQ.
For the Firm

MFS/VF
cc: Mr. Rising

[

NOTICE THAT PAYMENT OF COMPENSATION HAS BEEN STOPPED OR MODIFIE

CHECK TYPE OF CASE: [X] WORKERS' COMPENSATION [ ] VOLUNTEER FIREFIGHTER [ ] VOLUNTEER AMBULANCE WORKER

ANSWER ALL QUESTIONS FULLY - TYPEWRITER OR COMPUTER PREPARATION IS REQUIRED

ALL COMMUNICATIONS SHOULD REFER TO THESE NUMBERS

1. W C B Case Number	2. Carrier Case Number	3. Carrier Code	4. Date of Injury	5. Social Security Number
[redacted]	[redacted]	[redacted]	[redacted]	[redacted]

	Name	Address to which notices should be sent
Claimant/Name of Deceased	[redacted]	[redacted] ..., NY 11727
Employer *	FEDERAL EXPRESS	2007 CORPORATE AVE., 3RD FLR. MEMPHIS, TN 38132
8. Carrier	FEDERAL EXPRESS C/O ALEXSIS	48 SOUTH SERVICE ROAD, SUITE 301 MELVILLE, NY 11747

* In VF and VAW benefit cases, the liable political subdivision (or unaffiliated ambulance service as defined in Sec. 30 VAWBL) is deemed to be the "EMPLOY

9. County Where Injury Occurred	10. Date Disability Began or Date of Death	11. Average Weekly Wage	12. Date First Payment Mailed	13. Date Most Recent Payment
SUFFOLK	5/2?/97	$ 684.25	7/3/97	

14. Description (Diagnosis) of Injury NECK

15. SUMMARY OF BENEFIT PAYMENTS

Indicate Type of Disability TOTAL/PARTIAL	PERM./TEMP.	Period(s) of Payment From	To	Less Days Worked	Number of Weeks	Weekly Rate	Amount
							$
		5/28/97	6/11/97 REIMBURSE EMPLOYER		2	400.00	800.00
T	T	6/11/97	8/14/97		9 1/5	400.00	3,680.00
P	T	8/14/97	11/22/97		14 2/5	250.00	3,600.00
P	T	11/22/97	4/27/98		22	250.00TR	5,500.00
		4/27/98	5/22/98		3 4/5	378.00TR	1,436.40
CHECK ENCLOSED		5/22/98	6/12/98		3	378.00TR	1,134.00

LUMP SUM PAYMENT (Include Lump Sum Non-Schedule Adjustment or Lump Sum Advance on a Schedule Loss Award)

DEATH BENEFITS	From	To	Paid To Or For	
	Lump Sum Death Benefit (VFBL and VAWBL only)			
	Funeral Expenses			
	State Treasurer (Sections 15-9, 25-a or 26-a)			
	Payment made into Aggregate Trust Fund - Date:			

TOTAL AWARD $ 16,150.40

PENALTY PAYMENT TO CLAIMANT $

LESS: a. Fees to representative: ATTORNEY $ 15.00

b. Reimbursement to: $

c. Other (specify): PREVIOUSLY PAID $ 14,735.00

TOTAL DEDUCTIONS (a+b+c) $ 14,885.00

BALANCE TO CLAIMANT $ 1,265.40

16. Have benefits been paid in full in accordance with an award of the WCB? ☐ Yes ☐ No If "No," check and complete items a-c, as appropriate:

a. ☐ Claimant returned to work. Date of return: ________ ☐ At pre-injury wages ☐ At reduced wages

b. ☐ There is a change in condition and/or earnings. (A medical report or other supporting documentation must be attached.)

c. ☐ Payments stopped or modified for other reason. (Explain below and/or attach explanation/documentation.)

17. ☐ **NOTICE OF TERMINATION OF TEMPORARY PAYMENTS OF COMPENSATION (Sec. 21-a WCL)** Employer or carrier is ceasing payment of temporary compensation. See special information box on reverse. Last payment was made on ________. Reason for termination of paym

Prepared by ROSEMARY FIORE Dated 6/1/98

Official Title CLAIMS SPECIALIST Telephone No. & Extension (516) 843-1741

C-8/8.6 (4-97) Prescribed by Chair Workers' Compensation Board SEE IMPORTANT INFORMATION TO CLAIMANT AND CARRIER ON REVERSE

STATE OF NEW YORK
WORKERS' COMPENSATION BOARD
175 FULTON AVENUE
HEMPSTEAD, NY 11550

(516) 560-7769

W97-0780 ✗
W96-0047

Robert R. Snashall
Chairman

State of New York - Workers' Compensation Board

In regard to WILLIAM [redacted], WCB Case #[redacted]

NOTICE OF DECISION

keep for your records

At the Workers' Compensation hearing held on 05/21/1998 involving the claim of WILLIAM RISING at the PATCHOGUE hearing location, Judge Mulligan made the following decision, findings and directions:

AWARD : The employer or insurance carrier is directed to pay $6,936.40, less payments already made by the employer or carrier, for the periods indicated below, unless employer or carrier files an appeal within 30 days after the date on which the decision was duly filed and served.

for disability over a period of			at rate	
weeks	from	to	per week	the sum of
22.0	11/22/1997	4/27/1998	$250.00	$5,500.00
- Tentative rate.				
3.8	4/27/1998	5/22/1998	$378.00	$1,436.40
- Tentative rate.				

Carrier continue payments at $378.00 tentative rate.

Fees	the sum of	To
As lien on above award payable by separate check by carrier TO CLAIMANT'S REPRESENTATIVE OR ATTORNEY:	$150.00	Scheine, Fusco,and

DECISION: I find prima facie medical psychiatric. I authorize cervical surgery as per Dr. David. Physical therapy authorized (post-op). Reimburse claimant $318.61 medical and travel audit. Authorize EMG/NCV's left upper extremities. Carrier toproduce consultants report on psychiatric.
Case is continued.

Claimant -	[redacted]G	Employer -	FEDERAL EXPRESS
Social Security No. -	[redacted]8	Carrier -	Federal Express Corp.
WCB Case No. -	[redacted]	Carrier ID No. -	W413785
Date of Accident -	05/27/1997	Carrier Case No. -	10247439/F4
District Office -	Hempstead	Date of Filing of this Decision -	06/17/1998

ATENCION:
Puede llamar a la oficina de la Junta de Compensacion Obrera, en su area correspondiente, cuyo numero de telefono aparece al principio de la pagina y pida informacion acerca de su reclamacion(caso).

EC-23 (4/98)

State of New York - Worke Compensation Board NOTICE OF DECISIO..

W.C. LAW JUDGE	DATE OF HEARING	DISTRICT OFFICE	HEARING POINT
Rubino	11/21/97	Hempstead	Medford

W.C.B. CASE NUMBER	CARRIER I.D. NUMBER	CARRIER CASE NUMBER	DATE OF ACCIDENT	SOCIAL SECURITY NUMBER
29715600	W413785	10247439/F4	05/27/1997	[illegible]

NAME OF CLAIMANT	DECISION DULY FILED AND SERVED ON	BY	FOR INFORMATION ON THIS CASE CALL:
William	12/1/97	MC	(516) 560-7769

William

27

Federal Express
Federal Express Corp
Scheine, Fusco and
Special Funds Cons. Comm
Finance Unit

TO ALL PARTIES IN INTEREST: READ IMPORTANT INFORMATION BELOW AND ON THE REVERSE SIDE

Please take notice that pursuant to Section 23 of the Workers Compensation Law and Board Rule 12NYCRR 300.13, this decision may be appealed by any party in interest by filing a written appeal with the Board within thirty (30) days after the filing of this decision. Such an appeal must be accompanied by the prescribed cover sheet Form RB-89, together with proof of service upon all parties in interest. A claimant who is not represented by an attorney or licensed representative is not required to file the cover sheet but may file an appeal in any written form. Please note: in order to be timely filed, the appeal must actually be received by the Board within the timeframe noted above.

Please take notice that pursuant to Board Rule [illegible] interest may [illegible] appeal [illegible] Board within thirty (30) days after service of the appeal. Such an appeal [illegible] accompanied by the prescribed rebuttal cover sheet Form RB-89 [illegible] proof of [illegible] upon all parties in interest [illegible] an attorney or licensed representative is not required to file the cover sheet but may file a rebuttal in any written form.

AFTER HEARING, THE FOLLOWING DECISION AND AWARD WAS MADE AND DULY FILED.

AWARD: THE EMPLOYER OR INSURANCE CARRIER ARE DIRECTED TO PAY $2,250.00 ,LESS PAYMENTS ALREADY MADE BY THE EMPLOYER OR CARRIER, FOR THE PERIODS INDICATED BELOW, UNLESS EMPLOYER OR CARRIER FILES AN APPEAL WITHIN 30 DAYS AFTER THE DATE ON WHICH THE DECISION WAS DULY FILED AND SERVED.

for disability over a period of			at rate per week	the sum of
weeks	from	to		
9.0 Tentative rate	9/20/97	11/22/97	$250.00	$2,250.00
Carrier continue payments at $250.00 tentative rate.				

Fees	the sum of	To
As lien on above award payable by separate check by carrier TO CLAIMANT'S REPRESENTATIVE OR ATTORNEY:	$125.00	Scheine, Fusco,and

DECISION: No Prima facie medical exists for the back, left arm or left shoulder. Case is continued.

CORRECTED NOTICE
REGARDING PRIMA FACIE MEDICAL EVIDENCE 12/29/97

EC-23 (2/97)

STATE OF NEW YORK
WORKERS' COMPENSATION BOARD

NOTICE OF DECISION

CLAIMANT

READ IMPORTANT INFORMATION ON REVERSE SIDE

DATE OF HEARING	W.C. LAW JUDGE	DECISION DULY FILED AND SERVED ON	BY
9/19/97	Rubino	9/30/97	MC
*WCB Case No.	Carrier ID No. W413785	Carrier Case No. 10247439/F4	
Date of Accident 5/27/97	Social Security No.		

Claimant

*Employer

Federal Express
2007 Corporate Ave
3rd fl
Memphis TN 38132

Federal Express Corp
C O Alexsis Risk Mgmt Svcs
48 S Service Rd
suite 301
Melville NY 11747-2335

Scheine attys
180 Froehlich Farm Blvd
POB 390
Woodbury NY 11797-0390

Special Funds
section 15-8
205 E 42nd St 18th fl
New York NY 10017-5706

TO ALL PARTIES OF INTEREST

PLEASE TAKE NOTICE THAT PURSUANT TO SECTION 23 OF THE WORKERS' COMPENSATION LAW AND BOARD RULE 13 ANY PARTY IN INTEREST MAY APPEAL THIS DECISION TO THE BOARD REVIEW BUREAU BY FILING ITS APPEAL IN WRITING ACCOMPANIED BY THE PRESCRIBED COVER SHEET FORM RB-89, TOGETHER WITH PROOF OF SERVICE UPON ALL OTHER PARTIES IN INTEREST, WITHIN 30 DAYS AFTER NOTICE OF THE FILING OF THIS DECISION. A CLAIMANT WHO IS NOT REPRESENTED BY AN ATTORNEY OR LICENSED REPRESENTATIVE IS NOT REQUIRED TO FILE THE COVER SHEET FORM BUT MAY FILE AN APPEAL IN ANY WRITTEN FORM.

PLEASE TAKE NOTICE THAT PURSUANT TO SECTION 23 OF THE WORKERS' COMPENSATION LAW AND BOARD RULE 13, ANY PARTY IN INTEREST MAY REBUT AN APPEAL BY ANOTHER PARTY BY FILING ITS REBUTTAL WITH THE BOARD REVIEW BUREAU IN WRITING ACCOMPANIED BY THE PRESCRIBED REBUTTAL COVER SHEET FORM [illegible] TOGETHER WITH PROOF OF SERVICE UPON ALL OTHER PARTIES IN INTEREST, [illegible] DAYS AFTER SERVICE OF THE APPEAL. A CLAIMANT WHO IS NOT REPRESENTED BY AN ATTORNEY OR LICENSED REPRESENTATIVE IS NOT REQUIRED TO FILE THE COVER SHEET FORM BUT MAY FILE A REBUTTAL IN ANY WRITTEN FORM.

After hearing, the following Decision and Award was made and duly filed.

AWARD: THE EMPLOYER AND/OR THE INSURANCE CARRIER ARE DIRECTED TO PAY AT ONCE

for disability over a period of: weeks	from	to	at rate per Week	the sum of	TO:
2.0 Reimburse	5/28/97	6/11/97	$ 400.00	$ 800.00	CLAIMANT
9.2 To claimant	6/11/97	8/14/97	$400.00	3,680.00	
5.4 Tentative	8/14/97 rate.	9/20/97 Carrier	$250.00 continue payments at	$1,350.00 $250.00 TR	LESS PAYMENTS MADE COVERING THIS PERIOD.
as lien on award payable by separate check by carrier to CLAIMANT'S REPRESENTATIVE OR ATTORNEY				$125.00.	Scheine, attys.
fee to DOCTOR for attendance at hearing.					

DECISION: Case was continued. Accident, notice and causal relationship established to the neck. Aevrage weekly wage established at maximum without concurrent employment. Physical therapy authorized to the next hearing. Reimburse claimant for medical and transportation expenses in the amount of $201.73, subject to audit. ***** Corrected notice regarding attorney's fee (11/28/97).

*In volunteer firefighters' and volunteer ambulance workers' benefit cases, the liable political subdivision (or unaffiliated ambulance service as defined in Sec. 30 VAWBL) is deemed to be the "EMPLOYER."

ATENCION:
Si no sabe leer ingles, puede llamar a la oficina de informacion mas cercana de la Junta de Compensacion Obrera (vease la lista de oficinas en el lado reverso) y pida informes acerca de su reclamacion.

WPEC-23 (6-96)

NOTES

NOTES

Program Schedule and Faculty

Program Schedule

Registration and a continental breakfast will be thirty minutes before the start of the program.

Morning Session: 9:00 a.m. - 12:00 p.m.

9:00
Introduction
Distinguishing social security from SSI; insured status: date last insured and onset of disability; types of benefits available: insured worker; dependents and survivors of insured workers: disabled widow/er, minor and disabled adult child, disabled divorced spouse. SSI: adult and childhood disability. Medicare/Medicaid. Ancillary benefits: work attempts/trial work period, extended period of eligibility (title II); Section 1619a and b (SSI). SSA redesign initiatives.

9:45
Disability Standards and Concepts
Statutory definition of disability; sequential evaluation; listing of impairments; medical-vocational guidelines; residual functional capacity; evaluating objective medical evidence versus subjective complaints; weighing medical opinions. (SSI disabled children). Ethical issues.

10:45 Break

11:00
Application and Appeal Process
Application procedure; stages of appeal; redesign experiments; disability evaluation pre-hearing and above; access to SSA file; submission of new evidence; timeframes on appeal; re-opening prior claims; res judicata. Ethical issues.

Afternoon Session: 1:00 p.m. - 5:00 p.m.

1:00
Preparing a Disability Claim
Initial client interview; forms and authorizations; obtaining medical (and vocational) and RFC evidence; developing new medical evidence; obtaining SSA's file; subpoenas; preparing claimant (and other witnesses) to testify; advocate preparation (what to do in preparation for medical or vocational expert). Ethical issues.

2:00
ALJ Hearings
Hearing notice; requesting adjournments; hearing procedures; role of medical and vocational experts; post-hearing evidence; issuance of decision; post-hearing processing. What ALJ's expect from practitioners; how do ALJ's evaluate claims? The new regulations for standards of conduct for claimant representatives. Ethical issues.

3:00 Break

3:15
Appeals Council
Deciding whether to appeal unfavorable or partially favorable decisions; Apppeals Council review of issues not raised by the claimant; "own motion" review; access to hearing tapes and exhibits of record; submission of new evidence; how the Appeals Council works; remedies; preparation and submission of argument; effect of Apppeals Council denial of review.

3:45
Federal Court Practice
Time limits and 405(g) jurisdiction; contents of a complaint; paupers petitions; service of summons; local rules for processing Social Security/SSI cases; whether to request reversal or remand; briefs and oral argument; appeals to Circuit Court.

4:15
Benefit Awards and Attorney Fees
Computing current and retroactive benefit awards. Administrative fees: 25% of what? Fee petition versus fee agreement. Federal court fees under the Social Security Act and the Equal Access to Justice Act.

Faculty

Co-Chairs:

Carolyn A. Kubitschek
Lansner & Kubitschek
New York City

Barbara Samuels
Citywide Coordinator, Disability Advocacy Project
Legal Services for New York City
New York City
Contributor, *New York Elder Law Handbook (1997)*

James M. Baker
Staff Attorney
Northern Manhattan Improvement Corp
New York City

Jill A. Boskey
Legal Aid Attorney
Center For Disability Advocacy Rights, Inc.
New York City

Tanya M. Douglas
Disability Law Specialist Attorney
Bronx Legal Services
Bronx, New York

Victor Fusco
Scheine, Fusco, Brandenstein & Rada, P.C.
Woodbury, New York

Hon. William Kirchgaessner
Administrative Law Judge
Office of Hearings and Appeals
Social Security Administration
New York City

Pamela Levine
Binder & Binder
New York City

Program Attorney: Janet L. Siegel